LED ZEPPELIN
ON LED ZEPPELIN

LED ZEPPELIN
ON LED ZEPPELIN
INTERVIEWS AND ENCOUNTERS

EDITED BY HANK BORDOWITZ

CHICAGO
REVIEW
PRESS

An A Cappella Book

Copyright © 2014 by Hank Bordowitz

First edition

Published by Chicago Review Press, Incorporated

814 North Franklin Street

Chicago, Illinois 60610

ISBN 978-1-61374-754-4

A list of credits and copyright notices for the individual pieces in this collection can be found on pages 430–35.

Cover and interior design: Jonathan Hahn

Cover photograph: Photofest

Library of Congress Cataloging-in-Publication Data

Led Zeppelin on Led Zeppelin : interviews and encounters / edited by Hank Bordowitz. — First edition.

    pages cm

  Includes index.

  ISBN 978-1-61374-754-4 (cloth)

  1. Led Zeppelin (Musical group) 2. Led Zeppelin (Musical group)—Interviews. 3. Rock musicians—England—Interviews. 4. Page, Jimmy—Interviews. 5. Plant, Robert—Interviews. 6. Jones, John Paul, 1946-—Interviews. 7. Bonham, John, 1948-1980—Interviews. I. Bordowitz, Hank.

ML421.L4L44 2014

782.42166092'2—dc23

[B]

2014017476

Printed in the United States of America

5 4 3 2 1

This one's for Mom and Dad, who
helped gestate the project.
All thanks and honor.
I love you.

CONTENTS

PART III   RAMBLE ON

ACKNOWLEDGMENTS

Cast and crew of the Music Division of the New York Public Library for the Performing Arts, Dorothy and Lewis B. Cullman Center.

Laura Moody, Jennie Thomas, Anastasia Karel, and Amanda Rabb at the Rock and Roll Hall of Fame Library and Archives.

My son Michael, for his research assistance at both places.

Mike Jacobs and Jeff Peisch, two vintage associates, and Cathy Carapella, a new one, even though that piece didn't make it in.

Maggie, David, John, Dan, Andy, Adam, Margaret, et al. at Bergen Community College.

Paul Cashmere, honcho at Australian music news service the Noise Network, for doing Australian legwork above and beyond.

Denny Somach, who knows more about radio and television syndication than anyone I know, and who recognized Alan Freeman's work and knew not only the provenance of the piece but knew the piece itself.

Peter Carlo Evangelista, who transcribed a lot of the recorded sources and stuck with this project for months.

Arthur Levy, one of my mentors in this stuff, who stuck a thumb into his stash of his classic publication *Zoo World* and pulled out a plum.

Chuck Eddy for understanding.

Dan Sheehan for being such a monster Zep fan that he was willing to read this in manuscript and comment on it.

All of the people whose work appears in this book. Once again, I am standing on the shoulders of giants.

Yuval Taylor, who postponed this book far more times than should be allowed. Amelia Estrich for her work throughout the book's production.

Mike (again), Larry, William, and even Caren.

FOREWORD

Enough people have recounted the Led Zeppelin story that it has fallen into folklore. Anyone who cares about the group enough knows that Jimmy Page got the group together to keep the legendary British musical breeding ground the Yardbirds going. This same audience also accepts that Led Zeppelin got its name from the Who's late drummer, Keith Moon, who thought the idea of a "New Yardbirds" would go over like a heavy metal blimp. Yet, as is the case with so much folklore, it ain't necessarily so.

Keith Moon did name a band featuring Page with the comment that it would go over like a "lead zeppelin," a more spectacular failure than a lead balloon—but that band wasn't the "New Yardbirds." In Pete Townshend's memoir *Who I Am*, he speaks of a 1966 rift among the Who following a fistfight between Roger Daltrey and Moon, which ended with Daltrey bloodying Moon's nose and Moon and John Entwistle threatening to leave the band. This period of discontent in the Who camp coincided with the Yardbirds' management's attempts to simultaneously capitalize on the band, let the members blow off some steam, and allow the members to revitalize themselves by having each musician record a solo project. Page and Jeff Beck wanted to record a rock instrumental entitled "Beck's Bolero," and they recruited Moon and Entwistle to provide the rhythm section. Page recollected the situation to *MOJO*'s Mat Snow thusly:

> This goes right back to the days when Simon Napier-Bell, who was managing the Yardbirds, was trying to get solo discs from each member. Jeff Beck and I were collaborating, and in those days with these solo diversions it seemed we should use other musicians, so there was Keith Moon, John Paul Jones, Nicky

Hopkins on piano, myself on 12-string electric, and Jeff—"Beck's Bolero" was what we were doing. After that session, Keith Moon was really fired up, and I don't blame him, and he said, "We must get a band together—how about it?" He was fed up with the Who at the time, and he wanted to take the Ox—John Entwistle—with him, with Jeff, myself, and all the rest of us . . . It didn't happen. But Keith's name for the band, Led Zeppelin, stuck in my mind.

It has also become Led Zeppelin cant that while Page and Jones were the old studio pros, Bonham and Plant had no real studio experience. However, Plant was recording singles as early as 1966.

Meanwhile, Page's hunt for a bunch of New Yardbirds had far more to do with business than tradition. When the group ran out of steam, it had outstanding obligations to play a series of shows in Scandinavia. Both the group's management and the only remaining member with any enthusiasm—Page—did not want to pass up this money-making opportunity, hence they had to put a band together in a hurry.

What Page could not have predicted was the way the guanine, adenine, thymine, and cytosine of him, John Paul Jones, Brummy singer Robert Plant (recommended by Page's first choice, Terry Reid), and Plant's long-time friend, drummer John Bonham, would combine and recombine to create a remarkable strain of musical DNA.

The band members spent a great deal of their post-Zeppelin careers trying to debunk the stories of backstage debauchery and hammered gods that followed in their wake. After the first couple of albums, they all were family guys. Plant often said that if you went to the hotel after the third album, you would be more likely to find him in his room reading Nietzsche than tossing the telly, and that stories of sharks and chain saws and the like, if they had any merit at all, were more likely the shenanigans of the crew than the band. By allowing the story to be told in the words of all four members, a clearer picture—less fettered by folklore—begins to emerge of the band and the way they perceived their history and legacy as they were creating it.

When Chris DeVito edited the second book in this series, his award winning *Coltrane on Coltrane: The John Coltrane Interviews*, he was faced with a monumental task: to collect every interview ever done with the jazz icon, get permission to use them, and then use the hard-won material to construct a viable biography of one of the genre's greatest players and innovators. When I was putting together the volume you now hold in your hands, the problem was different: even after the first cut, this book was three times its current size!

This is not to say Led Zeppelin were press whores—quite the opposite. They were notoriously wary of the press, especially the American press. That attitude permeates this book. *Rolling Stone* didn't really warm up to them until very close to the end of the band's existence. More frequently, they savaged the group. As John Paul Jones told Mat Snow in Q magazine:

> We got to America and read the *Rolling Stone* review of the very first album, which was going on about us as another hyped British band. We couldn't believe it. . . . After that we were very wary of the press, which became a chicken-and-egg situation. We avoided them and so they started to avoid us . . . If you did an interview you'd get misquoted, and if you didn't, they'd make it up anyway. . . . [W]e didn't do singles, and a reason for that was so we didn't have to do television or interviews.

There was interest in the members of Led Zeppelin even predating them actually coming together as a band—the dissolution of the Yardbirds was covered desultorily in the British music press. So, for the first couple of LPs (as Page liked to call them), Led Zeppelin was referred to as "Jimmy's Band." They caught on so quickly and with such force that they dominated the British press in a period that saw the disbanding of the Beatles and the quest for the next new thing, which turned out to be Led Zeppelin.

This brings up another point: while the other books in the *Musicians in Their Own Words* series have dealt with solo artists—John Coltrane, Jimi Hendrix, Tom Waits—this collection deals with a band as a single entity. But if Led Zeppelin was a single entity, a creature of its recombinant do-re-mi, then it was a beast with four heads, each with a distinctive personality that informed the band as a whole. These different personalities and perspectives need to be explored if we are to get a picture of—to torture the metaphor—how the band's musical DNA evolved along with each member of the band.

For example, when Robert Plant started talking to the press, he did it with a hyperlexic stream of consciousness reminiscent of Robin Williams. Plant even alluded to his verbosity when he and Page reunited and sat down for a drink with, once again, Mat Snow:

> Jimmy: See what happens when you're at a loose end for too long?
>
> Robert: You got a birdie this morning, ha ha ha! We'd be all right on talk shows after all.
>
> Mat: A double act?
>
> Robert: A bit like Mork and Mindy!

Jones, while regarded as "the quiet one," also proves to be a very thoughtful and articulate fellow, especially when discussing his music and motivations. He was quiet, he maintained in an interview with Snow in 2009, because "[Robert and Jimmy] just loved to talk. Singers are like that anyway; that's their job. And most people wanted to talk to the front men and not to me, which was fine by me. Bonzo didn't talk much either. Believe it or not, he was shy too."

Yet even Bonham displays a playful, homespun eloquence when he sees fit to acknowledge the press' existence . . . and more often than not, he would buy them a pint.

While I did not get my hands on every viable interview that the members and former members of Led Zeppelin conducted, I did manage to find some gems from every stage of their careers, both as a band and as post-breakup legends trying to present their individual artistic visions. There are some brilliant ones that I could not use for one reason or another, like:

- Jaan Uhelszki's "Led Zeppelin: Sodom and Gomorrah in a Suitcase," (*CREEM*, July 1977) which she hopes to use in her own book soon

- Dave Schulps's classic piece, "Jimmy Page: The *Trouser Press* Interview," (*Trouser Press*, October 1977) which was too retrospective for the book's purposes

- Angie Errigo's "Ask the Answer Man: Jimmy Page" (*CREEM*, February 1978), which we just couldn't come to terms on

- Andy Secher's "Led Zeppelin the Second Coming?" (*Hit Parader*, July 1982), for similar reasons

- Karen Karbo's "Stairway to Heaven: Is This the Greatest Song of All Time?" (*Esquire*, November 1991), which just did not fit this book's format

There are quite a few more that I haven't listed here. Remember, at one point this book was three times as long as it is now.

On the other hand, the material in this book is incredibly good, some of it not seen, heard, or read since it was originally published. Taken as a whole, these articles paint a vivid picture of what was happening with the members of Led Zeppelin as they experienced it in real time. This is powerful stuff—the facts as they saw them, at the time they discussed them. Now we can start to replace some of the folklore with home truth.

PRELUDE

In Which a Future Rock Star Considers a Career in Biology

Huw Wheldon: [*Laughing.*] Now and you're called what?

Jimmy Page: JG Skiffle Group . . .

HW: And you're just learning to play the guitar?

JP: Yes, from a teacher.

HW: From a teacher. You play anything except skiffle?

JP: Yes, Spanish and dance.

HW: Well, what are you gonna do when you leave school? They have skiffle?

JP: No, I want to do biological research.

HW: What do you mean by biological research?

JP: Well, [a cure for] cancer if it isn't discovered by then.

HW: You mean be a doctor?

JP: No, no, I haven't got enough brains for that sort of thing . . .

—Sir Huw Wheldon interview with young
Jimmy Page, BBC *All Your Own*, 1957

PART I

WHOLE LOTTA LOVE

"A tour, using the name the 'New Yardbirds' was undertaken—
'purely to fulfill old engagements' through Scandinavia—and,
that completed, the band promptly became Led Zeppelin, and
recorded an album in surprisingly quick time."

—Jimmy Page to Nick Kent, *CREEM*, May 1974

JIMMY PAGE IS JUST WILD ABOUT LED ZEPPELIN

December 27, 1968, *Go!* magazine

One of the first things the New Yardbirds did after a few desultory gigs in Europe was play some dates in America. And one of the first people they encountered there, and the first to publish a story about the new band in the US, was English expatriate Robin Leach, who created a broadside magazine called *Go!* that was distributed free. It was the same publication in every city except for the middle four pages. These four pages were sponsored by local radio stations (in New York it was the WMCA Good Guys) and included playlists and promotions for the station. For the two years the periodical lasted it was able to brag that it had "the Largest Circulation of Any Pop Weekly." —Ed

Jimmy Page walked into the office, smiled, and sat down. His slim build was covered with clothes, cornucopia of color, topped off with a silver velour jacket. The impression that his clothes made on others didn't even seem to faze Jimmy, as he talked about his new group, Led Zeppelin.

Jimmy Page is a well-known musician all over Britain. He is probably one of the best studio musicians ever to come out of the English recording studios, being in the backup bands for Engelbert Humperdinck and big groups.

From this background he joined the Yardbirds and stayed with them for two years as lead guitarist. After two moderately successful years with the Yardbirds Jimmy split, since he found too much friction working with them.

"They were too much into their own bag. They were great at experimenting, allowing me to move in and out of the expression every good musician needs—but then they started to get erratic.

"Sometimes we would play at concerts and the audience would want to hear some of our older songs—the ones that were hits—but the guys didn't want to do them. They just wanted to do their own stuff, solos and the like."

When Jimmy left the Yardbirds, the group just broke up. After that he tried reorganizing. The New Yardbirds took a little while to find, because Jimmy wanted to get the best.

After three weeks of constant searching he still had nothing, but one week later the whole group was formed.

The New Yardbirds consisted of vocalist Robert Plant, John Paul Jones on bass, John Bonham on drums and percussion, Jimmy Page on guitar and just about any other stringed instrument, except maybe the piano.

The New Yardbirds were already into recording an album when they started wondering about their name. "We originally thought that by calling ourselves the New Yardbirds we would be able to keep a sort of continuity from the early days of the old group, but midway through the album recording we figured it would be better to find a new name.

"A friend of mine had a name, but no group, so we took his name, with his blessings, of course. Actually, we kind of liked the sound; the Led Zeppelin sounds sort of groovy, doesn't it?"

The Led Zeppelin had its first concert in Scandinavia. "They don't cheer too madly there, you know? We were really scared, because we only had about fifteen hours to practice together. It was sort of an experimental concert to see if we were any good, I guess.

"We did the concert, and at the end we got a tremendous ovation. It was more than we ever expected, and it's really given us a great lift."

The Led Zeppelin will have their first album released during the third week of the New Year. This release, on Atlantic Records, will fall in the middle of a six-week tour which they begin December 26, in Denver, Colorado.

"The tour is scheduled for six weeks, but if we're having a good time, and the people like us, then we'll probably extend it."

Talking about the type of music the Zeppelin will do, Jimmy was animated as he said: "All of us are good musicians. We do what is pleasing to us and an audience.

"We can do all kinds and styles of music, so we're not restricted to any one thing. We want to get an act that will allow free movement. I mean, we play something and, say one of us just feels like playing one type of piece likely as not we will all join in after a few minutes, so we can all do it together.

"These things aren't planned. It's a feeling you get when you work together. Basically, we like to play blues with innovations, but we're not restricted. The old Yardbirds were restricted like that, by themselves. When they found something they liked they didn't do anything else for long stretches of time."

COMMUNICATION BREAKDOWN

"[The Yardbirds] were a happy group and used to get on well socially until we got on stage and Keith [Relf] lost all enthusiasm . . . I think it did us all a favor because the new chaps are only about 19 and full of enthusiasm."
–Jimmy Page to Chris Welch, *Melody Maker*, October 12, 1968

LED ZEPPELIN CLIMBS BEFORE ITS FIRST LP

Ritchie Yorke | January 11, 1969, *Globe and Mail*

Ritchie Yorke was a major voice for Led Zeppelin early on in their career (and his). His 1976 book *Led Zep: The Led Zeppelin Biography* was certainly one of the first books about the band. It was edited into *The Definitive Led Zeppelin Biography* in 1992. –Ed.

Much to their surprise—and delight—record companies have discovered that they can sell stacks of albums without getting once-vital radio exposure. They have even found that they can sell a group's LP even if it has never made a record.

The truth of this unlikely situation is borne out by the orders for the first album by Led Zeppelin, a new English group headed by guitarist Jimmy Page.

Although the LP is still more than four weeks away from its release date in the United States, it reportedly is much in demand in California, with orders for more than 50,000 copies.

How can a group command this kind of attention when most people have not even heard of the album? The answer seems to lie with the popularity of individual musicians.

In the case of the Led Zeppelin, Jimmy Page is the attraction. The 23-year-old former art student is known for his stints as bass guitarist with the Yardbirds, and later as the group's lead guitarist.

Although the Yardbirds have split up, their influence continues. Between the Yardbirds' breakup and the formation of Led Zeppelin in October, Page worked as a recording session musician. One of his more memorable efforts was the guitar gymnastics on Joe Cocker's single, "With a Little Help From My Friends."

"I only did a few sessions, because I didn't want to fall into that trap of playing on every disc coming out in England," Page said from Los Angeles, where the group has started a North American tour.

"Since I split from the Yardies, I've been searching around for some guys for a new group, the right group." The standing ovations received by Led Zeppelin at the Whisky a Go Go in Los Angeles indicate that Page's search may be over.

Led Zeppelin's other members are: John Paul Jones, 23, on bass, organ, and piano; drummer John Bonham, 20, who played with Tim Rose; singer, Robert Plant, 21, a former member of the Band of Joy.

The name, Led Zeppelin?

"Keith Moon, of the Who, thought it up," said Page. "You know the expression about a bad joke going over like a lead balloon. It's a variation on that; and there is a little of the Iron Butterfly light-and-heavy music connotation."

Led Zeppelin landed in Denver two weeks ago, starting a two-month tour that brings them to Toronto's Rock Pile on Feb. 12.

"The reaction has been unbelievable so far," said Page, who is recovering from a bout of Hong Kong flu. "It's even better than what we got with the Yardbirds. It's really exciting to be back on the concert trail.

"My original concept was to put together a group in which every one was proficient enough to be able to take a solo at any time, and it's worked.

"We cut the album at Olympic Studios in London early in November. It's all original material, except two numbers: 'You Shook Me,' a traditional blues, and 'I Can't Quit You, Baby,' the old Otis Rush thing."

The album, simply titled Led Zeppelin, will be released later this month. I obtained a copy from New York this week. The LP seems to live up to claims that Led Zeppelin will be the next super group in the United States.

It's a mixture of heavy, earthy blues ("I learned a lot from B. B. King, Otis Rush, and Buddy Guy: I used to listen to their records over and over, and then try to play exactly like that") and wailing psychedelia.

It's not quite as free-flowing as Cream, but in the process of adding more instrumentation and vocal harmonies, Led Zeppelin has emerged with a positive, driving, distinctive sound.

Page's guitarwork skims across the melody with a simple joy. Jones's organ rhythms are forceful and invigorating. The whole is a rare pop experience. Unlike many groups, Led Zeppelin has managed to maintain simplicity while striving for depth.

I find this the best debut album by a group since the 1967 release of *Are You Experienced?* by the Jimi Hendrix Experience.

"I'm really happy to be back into it," said Page. "There's room for everything on the scene; you don't have to follow any bandwagons. You just get out there and do your own thing.

"It's a good period for guitarists. I think every good guitarist has something unique to say musically. My only ambition now is to keep a consistent record product coming out.

"Too many groups sit back after the first album, and the second one is a down trip. I want every new album to reach out farther. That's what I'm doing here."

COMMUNICATION BREAKDOWN

Chris Grant: Okay we are in the studio with Led Zeppelin in person. First of all let us speak to Robert Plant who is a lead vocalist and also plays harmonica. How long have you been in the group?

Robert Plant: I am not sure how long it has been but I eventually got here.

—Chris Grant interview with Led Zeppelin,
BBC *Tasty Pop Sundae*, June 16, 1969

LED ZEPPELIN: PLANT

Mark Williams | April 11, 1969, *International Times*

As people started to take notice of the band, people also started to take notice of the band members. For the first year or so, they were Jimmy's group, the latest iteration of the veteran group the Yardbirds. Yet as far as the quartet was concerned, they were something else entirely. Mark Williams of the *International Times*, the revolutionary underground London newspaper, caught up with one of the other members of the band, Robert Plant. –Ed.

It's not hard to suss that Led Zeppelin are well on the way to becoming a "Supergroup," in the best tradition.

They have tremendous drive, the currently trendy "heavy" sound and they look good. They also play rather well. What does appear to be happening, even at this early stage of the game, is that guitarist James Page seems to be evolving as the dominant personality of the band, as far as publicity and teeny-appeal go. Which is sad, because all the group are excessively proficient on their own scenes and I personally don't think that Page has sufficient character as an individual to rise above the others in terms of "Star Appeal" (ugh!). The gent who really has that mysterious something, both as an artist and as a person, is Robert Plant and I can well see him causing a severe outbreak of knicker wetting.

Robert Plant wasn't feeling too clever last week when we went along to a soul searching, probing (finger popping?) in-depth interview, having just escaped with his life, (he said), from a crash landing plane at Heathrow. "The captain came on and told us there's going to be an emergency landing and then, from being way up in the blue one minute, we're suddenly going down, but very down. My scotch went up in my face and the next thing I know there's some guy asking me to help the older cats out of the plane, and there I am doing the Boy Scout bit while everyone else is running away!"

As we got onto musical topics I remarked that I was very happy to see that after years of getting virtually nowhere fronting Birmingham groups that were well ahead of their time (for that area), he was finally starting to be appreciated. Robert's last group, the Band of Joy, had some very interesting things going, nice arrangements of Buffalo Springfield, Moby Grape, and odd Negro pop numbers, that provided a useful background for his very distinctive, blues inclined vocals. "There were very few other groups around at the time doing that sort of thing, but eventually we were getting 60 and 75 quid a night. In the end, however, I just had to give it up. I thought 'Bollocks, nobody at all wants to know.'"

At that time, I remembered, he was very disenchanted with the whole business and gave the impression he might give it all up.

"I met Terry Reid, who I'd played one or two gigs with in Band of Joy days, whilst I was down trying to get something together with Tony Secunda and he told me that the Yardbirds' singer had just left and suggested that I try and get into that scene. I knew they'd done a lot of work in America, which to me meant audiences who DID want to know what I'd got to offer, so naturally I was very interested. I went down to Pangbourne where Jimmy lives, it was the real desperation scene man, like I had nowhere else to go. There I was with my suitcase getting off the train and suddenly this old woman starts slapping my face and shouting about my hair. Well, I was staggered, so I called a cop and he says it was my own fault for having long hair. So much for British justice! Anyway I got to Jimmy's and we found we had exactly the same tastes in music."

So Led Zeppelin was beginning and Bob managed to persuade Jimmy that the group needed John Bonham as a drummer and managed to persuade John that he needed Led Zeppelin instead of the nice steady job he had backing Tim Rose, which is what he spent most of his time doing after Band of Joy disbanded. The addition of well respected session man John Paul Jones on bass and organ got the whole thing grooving and the rest I'm sure you've all read about.

Plant's style is, thankfully, pretty hard to categorise. "The first music that appealed to me, when I was at school even, was stuff like [Bob] Dylan's 'Corrina, Corrina' and when you look deeper into that sort of thing you find there's a lot of the same feelings that are in blues music, like Leadbelly's stuff and then you realise that the blues field is a very wide one. There's a lot of shit of course, all the old guys, such as Bukka White, who originally recorded in the late '20s, are suddenly being grabbed a hold of and shoved into a studio to do an ethnic blues recording. They think, 'Well it's 200 bucks, that'll keep me in firewood for the next three months,' so they get into their wheelchairs, do the thing, and all the blues freaks say; 'Well man, this is the real blues,' and it's really a load of bollocks."

Onstage, Plant has a terrific empathy with the music he's singing to, moving and flexing to every progression and chord change. He presents, I should imagine, (says he carefully), a very desirable image to young ladies with an interest in musical gentlemen. The groupie thing, whilst, by cunning contrivance, we're on the subject, is of particular interest to Robert, never having really experienced that scene on the scale it is in the States.

"It's an art over there, it really is. Take the Plaster Casters in Chicago, it's the only thing they've got in the world man, because they couldn't pull a fella if the fella was blind and pissed, 'cause they're so revolting, but they can turn round and say, 'Well, I've got so and so's plaster cast.' When they came round to see us they came in with the wooden case, suitably inscribed, all very ceremoniously, it was SO funny. So one of them starts this big plating scene, 'cause, to them, that's all part of their ritual, and she goes on doing it for an hour, a whole hour. All of a sudden she stops, having decided that it's just not going to work. Then she starts taking her clothes off, because she feels that she's got to do something having wasted the last forty minutes. And she's rather large, no doubt about it, she's rather well built and there she is standing there as naked as the day she was born. So then she got covered in soap from head to foot, then she got cream doughnuts and then whisky all rubbed in together and there she was a moving mountain of soapy flesh. At first she dug it but soon she got rather afraid and her friend, a virgin who'd just come along for the ride, was trying very hard to disappear under the bed, like she just didn't know where it was at. Eventually she got into the shower, grabbed her clothes and split. A few days later we heard she'd quit the Plaster Casters—had enough! It's so sad that people like that exist, man. It wasn't as if it was a perversion she enjoyed, which would have been OK. It was just a ritual she had to do to get herself noticed. A very weird scene."

And so on that, decidedly unmusical note, we repaired to the Marquee where Zeppelin performed to quite the largest audience I've seen there since the Nice ended their residency and, apart from a little untogetherness in the first few minutes when Jimmy had trouble with his lead, they were absolutely total. Robert was wailing and swaying, like some energetic modern ballet dancer caught in a tornado and the band swung like fuck until the audience had been whipped up to a pitch equal to that which Mr. Hendrix used to be well-known for producing. Robert was the tiger teasing his prey, quite capable of pouncing but never going quite that far. The music did that for him.

COMMUNICATION BREAKDOWN

"Most places here they just go to have a dance or to have a drink, not to listen. They don't care who is on . . . [In Cardiff] they wouldn't let the group in because they didn't have ties. Robert Plant and John Bonham had to call the manager to get in . . . We'd been told that we'd have to do an exact 45 minute spot, and if we went a minute over that was it. So we cut it down and when we started the last number, if we'd been allowed to complete it, it would have over-run by six minutes. They turned on the revolving stage as we were playing and the deejay came round. The audience was whistling and booing."

—Jimmy Page to Nick Logan, *NME*, May 10, 1969

FORGET BLIND FAITH, LED ZEPPELIN'S THE BIGGEST

Ritchie Yorke | August 14, 1969, *Globe and Mail*

When the Beatles began to implode, the title of World's Greatest Band was up for grabs. There are those who say Creedence Clearwater Revival earned the distinction in 1969 by releasing three albums and a slew of global hits. Some say it was Led Zeppelin because of the high energy burn they left on popular music in their first year (and thereafter). What Ritchie Yorke thought becomes obvious as soon as you read the title to this piece. –Ed.

Jimmy Page, the lithe, lean lead guitarist of Led Zeppelin, was sitting in the mixing room of A & R Studios in New York, sipping tea and munching a prune Danish pastry. His hair hung six inches below the collar line, and his red velvet bells harmonized with the burgundy patent boots—if not with the pink brushed velvet Edwardian jacket.

Page had flown in from Salt Lake City, and he would be returning to the airport in an hour to catch a flight to Los Angeles. It had been a long day, but the 24-year-old guitarist was in lively spirits.

The track he was mixing (called "Bring It On Home") sounded like Sonny Boy Williamson mixed with Jimmy Page. Actually, it was Led Zeppelin's lead singer, Robert Plant, trying to sound like Williamson and doing a pretty fine job of it.

Page was racing against time to get this, the band's second album, out by the end of the month. Led Zeppelin's first album, released last January, has sold 500,000 copies and earned a gold record. And so Page felt the time had come for a new album.

"We've been so busy," he said, "that we just weren't able to go into the studio and polish the album off. It's become sort of ridiculous. I mean, we'd put down a rhythm track in London, add the voice in New York, put in harmonica in Vancouver, then come back to New York to do the mixing.

"When we got together last November, we never expected to be as big as this. We just wanted to be able to come over here to work a couple of times a year. But it's almost got out of hand."

In the past couple of months Led Zeppelin has emerged as the most important English group working in North America.

The quartet's second tour, which brings it to Toronto for two shows with Edward Bear at the Rock Pile on Monday, has been breaking attendance records with amazing ease. More than 10,000 people in Dallas, 10,000 in Chicago, 10,000 in Los Angeles; an incredible 8,000 at Santa Barbara against Blood, Sweat & Tears and Johnny Winter at a nearby location the same night. There can be little doubt that Led Zeppelin is *the* English band of the moment, including Blind Faith.

One reason is the emergence of singer Robert Plant as the most significant sex idol since Jim Morrison. Initially, Led Zeppelin was all Page but now, with Plant doing a great job of turning on the girls, the band has found a much wider acceptance.

Despite all the raves and monetary return (the band will earn more than $350,000 on this tour) that have come Led Zeppelin's way, Page has remained remarkably modest and honest: "There are so many guitarists around who are better than me. Everywhere I go I hear some cat who sounds better than I do. That's the trouble: everyone's good these days."

Early next month Page is taking a month off to relax. He intends to travel through Morocco and Spain. Then the band returns to North America for a short tour, which is kicked off by two concerts at Carnegie Hall. They were sold out weeks ago.

"This tour has been fantastic, but you can never be too sure. We've got to work even harder now. You can't rest on your laurels. It's easy to go down just as fast as you went up. I think what did it for us was the stage thing. We came here unknown on the first tour, did our number, and the word got out that we were worth seeing. We tried as hard as we could on stage and it worked."

COMMUNICATION BREAKDOWN

"It's impossible to convey just how big Zeppelin are now in the States but if I tell you that our album sold 20,000 copies in three days last week and is still pounding along it might give you some idea. You can turn on the radio and hear a Zeppelin track played three or four times a day."

—Keith Altham, *Top Pops*, September 13, 1969

COMMUNICATION BREAKDOWN

"It is a big prestige thing being asked to play there," said Robert with pride. "You have to wait until you're asked to play at [Carnegie] Hall by a committee that runs the place. I don't know why they asked us. Could they think us a nice group?"

—Nick Logan interview with Robert Plant, *NME*, October 11, 1969

JIMMY PAGE TALKS ABOUT LED ZEPPELIN

Valerie Wilmer | 1970, *Hit Parader*

Valerie Wilmer is best known as a writer and photographer covering jazz, renowned, in fact, as a keeper of the musical history of people of African ancestry living in Britain and in the United States. One of the lesser known facts about her is that she was *Hit Parader*'s "girl in London" for many years. Note, however, that she catches the jazz influences that all members of the group—particularly John Bonham—had. –Ed.

Led Zeppelin may sound a pretty incongruous sort of name to Americans unfamiliar with the British sense of humor, but when Who drummer Keith Moon dreamed up the title for Jimmy Page's new group he was recalling an ancient British saying. They say that when a joke falls flat, it "goes down like a lead Zeppelin"—(named after the World War I airship)—but Page's new combo seems in little danger of flopping.

For their recent appearance at London's Marquee Club, the ex-Yardbirds guitarist whipped his men into a commendable frenzy which was not without its moments of inspiration and extensive improvisation. "Our music sort of resembles jazz, as far as the improvisation is concerned," explained the leader. "All I can say is that we're just sort of moving on and throwing ideas to each other.

"We usually have the beginning part worked out in advance and the ending, and we might have a couple of cues as to what the thing is going

16

to go into, but we might go off into anything—who knows? We do have some numbers that are more or less the same from beginning to end but they're mostly the shorter ones, and anyway, it's more of a challenge to experiment."

Led Zeppelin, which has been flying high since last October, was more or less formed overnight. Jimmy explained that he had several old Yardbirds dates to fulfill in Scandinavia, but was without a manageable group. "We had a singer and Chris Dreja from the old Yardbirds was going to play bass, but I thought we'd have to cancel out. Then suddenly everyone phoned up at the same time and Chris decided to drop out in favor of John Paul Jones. He's going into management, anyway, and as he liked John, he thought it would be a good idea to have him in the band."

Jimmy's other henchmen are singer Robert Plant, a powerful, progressive vocalist in the Jack Bruce mould who also doubles on harmonica, and drummer John Bonham who has obviously listened to some of the "guv'nor" percussionists in the jazz world. John Paul Jones is, like Jimmy, a former session guitarist of nationwide reputation, and this stint represents the first time he has worked with a name group on a fulltime basis. "John had worked with some groups on his road, but mainly just for the chance of playing and because it was easy music to fit into. Before he came with us, he was working on sessions with Donovan and people like that. But I'm very happy with all of them as people," said Jimmy.

Jimmy Page is one of the most affable and easy-going people in the world of progressive music; as relaxed and beautiful off-stage as he is tormented and angry in front of the crowd. When I caught the Led Zeppelin at London's Marquee Club just before Christmas, I thought they had a tendency to go on for too long and destroy effective climaxes by trying to top them with a further musical climax. Jimmy took this criticism kindly. "It's funny you should say that, because when we played here at the Roundhouse, the reaction was so good that I asked people what they thought of the group. Nearly everyone I spoke to said 'oh, it was great, but you could have done longer!' It seems to be the scene now."

I asked whether he thought extended improvisation in pop was the inevitable course for all groups to pursue. "Well," he replied, "I haven't really heard that many bands lately, but on that Cream LP where they do the live things, there's a very long track called 'Crossroads' and maybe that's it. I don't think you plan these things; you just sort of get into it.

"If it gets boring, then obviously it's no good. We try to change it around a bit and if it goes in one way for too long, then we try to think of something else."

He agreed that he knew what I meant about the repeated climaxes. "You see, you take a chance with all this Free Form stuff. I suppose that if everything was really clear-cut and rehearsed and you know exactly what note you were going to play, then it wouldn't be free. It would be more like the Hollies or someone like that."

Jimmy himself attracts a lot of attention from aspiring guitarists, who marvel at the ease with which he bends the strings on his 1958 Fender Telecaster. "Mainly they come along and they ask what sort of strings you use, but all I can say is that they're very, very light. It foxes them because if they haven't been playing very long and they've got heavy strings on, it's such a physical effort. The main thing is to have them strung very light, you see. Sometimes they come up and ask how did you do so-and-so on a record and you try to show 'em, but you can't always explain it!"

His most impressive feat on the night I caught the group, was bowing his guitar strings in harmony with the vocal on a number called 'Days of Confusion.'* Surprisingly, I discovered that he first tried out this feat more than three years ago. "With the voice we try to do a lot of answering phrases and so on and that usually builds up into quite a thing with the voice following behind," Jimmy explained.

"The bow thing came about when I was doing sessions. One of the violinists came up to me and said 'why don't you use a bow on it?' I said 'oh, it can't work at all', but I tried it and it was working. As soon as I joined the old Yardbirds, we used it then. There is someone else who started out at about the same time as me—a guy with the Creation—but I don't know if either party knew about the other until some time later."

According to the guitarist, British audiences are more critical and narrow-minded than their American counterparts. "They all have their idols like Eric [Clapton] or Jimi [Hendrix], and if you're not careful they

---

*The actual song title is "Dazed and Confused."

accuse you of copying all round. They say 'hey, that's an Eric Clapton phrase!' or 'that's a Hendrix phrase!', so what I do now is to listen to classical music for pleasure so that I don't get caught up in this kind of danger. It seems that in America they're fairer in that they accept more than one person on the instrument."

He went on: "I had this thing the other day when I wanted to do some hard practicing and I didn't know how to go about it! Now I know that when I go on stage, whatever I do is just something that comes out, it could be blues or whatever. I think that if you really just sort of lay yourself open to all sorts of media, different styles of music, it will all go in and come out on stage without you actually having to religiously copy a phrase at home and try to repeat it on stage the next day."

Jimmy, who apart from his black-necked Fender Telecaster (custom-wired and the first of its kind, incidentally), uses a custom-built Tonebender fuzzbox and a standard wah wah pedal and an assortment of amps. He is more interested in what he manages to play than in what he actually plays it on, but he had this advice for aspiring young guitarmen: "As usual, keep practicing.

"At the beginning you have to get it off records because that's about the only way of doing it. If anything really foxes you and you can't quite get it off, go along and see if you can spot the player doing it. It would be pretty difficult with someone like Hendrix, but with someone like Jeff Beck who plays all over the place, you can look and see if it's a trick of the trade or whatever. That's more or less how I started doing it, anyway. I'd practice and then say to myself, well, how can I go on from that phrase? Then you'll start working in your own things eventually."

Led Zeppelin had just completed their first album when I interviewed the leader who declared himself to be "quite pleased" with the results. "At least there's nothing on it that I'm ashamed of," he smiled. "But I do have a pretty restless mind."

Right now he is itching to get to work on his latest acquisition, a flat pedal steel guitar of the kind used by C&W players. "I don't know what other instrument uses this system, but it's pretty effective. It works on a system of rollers and when you push down on the pedals, the strings sharpen or flatten accordingly. It's just a real piece of machinery, actually, and I've been playing some blues on it. You play it with three picks, (two fingers and a thumb) and it's a hard instrument to learn. It's tuned to a chord and you put this steel bar over the top and change the chord with the six-foot pedals. You can get quite a few varieties of chords from it."

As to Led Zeppelin's future, Jimmy maintained that his prime aim was to "get off a lot of new ideas quickly, especially with workable combinations of instruments—not ones that you can't reproduce on the stage. On all the stuff we've done so far, I've worked out the arrangements because of the time factor, but as from now on, everyone will be contributing to what we do."

COMMUNICATION BREAKDOWN

"I don't feel any kind of pressure to do something because I don't think at this moment people are that familiar with what I do. They've seen me once or twice or something; it isn't looked upon as a show. I think people are still saying he's a good singer as opposed to what they say about Jim Morrison, that he's a sex symbol or something, although I don't know how they'd say that. I don't mean any disrespect. I suppose he's very nice, but it's strange. I don't like the way he plays on everyone's head. . . . I think entertainment should be light. He seems to take himself too seriously."

—Robert Plant to Jacoba Atlas, *Circus*, March 1970

COMMUNICATION BREAKDOWN

John Bonham: I think that they're coming to listen to what you're playing and not just to look at you and see what you are. I mean, I remember when I was—let's go imagine a few years—when I first went to see the Beatles, 'cause we've mentioned them a few times, it was to look at them. You didn't really bother what you were listening to and today it's not what you are, it's what you're playing. . . .

Robert Plant: To have money at last is just another figure in my mind of mass acceptance which is what we all work for. I mean everybody, no matter how much they want to deny the fact, really wants, in the end, to be accepted by the majority of people for being either a talent or a commodity, and I think that we've reached that stage now. It's left to us to keep on coming up with something good so we'll be at the *Melody Maker* for winning these awards blah blah blah.

—Brian Ash interview with Led Zeppelin,
BBCTV *Nationwide*, September 16, 1970

ASK-IN WITH A LED ZEPPELIN: BASSIST JOHN PAUL JONES— "MOTOWN BASS DESERVES A LOT OF CREDIT"

Ritchie Yorke | April 4, 1970 | *NME*

The next four interviews offer a base and bedrock look at Led Zeppelin as four individuals. Ritchie Yorke spent quite a bit of time with the band during this period, shortly before spending a similarly immersive amount of time with Jimi Hendrix just before Hendrix's passing. Beyond everything else, this was the first major interview with bassist John Paul Jones. —Ed.

The only really encouraging thing that happened during 1969 for me was the unveiling of Led Zeppelin, Britain's latest weapon in the war against American rock. By year's end, Led Zeppelin—a group of unknowns apart from guitarist Jimmy Page—had become the most important new band since the Beatles, surpassing even Cream in popularity.

The group's sudden success came after Cream curdled and Hendrix fell victim to well-fed delusions of grandeur. There wasn't much of music's usual hype, and there was even less critical acclaim for the Zepp [sic].

Even now, it's very much in vogue in rock critic circles to rip off Led Zeppelin as a noisy bunch of weirdies from England. Even some of rock's upper echelon of publications still seem to deny the existence of the

Zeppelin. Initially, there wasn't much serious critical evaluation of Led Zeppelin. They were just another band into blues from England. Sure, they had a guitarist from the Yardbirds, but wasn't Jeff Beck the man to watch from that trip? Skepticism, apathy, ignorance. Meanwhile, the Zepp [sic] had arrived and hit and left the charts coated with the debris of a hard-rock hurricane.

The band's concert price zoomed from a low of $250 in January of last year, to $25,000 at the start of their fifth tour. Both albums had sold in excess of one million copies by Christmas. And a single, "Whole Lotta Love," went very close to a million. The new tour will earn the group more than $800,000.

Right now, what's happening in rock is very much in the hands of Jimmy Page, John Bonham, Robert Plant, and John Paul Jones. Without question, Led Zeppelin is the world's most popular group, outside the Beatles, and no-one knows any more if the Beatles still are a group.

In Toronto recently, I rapped with each member of Led Zeppelin and compiled a four-part profile-through-interview report on the group. We start with bass player, John Paul Jones. one of the finest technicians in the field.

Ritchie Yorke: What were you doing before Led Zeppelin formed?

John Paul Jones: Vegetating in studios in London mainly. Jimmy's also done his share of that. But he got out and went into the Yardbirds. Just before joining the band, I had gotten into arranging and general studio directing, which was better than just sitting and being told what to do.

I did a lot of Donovan's stuff. The first thing I did for him was "Sunshine Superman." I happened to be on the session and I ended up arranging it. The arranger who was there really didn't know about anything. I sort of got the rhythm section together and we went from there.

"Mellow Yellow" I did entirely on my own. I was pleased with it; it was different to what was happening in the general session scene.

RY: Were you surprised at the success of LZ?

JPJ: Yes, I was surprised as to the extent of our success. You see, we'd been doing all this for a long time and, after a while, you can see how a group breaks up and what causes all the ups and downs. You reckon that if you should consciously put together a group that won't have a lot of stupid troubles; and the basic thing of what people want to listen to; good musicianship; and a certain amount of professionalism; the right promotion—with those things you figure you must stand a good chance. But to what extent, nobody knows. To this extent, it's unbelievable!

RY: Do you think your success came because there was a gap in the rock scene after Cream and a perennial need for a hard-hard rock band?

JPJ: If you think from a pure popologist's point of view, you could say it was foreseen, inevitable, predictable. There was a gap there and we filled the gap. But there's a lot of other things which may do it.

I think the business did need something different because Cream was going around in circles. They never talked to one another, it seemed. The groups that did have a good sound were successful but they always seemed to have internal troubles; while the groups that did get on never got heard, and somehow you had to get the two together. An amicable group, a good sound and exposure.

RY: L Z seems to be a group which gets on well?

JPJ: Yeah, especially as we're all different people. Robert and John have got the Birmingham band thing in common. Nobody had actually worked together before LZ though. We just got together in a 6 ft. × 6 ft. room and started playing and looked at everybody else and realized what was going to happen.

RY: Who influenced your bass playing?

JPJ: Not a lot of people because it was only recently that you could even hear the bass on records. So apart from obvious jazz influences—like every good jazz bass player in history; [Charles] Mingus, Ray Brown, Scott LaFaro . . . I was into jazz organ for quite a while until I couldn't stand the musicians any longer and I had to get back to rock 'n' roll.

I listened to a lot of jazz bass players and that influenced my session playing, and then I cannot tell a lie, the Motown bass players! You just can't get away from it. Every bass player in every rock group is still doing Motown phrases, whether he wants to admit it or not.

RY: It's a shame that so few artists have credited Motown as an influence?

JPJ: Right. Yet it's been one of the Motown sound's biggest selling points. I used to know a few names of Motown bass players, but I can't remember them. Motown was a bass player's paradise, because they'd actually found a way to record it so that you could hear every note.

Their bass players were just unbelievable; some of the Motown records used to end up as sort of concertos for bass guitar.

RY: What do you think of Jack Bruce's playing?

JPJ: Jack is very good. I'm not too keen on the sound he has, but that's his personal taste. Being a bass player, I obviously have more idea of the sound I like than someone who just listens to records. I like his LP *Songs for a Tailor* though.

RY: What about Paul McCartney?

JPJ: Well, I think he's perfect. He's always been good. Everything he's done has always been right, even if he didn't do too much, it was still just right. He's improved so much since the early Beatles days, and everything is still right.

RY: How about Ric Grech?

JPJ: I don't know anything about him.

RY: Bass has really become important in the past two years.

JPJ: Bass players have really got annoyed and said to engineers, "You've got to get it through." Then they went to the people who cut the record, because you can get it on tape and then lose it on record. The cutters start screaming that it won't play with too much bass and people's expensive magnetic cartridges will jump up into the air every time you hit a bottom string.

I think [Jack Casady] did an awful lot, and he's still doing so. He designs bass guitars which are utterly unbelievable.

RY: Did you hear Moms Mabley's record of "Abraham, Martin, and John"? That had fantastic bass reproduction.

JPJ: No, I didn't hear that. The Motown record that really impressed me was *I Was Made to Love Her* by Stevie Wonder. When it came out, I just couldn't believe it.

RY: You must be one of the few people who actually sits down just to hear a bass pattern on a new record.

JPJ: Bass players are always like that. The first record that really turned me on to bass guitar was "You Can't Sit Down" by Phil Upchurch, which had an incredible bass solo and was a good record as well. Very simple musically, but it had an incredible amount in it.

RY: After years of session work, how does it feel to be in a group?

JPJ: It's a strain, but it's a different kind of strain. I much prefer it. In sessions you just vegetate and you reach a certain period where you're working a helluva lot and that's it. You can't do anything musically and it's horrible. You become a well-used session musician with no imagination.

I used to be the only bass player in England that knew anything about the Motown stuff so I used to do all the cover versions. I often used to almost be in tears at the sound they'd get and the way they used to mess up the songs.

RY: The English session scene is rather unique in that they really only have one man for each instrument, and if you're the man, you get to do every session going?

JPJ: Right. But it's not specialised, which is the strangest thing. You can do anything. Every record that's been made in England you could have been on, if they used your particular instrument—from Petula Clark to visiting Americans. I remember one day—firstly at Decca Studios with the Bachelors; then Little Richard, who'd come over to do a couple of English sessions—and it was bloody awful.

RY: It must have been rough at first, though with people only thinking of LZ as Jimmy Page's band?

JPJ: Well if Jimmy had been incredibly insecure and really wanted to be a star, he would have picked lesser musicians and gone on the road and done the whole star trip. Everybody in the band recognised that at first having Jimmy's name was a great help. In fact, it opened a lot of doors, and once you realized that, and became aware that you had a job to do, it worked out all right.

I've been playing bass for ten years now. I've been on the road since I was two years old—my parents were in the business, too . . . in variety. They had a double act, musical comedy thing. I was in a professional band with Jet Harris and Tony Meehan. That was when I was 17.

RY: What do you think of Robert Plant?

JPJ: Robert is unique. We're all unique really, but Robert is really something. I couldn't imagine any other singer with us. I just couldn't. Robert is Robert and there's nothing else to say.

RY: How about John Bonham?

JPJ: John is the find of the year as far as British drummers are concerned. I can't remember anyone like him either. It's obvious why these people have ended up in the same group. We've all the right people. If anybody had to leave, the group would have to split up. Each of us is irreplaceable in this band.

RY: How about Jimmy?

JPJ: For years and years, I've rated Jimmy. We both come from South London and even then I can remember people saying "You've got to go and listen to Neil Christian and the Crusaders, they've got this unbelievable guitarist." I'd heard of him before I heard of Clapton or Beck.

I probably listen to more of Clapton through Jimmy telling me to than any other reason. I've always thought Jimmy to be far superior to all of them. It sounds like a mutual admiration society; people don't believe me when I say this, but I mean it.

RY: Why do you think English bands are beginning to be stronger chart-wise, than American bands again?

JPJ: The Americans have got lazy. They've had it their way for so long. As soon as some competition comes along and does well, the not-so-good bands get uptight because they think they're missing out on all the work. The better bands pull their fingers out and really come up with something great, and they do as well as the best English bands.

RY: Do you think we're in the middle of a second English invasion of the US charts?

JPJ: I think it can be taken as a criticism of American bands that so many English groups are getting into the U.S. charts. American groups should look at themselves and their music if this is the case, and ask themselves why all these foreigners are going so well when they're not.

And I'm sure if they looked hard enough they'd come up with one reason or another, and they'd be able to get it back together and make it again.

ASK-IN WITH A LED ZEPPELIN: "THINKING AS A SEX SYMBOL CAN TURN YOU INTO A BAD PERSON"– ROBERT PLANT

Ritchie Yorke | April 11, 1970, *NME*

Last week, I reported the sayings of bass player John Paul Jones. Continuing NME's four-part series on Led Zeppelin, I turned to lead singer Robert Plant, who is regarded in some quarters as rock's most provocative sex symbol since Jim Morrison (but wait till you hear what he has to say about that!).

I interviewed Robert in Toronto and his frank replies to my questions are below . . .

Ritchie Yorke: Did you expect to meet with such staggering success?

Robert Plant: Never! I don't think anyone could expect that, really. Not Jimmy, and Jimmy already knew that American audiences were much more responsive to hard work. But none of us really expected this. Just bang! And we really never knew how big we were.

You can't really realize it until you come to each individual town that you have never been in before and people are running down the street banging on your car windows and all that. And when you get a fantastic reception the moment you walk on stage, you start to realize just what's happening. I could never have dreamed of anything like this.

RY: What were you doing before Led Zeppelin was formed?

RP: I was working immediately before LZ with a group called Alexis Korner and we were in the process of recording an album with a pianist called Steve Miller, a very fluid thing—nothing definitely set up. We were going to do a few festivals in Germany and that sort of thing. Before that, I hadn't done much at all. I'd cut three singles which I prefer to forget. I want to leave them in the dimmest past!

John Bonham and I worked together for a total of 2½ years. It was a period of trying to find what I wanted to do musically. You know, you go through the initial thing where you want to get up on stage and scream your head off, and the next minute you want to play blues, and you finally find that everything is a means to an end to what you really want to do musically . . . once you've reached it.

So I feel my first four or five years were finding out what I wanted to do. You could either end up going completely into the pop field on a commercial trip, or just stick to what you liked musically.

RY: Have you now found your musical niche?

RP: I think I'm finding it. The first year of LZ has made me see a lot more of what I want to do. I think this year has been much more valuable to me than the other five because for the first five years nobody really wanted to accept what I was doing, even though we were doing a sort of Buffalo Springfield–Moby Grape sort of thing.

In England, nobody really wanted to know, they just said it was a noise with no meaning; and to me, it was the only noise with meaning. The Springfield and the Grape really knew what they were doing.

LZ has given me a chance to express that in lyrics on the second album, and when we do the third album I hope to get that thing even more to the point of what I'm trying to get into. Gradually, bit by bit, I'm finding myself now. It's taken a long time, a lot of insecurity and nerves and the "I'm a failure" stuff. Everybody goes through it. Even Jimmy did, when he was with the Yardbirds, but now everything's shaping up nicely.

RY: When you started though, everyone in North America thought this was Jimmy Page's band. That was the impetus which launched you here. It must have meant you all had a great responsibility to prove yourselves individually, as both people and musicians.

RP: Yeah, but it was really good, because, well, obviously we owed a lot to Jimmy in the first place because, without him, we couldn't have gone into the right places initially . . . Because people like Spooky Tooth have had such a hard time trying to get any sort of reputation in the States, and eventually all their inspiration goes.

Spooky Tooth came over here in the summer and did about seven gigs in as many weeks. It was very bad for the band.

With Jimmy's reputation, we could go into the proper clubs, but had Jimmy been the only member of LZ who was any good at all, it would have been pointless. Fortunately each of us shone in our own little way, if that's what you can call it, and the audiences said: "Wow, there's Jimmy and he's brilliant" and they look around and they take everybody else how they want to.

Obviously on the first tour, it was all Jimmy, Jimmy, Jimmy, which is fair enough because he deserved it, and then on the second tour people started taking an interest in the other members of the group and then with our stage act, well we've had some criticism of that.

The thing is that after a while you personally start going out on the stage and you can feel what's going to happen. The moment you set foot on stage you can sort of let go, and the audience is like a piece of blotting paper and what makes it is what you give it, and you've gotta give it good.

Each of us has a different personality which comes to the fore. Like John, when he jumps into the air above his drums. Everybody now knows each member of the group for his musical ability and for himself, I think.

RY: Robert, you have been described as the most important new sex symbol in pop since Morrison. Does this really get to you? Or do you take it lightheartedly?

RP: Yeah, well, don't you think it's the end of your life once you take it seriously, that sex symbol thing. If any musician goes on stage feeling that;

I mean, you can take in all that applause at face value and it can turn you into a bad person, really it can.

Terrible Harm

All this sort of popularity can do you terrible harm and I really thought that it would do once we started getting off. I thought, "God. If this keeps going what the hell will happen to me?"

You can go right off your rocker and you can start to think—"Here I am and I'm the greatest singer in the world" and all that. But it's not worth doing that because there's always someone who can come along and will sing better than me and I fully realize that, so all you can be is honest and be yourself.

If there's some nights when I don't want to say anything to the audience then I don't. But I don't make it noticeable.

I don't really know how people think about sex symbols. If they can see your pelvis then that must make you a sex symbol . . . because I'm the only one of us that doesn't have a guitar or drums in the way of mine. I suppose I started with a bit more chance than anybody else in the band.

You can't take it seriously simply because you read all these things about it. You just get into your music and the sexual bit isn't an apparent thing. It's not what we're there for.

RY: Your stage act seems to be going through some changes as compared with the first couple of tours.

RP: Yeah. I think that what we're doing now is what each one of us wants to do. I think people expect us to be a lot more arrogant than we are. A lot of people say "Yeah well they're alright but what about all that laughing and jumping around they do."

There seems to be a label that goes with music that's intense. People are expected to stand there looking as though they're out of their minds. If ever I was to go out of my mind, I'm sure I wouldn't just stand there like that—so it's like a big play act and we mustn't play act otherwise we'll run away with ourselves like Jim Morrison did.

RY: Do you think Morrison takes himself too seriously?

RP: Oh yeah. We only played with the Doors once in Seattle and it seemed like he was screwed up. He was giving the impression he was into really deep things like Skip Spence of Moby Grape. You can get into a trip of your own that you don't really realise what's going on in the outside world.

Morrison went on stage and said "F— you all" which didn't really do anything except make a few girls scream. Then he hung on the side of the stage and nearly toppled into the audience and did all those things that I suppose were originally sexual things but as he got fatter and dirtier and more screwed up, they became bizarre.

Over all our Heads

So it was really sickening to watch. My wife and I were there watching and we couldn't believe it. I respected the Doors' albums, even though they're not brilliant musicians, and, as I said, that doesn't matter. What Morrison was doing on record was good.

The track "Cancel My Subscription To The Resurrection" ["When the Music's Over"] was great, but now he doesn't get into any of the things from the past, and the sexual thing has gone. He was just miles above everyone's head. It seemed that he realized the Doors were on the way down.

He went on stage with that opinion and immediately started saying all those strange things which nobody could get into. There were one or two people there crying: "You're God, you're King," and I was thinking, "Why?"

Then the Youngbloods went on stage and wiped the audience out because they were so warm. They'd laugh and the audience would laugh. That's how music should be. It isn't a real serious thing. We're not over here to have a bad time. We're over here to have a good time and people pay money to have a good time as well.

RY: But there has to be something else going down. Jimmy and I agreed on a theory about a gap in the scene for hard rock.

RP: You could say that and then again you couldn't. There was such a difference, even on first hearing, between us and the Cream. There was an intense difference. There were other groups in the country at the time who could have filled the Cream's place more specifically than ourselves.

RY: But you're into hard rock?

Different Things

RP: Well, I think individually, offstage, we're into different things but it all comes out in the music. If you noticed, we had a C&W half hour the other night.

RY: There seems to be a lot of younger kids turning up to your concerts?

RP: Yeah, the spreading of the gospel I suppose! It beats me why they come. I really think that the first album wasn't commercial at all. You know, CS&N [Crosby, Stills, & Nash] are far more commercial than LZ in as much as the vocal thing is there to hang on to. With LZ there was all sorts of different things going on. Every member of the group was doing something different so it doesn't strike you immediately as something . . .

RY: Obviously you did what you wanted and the public liked it at the same time?

RP: Yeah, that's why I can't see why the kids that came along got into it as strongly as we did and as strongly as the original audiences who came to see us when we first came over here. So you've got this stronger thing now. The audiences are really strange now. It worries me sometimes to see how it's turning out. Go to concerts by Janis [Joplin] or the Youngbloods or Neil Young and you'll still get the same people. So I suppose the audience is just fanning out more and more.

RY: You made it in America first and then Britain. This has got a few people uptight?

RP: Yeah it has. You can imagine that England being the conservative place that it is, the conservatism goes into the music as well. The musical journalists are still sort of dubious about this sort of music and they were thinking that it was a flash in the pan and they didn't think it had any social relevance, which it does.

Groups who go on stage and play music at festivals that says: "Down with the establishment" are immediately in the majority now—even in England.

RY: Who are your greatest influences?

RP: There was a guy called Tommy McClellan, who recorded on the Bluebird label for RCA in the 30s. His rapport, the way he completely expressed himself on record, was great 'cause it was though he was saying "To hell with you," all the time, and he was just shouting out all these lyrics with such gusto that even now, you could sit there and go "Corr."

It's the same with Robert Johnson. His sympathy with his guitar playing, it's just like when you're a vocalist you have to be sympathetic with the musicians you're playing with.

RY: B. B. King?

RP: Not really. I like B. B. I like to listen to him, I like to hear him sing and I like him stalking and leading up to things like "Don't Answer the Door," where he does a big rap like that Isaac Hayes album, where he does a big thing for a long time. But B. B. King is a guitarist's sort of singer really if anybody is sort of going to take things from him.

I always respected Steve Winwood I must admit. He was to me the only guy. He had such a range in the early days when Spencer Davis first became popular. They were doing things like "Don't Start Crying Now" by Slim Harpo and "Watch Your Step," and "Rambling Rose," Jerry Lee Lewis, and the whole way. Steve was one of the first people who wasn't sticking to the normal, like the Hollies and all those groups who had been "dot dash, dot dash, follow the lines" and sang all the same thing every night.

And along came little Winwood, who was only a bit older than me, and started screaming out all these things and I thought, "Gosh, that's what I've been trying to do."

RY: What do you think of John Paul Jones?

RP: What a question! As a musician, incredible. His imagination as bass player is very good. Also as a pianist and organist, because he looks at the whole thing in a completely different way to me. I mean, the five lines and four spaces were never of any importance to me because I was a vocalist and I just hung onto the fact that it was an easy way out being a vocalist. You don't have to know much, you just have to sing.

He comes from a different angle altogether and even though it doesn't apply to my singing he can be a definite influence on the group—if he cares he can be which is an interesting thing. Jimmy can read music and all that, but he's more basic, more into blues and whamming out and writing the sort of thing I want to write, but John comes in and his rhythms and his whole thing from Stax and soul side of things, they give you the backbeat that you need so I appreciate that.

RY: Bonzo?

RP: He's a good sparring partner! [Laughs]. We played together for a long time and I think this is the only band we've ever had, obviously, any success in. If I didn't like him as a drummer I suppose he wouldn't have been the drummer, because someone would have said no. So he's got to be all right. Besides, he's phoning his missus in the morning to send a bunch of flowers to my wife.

RY: Jimmy?

RP: To begin with, when someone comes along and says: "Come with us; you're going to make a lot of money," you think he's got to be joking, so you say okay. But in the beginning I held myself a long way off from him. The more you get into the bloke, although he seems to be quite shy, he's not really. He's got lots of good ideas for songwriting and he's proved to be a really nice guy.

ASK-IN WITH A LED ZEPPELIN, PART THREE: JOHN BONHAM, DRUMMER EXTRAORDINARY KNOWN AS BONZO

Ritchie Yorke | April 18, 1970, *NME*

The third member of Led Zeppelin to be interviewed in-depth in our four-part Ask-In profile of the group is drummer John "Bonzo" Bonham, surely the finest drummer to emerge since Ginger Baker. Once again, like co-Zepps John, Paul [sic] and Robert, he answered my queries frankly and willingly. I saw him in Toronto.

Ritchie Yorke: What were you doing before LZ?

John Bonham: Five months before LZ appeared I was playing with Robert Plant in a group called Band of Joy. We did a tour as a supporting act with Tim Rose when he was playing England. Then Tim went back home and we continued for a bit longer and then we broke up. Tim Rose was coming back for another tour and he remembered me from Band of Joy and offered me the job and I took it.

So Robert and I lost contact for about 2 or 3 months. The next time I saw him I was with Tim and he'd joined what was then the Yardbirds. He said they needed a drummer for a new group. About two weeks later he came with Jimmy Page to one of Rose's concerts, saw me playing and then I got offered the job.

RY: Were you surprised at LZ success?

JB: Yes, very surprised. At the time, when I first got offered the job, I thought the Yardbirds were finished, because in England they had been forgotten, but I thought: "Well, I've got nothing anyway so anything is really better than nothing." I knew that Jimmy was a good guitarist and I knew that Robert was a good vocalist so that even if he didn't have any success, it would be a pleasure to play in a good group. And it just happened we had success as well.

RY: How long have you been playing the drums?

JB: Six years.

RY: Which drummers have influenced you?

JB: Loads of drummers. I dig listening to drummers I know aren't half as good as perhaps I am. I can still enjoy listening to them and they still do things that I don't do, so therefore I can learn something. I like Vanilla Fudge's drummer, I like Frosty with Lee Michaels.

I walked into that club last night (Toronto's Penny Farthing) and there was a group (Milkwood) whose drummer was great. He had such a great feel to the numbers. You know things like this happen all the time. You go somewhere and see a really knockout drummer.

RY: How about [Ginger] Baker?

JB: I was very influenced by him in the early days because when I first started Baker had a big image in England. He was the first rock guy, like Gene Krupa. In the big band era a drummer was a backing musician and nothing else. And in the early American bands, the drummer played with only brushes in the background. Krupa was the first drummer to be in a big band that was noticed.

You know, he came right out into the front and he played the drums much louder than they were ever played before and much better. Nobody took much interest in drums really up until that thing and Baker did the same thing with rock.

Rock had been going for a while but Baker was the first to come out with that . . . a drummer could be a forward thing in a rock band and not a thing who was stuck in the back and forgotten about. I don't think anyone can put Baker down.

I don't think he's quite as good as he was, to be honest. He used to be fantastic, but it's a pity Americans couldn't have seen the Graham Bond Organization, because they were such a good group—Jack Bruce, Ginger Baker, and Graham Bond—a fantastic group.

Baker was more into jazz I think. He still is—he plays with a jazz influence. He does a lot of things in 5/4, 3/4. He's always been a very weird sort of bloke. You can't really get to know him. He won't allow it.

RY: What did you think of Ringo [Starr]'s drumming on *Abbey Road*?

JB: Firstly, I wouldn't really guarantee that it's Ringo playing because Paul McCartney has been doing a lot of drumming with the Beatles, I hear. Let's just say I think the drumming on *Abbey Road* is really good. The drumming on all the Beatles' records is great. The actual patterns are just right for what they're doing. Some of the rhythms on the new album are really far out.

RY: Are you playing music that you like?

JB: Yeah. I think we do a bit of everything really. We go from anything in a blues field to a soul rhythm. Anything goes.

Jimmy will do a riff and I'll put in a real funky soul rhythm there or a jazzy swing rhythm or a real heavy rock thing. It's really strange.

RY: You seem to hit the snare drum harder than anybody around. How many skins have you broken on the tour?

JB: None. You can hit a drum hard if you take a short stab at it and the skin will break easily. But if you let the stick just come down, it looks as though you're hitting it much harder than I am. I only let it drop with the force of my arm coming down.

But I've only lost one skin on this tour. That was a bass drum skin and that was because the beater came off and left the little iron spike there and it went straight through. But that snare skin has been on there for three tours.

When the bass skin went, we were into the last number, "How Many More Times," and Robert was into his vocal thing just before we all come back in. It was a bit of a bummer.

RY: How did you start playing solo routines without sticks? Did you break them one night?

JB: It did begin with something like that. I don't really remember. I know I've been doing it an awful long time. It goes back to when I first joined Robert, I used to do it then. I don't know why really. I saw a group years and years ago on a jazz program do it and I think that started me off. It impressed me a helluva lot.

It wasn't what you could play with your hands; you just get a lovely little tone out of the drums that you don't get with sticks. I thought it would be a good thing to do, so I've been doing it ever since.

RY: What do you think of Robert Plant?

JB: I could talk about Robert Plant for days because I know him so well. I think we were 16 when we first met, which is six years ago. That's a long time. He knows me off by heart and vice versa. I think that's why we get on so well.

I think when you know someone—when two people get together and know each other's faults and good points—you can get on with them for a long time because nothing they do can annoy you when you're already accustomed to it.

RY: How about John Paul Jones?

JB: We get on well. The whole group gets on well. We have our differences now and then.

But to me some groups get too close and the slightest thing can upset the whole group. In this group, we're just close enough, without getting on stage and someone saying something and the whole band being on the verge of breaking up. That's what happens when a group gets too close. You can get more enjoyment out of playing with each other if you don't know everyone too well.

That's why so many people like jamming. Sometimes it isn't any fun anymore to play with a group you've been in for years. But with LZ, we're always writing new stuff, doing new things, and every individual is improving and getting into new things.

RY: What do you think of Jimmy Page?

JB: I get on well with Jimmy. He's very good. He's quite shy in some ways, too. When I first met him he was very shy. But after 12 months at it, we're all getting to know one another. That's why the music has improved a lot, I think. Everybody knows each other well.

Now there are little things we do which we understand about each other. Like, Jimmy might do a certain thing on his guitar, and I'm now able to phrase with him. But in the early days I didn't know what was going to come next.

But I still don't know Jimmy all that well. Perhaps it takes more than a year to actually sort of know someone deeply. But as far as liking goes, I like Jimmy a lot. To me, he's a great guitarist in so many fields. He's not just a group guitarist who plugs in and plays electric guitar.

He's got interests in so many kinds of music. So many guitarists won't play anything but 12-bar blues, and they think that's it. And they have an attitude of when they hear a rock record of saying, "Oh that's a load of rubbish."

Blues has got to be pure and they're pure because they play it, but really that's not true either. Some of the greatest musicians in the world have never played blues so you really can't say that.

When we first came over here, the first American drummer I played with was the Vanilla Fudge's drummer. He was one of the best I've ever seen in a rock group yet so many people put them down. Nobody wants to know, thinking they're a bubblegum group.

Perhaps they were, but you can't get over the fact that they're good musicians. No matter which way you look at it, they're still good. Although they're playing music that I don't particularly like, I still admire them.

RY: Are you fed up with touring yet?

JB: No, not really. Sometimes it gets a bit wearing, but that's only because I'm married and got kids at home. But I've never got browned off with the actual touring. I enjoy playing; I could play every night. It's just being away gets you down sometimes.

I enjoy going through different towns we haven't been to before. But you get fed up with towns like New York, where you've got to spend a lot of time. It just isn't interesting any more.

JIMMY PAGE ANSWERS THE QUESTIONS IN THE FINAL LED ZEPPELIN ASK-IN

Ritchie Yorke | April 25, 1970, *NME*

The last part of our four-part series on Led Zeppelin is an interview with the man who made it all possible in the beginning, guitarist extraordinary Jimmy Page.

Jimmy's reputation as rhythm (can you believe rhythm?) guitarist with the Yardbirds and his stupendous session work in London (Joe Cocker's classic, "With a Little Help from My Friends" features Page's picking) was enough for Atlantic Records to sign Led Zeppelin unseen. The intuition of Nesuhi and Ahmet Ertegun and Jerry Wexler, the fathers at Atlantic, is too incredible to be believed.

As before, I am represented by RY below and JP is Jimmy. Here is how he replied to my questions in Toronto, Canada.

Ritchie Yorke: Where do you think your following lies?

Jimmy Page: It's hard to pinpoint really. At the beginning it was the underground clubs because that's where we started. Obviously it's spread by the amounts of people who come to our concerts. People are coming all over from schools and I don't know where. The turnout is getting so big you wonder where everybody does come from. I suppose basically it was from the underground thing.

RY: There seems to be a lot of young people into your music now?

JP: I don't really know why this happens, especially for our sort of music. But I do know that when the Cream did the Madison Square Garden concert there were people of nine and 11 in there. This is really quite amazing. I'm not really quite sure of their motives.

I'm sure they can't really be into the music—they can't understand it. But then again, you find in England, kids (I don't like to call them that), people of 13 are buying underground music and apparently know what's going on in the music.

I know a source, a fellow who runs a record store near where I live who keeps me up to date on who's buying what . . . the English charts are so strange, such weird things get in, it often amazes me who buys what. So I do a bit of research and yes, 13 year olds do buy these records.

RY: Did you have any idea of where you were going a year ago?

JP: Yes, the whole thing at the times was hard rock core which you can hear on the first album cos it's basically what it is. Obviously, there's a couple of blues as well—hard rock and blues, the whole thing.

That was the whole idea of it and it still is really. But now we've had more acceptance, we can open up on other things which we probably wouldn't have done to start with. Things like "Thank You." Really there's so much we can do, it's just a matter of time getting it all out.

RY: Were you surprised at your tremendous success?

JP: Oh yeah. The Yardbirds at the end were getting probably $2,500 a night and I thought LZ would probably start off at $1,500 and work our way up to that and have a good time. But that was all I expected. It's really frightening actually the way it has snowballed.

Second album

JP: The record sales of the second album . . . it really surprises me, it's beyond my comprehension that things should go this well. Because it wasn't a contrived thing. Obviously, it was time for our sort of group, what with the Cream breakup and Hendrix hadn't been doing much. They had been the two real big ones at that time so I think it was just good luck that our timing was right. And in we came with the hard rock as well.

RY: What do you think of the American pop scene?

JP: Well, one always gets inspiration from people like Love, but I believe they've broken up, which is unfortunate 'cos Arthur Lee was a tremendous writer. And of course Buffalo Springfield and all the offshoots of these things will be and are great. There are groups over here doing really good things.

Blood, Sweat, and Tears aren't my cup of tea. Spirit do some really nice things on albums. They give a nice atmosphere when they play and I always enjoy seeing them.

RY: How about the Doors?

JP: Actually, I was surprised after hearing a lot about the Doors and we got a lot of advance publicity in England about how sexy Jim Morrison was, how virile and whatever. I was surprised to see how static he was live on stage. I admire his writing ability and when he gets it together in a studio, he really does. But on stage, he's not really for me.

He doesn't really come across in any way like I'd like to see. Being dressed in black leather can only go so far but standing there like my father would on stage doesn't really come across for me.

RY: What do you think of the opinion that Robert Plant copies Jim?

JP: How could he have done? They're completely different. If you want to relate Robert to a sexual image . . . and a lot of people are doing that, he's all those things one would associate with it. He's good looking (I'm not saying Jim isn't), he's got the virile image, he moves very well on stage and he looks right and he sings well—his whole thing is total sexual aggression.

As far as I could see, the Morrison thing is just an embarrassment towards the audience. He would actually insult them and swear at them and his sexual thing is more of an introvert thing—it isn't so extroverted as Robert's.

RY: You're doing a lot of personal appearances in North America now. How did it all start?

JP: We started off at less than $1,500 a night actually. We played for $200 one day but it was worth it because we didn't care, we just wanted to come over and play the music. In England, we had such a bad time and bookers were saying, "LZ used to be the Yardbirds, we'll book them but we'll put them as the new Yardbirds." It was just a joke in England that they wouldn't accept you. They won't accept anything new.

Over here, we were given a chance. Bill Graham booked us in both the Fillmores and all the underground promoters like Russ Gibb and these people all booked us and gave us a great start and it was on our own shoulders. You know, come over here, work as hard as you can, give them all you can and if it doesn't work, go back to England and start again. But obviously no one would have had us back if we had died. It was just up to us.

RY: You're earning fantastic money now. What's the most you've ever made?

JP: In Boston we got $45,000 for one gig, which was just incredible. It just depends now—the artistic side can go so far, then the managers take over on the business and you start working on percentages above guarantees and it obviously depends on how big the place is and that was the biggest place we played. There were about 17,000 people.

RY: Some critics think your violin bit is gimmicky.

JP: It's important to me, actually. Unfortunately, it does look gimmicky with the visual thing of the violin bow but, in fact, good things can be done with it. It's pretty hard to do. It's not as easy as it looks in actual fact. I would still include it whether people hated it or not.

RY: Do you think you've improved your guitar playing since joining LZ?

JP: I don't know about LZ as LZ, but playing with these people has been fantastic. I've never played with such good musicians before in a group and I'm sure everyone's improved within themselves.

RY: What do you think of Jeff Beck?

JP: I think he's great. When he's having a shining night, he's really fantastic. He plays things of sheer genius.

RY: I've heard that the Vanilla Fudge is joining him?

JP: Yes, I've heard that. I don't know how it'll go temperament-wise. He's got a funny temperament.

Eric Clapton?

RY: Eric?

JP: He's a very tasteful player. I haven't seen him play since John Mayall days. I didn't see Cream, I didn't see Blind Faith shows. That day is over isn't it? Everybody says so.

RY: What bands do you like?

JP: Unfortunately, I haven't seen all the bands I'd like to see. I'd like to see Crosby, Stills, Nash, & Young group. I really would. There's a friend of mine, matter of fact he got my guitar for me, called Joe Walsh, who's got a group in the Cleveland area called the James Gang. I heard them and they were very good and went down well. I expect we'll hear more of them.

RY: Who has inspired you?

JP: Even now I don't listen to current guitarists . . . whether that sounds right or not. I was really listening to the old blues people. I thought, "Well, they've got their thing out of it, I'll get my thing out of it too." I thought that if I started to listen to everybody else like Eric [Clapton] and Jimi [Hendrix] then I'd get bogged down with their ideas and start nicking their phrases which I probably did do subconsciously and I think everybody does.

You can hear Eric's phrases coming out on Jimi's albums and you can hear Hendrix phrases coming out on Eric's records. I was really listening to acoustic guitarists like Bert Jansch. He's my all time favorite. I was listening to that more than anything and that's what I play a lot of at home. I would really like to develop the acoustic guitar into something much better. The finger style, not like C., S. and N.

RY: How about blues guitarists?

JP: They're great. They've all got their trademarks. It's so easy when you're learning guitar to get all your trademarks off them and suddenly a style of your own develops out of this. I still listen to a lot to Otis Rush more than any of the others. And a guitarist who came to England called Matt Murphy. Buddy Guy, of course. I could relate to them more than B. B. King at that time. Now I think that B. B. is very up-to-the-moment.

At that time, his records were recorded in the '30s and it was hard to relate to them. Yet, I knew that people like Rush and Guy had drawn from them but that was today's statement of that thing. And it wasn't till B. B. King became more well-known and more records became available that one was able to say B. B. King is there as well.

RY: Johnny Winter?

JP: I like his steel playing very much. His bottleneck Robert Johnson things. He's really got those things off to a tee.

RY: Some people accuse you of having no taste?

JP: Maybe I haven't. I don't know. I just play how I feel. If I feel tasteless, I play tasteless. I've heard every guitarist attacked that way—it depends on what they can do. If I sat down with a guitar I could probably play a lot of things that a lot of other people couldn't play—you know, classical things and people might say, "That's really tasteful, man."

RY: How about the Stones?

JP: I don't know really. Did you see that Hyde Park film? Some of it started off really good, but then they got into things like "Satisfaction" and it sounded pretty weak. I don't know why. Maybe it's because they hadn't played for so long—it was such a big ordeal playing for so many people, they must have been as nervous as hell. I think it will be good because Jagger is so fantastic, and his songwriting—the words are incredible.

Beatles?

RY: And the Beatles?

JP: They just turn it out, don't they? It's always good and always sounds fresh whether it is or isn't. They've done some good things. It's amazing the way their guitar styles come into it.

RY: What about George [Harrison]'s playing on *Abbey Road*?

JP: Was it really George? It might have been Paul. It's nice actually.

RY: In what direction are you going?

JP: It sounds corny, but we've got something we want to try out but I don't want to tell you about it in case it doesn't come off. It's an idea for a really long track on the next album. In so much that "Dazed" and "Confused" [sic] and all those things went into sections—well, we want to try something new with the organ and acoustic guitar building up and building up to the electric thing.

It will be probably a 15 minute track and I'm really looking forward to doing it. I can't really tell you more about it in case it doesn't work out. But I think it will.

RY: What do you feel about the second album?

JP: It took such a long time to do . . . on and off—having no time and having to write numbers in hotel rooms. And hearing the initial numbers we did so many times playing them to different people by the time the album came out I was really fed up with it. That's why I had lost confidence in it by the time it came out. People were saying it's great and I thought, "Oh good."

RY: Do you like being the producer?

JP: Writing a lot of it, as it's only album tracks, it's nice to have a free hand in what you've written. A producer, in fact, would probably say, "Well, I like that idea but why don't you try this?" and he'd start taking over. So it would be a bit of a battle if you'd written it yourself. It would be different on a single because I guess the producer would know.

That's why [I've] been the producer most of the time because the songs have been either written by me and Robert, or the rest of the boys. It's more personal really.

A single?

RY: Do you have any plans for a single?

JP: Yeah, when we get back. We've got two ideas but then when I say ideas, an idea usually amounts to a chorus or a couple of verses or a few riffs. It's just a matter now of going back, have a week off or so and everyone's going to think about singles and ideas for such.

Then we're going to come together and amalgamate all the ideas to see what comes out of it, I should think.

RY: I hear that you really can't tolerate straights.

JP: Oh yeah. I really hate all of that narrow mindedness . . . But I think anyone does with long hair, or anyone with genuine feeling. Even if they're not, even if they appear to be a straight person, if they're sympathetic to other people, they would be fed up with hearing people making nasty comments to them.

You're really discriminated against all of the time. If I was colored, I'd really be able to kick up a stink and I'm not, so I really have to put up with it. And I know everyone else with long hair does. It's a bit of a drag.

RY: Any particular instances?

JP: Well, restaurants where you get a bad time. Try to check into hotels where they don't like the look of you and they don't want you messing up the swimming pool. You know how it is. It's just a hostile sort of age.

COMMUNICATION BREAKDOWN

"We are all happier now than we have ever been. And I want everyone to know it . . . At the moment, the four of us are enjoying making our third album and taking it easy at home between sessions . . . Just because we are doing it all very quietly, some idiot thinks that we have packed it in and so all those false rumors start to circulate . . . To put a complete end to all the breakup rumors, anyone who goes to Bath will see and hear Led Zeppelin play as they never heard us play before."

– John Bonham to Roy Carr, *NME*, June 27, 1970

COMMUNICATION BREAKDOWN

"After going down well at a concert in the States, someone wandered up to me and said in all seriousness, 'how do you feel about being the biggest sex symbol since Jim Morrison?' I was so amazed I just replied 'Have you got a cigarette?' Well . . . what can you say? You know, someone actually called me a sexual beacon!"

–Robert Plant to Roy Carr, *NME*, July 4, 1970

JIMMY PAGE: ZEP COME TO THE PEOPLE

Keith Altham | February 27, 1971, *Record Mirror*

Led Zeppelin made their reputation on their live shows. Even before the first album came out, they were the talk of the Bay Area because of their opening slots at the Fillmore, and word spread like warm butter on toast. After two years, they were already playing stadia around the world. So, as a treat to their fans in England, they decided to do a longer tour of smaller venues. —Ed.

"What do you want if you don't want money?" was the lyrical question once put [to] but never answered by a certain Adam Faith née Terence Nelhams which seems more relevant to those super-stars of today who like Zeppelin can make 37,000 dollars out of one concert in Anaheim, U.S.A.

Messrs Page, Plant, Bonham, and Jones have clearly defined one priority as musicians by electing to play those clubs, pavilions, and ballrooms which gave them their initial identity and provided close contact with an audience which has been moving further into the distance with each Festival.

"The audiences were becoming bigger and bigger but moving further and further away," Jimmy Page told me. "They became specks on the horizon and we were losing contact with people—those people who were responsible for lifting us off the ground in the early days.

"We are playing those clubs like the London Marquee for exactly the same amount as we did in the old days as a thank you to those promoters and the audiences alike. By doing this we will be able to tour the entire of Britain and not just those cities who are fortunate enough to contain large venues.

"We will establish contact with our audience and re-energize on their reaction while they will have a chance to see a group which in the accepted tradition would be appearing only at high prices in large auditoriums.

Hope

"The only aspect which troubles me is that there will obviously be a large number of people who will be turned away on the night and I get a pang of conscience every time I see someone who has trekked miles to see us being sent away. I can only hope that the club owners will distribute tickets fairly and preferably on a first come first served basis.

"We have kept our price down and we expect them to do the same with their admission charges. It is my opinion that the real excitement and life's breath of progressive music comes from these small clubs—we hope our appearance will give them a shot in the arm and close contact will revitalise our enthusiasm."

Was a time some four years ago when Jimmy would not say 'boo' to a road manager but time and experience have given the ex-Yardbird a self-confidence and assertion which shows in his positive attitude towards the group's musical policy and direction. Having sampled wealth and fame he is better qualified to assess its worth.

"If I thought about the money coming in or the money going out I would go stark raving bonkers," said Jimmy. "We have managers and accountants to take care of our business problems and leave us with what concerns us most—the music."

Objective

"My ultimate objective and challenge is to excel in all spheres as a guitarist and I want to attempt all styles. Maybe it will mean I will end up as a Jack of all trades and master of none but at least I will have sampled the different sweets available. I don't want to be better than any one particular guitarist just more versatile."

It seems more than likely that the Press will wish to attend at least one of the smaller venues which Zeppelin intend to play and as the crush is likely to be far from comfortable for armchair reviewers I asked Jimmy if he was concerned about the reaction this might cause from a jaundiced journalist sandwiched between fans.

Message

"If they expect red-carpet treatment then my advice is don't bother to come" said Jimmy, "Because they are taking up valuable space which someone who really wants to hear us would otherwise occupy. We are not playing for the sole benefit of the Press—or those particular critics who we all know review most of the shows from the beer tent, or the bar!

"There are plenty of new young faces on the musical papers now who would enjoy to come and hear us play and I hope they do. My message to the journalists looking for V.I.P. treatment is don't bother to turn up."

In addition to their tour of the mini-venues Zeppelin intend to play at least one charity show for "Release"—the organization which has done so much to help young people over drug problems.

"Release is the one organization which most young people would automatically turn to if they found themselves in trouble with drugs," said Jimmy. "Caroline Coon and her helpers have done more to help young people in that area than anyone else—they do good work."

What are the economics of putting a group like Zeppelin on the road?

"Oh goodness knows—for a start we have to lay out £8000 for a new P.A. system because someone left our old one out in the rain! Then we have to buy a new van which will probably mean another £2000—two roadies, a tour manager, and our personal manager. The only major difference is not having to worry about someone levelling a gun at your head as they do in the US so there is less emphasis on security."

Difference

By playing the clubs there is a strong likelihood that the "jammers" will descend upon Zeppelin to "sit in" and play with the band. They are not likely to receive a warm welcome and Jimmy made a valid and important point on this issue.

"Let me give you an example," said Jimmy. "A year ago I went to see Howling Wolf perform in London and I was really looking forward to hearing him. I stood at the side of the stage and the whole time the management were pestering me to go in and jam.

Potential

"'We can get him off now if you want to go on!'"

"Now I hadn't come with the intention of playing and the people there had not turned up in the hope of hearing me. Howling Wolf had a lot to offer and we wanted to hear him. It's the same scene with us—we have a lot of new material and new numbers to offer. It won't be the same kind of program that we will play in the clubs as we have been in concert.

"John Paul Jones is playing a lot more piano on our forthcoming album and we intend to feature him. There will be a new sort of dynamics about our music now. There is so much potential and so many new combinations which the group has to offer that we want people to hear them before anyone else gets into the act!"

ROBERT PLANT

August 14, 1971, *Rock Magazine*

Fresh out of the studio after recording *Led Zeppelin IV*, the Runes Album, *ZOSO*—take your pick about what you want to call it (Zep don't mind)—Robert Plant encountered a writer from *Rock Magazine*. As with so many writers, s/he (there is no byline) tries to breach the light/heavy, acoustic/electric dichotomies, and Plant toes the party line and denies they exist.

Led Zeppelin was not simply a "heavy" rock band. There was a lot more going on. —Ed

Rock Magazine: You've just come from the studios. Were you recording for the fourth album?

Robert Plant: Yes, it's that long dragging-out thing of mixing a lot of tracks. The intention originally was for a double album, and then we thought, "Well, not this time." But then we've been saying "not this time" since the second album. Jimmy took all the material over to Sunset Sound in Los Angeles with a very famous producer who said it was the studio, and did the mixes. We finished recording in February and the idea was to mix it there and get it out in March. But he brought the tapes back and they sounded terrible, so we had to start mixing all over again. It's a drag having to do it twice, but we're coming to the tail end of it now.

RM: So it's basically Jimmy who's producing the album?

RP: Well, we all discuss the thing, but when it comes to putting it right down, he's usually the one to do it. I'll be there as often as I can, because I know exactly what I want, but if I'm not there then we know each other well enough to know exactly what we both want. But for me it's really a case of getting to know things at the moment. I can go along there and sit for twelve hours and suggest things, but I like to be of some practical use. Still, it's only three years now that I've been in a position to get accustomed to recording studios. It's growing pains that I've got now.

RM: The first two albums were very hard musically, but on the third there was a lot more acoustic stuff. Is the new one following on in that sort of direction?

RP: I don't think there's any set thing. We don't get into any mould and stay there. People might want us to, and other people might not want us to. Most of the mood for this new album was brought about in settings that we hadn't come across before—we were living in this old falling-apart mansion somewhere in the country, I can't quite remember where, and we had the Stones mobile truck, so the mood was . . . bang! Like that, and we could hear the results immediately. There was no big scene about going back into the studio and doing it again because we had time to experiment, especially with the drum sounds.

We did this thing called "When the Levee Breaks," which is an old Memphis Minnie number, a Kansas Joe McCoy thing, and the drums on it sounded incredible. There was a secret to it which we just stumbled across really, which was just one microphone, just one—and the revelation of finding out that one microphone did more than about 35 in a studio set the mood really; it was enthusiasm.

Out of the lot, I should think there are about three or four mellow things . . . they're really improved a lot—there's a thing called "Stairway to Heaven," and a thing called "Going to California," but also there's some nice strong stuff, some really . . . we don't say "heavy," do we?

RM: You can say heavy if you like.

RP: Well, I don't know whether we do. But it's strong stuff, and it's exciting, and the flame is really burning higher and higher and higher. But it's probably best that we keep out of the way and quiet, and then when the album comes out we'll wait for the torrent and the retort.

RM: Do you think that sort of music succeeds on an album? I mean obviously it gets people going on stage and you get the feeling, but when it's just coming out cold off an album do you think—

RP: Yeah, but it isn't as simple as one/two/three/four and away we go—I don't think it ever has been like that, because "Communication Breakdown" at the beginning wasn't one/two/three/four, and we'll see you at the end. There's groups who do that who are supposed to be copyists of us and things like that, but you listen to people who are "copyists" of yourself and there's nothing going on. I mean, to have people coming along and saying Grand Funk [Railroad] are the Led Zeppelin of America and they're really knocking Zeppelin off their position—you're going, well, "Please stop. I think you've got it wrong."

RM: Do you really enjoy doing those acoustic things?

RP: I do, because I manage to plonk guitar on about three numbers on this album and it means so much to me to be involved more than just vocally, to know that I've been able to contribute something a little more. But they can be so good because they can start off in one vein, and when you come to do them on stage they're nearly always like a stomp type thing, and it gets really close to the people. That's all it is really with us, I think— just saying, "Well, good evening, and if you don't laugh and if you cry, and if you don't shout, and if you don't moan, and if you don't argue, then you haven't had your money's worth. There's no story."

Everybody's getting hung up on critics and things, but if they just let people get on with it, and let audiences pay their money and just come out saying something and laughing, then whatever it might be, so long as people get something positive out of it, then we've done our job.

RM: Have you ever thought of doing a solo album that maybe doesn't come out through Led Zeppelin, or are you satisfied with Led Zeppelin as a vehicle for everything you want to do?

RP: It can be the vehicle for anything that any of us want to do. John Paul's delving very deeply into electronic stuff now, which to begin with I thought was a bit harsh. But listening to him a bit more and watching him a bit more and knowing him a bit more . . . it all fits in. We don't get on each other's nerves because each time we feel as if we're going to do that we just say, "See you in a week," so every time a new idea comes up it's chewed and chewed. That's why people can't expect us to keep to "Whole Lotta Love" and things like that, because somebody might arrive at a rehearsal or session and say "How about this?"

The idea of a solo album occurs, obviously, to everyone, but the thing is who else could play on it apart from me? They'd only be three other people, and that's Bonzo and Jonesy and Jimmy, because they're the most accustomed to what I do—vocally and everything else. I've sung with other people, people who I've admired and things like that, but there's a thing that spurs up in me when we are doing something good and it gets into a good thing. I don't mean repeating "Whole Lotta Love" every night, but there may be a section in the middle that has never arisen before, and at that point everybody just looks around at each other and goes "Right," and we go from there.

RM: You tend to do things like "Whole Lotta Love" a lot though. Is this because you really like it or because you feel it is expected of you?

RP: Well, it is expected isn't it? But it isn't just "Whole Lotta Love," because that lasts on stage maybe four minutes, and for the rest, the construction that comes at different parts in that four minutes spreads, spreads into a ten-minute thing. But within that ten-minute thing, there are parts where the audience are up and applauding, there are parts when they'll maybe be quiet, and there are parts where they're shouting their heads off. That's how all that started, really, with things like "Dazed and Confused" and "How Many More Times"—when we recorded "How Many More Times" we just didn't know what we were going to do; we knew the basic riff, but we didn't know "The Hunter" was going to come into it, or "Rosie"—they come on the night or they come out at the session.

I think that's why we're still together and we're not bitching at each other or anything like that, because we know that wherever it is—even if it's in Iceland—if we suddenly hit on something . . . you can feel it coming from behind—the bass and drums suddenly knit together and it's like a big handshake between the two and they go off, and Jimmy and I'll stay doing something else. It's like a good jigsaw puzzle. That's why a solo album would be useless because you wouldn't get half of it together. You could bring in all the incredible musicians you liked—the Memphis Horns, anybody—but you wouldn't get such strong buzz. I wouldn't anyway.

RM: Do you ever feel held back by what your audience expects, or do you feel that what they want is what you have to play?

RP: Well, I don't think that what they want is what we have to play, because we didn't have to play "Bron-Y-aur Stomp" or "Friends" and things like that because it wasn't expected of us, was it? We did get a bit of knocking for it, although personally I think that album (*III*) is the best thing that we've done. But you see, you can get upset momentarily by the remarks, and probably all the way through this interview you'll get this one coming from me, but for all the people who griped and took the trouble to write gibberish to the music papers, there were a lot of people who were surprised that we'd taken that much trouble to go that much farther.

RM: Well, certainly when I heard you were doing things like that, I thought good, now they've made their name they're going to start thinking about a wider scope of music.

RP: It's been there with James from the word off really, because really it was his conception; compared to mine, his alternatives were numerous. I think he probably could have started doing something like that, but that probably it wouldn't have been as largely accepted. It's nice to have an audience and to say, "Right, we want to please people," and get the ultimate kick out of it ourselves, because really there's very little else to get kicks out of apart from music, and the arts generally. You can't really turn up one day and decide to do a completely acoustic album and write twelve acoustic numbers three minutes long. But it isn't as if it has to be acoustic . . . on this new album the electric numbers are, in my eyes, a lot better than the ones before. They may not be as instantly commercial, but if you listen to them long enough I think there's a lot more thought and a lot more maturity in them.

RM: How much is Led Zeppelin as a whole aimed at a commercial market? I mean, how much does that enter your thinking when you're writing a song or making an album or doing a stage appearance?

RP: Well, they are three vastly different thing[s]. Writing a song, all it is, is that you're in a certain mood and something starts to come out. It might never reach an audience and there are things that haven't reached audiences. If at the end of a song it's a gas, then it's on the LP, and if it's a gas that we want to think about a bit longer, then it's not. Or maybe there isn't room for it on the album. Writing a song is the last place you're going to start thinking about 2 x 20,000 people in Madison Square Garden. What was the second one?

RM: Making an album.

RP: Making an album is a case of making your own personal idea of what is perfection at that point. I mean with the third album, I shed a couple of tears because I was so happy with it, but a lot of people weren't, so there's one proof of the pudding.

RM: You don't consciously think, "We can use that because . . ."

RP: Oh Christ! It would be pointless me having a word with you if that was the case wouldn't it? If that was the case I'd want to be on the cover of magazines every week. I've seen people, mind you, who worry about the position of their guitars before they go on stage at *Top of the Pops*—and there's another farce. Bonzo and I went there the other night, and we went into the bar, and there were record pluggers everywhere. There was nil conversation—the whole thing stank. I'm afraid we became objectionable, because the more it went on the more I was thinking "Why?" and "When's the train to Worcestershire?" and "How did I get in here anyway?" And I got in because I said I was Mickie Most anyway, and they didn't know I wasn't. I'm going to get shot next week now. But the whole thing typified exactly what you were saying do we think about—and we don't. You can't, because if we did I'd have done something really silly to myself now. That is The Business.

RM: How about when you're on stage, and there are all these people who've come to see the Led Zeppelin that they know; don't you ever feel tempted to shock them and do something that is completely unexpected from you? Or is it very important to you to play to what they want?

RP: I don't think you can decide when you go on stage. I mean, you can't deny that when you're in a position to impress them, you give them all you've got—everything, everything that you've got. But the mood changes so often through three hours—you get knackered in one place or maybe your head's spinning round and round—but there's a part, five minutes on as it's building to it, that you suddenly get caught up, and you go right up with it and you take off somewhere.

It's just a case of light and shade really, and the audience are there as a backcloth to your light and shade so they can either get off on it or please themselves. There's no premeditation—there is in the fact that "Whole Lotta Love" will come somewhere towards the end of the night—but not really otherwise.

RM: Yes, but would you leave out "Whole Lotta Love" for instance?

RP: No. Because a lot of people have come because they enjoy that, and they haven't really had the time to get into "Friends" and "Celebration Day" . . . but "Whole Lotta Love" has to be there to get everybody in. Ah, that's a rash statement. To get the people in who wouldn't have come just to hear the other things.

RM: You think that by doing "Whole Lotta Love" you can lead people to things that maybe they wouldn't have thought of?

RP: To give them the chance of hearing things that we reckon are worth hearing, as opposed to just the cliched . . . what has become our National Anthem. But don't forget that in the past year in the eyes of the Press I've gone from a Pre-Raphaelite fucking entity to a Viking warrior or something— so really it would be nice for them to stop thinking about all that and just have a listen to things they might not have given a second thought to before. I'm so much more adamant now when I'm singing things like "That's the Way" than I ever was when I recorded it, and I've seen people get off on the fact that I emphasize the parts that I feel need emphasizing, and I feel it come back.

But then I feel it come back from "Whole Lotta Love" because it's a climax—it's not the best climax the group will have, but it's nice to see people climaxing in every possible way around you. Really, when people pay money—and you can't really say that they can get away without paying money—they should be able to have every aspect, every mood, every angle, for three years: you. Not "how does it look?"

RM: There are times when your stage act, the way you move around, does look a bit contrived—all that stuff with mike stands. I admit it's not so much now, but in the early days, like that first tour with the Liverpool Scene and Blodwyn Pig . . .

RP: Yeah, well that was the first one we ever did. At that stage I was a vocalist, full stop. What could I do when I had three people around me who were really getting it on? I got excited, and when you get excited you can run round and round in circles—I mean I've run behind the amps and leant up against the amps and blown one because it's been so good—but you can't go around and have a little guide book to original poses when you're getting excited. If I didn't get excited I'd leave the group tomorrow. So really these pre-meditated things are just . . . well, I know damn well they're not and I don't think they look that way either. It's just another extension of this vocal-thought-motion-audience thing—it's the supreme contact. We've lost a lot over the ages of contacting one another, reaching each other through means apart from speech, and it's not a page out of some book on erotica when I'm dancing around, it's just "Well great!"

RM: How do you feel now about singing a lyric like "Squeeze my lemon 'til the juice runs down my leg"?

RP: I think that was poetry at one time. In its original context, that Robert Johnson album, *Travellin' Riverside Blues*, I was playing the album the other night and I felt so proud of owning it, and that line was just so indicative of that person Robert Johnson. We recorded that in L.A. and it was a time when there was a lot of looning—and there was a lot of looning going on—and it was one of those states of mind you get into when everything's rosy and shining, and so a lyric like that comes zooming in. It's borrowed, admittedly, but why not? I really would like to think that someone who heard that and then saw some clever critic writing about Plant living off the far superior Robert Johnson, or whatever they have to say to keep their jobs, would go and listen to Robert Johnson as a result. But I wish I'd written that, I really do. Sometimes I wish I'd been Elvis . . . or Superman, or that fella in the San Franciscan cartoons who always ends up in an alley with some chick with her legs up in the air.

But Robert Johnson . . . just him, the sympathy between guitar and vocal, the whole atmosphere of a record that was done in some back room—you can do that with John Lee Hooker and it's forty minutes of boredom half the time, sometimes. But this Robert Johnson thing was a complete and utter statement. He was almost the innovator of the walking bass and all that sort of thing that Tommy McClennan and Muddy Waters grew from. Tommy McClennan especially came along afterwards and said well, that's it, that ultimate personal blues. But "squeeze my lemon"— I wish I could think of some thing like that myself. But it's not cool to do that these days, you realize that don't you? If I'd been Elvis Presley I could have done something like that, but he cottoned to Arthur Crudup instead. I could have been a Robert Johnson bloke.

RM: What do you think Led Zeppelin has achieved after three years of phenomenal success, in terms of stardom, or whatever you like to call it—audience reaction?

RP: Well I hope we've made the impression by now that nothing is the norm, that nothing need be the same next time. We haven't categorized ourselves. And I don't think we've thrown ourselves at the public as much as a lot of other people who say they haven't—we don't put ourselves in the way of glory. But three years is such a short time to start making any grand assessment. We've had the opportunity to be superduper incredible stars, and we could have lived on that much more than we have done, but I think it's just a case of holding back all the time, because if you take the reins that are given to you, you end up destroying yourself—overdoing it, over playing it, over living it, and suddenly finding out that the things from your past don't fit in at all with what you're doing now. Therefore it's much better for me to go home and be as I have been for years and years and years, than make some new being out of myself . . .

I haven't set myself any sort of position, and I don't look up to myself as being this, that, or the other. It's easy to say you don't, and do, but I think if I just carry on like this, then our success will carry on for a long time, at least I hope it will. But anyway, our ability will increase and that's the main thing. I'm not going to lose sight of dry land, I don't think, though I've seen a lot of people do that.

LED ZEPPELIN: VANCOUVER 1971

Rick McGrath | Fall 1971, *Georgia Straight*

One of the longest running "underground" periodicals in Canada, the *Georgia Straight* (named for the body of water that separates the city from the rest of British Columbia; the founders figured they would get free advertising from the local weather reports "with winds coming off the Georgia Strait") has been published in Vancouver since 1967. It was the only periodical invited to opening night of Zeppelin's 1971 North American tour. While talking with Rick McGrath, Robert Plant finally started firing back at the press, especially in the wake of the generally lukewarm reception to the *Led Zeppelin III* album. –Ed.

I got to watch the concert from the stage—about 10 feet away from Page. It was one helluva show, culminating in "Dazed and Confused," which was their big final encore number (this was prior to "Stairway to Heaven").

After Led Zeppelin's tumultuous second encore I waited for the crowds to disperse and then slipped backstage: Lots of cops, a few groupies (these surprisingly more sophisticated than the usual fare), and the now-familiar faces that appear backstage after every concert.

I had previously made arrangements with Led Zeppelin's manager, Peter Grant, to get in and see the group after their show. For some reason *The Straight* was the only segment of the Vancouver media to obtain an interview. After waiting a half hour or so, the door opened, Peter looked out and motioned Tracey and I inside the dressing room.

They looked like they were having fun, as well they might. Vancouver was the first date of a long North American tour, and spirits are helped considerably if the first night is a winner. I guess they figure 20,000 people can't be wrong.

Once inside the dressing room, Peter motioned me over to Page and Plant who were sitting off in a corner discussing, I thought, either a new song or part of an old one. Page was playing and singing and Plant was listening intently. Jones and Bonham were in the opposite corner, flailing away on acoustic guitars and loudly singing old rock hits like "Save the Last Dance For Me," "The Bristol Stomp," etc., etc. They got louder, in fact, and as I started talking to Plant, Page joined them and on occasion during the interview Plant would leap to his feet and join in on some chorus.

I did come away from the experience with a few observations. First, these people are not stupid. Plant is extremely articulate and certainly is his own man. He has definite ideas about his work, his public, and his critics, and at 23 (his birthday is August 20) he is a seasoned performer who is trapped somewhat by the wishes of his audience and the wishes of his own creativity. If pressed, he is defensive about Led Zeppelin, but that I find understandable. It is, after all, unique in a much more valuable way than the music of, say, Grand Funk . . .

Rick McGrath: It was pretty hot out there . . .

Robert Plant: Yeah, sometimes it gets a bit scary when we see half the stage disappearing . . .

Jimmy Page: It was a bit rough.

RM: Let's talk about what you've been doing since you were here last.

RP: We've been to Italy, Switzerland, Denmark. We did a tour of England, intending to go back to all the old clubs that we played in the beginning.

RM: . . . around Birmingham . . .

RP: All those sorts of places. In some way it was a successful move, in other ways it was a bit of a dead loss, because you'd be playing in places that only hold 250 people.

RM: Isn't that what the club trip is like in England? A lot of smaller halls and stuff?

RP: Yeah, that's what it used to be like at the beginning. But there's always something bigger than a club in each town, a hall or something. Not so much a Coliseum, though.

RM: And you've finished your new album?

RP: We finished that, and we did it in our own home. Well, how it went was that we used a mobile truck for our recording unit and we went to an old manor in Surrey. There we put up all the equipment in one room and stuck all the mike leads through a window. Straight into the recording van. So anything that we did just went straight down on tape. Bit by bit it grew up into a great collage of numbers.

RM: Do you like it?

RP: [Nodding head.] Yeah. It was another atmosphere altogether.

RM: What are your thoughts on *Led Zeppelin III*? It didn't seem to have it the way a lot of people thought it would.

RP: I thought it would as well. I was really happy with it, because to me it was just one step in growing up.

RM: Well, it got some bad press. That's something we should talk about later. But there was an incredible wave of Led Zeppelin mania, or whatever, and you had just finished a very successful tour, and then the album came out and nothing happened.

RP: Yeah, but to me, personally, that album was certainly a large step after the second one. Because you can't keep turning out the same thing. If you do that, you can't do anything for yourself. We know we can rely on things like "Whole Lotta Love" and it is quite easy to work within the same framework all the time. But who does that? Just people who haven't got anything going for them in the brains, that's who. And I think the third album was an essential thing, I don't care if it sold any copies at all, because it showed there was a bit more attached to us and it than "Shake Your Money Maker" sort of stuff.

RM: Which leaves you in the bind of wanting to progress, when the audience doesn't want you to.

RP: I daren't say they don't want you to, but it seems they're not ready to accept, or even give it a fair try because I think if people play the third album and listen to it with the same amount of justification that they gave the second one, they might see what's going on.

RM: What about rock critics? They seem to be the other extreme. On one hand you have the audience screaming "Whole Lotta Love," and on the other a critic saying the opposite.

RP: Well, a critic who's been a critic in one position for more than six months gets a bit cocky, right? He feels pretty cool. So he suddenly starts making assumptions and statements that aren't his to make, man. You can't condemn something just by . . . a critic can't fucking state what he wants to . . . like if he goes to a concert, like tonight, and he goes away and writes, "Well, I don't know what to say because it wasn't too good at all." For 17,000 people going it was fucking too much, but that one guy could get quite a reputation for decrying it. And unfortunately that seems to be the general system of critics . . . to make themselves a name. Instead of just transposing what happens, and saying it was accepted, they suddenly start becoming an entity for themselves, instead of a courier for the people.

And just as a new society is growing and moving, we've got to eliminate all this old crap, and we've got to be fair with each other. Because if we get all these blasé attitudes at an early stage where we're still trying to prove to a lot of people that it's a wholesome, positive thing and they keep tearing away inside it, well, it'll be ruined before it's even gotten halfway. Because that attitude doesn't stop just at music, but it goes everywhere. And that attitude of somebody in a position to influence somebody else is open to somebody with no talent but a pen and a job. And it worries me, really, because I don't just see it for us, I see it for people who I really fucking admire. They've given something and are working really hard. And people are digging it and going out and getting some satisfaction from it. But that guy, well, he's on another one altogether, isn't he?

RM: I'd have to agree, even though I've been accused of the same thing on a few occasions.

RP: Well, you've only got to be fair.

RM: Right, the way I look at it is that a critic is no good unless he's honest with himself. And if he has constructive things to say. That's part of criticism. It should help more than hinder.

RP: Yes, but things like *Rolling Stone* get out of hand. Even in England people buy it because it's been around for such a long time. It gets to be a habit. And what they read is something else, man. Because it's always down, down, down. Why don't they stop all that and start being nice? Is that such a hard thing to do?

RM: Yeah, but they're in it for the bucks and controversy always sells more than good news.

RP: Yeah, but we're in it for a buck as well, to an extent. But we go out there and there's no bad ones. People could throw a fucking bottle and it would still be cool because they're there and the thing incites them to do that. So you just ride along with it.

RM: They ripped the doors off the front of this place tonight.

RP: They've been eating good breakfast cereals or else they've captured energy in long hair. I wonder if any of them were in your Gastown thing. We heard about it, but see, when you're in our position, mate, you're in so many fucking places in such a short time and everybody's going look at this, and people keep coming up and saying what do you think about them saying this and what do you think about them saying that? Half the time you miss it or you just don't even know it's there. Because if you get affected by these things, well, you just go on stage shivering, more or less.

RM: I've noticed the stage act has changed since you were here last. It seems to be getting back to a hard rock and blues thing.

RP: Well, it ain't wanting to change, it's just how it goes. Tomorrow is another day. It's like with albums. People say "Do you follow in the same pattern as before?" And you talking about the third album. The third album, to me, was a disappointment in the way it was accepted because it wasn't given enough of a chance.

After "Heartbreaker" and "Bring It On Home." And thunder, which was what it was. So we say try this for size and I thought when we were doing it that I was able to get inside myself a little more and give a little more on the album. I thought the whole thing felt like that. I was pleased with it, and I'd play it now without hesitation and dig it. And you can't always do that to an album that you've played a million times. But I really thought it stood up and then everybody was saying, well, noo, and they'd leave it and then come back in a couple of weeks time and say, well, we can see . . . but nevertheless, we think it's best. But that's what people say because the simple, heavy thunder is much easier to assimilate, much easier to react to in every way. But you can't just do that, otherwise you become stagnant and you're not really doing anything, you're just pleasing everybody else.

And the whole thing about the whole music scene now is that we didn't follow Sam the Sham, we didn't follow all those people. We came over here and nobody knew who we were and we weren't following anything. We weren't saying "It's Gary Puckett for us," and come over here . . . do you know what I mean? And it's just by playing what we had to do, with all the bollocks that we got, that people said fair enough. And anything we can do new on an album I think is a good move.

RM: What direction is your new material taking?

RP: It really varies, because having that place in the country . . . it's that old cliché about a place in the country . . . but it was really great. The mikes coming in through the windows and a fire going in the hearth and people coming in with cups of tea and cakes and people tripping over leads, and the whole thing is utter chaos. Bonzo's drums are in the hall, in the entrance hall, with one mike hanging from the ceiling. And things like that. And everyone's going . . . and we set up another set of drums and I was playing drums . . . and it was a good feeling, and we did it as easy as pie. So this album's got a lot of feeling to it.

RM: You write the lyrics. How do you get them to music? Do you make them up as the music goes, or what?

RP: Sometimes, like now, there's a few things. Like we went to Milan, and there was a big music festival with people from all countries contributing.

They travel around, and we just came for one gig. And we were told that it was a cool thing and even though there was a reputation for bottles being thrown in Rome, we were assured it wouldn't happen to us. Anyway, we started playing in a big cycle arena, and they'd been booing everybody else, and as soon as we walked onstage, I noticed some smoke at the back of the arena. And there's all this smoke and there's firemen behind us and I was going "Fire! fire!" in my finest Italian.

Anyway, nobody took any notice of me and we carried on for about a quarter of an hour and the fire had gotten all around us. And I turned around and looked at everybody and Peter (Grant, the manager), his eyes had all gone big and red. And everybody was suddenly coughing. People suddenly appeared with masks and things like that and suddenly there were bombs going off, everywhere. And the whole thing about what I'm doing is that I've been doing it seven years and I'm . . . what time is it?

RM: Midnight.

RP: I am now 23.

RM: Your birthday? Well, let me be the first to congratulate you. (We shake hands.)

RP: And so it's been seven years and suddenly I find we've been tear gasse[d]. So I got an Italian guy to come on and I told him to tell everybody to (Robert purses his lips and blows several times). And everybody's blowing. And everyone was just sitting down and coming around and digging it. And I was getting so I couldn't sing, and the feeling, if you've ever been tear gassed, is that if you move, you've got 15,000 kids who are going to freak out. So you don't move and you become so nauseated. Anyway, it finally broke up and there were kids running everywhere.

There were 250 stormtroopers there, in line, and I forgot to tell you, as we got there, there were wagons all alongside the road, and there were all these guys lined up by the front door. So I jumped out of the car and I was saluting and shouting and checking the uniforms and walking up and down the ranks going (makes faces) and I saw something I've never seen before, because they were completely devoid of anything human. They just looked at me as if to say "Objective number one" or something.

And suddenly everyone was running. And the kids came running over the stage, and we split and ran down a passage under the cycle arena. And then they tear gassed the passage. So Peter, who can't run very fast, was in trouble. So we found a room and we barricaded ourselves in. Broke into a medical cupboard and had all these fucking weapons and stuff. They were bringing the roadies in unconscious. We had one nurse and some oxygen and we looked out the window into the streets and there was fighting and shooting and cars being smashed and driven into trees and the whole thing was like a war. And it was because we stood up on stage. But that was not the real reason for it all. There were 250 people who just didn't know what the fuck was going on. 15,000 people are jumping in the air trying to escape the fucking tear gas and they don't understand.

And as we drove back to the fucking hotel, round the wrecked cars and round the fights and all that, there were roadside hospitals all the way to the center of Milan. I've never seen anything like that.

And I got up the next morning and got the papers and the driver translated and just told us that the kids had caused a riot and the police had had to move in and do the fucking honours. People lost their sight. I cried for days and days and everything I think about it, or I think of something gentle, I even saw a silly film with Cary Grant in it, and he was going on about what man must do to be man, and I was fucking crying. Because it just fucking hit me and if I'm ever down in America all somebody has to do is say. "Are you a boy or a girl" and I'll fucking dive at him. Because it's an animal reaction. I've already been in a rathole once.

And I know it's not just because we're radicals or rock 'n' rollers. It's because there's nobody understanding. And our side of the fence are going over there and saying "Fuck That," and that side is coming over and saying "Up Yours," and it's the wrong thing, you know. The concerts should be in twice as big a place and everybody should bring their parents. And then we can get it together. What we need is more of a bridge between the two sides . . . and in Milan? What are you going to do?

COMMUNICATION BREAKDOWN

"We were over in the States doing as well, if not better than the Stones and yet there wasn't one line in the British music papers. It was all the Stones, "the Stones this, and the Stones that," in every paper we looked in. We just got a bit pissed off and we might as well be in like in a bloody Lancaster, playing there, and we might as well have been in Ceylon, playing there, because the kids didn't even know where we were, or anything. It came over a bit wrong because it might sound as though we thought the kids—we've been neglected as a group, not just by the papers . . . I think now in the beginning, nobody could say a bad word for us. Now, all they want to do is sort of find a way in which they can knock us. Like you get letters sent up in the back pages that would say "Led Zeppelin are not playing anymore, they're too busy buying country mansions and Rolls-Royces." There ain't one in the group who owns a Rolls-Royce for a start, so it's all false information that they've read at a different article, the people who have assumed that's what we're doing. You know, I'm living in that same bloody house now as I lived in from the word go, and so is Robert."

—John Bonham to Roy Carr, *A Talk on the Wild Side*, July 1972

LED ZEPPELIN RADIO INTERVIEW, SYDNEY AUSTRALIA

David White | February 27, 1972, Radio 2SM

The 1972 tour took the band to Australia for the first and only time. During the trip, they sat down with several DJs at Radio 2SM, which was, in the days before many people had FM radios, the last word in rock radio Down Under. One of the interviewers, David White, recalled the evening:

The 2SM I was part of dominated the Sydney radio scene. Back in the days before FM, 2SM was an AM Rock powerhouse, much like the legendary KHJ that once ruled L.A. At its peak 2SM rated a huge 24.8 percent of the market and no one has ever topped that.

Amazing stuff . . . from the audio I can recognize some of the jocks who were present while we chatted. There was Greg Reece, maybe Groover Wayne—can't be 100 percent sure on that though and others who drifted in and out. Plant and Page came in to 2SM's studios in Clarence Street, Sydney, and emerging from the fog of rock 'n' roll memories is all of us seated around a massive collection of rare singles and LPs (remember those Stone Age artifacts?). They belonged to our music director, now true radio legend, John Brennan. Anyhow to cut to the chase, during the interview the Zeppsters found a heap of vinyl they loved and when it concluded they and the mass of singles and albums they fancied . . . went with them. Brenno spat the dummy big time because they were from his personal collection and I remember calming him down saying, "Mate, how many people can say Led Zeppelin loved their taste in music and decided to help themselves?" I do believe the interview took place in 2SM's basement studio, which played host to many legendary interviews.

This explains references to various records during the course of the interview, like Teresa Brewer. Also, keep in mind that in 1972, people still argued about the "validity" of artists like Joe Cocker.

Because of all the people "who drifted in and out," the audio on this is a bit dodgy. The variety of hosts on this are noted as "Host," "Host Two," etc. –Ed.

Host: So I heard about the [Small] Faces and then there was nothing about them for a long time until Rod Stewart*—

Robert Plant: It was a shame really because I really, really, really did like Steve Marriott, you know. When they first started he could play about two chords on the guitar but the whole thing that they built up on stage—they got one record out, *What'cha Gonna Do About It*—and they went on stage and they really, really . . . they had all that fire, you know, they were really exciting! Probably as exciting, or even more exciting than the Who, who had just been around a little while that time you know, and they had the Union Jacks on the box equipment and they were really fine! Things like "Itchycoo Park" and "Tin Soldier" were really good things. And then they went through all the old crap and I don't know what they did. I thought they were good.

But nowadays old Stevie Marriott went off to do something else. It's a pity really 'cause they did all mix well musically, you know they did—and being all the same size as well you can say, you just go. [*Laughs.*]

Jimmy Page: [*Having just discovered John Brennan's pile of vinyl.*] Can we crate these back to London or what? [*Laughs.*]

RP: Yeah! There's a bit—there's a few too many in here for me to leave it! Quick, get a grip on it—

---

*At this point, Steve Marriott had been away for about three years, but bassist Ronnie Lane was preparing to leave the band, and Rod Stewart was considering going solo.

JP: —that's amazing—

RP: Actually these are really old things . . . you wanna scrap these quick. Yeah. [*Laughs.*] Stevie can send them later.

Host: Have you heard any Australian music or any Australian bands at all?

RP: We've seen a fantastic television show.

[*All laugh.*]

Host: *New Faces?*

RP: *New Faces,* yeah! [*Laughter.*] If that sums up the— [*notices a record*] Teresa Brewer? [*Laughter.*] If that sums up what's going on, you know—

Man: I'll see you guys later. [*Readies to leave room.*]

Host: See you in a bit!

RP: Bye-bye!

JP: Farewell.

Host: What about people like Cat Stevens? D'you go for that sort of stuff?

RP: Yeah! I think he's quite good.

Host: Anybody else from that similar band? Sort of the ol'—

JP: Have you heard Roy Harper? No? Have you heard that album—the last album, *Stormcock* was his last album and that was . . .

Host: You do something about him on the last album—

RP: "Hats Off to Harper," yeah. Oh he's—blimey!

JP: Ah, so yeah! Let's . . . let's carry on with the thing without interrupting. Yeah Harper is a really amazing character all around. He was in the RAF* for about nine years. He learned to play snooker with both hands and discharged himself; he was insane in the end. But he's upset, he's got

---

*Royal Air Force.

on the BBC and really said things he's not supposed to say and all that about, "Well, here I am in the middle of everything I hate, man, and I don't really know whether it's there but it's cool and everybody listening will understand," and like . . . "beep," "bleep," "bleep," you know, get him off! [*Chuckles.*] But he does create some amazing music.

Host: Yeah. I'll bet you're doing a three and a half hour concert. When did you start doing that? After the second album was released—

JP: No, all the time!

Host: Right from the very beginning you said—

JP: I don't—we weren't doing three hour songs, were we? 'Cause, like, the early days we'd do two sets—

RP: Oh, crikey, yeah . . .

JP: The thing was, as we got more material together we didn't want to sing anything else. We just kept growing.

Host: Yeah. Listen, your first album, and I saw you when the Yardbirds came here the first time. What are your impressions of those the very first group you came on with?

RP: Well, I just enjoyed it you know. It's just a big loon for me. I wasn't really looking at it in any sort of social stance at all—

Host: As soon as you got up on stage then you sit up in the crowd at the stadium, remember that old place?

JP: Yeah! That was great there, actually! Really fine atmosphere!

Host: Yeah! Yeah! You did the—the bit with the bow on the guitar that stage. The thing is incredible, were you doing it long before that, before you joined the Yardbirds?

JP: Well, not really because I was doing session work before that. I did one session with it, but it never got released, but once I joined the Yardbirds I started doing it. I don't think anybody else is doing it just at that particular time.

Host: The group broke up after happening ten years' time ago, that was the last thing—

JP: No, no, no, no. No, yes! Probably with Jeff Beck, yes. And, and the group that you saw over here was one that was just a remainder. Just four of us instead of five, it had always been a five-man group up to that point and we recorded with, um, Mickie Most. The less said about that the better.

Host: Why, why is that? 'Cause I mean—

JP: Because he just—

Host: —he's pretty successful . . .

JP: Yeah well, I'm afraid that—that Herman['s Hermits] and the Yardbirds aren't really the same sort of background, are they? But he really messed it up. You see, we had an LP to do and we finished it in about ten hours I think. So much so that we had a pianist in, Stu [Ian Stewart], who was the road manager for the Rolling Stones and he still plays on their records even now. We did two blues things and we didn't even hear the playback of the first number that we did. He said, "All right! Straight on to the next one! Straight on!" And old Stu just couldn't believe it. He said, "I never worked like this in my life!" So there you go.

Host: You guys were telling me [John] Dankworth was coming up—this Adelaide festival and Cleo Laine—do they still pull a young following?

RP: No, no I don't think so, no. Yeah, it's more of the cabaret type thing I should imagine, for the main part. I mean John Dankworth has written some really good stuff—you know, really fine stuff—but nowadays I think that kids are really moving towards something with a little bit of life in it you know, and . . . Cleo Laine's headline . . .

Host: Well, I guess they're just starting to have to discover the fact that Cleo Laine in Australia has a voice. People have just heard it on the radio but we've heard a lot of English records.

RP: Mm, yeah, right.

Host: I just wonder whether there was any kind of return at all to that scene?

RP: Not really, no.

Host: You mentioned before, Jim, the Stones. What do you think of, say, a lot of people reckon that Jagger's gone beyond the thing of a pop star to sort of a cult hero and the music is suffering because of it? Do you think that's right?

JP: Why, I don't know really. He seems to have got into the jet-set scene, I really don't know what he's doing. See, I don't know how you relate that to a cult hero.

Host: Uh, he—the way he sort of you know made it to *Newsweek* covers and stuff, and—

RP: Made it to! [*Chuckles.*] You mean, you mean "reached it!"

JP: When he had his Catholic marriage, I think I've—

Host: What about his role in *Performance*? Have you seen the B-side of that?

JP: Yes, we've seen that.

RP: It was good.

JP: It was *really* good. Haven't you seen that here yet?

Host: No, they banned it . . .

JP: It ain't, is it?

Host: Yeah.

RP: Oh it's fine! It's really fine! They banned things like that; they banned Uncle Dirty and Wild Man Fischer and all that. What they don't know is that they can ban—it's not the filth they've got to worry about, you know.

Host: Yeah but it's the intelligence of the guys who banned it, you see.

JP: Yeah.

Host: Did you like—

JP: You'll have to change it then, won't you?

RP: Yes we'll help you do that. Just don't mention our names. [*Chuckles.*]

Host: Do you like the Stones' last album?

RP: Um, yeah it was all right. There are some good things on it, actually.

Host: Any particular style and stuff that you like or—

RP: *Beggars Banquet* I really like.

Host: "Sympathy [for the Devil]"?

RP: Well, yeah, the whole—the whole thing really, or most of it is really good, you know. That's where the Faces come in, you see, that sort of sound you know, "Stay with Me" is a little bit like that, do you know what I mean? The um—

Host: Shuffle—

RP: Right! The sort of rockin'-along thing—

Host: Yeah.

RP: Which the Stones have been doing for quite a while and Chuck Berry even did it.

Host: Right, the boogie type feel.

RP: Mm.

JP: Well, I always liked [*Their*] *Satanic Majesty's Request* because that was more or less the last complete one with Brian Jones, wasn't it? Or was it not? I don't know, but it was a good one and is it has become sort of fashionable to put them down, and everybody has sort of—

Host: Well people have the stance following [*Sgt.*] *Pepper*['s *Lonely Hearts Club Band*] and being on the heels of the Beatles with the electronic, freak-out sort of thing that they got into with *Satanic Majesty*. They seemed to track the Beatles would do something and they'd sort of—

JP: I'm sure they'd be the first to admit it, too. They did! They did seem to be following what the Beatles were doing.

Host: Do you find the lyrics are pretty important with what you're doing now? Like yesterday you said that, "People said that 'I was a millionaire but I'd spent more than a million.'"

RP: Ah well! That's—that's a bit—I would never—I love that song. If you—has Howlin' Wolf got any records out over here?

Host: Yeah, there's Howlin' Wolf's London sessions—

RP: Ah, yeah, well, forget that. There's an LP in England called *Goin' Down Slow* and those are the lyrics of "Goin' Down Slow." "Please write mama, tell her the shape I'm in / Tell her to pray for me, forgive me for my sins," yeah. Damn! Those Chess [Records] sounds were so fine! You know, the recording, the riffs, you know, the whole *feel* of the thing and Howlin' Wolf's voice! And everybody's just, well, "Smokestack [Lightning]" and "Spoonful," "You'll Be Mine." Even Marc Bolan's pinching bits of it there, you know, that [*starts singing T. Rex's "Jeepster"*] "you're so sweet" and all, that's Howlin' Wolf!

JP: Yeah, sure.

Host: Marc Bolan's music and T-Rex stuff yeah—

RP: Well, if anything, I reckon it's better than before except for the lyrics have suffered terribly you know. But then again, I say he's filling a gap that a lot of people have declined to associate themselves with for a long time, and you've got a lot of kids who don't really wanna look at David Cassidy or whatever his name is, you know, and old Bolan comes along with a few sequins and takes over!

Host: Yeah. I reckon there's sort of a mini-phenomenon now in England and sort of T. Rex and Slade are sort of battling it out or—

RP: Oh no! Slade I've known for years and years they lived not far from me and I don't think they could ever take over anything. [*Chuckles.*] They're really great blokes, you know, but . . . I don't know.

Host: I reckon Noddy Holder has got a pretty sort of incredible way of resolving lyrics to almost—

RP: Yeah, but he's always been doing that and he's never been cool to do it before! [*Laughs.*]

Host: Since "A Whole Lotta Love" [sic] do you think that you have set off deliberately in another direction to get away from that title or—

JP: No, no, no. You can't say direction is a—is something that people can only talk about if they're not involved in it, you know, because direction is really a strange word, in fact, when it comes to creation.

Host: So many kids in a place like here, in Australia, we get these things a while after you put them out, would hang so long on a thing like "Whole Lotta Love" and they keep on looking for something else that's going to vindicate their deep, strong feeling like that you know, maybe it came up in that, um—

JP: Well, yeah, but what about "Immigrant Song"? The "Hammer of the Gods"?

Host: Yeah. Yeah. Well, it tends that way.

RP: The "Hammer of the Gods," man's anatomy, fine! [*Laughs.*] It depends what you wanna—I mean, a lot of people used to boo during "Whole Lotta Love" and I don't know what else. That record must have been a part of so many little scenes. [*Laughs.*] But I'm sure we've—

Host: But it's a far out bit a part of what they're really, y'know, hoping to strain for. They keep looking for that all of the time. I think the far-distance loss thing—give us more of that.

JP: Ah, but it's there really, but it doesn't come necessarily electrically, you know. Things like "Friends," on the third album, which I reckon had as much bite, and it got through just as easily.

Host: There's a lot of things that are really obvious you know, that sort of hits you smack in the face and I can grab hold of, and I've got a pole to climb on straightaway.

JP: Yeah.

[*Coughing obscures audio.*]

Host: A lot of little kids say that. When you were pretty much a young boy and you're listening to radio and bopping around, what was the record that really got to you and had a special, sort of—where something happened where a record really stood out in your mind, say back in the rock era or some record that really grabbed you for some reason—that was a really personal thing to you. Can you remember a record like that, that stands out?

JP: Oh there were so many. From when I—I had a record player in 1960 and I was a lot younger than that, than this, then, and the first things I did was try and get the records that I'd only heard little bits of, in the initiation stages, you know, and I suppose it was the early Presley things were the things. The things like "Lawdy, Miss Clawdy" and "Trying to Get to You," you know, I mean we did "Lawdy, Miss Clawdy" yesterday.

Ah, it's just that there was such a sound about it, again. It was on a par with those Chess recordings and Howlin' Wolf. It was a sound—not on its own, but it's such a refreshing sound for white people to turn out at the time, when there was nothing else but Rosemary Clooney and—

[*Audio inaudible due to coughing.*]

Host: [The] Drifters' "Up on the Roof" and things like that? Did you get into that stuff?

JP: Well, I did—

RP: *I* did! [*Laughs.*] Yeah!

JP: I really liked "It Might as Well Rain Until September" and things like that, and—

RP: I was still praying for Ricky Nelson and these people to keep—keep it going.

JP: [*Laughs.*] Oh I wasn't totally a softie then! It was . . . it was just a little something about Bobby Vee's voice. I like to try and mimic people sometimes and I find it anyway to do that is to roll your jaw from left to right about ninety degrees [*makes yawning sound*] to sing "Rubber Ball" and things like that, "More Than I Can Say" . . .

Host: I remember the other day at John's place, we were listening to that Bobby Darin thing . . . like "Mack the Knife."

JP: Yeah, nobody came.

RP: No, he came off there—

JP: As soon as he got to "Mack the Knife."

RP: As soon as he got to the old schmaltz, we took it off—And "Splish Splash," they were all right . . .

Host: Did you uh, did you ever dig Buffalo Springfield?

RP: Oh yeah, very much so.

Host: Oh.

RP: The whole—all that groove really. But really they were at their best when they were *Buffalo Springfield Again* you know, "Rock and Roll Woman" and things like that. Now, if you're talking about West Coast music, have you heard of Moby Grape?

Host: Yeah. They're good.

JP: Yeah, they're—I really like them.

Host: Do you remember that scene, like in '65 when the Byrds came on and it all started to really roll—

RP: That's—that's it! That's when it—well you know, I mean, I wasn't really doing too much at all you know, 'cause being up in Birmingham, me and Bonham weren't the easiest blokes to sort of usher into a night club and be told to play what were gonna play. So we listened to sounds like that to get a bit of inspiration, along with Jerry Lee Lewis and all those people. But Moby Grape and Love—bits of them, not *all* of it! But a lot of it did me the world of good.

Host: I went to a concert in San Francisco last year—to the West Coast [*inaudible*] and the Family Dogg. Have you played there?

JP: No.

RP: They're a really different group—they're pretty wild. The Family Dogg when they were playing with, backing up the Who.

JP: Was that last year?

Host: Uh, 1970.

JP: Oh yeah?

RP: And I saw Kaleidoscope there.

JP: Did you?

RP: Yeah.

JP: Oh yeah. They were—they were brilliant!

Host: And the Family Dogg.

RP: The most exciting gigs that I ever saw. Because you just didn't know what they were gonna play next, each number was so different and changing instruments. And they were so accomplished on the instruments, too.

Host: With the Who and the Family Dogg, it was almost too much for the building, right?

[*Chuckles.*]

Host: Have you got plans to do anything like the Who did with *Tommy*? Like the walkoff type thing? Or are you just going to keep on—

JP: I don't know.

Host: Is it true that—

JP: Who knows where you're going? I suppose— what do you think? Record-wise we work about a year ahead, don't we? Or eighteen months…

RP: Yeah. We've got a lot of ideas are turning around, a lot of Jimmy's ideas musically that—that could be built into amazing things but I don't think that they could be classed alongside a rock opera or anything like that 'cause they're another thing altogether. You know, they've looked to be an amazing thing to get into but it's just—

Host: Almost too pretentious, maybe.

RP: Well I don't know, because you don't really know how they work.

JP: It's just this classification thing. I mean, I don't really know what you . . . well, try to classify our stuff, I'm—I'm playing it!

Host: Yes it's so emotional. You look like Stan Kenton trying to find a place for his kind of jazz and there's nowhere for it . . . your sound straining to achieve something new . . .

JP: Actually you said about the only name that I can relate to out of all those bands, eight mental breakdowns and all that.

Host: You listen, you listen for a certain peers now, not Stan Kenton—

[*Overlapping speakers.*]

JP: But it isn't, now, it isn't.

RP: Yeah, it's schmaltz.

JP: It isn't now, I'm afraid; no, it's not it's just not good. I really hate to see so many musicians when you see a brass section and everything, and they all do the same sort of thing, patented down phrases, every time. So much could be done with those instruments.

Host: And on stage you're all pretty happy with what you do. When you were recording, what happened?

RP: It's more just the same really. We spend most of the time laughing all the time anyway. [*Chuckles.*]

Host: Yeah. I don't know if you'd dig this at home, but if I got some, say, of the latest Aussie records and put them on, would you listen and give some of your comments, of what you think?

JP: You mean *Juke Box Jury*?

Host: Yeah, I mean some of the latest groups: could you tell us what you think of the music?

RP: If you got a buzzer, yeah!

JP: And a bell—

[*All laugh.*]

JP: Yeah, if you like! You see, we haven't really heard much of the Australian music at all, 'cause I, for one, can't stand the radio going on all day. It seems that over here you gotta combine the good with the bad, you know what I mean?

Host: Like AM in America—

JP: And I can't really handle the bad.

Host: But if I just get a couple of records, and [put] them on.

JP: All right then.

Host: Keith, when he drove you back the other day, was saying you were talking about the [*unintelligible*] record. Y'know, the "Day by Day" thing?

RP: Oh crikey!

JP: What about it?

RP: We're only talking about it.

JP: Well, actually somebody said that it was written by Ray Davies. That was basically the essence of the conversation.

RP: We couldn't believe that Ray Davies could write a song like that.

JP: Godspell! Right! Somebody said that, that's why we were going on about it, because somebody said that he had.

Host: There's a studio down in Melbourne run by a respected producer in the business, he says it's the worst produced record he'd ever heard.

JP: Worst produced?

Host: Yeah.

RP: I don't really like it—

Host: Do you find you get a lot of rumors, like what I told you in the car, floating around? [*Unintelligible audio.*]

JP: Oh, there's so many things going around, but, well, what can you say? Somebody's always gonna talk about somebody, don't they? It's either that or the queen.

Host: The Family, is that group still operating?

JP: Yeah.

Host: Are they— do they enjoy any acclaim?

JP: Well, yeah! Really they've been a very constant group. I can't really understand why they haven't done a lot better than they are doing. But then again, they're not doing badly, you know. They're working constantly for a good amount of bread. We didn't really know when things had taken off that they'd taken off, 'cause you can't really tell, you know what I mean? 'Cause you go to one town and get a reaction but there's ten million other towns.

[*Unintelligible audio.*]

Host: At the concert yesterday, there was this 14-year-old Swedish girl who flew all the way from Canberra.

JP: Well, why didn't you tell us? [*Chuckles.*] You've been— you've been telling us all these stories of all these great birds you saw—

RP: And we believed that, we really do. Incredible!

Host: What about people like . . . Joe Cocker?

RP: Yeah! Why don't we talk about Freddie King?

Host: Yeah.

JP: Cocker is good, though. Don't dismiss him out of—

RP: Yeah.

JP: Cocker's great.

RP: It's just that Leon Russell . . .

JP: Yeah, right.

RP: No, no—the way it's gone about. You see the only reason that we don't work all that often and we're a little bit indecisive—not indecisive but we'd totally please ourselves—is that that's the only way that you can really enjoy it and still remain in control of your faculties, you know. And there's some people who move in, like big businessmen, on the scene and they just happen to be musicians too, you know. And of the one or two that are around, you know, you've mentioned a couple. [*Chuckles.*]

Host: What do you think about Joe Cocker then?

RP: Well goodness knows, but I really, really . . . They say he's gonna do something again now?

JP: Yeah there's Chris Stainton, who's the pianist, but he also played bass unbelievably well. He, um—oh cheers—he started a new band with Glenn [Ross] Campbell from Juicy Lucy, the steel player, and apparently Cocker is joining that. That should be really good.

Host: It's like his old record, in some ways. Would you like to hear his stuff then?

JP: Yeah!

Host: These are the La De Das, one of the top groups, one of their own songs.

JP: Where is it then?

[*Record plays.*]

RP: It reminds of "I Wish I Could Shimmy Like My Sister Kate," "I'm In with the In Crowd," and "Ticket to Ride"—fantastic! [*Chuckles.*]

JP: Bloody fantastic!

RP: I don't know, you must have a lot of the Olymp— have you heard of the Olympics over here?

Host: No.

RP: Old American vocal group. They did "Western Movies" and "The Twist" and all that sort of thing.

Host: I've heard their version of "The Twist." They were on Top Rank.

RP: Yeah, and "The Bounce"! No, No, No, No, No! Well there's two on Top Rank.

Host: A thing called "Western Movies."

RP: Yeah, yeah, well that's it.

Host: It's a direct tag on them?

RP: Well, it's the way they end it.

Host: Well then you feel the song doesn't matter?

RP: No, but I mean, why not? I mean if we heard it in a club and we were all half-canned it would be the finest thing of the night probably. We wouldn't relate to it as a bit of individual getting together.

JP: But can we look at the records first and then come back in case the library shuts, 'cause then we can do it—we get to be curator. We could run out! [Laughter.]

Host: We've got one section for imports after all. How about musical groups like Yes and Wishbone Ash and people like that? What do you think of them?

RP: I saw a good group called Home in England, I don't know whether they've had any records out over here. They were on CBS in England, sort of like, you know Poco? Sort of along those lines, but they were younger and their approach was an English approach. They were pretty good but as to others, I don't really know.

Host: Say, in the more commercial field, some of the big names today. Do you have any likes or dislikes? We have some Joni Mitchell. I mean, we could play a track of hers and more things she's done.

RP: Well, yeah, it's really hard to sort of whittle it down to one. She's really so good, in so many ways, that there's so many different things that she does that you can like her for.

Host: A group in England about twelve months ago that looked like they were going to be a fantastic new group, called the Nice . . .

RP: I don't know much about them at all. The Nice?

Host: Did you see them when they were together at all?

JP: No—to tell you the truth I think I saw about ten minutes of them once. The organist, Keith Emerson, was the mainstay of the thing. It's what they built everything around really and he's a pretty good organist. He's got all these devious methods of playing the organ, standing on it and throwing knives into it to hold the octaves, you know, *tschunk*! With a dagger! Then he'd play a little bit then *tschunk*! With a machete and when he got down to a chain saw I think—

[*All laugh.*]

Host: Emerson, Lake, and Palmer, what do you think of the things they're doing, like "Tarkus" . . . ?

JP: Mm, okay. "Tuchas" did you say? [*Chuckles.*]

RP: Tuchas! Right! The tuchas! Incredible String Band is another kettle of fish. Nothing to do with Emerson, Lake, and Palmer, but . . . I appreciate them a lot more.

JP: They're like a breath of fresh air every time you go and see them. Really good.

RP: 'Cause it's like—it's more like a renaissance sort of a medieval travelling troupe you know, and they— I suppose they must please themselves entirely, what they do, but they always hold the audience in the palm of [their] hand. They do pantomimes and all these mime troupe things. Really, really good.

Host: Like old English folk music, back in the days . . .

RP: Right! Yeah! But they add something to it like a magic that not many people possess these days.

Host: Are they very big in England?

RP: Well, it's not a thing like that at all really, they just . . . well they wanna do something similar to us on another plane altogether you know, when they want to *do* something, they go out and do it.

JP: And everybody's here to see them, but there's no big sort of hysteria built now.

Host: Sounds very nice.

JP: Yeah, yeah. You don't need critics for shows like that.

RP: 'Cause they wouldn't know what they were seeing anyway, half of them.

Host: What about American bands? Have you got sort of preferences among them? Did you see Grand Funk [Railroad] when they were over there?

RP: No, no, I haven't seen them.

JP: No we did play with them, though, didn't we? Years back?

RP: Oh yeah! That's right. Boston, wasn't it?

Host: A lot of people, they give them sort of a severe rubbishing out of any group I've ever heard about. Lately people are just putting them down as being crap, y'know, just . . .

RP: They sell so many million records you know [*clears throat*]. So did Perry Como. But they fit in somewhere along the line, don't they?

Host: Have you heard any of their stuff at all?

RP: Yeah I've heard bits of it.

Host: What do you think of what you heard?

RP: Well, I didn't really like it too much at all. I don't know—you gotta go a little bit further than that. You know, you can't just play one thing for about half an hour. But maybe they are going further may—they—apparently I don't think they've been on the road for a year or something like that. You know, they've just said "Right, we're not gonna do anything at all."

Host: How about groups like Chicago? You don't like them?

RP: Not really, no, I don't. To employ brass into something and still possess *real* balls you know, real excitement, it's a very . . .

[*Someone enters the studio, carrying more records.*]

Host Two: Hi all!

RP: Oh blimey!

[*Laughter.*]

JP: Oh, mate!

RP: Fantastic!

[*JP and RP start sorting through the new batch of records.*]

RP: It's a very hard thing to . . . Oh shit! Look at this! [*Laughs.*] It's a very hard thing employ brass and get away with a little bit of funky.

JP: I think they're one of the best of those sort of groups though, aren't they?

RP: Yeah.

JP: I mean when you weigh it up what else is around? They all sound pretty similar.

Host: How about Yes?

JP: You keep asking that, aren't you?

Host: Yeah.

JP: They're good! They're good.

Host: I think they're a good band. Have you seen them in action?

JP: I only saw a television thing, they did a sort of an hour thing, a live-in-concert thing, but it was taken on the road. At one university I think that they played at, and then everyone was sort of interviewed in their home, and it was quite good.

RP: Actually everybody said to me "Oh you're gonna like [Australian '50s revivalists] Daddy Cool," and almost everything I've heard I have liked.

Host: You like them?

Both: Yeah, cool.

RP: I'd like to see them on stage very much. [*To program director John Brennan.*] Can I have that Elvis EP back please, Jack? [*Laughs.*] Elvis!

Host: What groups do you—as a group—admire most? What are the groups that you dig most, you know, modern groups, new groups today?

Host Two: Ones that consider have potential, that are going to be big or what . . .

JP: No. Most of the groups that I really liked a lot have broken up, like Kaleidoscope and Fairport [Convention]—

RP: Yeah!

JP: From those particular eras and Fairport [Convention] with Sandy Denny was a good one. But I like Yes. I must admit I do like them.

RP: Have you got the album Sandy Denny with um—

JP: *Leige & Lief.*

RP: Yeah, *Leige & Lief.* That is a fine album!

Host: Isn't she with Fotheringay now?

RP: No, she's left them to do a solo album. And Richard Thompson who was the guitarist with Fairport [Convention] is back with her again. The first album by Matthews' Southern Comfort I really liked.

JP: Mm. One side of it was very really, really good.

RP: Yeah, right, did you hear that?

Host: Yeah, yeah, those were a couple of Australian guys in that group.

JP: I don't know. That thing, "seems to me that I've been floating on the same wind," what's it called? "Colorado Springs (Eternal In My Mind)!" Really—a nice album, that was.

Host: Can we get the thing from the light to the more . . . there's a lot of the stuff which is very heavy which side of the audience wouldn't be as aware of as if we could perhaps—

JP: Well that doesn't really matter does it? 'Cause that's not—

RP: That's not our—our fault or your fault really . . .

JP: 'Cause you're—you're asking us what we like, and that's really what we like! We can't really say we like—

Host: Well what I'm asking perhaps is, what do you like . . . that is commercial?

RP: Well, we—we like anything! You can't really do—I don't really know where commercial begins and stops because—

Host: The stuff that you hear played on stations, or on Top 40s, or—

RP: Well this is why I stated in the beginning, I try and avoid listening . . . You see, there are people who turn out really good stuff who have to be ignored because there isn't a palatable audience for it. Now there really is you know, I mean it's up to you to give them a really good cross-section of good sound, you know. I mean this is the problem in England really, the kids have had to go out and they have to go on hearsay so much—

JP: Yeah.

RP: So that reputations are built on hearsay, you know, people like Fairport Convention. The original Fairport Convention were really good.

Host: Well, even Yes had trouble when they started to get their gig.

RP: Well we—

JP: *We* did!

RP: We went to America because nobody would bill us as Led Zeppelin! We were the New Yardbirds, you know. As soon as we got our first rehearsals under way and we went in the studio, we knew that we weren't the New Yardbirds. But they weren't prepared. Nobody's prepared to sort of say fair enough off they go and this is a new group called Led Zeppelin.

Host: Which record gave you your identity?

JP: Well, the only one—

JP and RP: The first one!

RP: If you know the history of the group properly, we've recorded in about, thirty hours or something like that, less than that. And that was three weeks after we'd formed. All these constructions on things like "How Many More Times" and things like that were Jimmy's baby really and they were so amazing that the other three of us were taken back by it, y'know. And it was the enthusiasm put into recording that first album.

JP: It shows, though, doesn't it?

RP: Yeah. I mean, it just went *bang*! And every night was such a gem! Every night was so good to be able to get out there and play it again! Because of constructions would lead to different things every night like they do even now, y'know.

Host: Actually, what you may be saying is that you'd like to see, in a way, not, maybe, FM radio, but radio with, perhaps, a freer access towards everybody. A special channel that would play records for the people that you're talking about.

RP: Mm, I mean I realize that you've got to keep your listeners and a lot of the listeners are probably into some things, but they don't really . . . The things that are going around on the radio, a lot are played, like, four times. I mean, every time I put the radio on, I hear one song four times and I go 'oh dear, dear,' you know.

Host: Do you think that radio can educate?

RP: Radio can *brainwash*!

Host: You think FM will ever get into England? I mean, they're having hassles now with, apparently they're supposed to be getting commercial stations too—

JP: Well that's gonna be worse than what we've got now because of people who are buying that, the ones who gonna get the licenses for that are the big sort of newspaper magnates, all these people who've got the bread. So it's just gonna be just as bad as it was before, really. It's not going to be a breakthrough for commercial radio; it's just going to be more channels.

Host: It doesn't sound like anyone's doing anything really.

RP: Yeah, but look at who they're using. You know. I mean John Peel really deserves the biggest pat on the back of all of them in England.

JP: They try to sweep him under the carpet, really. You know, they try to put him on at hours when they hope nobody's gonna be listening.

RP: Oh! He's the one who virtually got everybody aware of what was going on.

JP: He was the first one to start giving people a chance, people that you would never normally hear in no way at all. They might just be playing in arts fairs.

Host: Like Medicine Head and things like that?

RP: Well, like everybody from the word go!

JP: Also, what's his name? The mad banjo player?

RP: Oh yeah! What's his . . . what's his name with the piano? All sorts of—well, you might as well call it like, the same thing as the Incredible String Band, that moving around and—and giving a show you know? On his programs he'd have a bit of everything, and the people were suddenly aroused, you know, re-aroused, like Presley arousing. You suddenly found out that there's a lot more content to it than met the eye because, like Radio 1, I reckon that they were doing the country a favor but really all they were doing was beating the music into the ground. Because you have to pass an audition to be able to play on Radio 1 and people like Terry Reid—who are really, really gifted—failed! Because of the material, not because of the fact that he was a brilliant singer—

JP: That's Top 40 for you.

Host: Yeah.

RP: And it doesn't even compare to the Top 40 of your standard, because at least you play the records *by* the artists, however good or bad they are. But in England you get like of copy of it you know, by somebody in the studio—

Host: No needles on.

RP: Hm?

Host: Because you've got no needles on.

RP: Yeah, and because they've got no insight, the people who are doing it.

JP: Civil servants . . .

Host: Listen, talking about identity, do you think—have you heard Deep Purple lately, live?

RP: No.

Host: Do you like them?

RP: Um, I don't know.

Host: Something that Ian Gillan said about Zeppelin, you know, when it came out here. He said that your songs weren't strong, you were suffering from—

JP: No! [*Chuckles.*] Well, what about their first LP? There's one thing on there that sounds like a direct nick of one of ours. And plus another one that's a nick of "Bombay Calling" by It's a Beautiful Day.

Host: Yeah but he also said that, up until that point, that they were too influenced by too many things by everybody and they didn't have an identity, and they were very worried about in fact that they didn't. They didn't sound like anybody.

[*All exclaim at once.*]

RP: Hang on—

JP: What an issue, eh?

RP: Sounds like the Houses of Parliament!

JP: Now that's a really silly thing to say, y'know. I mean as far as we go they can please themselves with what they think, as what we write is improving by the day. I reckon that their first album can't be put down in comparison to our *fourth* album, because there's no comparisons, really. We're the same group and there's a little bit of this and a little bit of that but it—

RP: We're three years doing it.

JP: Yeah. We're here and there. Whereas there's a lot of groups and I'm not saying them, but a lot of groups just get one riff and they beat it into the ground. They'll play that one riff for about ten minutes and . . . I suppose you can mummify the kids after a while. That seems to be what Sly Stone does, but he does it really well. I mean, they're totally amazing, but it's still that really constant turning over of one thing.

Host: What do you think of "Black Night"?

JP: All right, but haven't we heard it somewhere before?

RP: I suppose we've heard everything somewhere before. We often sit down and say, "Wow, we've heard that before somewhere." It was—

Host: How about Free reforming?

RP: Mm, yeah. They were pretty good.

JP: Yeah, but that's another group that I can't see going on the same plane you know. I think that's why they broke up really. But then we'll see what happens when they get back together again—

RP: That's great! 'Cause we did it! Their first two albums we were raving about it, by the fourth it was very—

Host: Is Simon [Kirke] on the new album?

RP: Really I don't know. You see—we met virtually all of them individually after the breakup and they were all complaining about various things. But a lot of it must've been the fact that they—that it was that same sort of [*hums a few bars*] that little bit of funk, but never taking it any further or taking it back anywhere And that's one of the things that keeps us happy with what we do ourselves.

Host: What about Jethro [Tull]? What do you think about their stuff today?

RP: Well we did about fifteen dates with them in America on one tour, and the whole setup of that group really amazes. Their manager wouldn't let them go out with us because we were decidedly tear-aways and hooligans and all that. And ol' Jethro* would sit in his room, he wouldn't even having nothing to do with the other members of the group. Every night he'd say the same quips in between numbers. And when it comes down to *that*, he'd hold his flute up and say, "How'd you like my phallic tin whistle?" "Jim Morrison's got nothing on me." And all that sort of thing, you know. But night after night after night, so that really stops you going any farther into listening to him.

JP: Yeah.

Host: It sounds like a completely rehearsed gig . . .

JP: Well that's just it.

RP: It was their management, God bless 'em, but . . .

JP: Well you see he's—you know, whoever's at the helm of the whole operation, you know. I mean, the thing is, it—that's the one thing with us, we don't go out there and do the same thing every night. We're constantly working on ways we're going to change it, every night, so there's a change.

---

*Plant is referring here to Ian Anderson, the leader of Jethro Tull.

I can't even envisage playing in a group where you'd have to do the same thing, note-for-note perfect. I never have, ever.

RP: We're very fortunate 'cause we haven't got a manager who can only look at it the way that people do and manufacture something. I mean he's into it, the changes, as much as we are, and he'll get off on the fact that we'll do something totally different then how we've done it before.

Host: What about Manfred Mann?

JP: It's a long time ago.

Host: The current lineup is interesting.

JP: Haven't heard anything.

Host: They came out here, the first big pop show that we had. It really sort of opened things up for big groups. I think it was the Deep Purple / Free / Manfred Mann tour. They were the first of the really big shows and it all sort of snowballed from there with everything.

JP: Mm. And what about the Who and Small Faces tour then?

Host: Ah, well with that—I'm saying that was a fair while ago, and there was some sort of a gap after that stuff and then Deep Purple was the first one that came after that.

RP: That was brilliant actually I should imagine that, the Who and the Small Faces . . .

Host: The Who were great.

Host Two: Yeah.

RP: Well I should imagine Small Faces were.

Host: They were too, Stevie [Marriott] . . .

Host Two: They got booed off the stage.

RP: Oh but they will do that! They'll get booed off stages anywhere, the Small Faces, because they're so . . . they're like—oh they just really—they were too much! Really, too much for people to take it at times.

Host: They came out on stage and said, "Fuck you." And the crowd booed and there were things flying and he said "Fuck you all I'm gonna get off the stage!" and walked off and later I saw him. [*Chuckles.*]

JP: Yeah, but when they really started laying it down when people said, "Well please yourself in what you say and do, just get it together." They really did that very thing, y'know.

Host: How 'bout with the old days of Stevie Winwood and the Spencer Davis Group and them?

RP: Oh yeah, the Shrines.

Host: Do you like those guys?

JP: Yeah very much so, yeah. Well, Winwood was a gem in those days. Well, he was for a long, long time. With Spencer, they used to start off with "Rambling Rose," a Jerry Lee Lewis thing, and they used to do this moody intro, and old Winwood clapping away, and he had this pickup Sellotaped to his guitar and all of that. They used to play in little closed— but the atmosphere was fine and Spencer's rhythm playing that "chink, chink" all the time you know. They were really fine, really good. We gotta go soon anyway.

Host: Say the first thing that comes into your head about the concert yesterday.

RP: Warm. Well, not . . . it was really warm, it was. Sounds like that chick who take photographs in *Les Girls*, isn't it? [*Chuckles.*] Well, the people were fantastic. I'm only upset that we couldn't have the stage farther back and that all those people who climbed over to see it properly.

Host: That was an incredible experience seeing all that.

RP: Yeah! As the afternoon went on it became more like it should be you know, the people getting in little groups and all sitting down. There was a guy doing gymnastics with a pair of swimming trunks on. I think if we'd have stayed there about another three hours and that somebody else like the Incredible String Band on as well—

Host: Yeah.

RP: We could've taken off! The whole ground could've just shot into space! And landed anywhere in the world and done a bit of good.

Host: Do you think you'd come back to the country for another tour?

RP: Well it—it depends on a few things, but I wouldn't mind at all.

Host: Have you been happy with the audiences?

RP: Very much so, yes. Auckland was a bit strange. No, not Auckland. What am I talking about? What was that other place we played? It begins with *A*. Adelaide!

Host: Oh Adelaide, you said it looked like an old sort of cow town in the old Midwest of the States.

RP: But then again it didn't! But then again it did. It was one of those—I don't know. I was at a bit of a disadvantage, really. I sort of went "Ooh." But there were people scrapping. There was one guy who was leading, he would stand up at different times and start clapping like that [*claps*] and then if somebody said "sit down!" he'd go *bomp!* you know, and the guy would be all bloody and all that and the guy would sit down again and . . . I suppose if you get somebody who you can see doing things like that it does look slightly . . .

Host: Which has been your best audience, most receptive?

RP: Well I liked Melbourne, Sydney, and Perth . . . and Auckland have been really, really fine, because you dig 'em all for different things. I mean, the one in Melbourne got off for me 'cause it started raining at different points and everybody knew that if we stood there too long we'd go *pfft*—we'd get electrocuted, y'know. [*Chuckles.*] And yet, when we said, "Well we can't do anymore" they'd say "Oooohhhh!" We had to stop for about ten minutes and put tarpaulin on the stage and come back on. And when we came back on there was about a forty mile hour wind blowing. The tarpaulin that was over the P.A. system was falling down all over the guy who was controlling the P.A., one minute he'd be there and the next minute he'd be immersed in this big tent.

Host: We had Creedence [Clearwater Revival] a two weeks before you. Have you managed to see them live at all?

RP: Mm.

JP: Mm.

Host: Yeah, what did you think?

JP: What did *you* think?

Host: Well I thought—

Host Two: Very disappointed.

Host: Disappointed. I mean their sound was recreated exactly as a record input. Well that's good, but then they got up on there and they just sort of do it, very unenthusiastically for us, and they just finished and said "Zap, that it!" They were only up for about three-quarters of an hour.

RP: Wow.

Host Two: There was a wall between them and the audience.

Host: And there was nothing getting through. There was something stopping it, you know? The audience appreciated it, but there was still a very sort of calm feeling and everyone went away saying "What happened?"

JP: There didn't seem to be anything extra there, really, when *I* saw them. I'd never seen them before and I just really wondered what it was gonna be like.

RP: They didn't transmit—

JP: That's another one of those things that we were talking about earlier on, just going on there and thinking about something else as they play. You can't really do that, but somehow it was just so note-for-note perfect to the records or you just wondered just exactly what—

Host: If they did anything else in the show differently.

JP: What kind of satisfaction *he* was getting out of it, really.

RP: Yeah.

Host: Have you heard any of their albums? Or I guess you must've . . .

RP: Yeah we were on the impression that he was a rockabilly fan, a real fiend, you know.

JP: A real fanatic.

RP: Incredible great record collection of all these people that he'd sort of pinch records off, like Roy Orbison's "Ooby Dooby" and "Any Old Sunday." I just thought he was really gonna know about these things.

Host: Did you get to talk to the guy?

RP: He's a bit too cool, actually.

Host: How did you get on with him?

RP: Well they invited us up to their "Mondo Bizarro" which I think is Spanish for "Bizarre World" or something like that and chatting to our hostesses.

JP: And wearing this raincoat.

[*Laughter.*]

RP: I don't know, the whole thing is different.

JP: His bunny club.

RP: We had a lot of good high spots in our time, like touring is really going on holiday. We like to have such a good time. I don't think we're at all pretentious or anything like that we just go out and . . . and have a fucking wonderful time until somebody tries to stop us! [*Laughs.*] And there's a lot of people who don't work like that you know, probably they might be the right way.

Host: Creedence seemed to be very uptight when they came out here. Didn't seem to enjoy themselves much.

Host Two: How many months of the year would you tour?

RP: Depends. However many we feel like. We worked out some kind of a plan for this twelve months.

Host: Yeah.

RP: Mainly all it incorporates is going places as we can get 'em, Bombay or Thailand along the way.

Host: Listen, have you still got that farm, that house out in the country? Are you very much into this whole ecological thing, where people who tired of the hassle of the city go out and—

RP: Well it isn't very much "into a thing," it's just a realization of . . . a lot of the . . . situation as it stands. I don't want to be classed as an ecological freak at *all* because I'm just totally aware of it the escalation of—

JP: It's no big thing, really. It's just common sense, isn't it?

RP: If somebody caught me in Adelaide and they said "Well Jimmy, what do you think of—" [*Laughs.*] We have it all the time, though, don't we? We even had a room booked in Auckland Hotel for Led Zeppelin you know. He got his own room, this guy! [*Laughs.*]

JP: Mr. Zeppelin. [*Laughs.*]

RP: So coming back yeah! But ecology is, um—what a new term, isn't, for the desire to stay alive?

JP: It's fantastic when—when you try and stop those wheels and you see what you're up against.

Host: Yeah.

JP: When it's obviously morally wrong, what's going on, and you just see what gains have been played beyond the scenes.

Host: I reckon we've about thirty years left if they keep it going at the same way.

RP: You see I've got a child, a little girl, and I've got another one on the way, and you just wonder whether you should even be responsible for bringing life into the world really. I mean we're in the position where we could take the reins and say, "Right, hold it! All God's children are going to have a choice, and we don't want it to go like this." But you start shouting out like that and it should give so much meat to people and talk about this to the critics, to the press, to the radio, to the media in general and they'd make it into a farce! You know, it could soon turn from what you really feel into the latest thing to talk about concerning Zeppelin. So you say as little as you can about it and you laugh a little more.

Host: Yeah.

JP: It's really strange. I'm involved in this issue at home, at the moment on Loch Ness, and it's a fantastic beauty spot and they're intending to put pylons all the way along one of the edges of it not all away along but a two-miles stretch, which is enough and it will be seen. And it will set a fearful precedent because there aren't any others around there. It's amazing, but when you see what you're up against and you speak to the press up there and they say, "Was there any idea of a publicity gimmick in this?"

RP: You see . . . we know how everybody has to be who earns their bread and butter out of saying things about other people. The unfortunate thing is that the number of people in the streets here in Sydney, or anywhere else, are totally aware of all these different situations, you know. Maybe they've got their spokesmen, but their spokesmen are shouted down. I mean even [John] Lennon, in his crazy ways, tried. Bob Dylan tried as well for a long time. Just at little stab points. The horizon is so great and what we have to either contend with or turn against. There's so much there that one man can't say it all, let alone sort of brandish the standard and bring everybody under the one flag and say, well, y'know . . .

Host: You virtually can't be honest.

[*All talk at once.*]

JP: Well you can be!

RP: You can, but you get shut up. You can't afford it!

JP: Oh! You can afford it, you can afford to be but it becomes . . . they can turn it into a very pretty thing!

Host: This is what I really mean, it turns against you. Listen, as a matter of interest—this is just by the way—what, yesterday, did you mean when you said something about San Francisco, except for some girl kicking a beer can or something . . .? Kicking that can over?

RP: Oh yeah, right.

Host: I just wondered what you meant by—

RP: Right. Well San Francisco, when I first went there—and Jimmy went a long time before me—when I first went there, I'd got so much out of people like Moby Grape and Love and the new feeling again you know, a revitalization of what sent me on musically, y'know. 'Cause they were singing about things and they were singing with a *drive* of a kind that I really wanted to be a part of, you know. I went there and I was so elated when we first played the Fillmore. It was like one of the biggest experiences ever, not because it was San Francisco and all the music was there but because the *people* were there, and the people were . . . God, you know, if you could've transported *those* people around the world you'd have done a lot of good, but we went back, as time goes on and we keep going back we keep—we find that that little subculture has been divided into . . . as a society, already in there. There's the different ranks you get like, if you haven't been around too long, nobody's gonna talk to you. You walk down the street and people don't smile at each other anymore.

JP: And that was a big thing about it; you could walk around and everyone would be saying "Hello!" didn't know who anybody else was but it was just this thing—contact with everybody.

Host: Mm.

JP: And I saw, when I went there before with the Yardbirds, it was—it was just a very, very small community and this whole thing is grand! It's fantastic!

RP: When you see something like that, it's fine to see it grow. I mean, unfortunate thing was, it got—I don't know what happened. I suppose it was all the drug abuse and all that sort of thing and like suddenly a guy who probably sat on top of a hill and blew a pipe now and again had got drawn into other things until he found out that he had to get out in the street to hustle to make sure that he got those things continually.

Host: Yeah.

RP: And then when man is revealed as the animal that he is, he forgets all the beauty that he created. It was a good feeling then, and I tried to relate it to, but also I tried to say that when you go back there now it's another story.

JP: Yeah.

RP: And just as I said that some chick threw something right into the crowd, you know!

JP: Yeah!

RP: Like a twisted beer can went [*makes flying noise*] and probably whoever was listening to me just got a bump on the head and carried on listening.

Host: Yeah.

RP: So that was it. And if everybody had turned around quick enough, which I hoped would've happened, they would have seen her arm up like that. I mean, a lot of people do it and you don't see 'em.

Host: It was like a guy, one of his fans, who had chucked an egg at Jagger, and they just happened to catch who it was, y'know. It was really incredible. He shook his mic and said, "You! You wanna throw eggs at me? Come backstage and I'll throw a bloody *bucketful* at ya." He scared the sap outta this poor cat. Not poor guy, he shouldn't have done it. They saw him: he thought he'd get away with it. They caught him in the act with it. The egg in the hand.

RP: Yeah, but what is all that about?

Host: Ah it's just something.

RP: I know! But, I know—

JP: People do get really hung up, isn't it?

Host: The cat is—it's probably just some guy who thinks "Ah . . ." you know that's—

Host Two: You get them at every concert.

RP: But they *should not be there*! They should not be there at all, you know.

Host: That's what you gotta fight against, you know, the whole—

RP: Well that's what the people who come had better fight against.

JP: Yeah, it's up to them to get it together. I mean every concert that we've had apart from yesterday wasn't quite so bad. The Sydney audience seemed to have it really together, actually, the whole sort of thing between them. I mean it's really disciplined. All this sort of running across, when they started to run towards the grass, I could see all the police and I'm going, "Well wait a minute, what's gonna happen here?" And they were really cool about it and the whole thing just mellowed down into a really good feeling. But the one problem we have come across, when the audience haven't got it together amongst themselves is the standing up and sitting down. The people want to stand up, and people want to sit down, you get all these people shouting out "Sit down! Sit down!"

Host: Yeah.

JP: It gets too much, especially when you're doing acoustic numbers.

Host: Yeah.

RP: But you see we spoke to the chief of police beforehand and this Hopper—and I tell you those two guys were as cool as anybody who was sitting down.

Host: Yeah.

RP: Because they—they realized the situation, they realized that you can aggravate something by sending in an element that is now . . . I mean if you've seen the police in Europe, it's, unfortunately you're asking for trouble! You know because it's like everybody's got a bad name [on] both sides of the fence to each other. So this guy realized that the stage should've been pulled back another fifty yards before day began—

Host: Yeah.

RP: Right, and if they expected that many people, then these people should've been accommodated, you know. Otherwise, you *do* get trouble 'cause people are jumping out the stands and running across. I thought this is gonna be another Perth, you know, and we were gonna have to flee quickly with ripped garments—

[*Someone chuckles.*]

RP: But no! They didn't do that, see, and that was where they *really* pulled it out for me, 'cause as soon as I sat down and went, "right," that is when the concert started. And we dug them as much as they dug us, I think.

Host: Have you got another album ready to go? After the tour?

RP: I won't tell ya!

Host Two: Right on, next question. [*Chuckles.*]

Host: You were saying in an interview that used a lot of symbols to stuff up the mass media just so they just couldn't label you, that was just the premise behind using all the symbols you had for the—for the fourth album?

JP: Well it wasn't *just* that, but that certainly came into it.

Host: One of the reasons.

JP: As soon as you saw them going, "Well, yes, well let's have more information on the title please and all this sort of thing, you realize there is more—more focus there.

RP: But those symbols carry a bit of weight.

JP: Certainly a little bit of chaos, sure they did you know, but don't worry.

Host: Can you explain some of those symbols?

RP: Um, well, I don't know. It would take another hour. I wanted to see us on the telly! It's too late now. Have you got a TV here?

Host: Yeah, we do somewhere.

RP: Why don't we cut it off now and come back after?

JP: Well we probably missed it, haven't we?

RP: Half past six.

JP: Oh is it? Oh let's go and watch that!

RP: Right! Over and out! Roger and out!

[*They adjourn to watch the 6:30 news on which they are set to appear.*]

[*Tape rolls again.*]

RP: A cup of tea would go down *really* well. Cuppa tea and we'll stay the night!

Host: You were saying about "American Pie" before . . . that the record itself, that listening, do you think it's all about the American rock scene and Buddy Holly and—

JP: Oh no! Well it's about the whole lot, by the sound of it and that includes the English you know. About how it began: "Did you write the book of love?" I mean when you start up a song like that then you end up where the music thing is now, on the second side. I think we were—can't we play those sides of it? One after another? 'Cause I'm sure that you—what you do is on a Top 40 station, or whatever this is, you're gonna play the one side you know, but the story is um—

Host: Yeah.

Host Two: But would you listen to the others?

RP: No, but the story really is really, uh . . .

Host: Yeah.

JP: I think because it's such a sort of—that chorus is so catchy and you relate it to other sorts of things that you've heard before like that, you bypass the notes. I must admit I did. The first time I dismissed the whole thing out of hand. Then, when I listened to the lyrics properly it's about a big revelation, what it was all about.

Host: Yeah.

RP: Yeah I really like to put that in to our thing just because of the fact that a lot of people would just say, "Ah there it goes" until they um . . .

Host: Yeah.

Host Two: You probably, um . . .

Host: That reference to "American Pie"?

RP: No, well there's nothing to do with "American Pie," it's just um—

Host: Oh, lyrics in general.

JP: Yeah!

Host: Mm, do you feel that a lot of people sort of say . . . you can do a lot of gigs today and you get up and a whole lot of people say "Yeah! Really great set there!" and you think to yourself "Well I played shit ass and I just conned them," because a lot of people try and say, "Yeah! You really sounded great!"

JP: Yeah you don't—

RP: Never *con* them.

JP: You don't think you've conned them, you just think—you just feel really cheated that you know that they thought it was good. Well, you know when the people say "Yeah! Great man!" you know they're just saying that 'cause they want to talk to you for about a quarter of an hour. Some people really mean it and they've missed it, you know they've missed it. Saying that you could've been a bit better really, and you just feel annoyed that you couldn't play better. I always get that way every night anyway.

Host: Yeah.

RP: I know I do, most of the time [*chuckles*]. But a lot of it has to do with the audience, because you can be playing incredibly well you know, and if the audience ain't quite how you like it, y'know, and you become as specialist as they are, well in fact twice as specialist as they are 'cause you're dealing with like tens of thousands of people . . . en masse . . . in one go. So to get that good flowing—that exchange of feeling, like we give them something, they give it back, and so we give them more and they give back more until you—

JP: —rapport just keeps building.

Host: Building, yeah. Have you ever considered cutting a live album?

RP: I wouldn't mind actually. It's just catching it. Some nights are out of this world, that we'd be totally happy with. And the band has played and there's not a recording machine in sight, except for some bootlegger with a mic and a broomstick [*chuckles*]. You're saying that making a lot of bread will make you sound bad so they swing the broomstick round in the air! [*Chuckles.*]

Host: Yeah, so have you had any of your stuff that's been known to be bootlegged, selling pretty well in the States?

JP: Yeah.

RP: Mm.

Host: This must really piss you off.

RP: Ah well, yeah, because it's a terrible reproduction, you know. *Live on Blueberry Hill* was dire!

JP: And especially when that one came out it was at the heyday of bootlegs and bootlegs were costing about double the price of the legitimate LP, which seem totally unfair 'cause they didn't have any overhead, like a proper record company. And the quality was bad. It should've been at least half price, shouldn't they? That would've justified bootlegs in some way, shape, or form, but as it is, they're still more expensive, I think, in England. Just a little bit more, but at that time they were double, and for double a LP, which is what that was, it was costing a lot of money.

RP: But we'd gladly rush out I know, Jimmy and I, we'd—

JP: Yeah!

RP: We rushed out to get a Dylan bootlegs! [*Laughs.*] "Quick! Let's get in there!" Y'know, we'd go in and then the guys would sort of go totally pale, 'cause they've got ours just next to the Dylan bootlegs, you know!

[*All laugh.*]

RP: So I mean . . .

Host: Oh! What was your reaction when you saw your first bootleg just lying on the shelf there?

JP: I mean I put it on. I was so disgusted with the sound, I threw it in the river. [*Chuckles.*] And I—and I tried to get another one from somewhere! [*Chuckles.*]

[*A woman walks into the room.*]

Woman: Hello.

RP: Hello!

JP: Hello!

RP: Welcome to "On the air!"

Woman: Sorry to interrupt.

RP: Okay, I'll tell you what I would like to hear in the middle of it all: got anything by Dion, any of the old stuff?

JP: You just—

Host: Which one?

RP: Something like "The Wanderer" or "The Majestic."

Host: Oh yeah. Somewhere in the back.

RP: Yeah! Baby yeah! 'Cause these people rock.

JP: Have you got "My Girl the Month of May," which was a Dion . . . they reformed about '66.

RP: Oh please, yeah! If you've got an album by you—

JP: Have you heard that? "My Girl the Month of May." It's great. They reformed and they just did this one—

Host: They did one this one album when they reformed and it's on that . . .

JP: That's right! It's an LP! 'Tis an LP, that's right, "My Girl the Month Of May" is a single, though.

Host: Yeah I know.

JP: It's good.

RP: Yes. Well he's still got a superb voice. It's really New York.

JP: Funny enough when you put on the Aztecs thing it reminded me of some of the singles that he started to put out . . . "Hoochie Coochie Man" and all those sorts of things—

RP: Yeah, I remember—

JP: It reminded me of that, although he was doing it acoustic—

Host: When I first saw—one of the old Chuck Berry songs—

RP: "Johnny B. Goode"?

JP: Yeah "Johnny B. Goode," yeah.

Host: That was unreal. Yeah!

RP: He's got a lovely voice. He really flows around the place like anything, you know.

Host: Is he—he's just doing acoustic stuff now, is he?

RP: Mm, yeah. We saw him, didn't we?.

Host: What—what's his act like now? Just "Abraham, Martin, and John" stuff?

RP: Well I should imagine it's changed yet again because I heard a track in England just before we came away which is a live album or a cut off of an album which was live and I think it was "Ruby Baby" or something like that. It was one of those things anyway, but it was so fine because, despite it being an acoustic . . . well it's like I was trying to say about "Friends" being as heavy as "Whole Lotta Love," you know. It was really, really, really good.

Host: He came out here a long time ago, Dion. A friend of mine saw him, sort of when he was 29 or 30, and he saw him when he came out. He reckons he was an incredible thing on stage and he had the big sort of baggy pants, and the whole bit, y'know. The Belmonts were there . . .

Host Two: Excuse me, Dave? I was wondering if you guys wanted to hear just the opening part of the special?

JP: Okay, yeah.

RP: Yeah! It's all good.

Host: It's really a good setup when they get it working.

Host Two: This next one coming up—

RP: It sounds like were being a bit cynical but you—the point is we ain't.

Host: No, no no.

JP: Yeah.

RP: 'Cause, I mean, there was a group we saw last night, [the] Chain . . .

JP: Yeah.

RP: And I mean, if you played something by them, it might be the worst thing they'd ever done but it would be better than what we're doing so far 'cause they were playing pretty good.

Host: Where'd you catch them? And what'd you see?

JP: I'll tell you what, that last number, that sounded a bit like something reminiscent of the very early Marmalade things.

RP: Yeah right! Yeah.

JP: Even though the Marmalade . . .

RP: Yeah, they were an amazing group. They had a lot of books thrown at 'em. But they pulled out of it you know. And as soon as they pulled out of it everybody, by that time, said "Oh, we don't want to know about them." But they pulled out and started doing good things. I don't know if you've heard any of the recent things?

Host: Like, give me an idea—

RP: Not "Ob-La-Di, Ob-La-Da"—

[All talk at once.]

Host: Right! Right! We're talking about post-"Ob-La-Di"—

JP: Is it "Rainbow"?

Host: Yeah, it was "Rainbow" I think.

JP: Yeah, that's one of the good ones.

Host: Listen, this next one's by Alison MacCallum. She's about twenty-four years old. It's a band, a young thing called "Superman."

JP: Mm.

RP: Yeah, we had this in the car didn't we, on the way up?

JP: Yeah, it's gonna be one of those you're gonna be playing a lot, in'it?

Host: Right, yeah.

JP: Not bad at all, but if it's written by the people who wrote the one before, that shows that they're well on the way to being pretty versatile, anyway. They've just gotta take it up a grade.

JP: That's by [Simon] Napier[-Bell], isn't it? He produced the record?

Host: Yeah. How do you feel about the chicks?

JP: He had something to do with the Yardbirds once.

RP: Well I don't know shouldn't imagine she sings like that all the time but, it'd be interesting to hear . . . You see, I'm so used to making assessments. I'm listening to an album, now.

Host: Same here.

RP: Yeah, then you get an idea of, you know, when somebody says "What do you think of the voice?" The chick's gotta sing it like that 'cause it's that kind of a song, isn't it? You know, you've gotta really lay it out.

Host: She's got a really ballsy voice, she sings of love, blues stuff, and ah—

Host Two: She's crutchy on stage.

RP: Crutchy? Hm. Can't be bad. Perhaps she'd like to come and do a duet. [*Laughs.*]

Host: What'd you think of the production on that—on that track?

Host Two: Jimmy was just commenting on that.

JP: That song might have something to do with the Yardbirds.

RP: He's not got anything to do with that, as well?

JP: If he's listening now, I bet he's sweating down the other end.

[*Plant laughs.*]

JP: 'Cause he knows what I ought to be saying.

Host: I see. Look—

RP: [*Laughs.*] Is he—is he doing well over here, then?

Host: This is his first production here.

Host Two: I think he charges all around the world just popping in and guest producing.

RP: So if we don't go to India . . . ? [*Laughter.*]

Host: You've heard Billy Thorpe, yeah?

Host Two: We played a Thorpe live track, yeah. Never played Spectrum. How'd you feel about that?

JP: I didn't really feel much at all, actually.

RP: It's a bit distorted, but I mean, nevertheless, it's got a lot of balls, y'know . . .

Host: That's what he's like most of the time. He just does rock stuff and the blues stuff and he's very laid out there. He's going to London and, he showed me, with the band.

RP: *I* don't go to London very much.

Host Two: How would you rate his chances on hearing that in London now?

RP: Well there's a bloke called Roy Young over there. The Roy Young Band has been going for years and years and he's really . . . I mean, when it comes to really hard, basic, slamming it out, then he is really, really, really the best. I mean a lot of rock 'n' roll revival and people are doing things like that but he's one guy who's been doing it all the time.

JP: Yeah, he was there right at the very beginning, doing a lot of rock shows. Hardly anybody heard about that, but they were really good. He's just done a version of "Rag Mama Rag"—it's unbelievable.

RP: Yeah. I mean he's really the guy.

JP: I mean you've got some competition when you're just banging out twelve bar blueses, really. I don't . . . I don't . . . I mean, what are their records like, his singles and things?

[*General murmuring.*]

RP: Hang on. Can you just put that one on the turntable that we passed? 'Cause there's a record that comes from England by a bloke who used to be with the Tornados. It summed up about 1963, I suppose, in England and it was quite atmospheric. I mean we all gonna have a little giggle but at the same time it's pretty good.

Host: What kind of nostalgia does that bring back to you?

RP: It was in the era when I used to stand with open mouth, agog, watching these artists. But there was a guy called Mike Berry, as well, who didn't really do much at all, but the recording sounds pretty amazing.

Host: I think about the death of Buddy Holly—

RP: The "Tribute to Buddy Holly," yeah. [*Sings*] "Snow was snowing . . ."

JP: Same recording plant as well—

RP: Yeah. There were some amazing sounds on the RGM thing. Michael Cox was a bloke who did—what as that hit he had, "Angela Jones," remember? [*Sings four note melody.*] And he did a "Sweet Little Sixteen," the Chuck Berry thing and the guitar solo was *absolutely* amazing!

JP: Yeah there's a sort Rick Nelson, really, wasn't it? That sort of vocal style?

RP: Yeah, so really it represents an era. It's not particularly brilliant, because the American counterparts were really lashing it out at the time. Frankie Ford—well, not exactly the same time.

"DON'T LABEL US": "ZEPPELIN" ON JAPAN TOUR

Lon Cabot | September 30, 1972, *Stars and Stripes*

You know something has achieved popular culture significance when the army catches up to it. Here, the US military daily *Stars and Stripes* reports on a press conference with the band before they launched into a week of concert dates in Japan. −Ed.

TOKYO—"We don't feel that our music can really be categorized or labeled because it encompasses a number of styles and types of music," said the members of Led Zeppelin.

The four-man British rock group opening a two week concert tour of Japan Monday held a press conference Saturday at the Hilton Hotel.

"Music falls into a certain category because people judge it the wrong way," explained the group.

"There's as great a variety in the music we play as there is in what we each like. As a group we have to draw influences from everywhere in the music field to get a well-rounded idea of what areas there are to explore and expand on," said Jimmy Page, guitarist and group leader.

Page formed Led Zeppelin in 1968. After a year of performances throughout England the group traveled to the US and made their debut at the 1969 Newport Jazz Festival. The group received immediate recognition and a short time later began the climb to success.

"We've received platinum discs for each of the four albums we've recorded since 1968," stated Page.

Platinum discs are presented when an album has sold over two million copies [sic].*

Zeppelin is working on a new album which will be released some time in November.

"When you start recording, you find that what it is you want your song to say takes time and a variety of styles to actually put it into music. I think that is the main reason we've only had album releases," explained Robert Plant, vocalist for the group.

Zeppelin has been together for nearly five years. Unlike most musical artists they have no desire or future plans to break away from their "group" success.

"We think alike and our tastes are all basically the same. We enjoy putting our music together and are generally pleased with the results. There is no reason for any one of us to quit the group and try it solo," Page explained.

While speaking out on controversial issues of the day seems to comprise a majority of the songs on the record charts today, Zeppelin is satisfied to express simply what they feel, "we're musicians not politicians," said Page.

Led Zeppelin will begin their two week tour of Japan Monday at 6:30 PM when they open for two days at Tokyo's Budokan Hall. Other scheduled performances include Oct. 4, 6 PM, Osaka Festival Hall; Oct. 5, 6:30 PM, Nagoya City Hall ; Oct. 9, 6 PM, Osaka Festival Hall , and Oct. 10, 6:30 PM, Kyoto Kaikan Daiichi Hall

---

*Actually one million in the United States, less elsewhere.

LED ZEPPELIN (PART 1): A WHOLE LOTTA ROCK 'N' ROLL

Nick Kent | December 23, 1972, *NME*

The long road finally found Led Zeppelin in their home country for a few pre-holiday dates. The next two pieces take us on the road with Led Zeppelin and Nick Kent as they travel through England. Here, Kent gives lie to the fomenting of destruction that supposedly followed in the wake of Led Zeppelin. –Ed.

It's way past the midnight hour and the room at the Angel Hotel, Cardiff, is starting to look a trifle the worse for wear since the entourage of Led Zeppelin—"a visiting pop group"—had decided to see the wee, wee hours through in its carefully antiseptic surroundings.

Stray bottles of beer, whiskey and coke are to be found strewn around the place, while redundant plates which once held sandwiches lie around the floor.

The room is comfortably full of people either talking intently, drinking, twiddling their thumbs, or staring at their feet.

Strange thing is, there's no actual wreckage—and that's one thing that the hotel authorities should be thanking their lucky stars for.

After all, you know as well as I do just what a travelling big-time rock 'n' roll band can do to a hotel room in the early hours of the morning.

And this, dear friends, is big-time rock 'n' roll . . .

Big money, big reputation, big business.

Those two tough, short-haired guys sitting in the corner aren't there to look picturesque. Oh, no. They're security, and the best at their job as well.

They've just finished working on the Osmonds' tour.

"Now that was different," says one of them adamantly. "With them, it was just young kids, y'know, but here it's more the sort who get . . . uh . . . jealous. Y'know?"

In the middle of the room is the toughest customer of them all—Peter Grant, a mountain of a man and Zep's devoted manager from the very beginning.

This is a character no-one messes around with. BUT NO-ONE.

He's been around and learned a few tricks of the trade, but at the same time he was once Gene Vincent's roadie which means he's a rocker, so that's O.K.

Others in the room are Richard Cole, who looks like a pirate, black beard earring et al, the slight frame of one B.P. Fallon publicist, and Messrs. Page, Plant, Bonham, and Jones.

All of which proves nothing less than the undisputable fact that rock 'n' roll is on the road again.

While the Faces are carousing around the suburbs in a good-time Bourbon haze, their stablemates from the weightier side of the Metal Zone, Led Zeppelin, are holed up in the fair capital city of Wales for a two-day extravaganza of pile-driving rock 'n' roll.

Tonight's show has been "average"—no more, no less, which means that the band got the colossal response they've registered as a customary reaction over the last few years, culminating in a mammoth rock 'n' roll medley, sandwiched in between "Whole Lotta Love" and three encores.

The set lasted over 2½ hours and was a constant showcase of how dynamics, musical dexterity, and sheer drive should be employed when playing hard rock.

By 1 AM the band had quite forgotten about it. Page's only remark afterwards concerned the number of guitar strings that had been broken throughout the proceedings.

Led Zeppelin are more popular and better respected than all their heavy bastard children put together, simply because they are the ace band playing this kind of music—and their audiences know it.

Yet how much do you know about Zeppelin beyond what you hear on record?

Sure, we all know the names of the members and the fact that Jimmy Page used to be in the Yardbirds. Otherwise the Zep Charisma exists almost solely in the music and the band's on-stage persona.

We all know Page, now out-front more than ever, the intense rocker playing definitive heavy rock guitar; John Paul Jones always in the background; "Bonzo" Bonham thrashing his kit and, out in the spotlight, Robert Plant the precocious lemon-squeezer himself.

Nowadays, when an audience goes to see the Stones it is largely to wallow in the enormous mystique the band has been parading before all of us out here in Mediaville over the years.

With Zeppelin it's the music and rock 'n' roll spectacle that takes precedence every time.

The people come to hear "Whole Lotta Love" or "Stairway to Heaven" or "Dazed and Confused."

You name it, the Zeps will usually always do it and what's more, improve on the studio version.

Offstage the band seem to take on different personalities. Plant abandons his hip-shaking narcissism to become just one of the lads again.

Bedecked in luxurious Little Lord Fauntleroy golden curls, yokel velvet smock with loose-fitting jacket, and jeans, Plant looks more in keeping with the renaissance balladeer syndrome until you see the rock 'n' roll-star-beat-up snake-skin boots on his feet.

He's just returned from a failed attempt to repair the magnificent white elephant of a car he'd just purchased; but is still enthusing about whatever comes to mind.

Mainly, it's music. Buffalo Springfield, the Incredible String Band, Love, Bob Dylan, Elvis Presley, Gene Vincent, Robert Plant's tastes knoweth no boundaries.

"*Forever Changes*. Now there was a great album. Have you heard "White Dog" on *Vindicator* (Arthur Lee, ex-Love's solo album)? Lee dedicated that for me, y'know.

"He just couldn't believe that I dug his stuff, so much so that he wrote the song."

Someone mentions Bob Dylan and Plant is off again.

"Those first two albums—[sighs of disbelief and sings a few tentative words to "Boots of Spanish Leather"]—I reckon it was these that brought me round to marijuana."

Plant, a good hippy boy if ever there was one, spends his non-rocking hours close to soil farming the land, as does drummer Bonham, another bluff son of Birmingham.

The conversation next touches upon such bizarre incidents as the time Page and Plant were led on an official tour around the brothels of Thailand.

"We were taken by this guy who spoke strictly Queen's English, y'know, and it seemed to be the policy to show all visiting rock bands the brothels. I mean, it was interesting and that [laughs] but they couldn't understand why we didn't do anything.

"The guy kept saying that all the other bands he'd taken round had enjoyed themselves. Eventually we were labelled as undesirables or something because we hadn't got involved. Anyway it's illegal to have long-hair in that country so . . ."

The scene changes to Texas where Plant was once cornered by the Children of God in an attempt at some sort of conversion.

"It was unbelievably heavy. I mean, they never give up. The first thing they actually said was, would you believe this, 'We've got Jeremy Spencer'!"

Back to music. Plant talked about lyric-writing.

"It's a shame that the whole solo singer-songwriter concept had to degenerate into that James Taylor thing of taking things so seriously. Actually there are a lot of good ideas going around now.

"Actually this'll probably sound strange, but ultimately I can envisage Pagey and myself ending up doing a whole Incredible String Band–type thing together. Very gentle stuff."

Jimmy Page, who looks as if he could still be 20 years old, looks even more rustic-influenced than Plant. His beard has now been sheared while hair has been cut to above shoulder length.

Tonight's stage costume of a black velvet rhinestoned jacket has been concealed under Page's obligatory Farmer Giles tweed coat, complete with elbow patches to add final touches of pastoral simplicity.

Page is one of rock's more articulate speakers, though there has yet to appear a definitive piece framed around his words of wisdom. Had this anything to do with the known Zeppelin *Rolling Stone* (the magazine not the rock band) feud from way back when?

"Well, the situation we found ourselves in with *Rolling Stone* was purely political and stemmed from their side all along. The reasons are basically so trivial that it's really not worth going into."

How did Page feel about journalists' concern with the guitarist's past achievements in rock 'n' roll?

"Everyone seems to ask me about my days with the Yardbirds, which I suppose is flattering but rather unnecessary, I think."

He also hedges away from talking about his now legendary work as a session musician between 1963–66, as if bored with bringing up old details.

"It was pretty much uninteresting work, a lot of which has been made more of than it should."

On the development of Zep's albums he had this to say.

"The changes from album to album were roughly these. The first record was made in roughly 30 hours. We went in with some riffs and worked out a set of tracks which were functional as to the sound we were looking for, things we could get off on playing, live.

"The second was recorded in between a lengthy series of gigs we were playing in the States and so obviously the album was affected thus.

"The third album was again affected by a change of pace in that we wrote some of the songs in Wales and there were all sorts of developments then.

"And the fourth was generally more laid-back in the way it was recorded. It's quite pointless saying 'Oh yeah, this is the Led Zeppelin Acoustic Album' and 'this is the Led Zeppelin Heavy Album' because there have been those elements in our music all along and we've never swamped an album with one particular style.

"People claimed that the fourth album was traditionally influenced, but then 'Babe I'm Gonna Leave You' is a traditional song and that was on the first album."

And about the occasional murmurs from certain aficionados that the band have been too concerned with pandering to the tastes of our cousins on the other side of the Atlantic, Page had this to say.

"It's complete rubbish that we concentrate our attentions on the States. If people could be bothered to examine just how much time we do spend in one country at a time you'll find that we measure out our touring schedule to take in as many countries as we can.

"This tour of Britain is no less than the tour we did of the States this year. We tried to play around as many countries as possible and everyone ended up saying 'Oh they're ignoring us,' which is rubbish."

LED ZEPPELIN:
THE ZEPPELIN ROAD TEST

Nick Kent | February 24, 1973, *NME*

Mayhem? Maybe just a little, but far from the legendary debauchery of Led Zeppelin backstage and in hotels. Nick Kent spent considerable time with the band and saw these scenes any number of times. In Scotland, he reports on the backstage doings of the group and practically has to shanghai the taciturn John Paul Jones into talking. –Ed.

"Robert Plant quits show business and joins National Dairies. There's a good headline for you. Print that as a news item in your paper, O.K.?"

Now why's a carefree son-of-the-soil like Bobby Plant saying such things to cast a sudden mood over the general bonhomie of the Edinburgh Zeppelin dressing-room?

Why, wasn't he just a moment ago working in cahoots with Bonzo Bonham to turn the place into the usual boisterous rough-house, specifically attempting to provoke a mock fight between Bonham and the Securicor representative, rejoicing in the nickname of "Patsy" and generally indulging in a pleasant blend of cajolery and ribald banter.

That is, until one of the road-crew suddenly appeared in the midst of the jollity to throw a moody and hand in his notice on the spot.

"Oh c'mon, man. Don't act like such a bloody queen," shouts Plant as the guy bustles out down the stairs.

The reason for the sudden resignation appears to be an incident during the gig in which John Paul Jones, required to play a Mellotron solo as an introduction to "Thank You", found what he says was a fault in his equipment and immediately rectified the situation by smashing it.

"God, showbusiness can really get you down," mutters the down-home boy wonder. "This sort of situation just pisses me off so much. I mean, I've been really happy over the whole tour and then things like this happen to mess things up."

John Paul Jones has disappeared, last seen looking slightly menacing signing autographs for the barely pubescent female Scottish Zep aficiandos who seem to somehow congregate around the dressing-room door, cruising for autographs and a quick look at what goes on behind the scenes in the glitzy world of rock 'n' roll.

One of them is anxiously asking after the whereabouts of Jimmy Page. With little success, it appears, for Page, looking most dapper in white suit and slicked-back jet black curly hair, had donned his farmer Giles coat and ushered himself out of the building as quietly as possible.

By now, he'll be on the road motoring back to his estate in mystical Inverness.

Meanwhile, back at the dressing room, the mood has reverted back to one of mirth and madness. A beer-fight breaks out among Messrs. Plant and Bonham against road-manager Richard Cole. The ubiquitous B.P. Fallon, publicist extraordinaire, intervenes and yours truly hides behind a troupe of young girls as soggy, toasted tomato-and-ham sandwiches, beer-cans, and bottles are thrown in all directions.

Finally, from the wreckage of furniture, a large bucket of ice-cold water descends over Mr. Fallon and myself and everyone leaves in a hurry. Slowly we pick up the last remains of the wine and head back to the hotel.

The Led Zeppelin British tour is in its final stages, before the grand lay-off. Robert Plant is already making plans: "First I'll be going up to Wales to try and get hold of this farm that's been up for sale. Then it'll be down to planting trees and getting into the whole farming gig."

Scotland itself has been O.K., if a little passive. Audiences are appreciative, getting more and more lively until "Dazed and Confused," Page's monster guitar rampage number which now has Plant throwing in a couple of verses from the [John Phillips / Scott McKenzie] flower-power classic "If You're Going to San Francisco (Be Sure to Wear Some Flowers in Your Hair" for good measure.

From there on, the powerdrive is in full operation, working through "Stairway to Heaven" and bursting out horrendously full blown on the "Whole Lotta Love" rock 'n' roll medley.

The most impressive numbers of the live show are the new songs, "Dancing Days" and "The Song Remains the Same / Rain Song."

The latter is quite frightening in its power, spotlighting Page playing his twin-necked guitar with a dynamism and fluency akin to that of John McLaughlin.

The new album has yet to reach your local record-store, for numerous reasons. The actual product has long since been completed, but numerous trivial set-backs have occurred to delay its release.

Details are cloaked in secrecy, with the title and other such valuable information being held back until a week before release. Everything is being handled in typical Zeppelin style—an innate sense of laid-back subtlety and studied professionalism that has held the band together as a musical institution for the continuing survival of rock 'n' roll.

During one particularly listless night in Dundee, after an Edward G. Robinson Midnight Movie, the Zeppelin entourage started dispersing to their rooms, leaving myself and John Paul Jones alone to rap away the hours.

In certain respects, Jones is the most intriguing member of the band.

On stage he fits himself into the role of musician with a capital *M*, coming on as the most consciously studious member, seldom moving, and acting almost as an alchemist, mating the dynamics and energy output of Plant, Page, and Bonham, while constantly adding a new dimension to sound textures with his keyboard work (pay particular attention to his electric piano embellishments on the Zep blues epic "Since I've Been Loving You").

Offstage he appears almost obsessively quiet, particularly when compared to Plant and Bonham's raucous joviality.

In this respect, his personality complements that of the subdued Mr. Page and, on further examination, the two have a great deal in common.

Their past musical experience coincides in that both were professional session musicians. Page was particularly well-known for his work, becoming one of England's very best before he was associated with the Yardbirds.

His age had a lot to do with it—he was only nineteen when he was working regularly in the studios earning up to £80 a week and making a name for himself from such performances as the weeping guitar solo on Dave Berry's "The Crying Game."

John Paul Jones was a more anonymous session-player, simply because his instrument—bass—was a more anonymous instrument. Yet his list of performances is quite staggering.

He played an integral part in producing whole areas of '60s English rock music—everything from working for Andrew "Loog" Oldham (who was then the Stones' Svengali and the golden boy of English rock) on his more bizarre efforts, the early Cat Stevens tracks, most of Mickie Most's productions (all Herman's Hermits' greatest hits, Jeff Beck's "Love Is Blue," and even some work with Jimmy Page's Yardbirds—remember "Ha Ha Said the Clown" and "Ten Little Indians"?) and on to arrangement work for almost every English pop producer around, whether it be Mike "Gary Glitter" Leander or Steve Rowlands.

Jones also flirted with the gig of playing in a back-up group, working behind [Jet] Harris and Tony Meehan and even such luminaries as Carl Perkins.

"By the time Jimmy came along with the idea for Led Zeppelin, I was in a position as top fee session arranger where I was completely snowed under with work.

"Being a session arranger is literally a 24-hour job—working out individual scores for horns and strings the night before, handing them out the next day, and knocking the finished product out whenever.

"That's how all the Tamla-Motown arrangers work—I mean, the things they do for the string parts are quite unbelievable.

"But eventually I became quite satiated by the work, which coincided nicely with Zeppelin. I left when I was on top though, which was good.

"But I've worked on some quite ludicrous sessions. Things like Alma Cogan's last work, after she had died. I came into the studio and all the musicians were in tears, having to put the backing tracks on. I couldn't believe it.

"And then there was another which had Mike Leander and this grandiose scheme of bringing a huge orchestra, something like twelve guitarists and seven bass-players. Jimmy was there, and Big Jim Sullivan—all the established musicians. And Decca [Records] decided to scrap the project after they'd heard the tapes.

"My reasons for joining up with Zeppelin were purely musical. Led Zeppelin have really only ever existed for the music—I can't really see anything image-wise that one can attach to the band.

"I suppose that's why we've stayed together—each of us fulfills a function. Also, we have very strong management—I mean, Peter's been with us on almost . . . well, actually, every gig we've ever played.

"As far as I'm concerned, *the* key Led Zeppelin gig—the one that just put everything into focus—was one that we played on our first American tour at the Boston Tea Party.

"We'd played our usual one hour set, using all the material from the first album and Page's 'White Summer' guitar piece and, by the end, the audience just wouldn't let us off the stage.

"It was in such a state that we had to start throwing ideas around—just thinking of songs that we might all know or that some of us knew a part of, and work it from there.

"So we'd go back on and play things like 'I Saw Her Standing There' and 'Please Please Me'—old Beatles favorites. I mean, just anything that would come into our head, and the response was quite amazing.

"There were kids actually bashing their heads against the stage—I've never seen that at a gig before or since, and when we finally left the stage we'd played for 4½ hours.

"Peter [Grant] was absolutely ecstatic. He was crying—if you can imagine that—and hugging us all. You know with this huge grizzly bear hug. I suppose it was then that we realized just what Led Zeppelin was going to become."

"America has always been very good for us. I can't really recall a place that hasn't accepted us, in the sense that we're absolutely loathed in that area.

"I remember reading in what I suppose would be termed the Underground Press some very derogatory remarks on our so-called 'capitalist rip-off' tactics, which I find highly offensive simply because I've always thought that we give an audience its money's worth in playing time, while keeping an eye on ticket prices.

"There was a time when it was us, the Rolling Stones . . . I think . . . Deep Purple who got this thing thrown at them.

"Compared to the way the Stones operate as a touring entity, we're very different. Unfortunately the band found itself appearing at gigs in the States that the Stones had played some two weeks before, and it was just total devastation.

"We always keep down the entourage to a minimum, simply because it's easier to transport a small number of people around. One has to either go completely crazy or else work very strategically at touring."

Among Jones' tentative plans as a musician are to work on a score for *Stranger in a Strange Land* (though David Bowie has already purchased the film rights), while he's also been working on an album with Madeline Bell back at his home.

"I'm really not over-enthusiastic about anything currently going on in music. People seem to expect me to say something grand, but there's no-one who really moves me to any heights of ecstasy. I used to quite like the Pink Floyd, but then they somehow started to go off.

"My influences as a bass-player? Actually I was asked this some time ago on KSAN radio and I answered Mozart, which seemed to put the interviewer off so much so that he never really recovered.

"I think I also said that I like Tamla-Motown bass-players as well, which seemed to disgust him even more."

COMMUNICATION BREAKDOWN

"In this band we're very lucky that everybody is more enthusiastic as time goes on. There is not fatigue or boredom musically at all. There's a bit of boredom when you're stuck in Mobile, Alabama, or places like that. A few lamp standards may fall out of the windows—things like that—but we move on and we keep playing that music . . . You see, my little boy's just started to walk, and I haven't seen him bloomin' walk yet. Those are the things that upset you about being on the road. The very fact that you miss fantastic occasions like that. I mean, the kid just stands up and starts strolling around—and here I am in Tuscaloosa or wherever."

—Robert Plant to Charles Shaar Murray, *NME*, June 23, 1973

PART II

WHEN THE LEVEE BREAKS

"Atlanta had like fifty three thousand people there and the next one Tampa, Florida, fifty seven, and suddenly I go, 'My goodness what's going on?' It's crazy."

— Jimmy Page to Alan "Fluff" Freeman

·

LED ZEPPELIN'S JIMMY PAGE: A HEAVY BLIMP THAT GIVES NO QUARTER

Arthur Levy | July 19, 1973, *Zoo World*

The night before senior editor Arthur Levy of renowned South Florida underground music biweekly *Zoo World* got some quality time with Jimmy Page, Led Zeppelin had played for 57,000 people, an all-time record for attendance at a single-act concert. The record they broke was from the previous night, in Atlanta, where they played for 53,000 people. –Ed.

"We did an English tour before this one and we had to make some dramatic changes, really, 'cause when we were over here before we were playing for about three hours. We're now also playing for about three hours but at the time we hadn't a fifth LP to contend with so we had to make some dramatic changes in England to accommodate the new numbers plus the old acoustic numbers we were doing as well. And before we came over we knew, well, we knew it wasn't going to be quite as intensive as the last time we were here because—this might not be exact but it's not far off—we did something like eighteen dates in twenty-one days, we'd only three days off or whatever. And we were doing much the same thing we're doing now, which is commuting from one spot, backwards and forwards, and by the time we got through we were absolutely *nakkered*: when we got home each and every one of us was laid up for about a week."

Sitting in room 1000 of the plush Doral Beach Hotel, command central for this Led Zeppelin 1973 Southern Wing Tour, Jimmy Page's portable stereo is tuned to the local oldies station—the Five Satins, Jimmy Reed, the Four Seasons, Chuck Berry—all these are coming across the room in waves as Page sits languidly sucking a warm beer, his eyes lighting up as each song begins (without breaking the stride of this conversation) then drifting back to the here and now. On the turntable is Volume 3 of Atlantic's *Blues Originals* series, *Texas Guitar—From Dallas to L.A.*, featuring T-Bone Walker, Guitar Slim, Ray Agee, Al King, and others, but for the moment the FM is shuffling oldies and Jimmy Page is resting on his fifth evening in America, having just played two nights before to the single biggest audience in the history of rock 'n' roll that ever showed up to hear one single act on a show, over 60,000* who packed the Tampa football stadium, May 5, 1973.

"So what I'm getting at is this: when we finished the English tour we thought 'well, let's readjust it yet again, try some new bits and pieces and see how they go over.' And the only things that were rehearsed, we've done so many numbers that we've never done before, like 'No Quarter,' we'd never done that before in England, the only things we rehearsed were certain links between numbers, to tighten the whole show up, as opposed to getting into a lot on one number, chat, another number, more chat.

"That seemed to be uneasy really, it just didn't seem to be hard-hitting enough for us personally, I don't know how the audience feels about it. But as far as we thought we were never managing to get into a flow of things, whereas we are now. Out there we were doing four numbers straight off and then we have a break and then into a new number. But the main thing is we wanted to go out there with a bit of fire as opposed to going out there and warming up gradually.

"And then with John Paul Jones' equipment, which seems to be like he used to change virtually an instrument for every number, we tried to rework it so he was on the bass for a section and then on the piano for a section, and then back on the bass, working a bit more like that. So the first half of the show is just like that, you get him on the bass then on the

---

*Attendance was actually closer to 56,800 people.

piano. And that's the sort of thing that we did have to rehearse and we did have to practice. Changing a program is a devil of a job, you know, because everybody out there wants to hear something different, everybody has their own tastes, that's the way the world's made up. And you can't possibly hope to please everybody, but all you can possibly hope to do is give a good cross-section of what you've done, starting from the first LP onward and then a fair representation of what you're up to now."

"We've always been very fortunate in the fact that people have always just watched and waited and seen what we're gonna come up with during the course of an act, and they don't start with the chorus of 'Whole Lotta Love, Whole Lotta Love' before you're through with the second number. But that's so rare, it happens so rarely and it's so easy to say, 'well, if you think we're going to go through a show for three hours and we're not going to play 'Whole Lotta Love,' well obviously we're gonna do it so just be cool, it's gonna come.'"

With more thought given to audience reaction, the staging of this year's Led Zeppelin concerts has taken on added importance. For example, the curtain of flat aluminoid reflecting strips behind the band, quavering in the breeze at the outdoor Tampa gig, was augmented at their indoor dates by an even more dazzling refractory mechanism. "The mirrored thing is there all the time. Unfortunately, one of the main things were using we were unable to use in Tampa and that's an eight-foot revolving disc. Like at the end of 'Stairway' you've got those mirrored balls which start spinning light every way, two of those at either side of the stage. And at the back of the stage there's this eight-foot disc, which is not quite a semi-circle, but it's convex and you've got broken glass over it plus a mirror wheel inside it and when that starts going at the end the light goes everywhere just about, over the whole building. But we couldn't put it up because the wind was gonna blow it down. Now that, along with the mirrored balls working along all these surfaces, you get light going everywhere and it's like being in the middle of a diamond."

There's an ease, a fluidity to Page's manner that bespeaks the advantages of living in one hotel and commuting to the various dates from out of one city via a chartered jet. Having a stereo to listen to, with records to take his attention away to his old masters leads to conversation about the

Texas Blues Guitar LP sitting on the turntable. There's also a copy of the Otis Spann *Memorial* LP with Otis Rush playing guitar on it. "He's one of my favorites, one of my favorite guitarists, and he really plays nicely on it, he really can cook. But T-Bone Walker's on that Texas Guitar record and he's quite interesting, too." The Otis Rush *Mourning in the Morning* LP is recalled, a terribly embarrassing album of Rush produced by [Mike] Bloomfield and [Nick] Gravenites in 1969.

"Yeah, you don't produce somebody like Otis Rush like that, really. But he did one on Vanguard, the *Chicago/[The]Blues/Today* set, that's really quite good stuff on there. I like his approach to the guitar, though, it's really one I can sympathize with. But a lot of his earlier work was done on Cobra [Records], which is defunct now." So Page hasn't at all settled into a style that keeps him from listening and playing as much as he did before, really.

"I think I *probably* do more playing than listening, now, more actual getting into the guitar and writing, when it gets right down to it. But I still do listen to a lot of other sounds, varied sounds, not just one sort of music at a time, but it's quite varied. Old rock—not this sort of old rock," he points out, referring to the vocal groups dominating the oldies radio station during the conversation, "I never really got into them very much, but mainly rockabilly things and traditional English folk music, any traditional folk music anywhere sounds good to me, no matter where it be from." The resurgence of trad folk bands coming out of England, though, is especially exciting to Page.

"Yeah, yeah, I'm pleased it's all come out, because what it really means is that a lot of all those old songs are going to be brought out of the archives, and there's so many good ones there, it's good that they should re-live again because it's part of England's old heritage, really, and those days have passed. But nevertheless it's still nice to get into those old songs . . . I personally don't get much of a chance to go round to the clubs anymore 'cause I live out in the country and going into London for me is quite a pilgrimage. I get in about once every fortnight."

Getting around to the 'round the world tour Led Zeppelin undertook last year, Page is well aware of the effect that so much playing together has had on the group since last August, 1972. "We've been playing together and working consistently since last August, that's virtually taken us right around the world, although most people don't know it. We've been to Japan, Scandinavia, France, Germany, and we did quite an extensive tour of Britain, the biggest one we've ever done, really, as far as venues go. We tried to get everywhere, through Scotland where people usually miss out, those areas.

"We didn't go to Ireland this time. We went to Ireland about two years ago, but the situation there is very heavy, very heavy. And at that time we went, about two years ago, I'm betting we were one of the last groups to play there, maybe eighteen months ago. There were riots going on in the streets as we were driving up to the gig, just like that, and at that time we had no idea that it was as bad as it was, it was just before the bomb incidents really started. And then after that everyone thought, 'well, as much as we'd like to play up there, it's silly to jeopardize the band!'" As near as memory would allow, this was before Rory Gallagher's New Year's Day, 1972, gig in Belfast that was played while bombs were exploding outside the hall in Ulster.

"Oh, come on, though, he's Irish! That doesn't really count, politically that really doesn't count at all. Why? Because he's Irish! Obviously, if an Irish bloke can't play in his own home town, regardless of political pressures, there's something a bit odd. But they consider us an *English* group, so obviously if they're trying to free themselves of English domination . . . there were bomb blasts but they weren't blowing up the hall he was playing in, were they? They didn't make a beeline for blowing up Rory Gallagher." Do you think . . . "who knows, I don't know, I don't know. I didn't mind taking the chance then, but the situation's gotten very bloody over there. It's a tragedy, really." Conceptualizing the effect Led Zeppelin has had on rock culture in general, one is led to the inevitable question of the identity crisis most supergroups seem to be falling uncontrollably into today.

"Obviously, when you play a date like Tampa you don't expect to walk out there and really see that many people, it's a bit awe-inspiring when you drive up and see all those people and it hits you that *you're* the people they've all come to see, to coin a phrase, it's your arses that are on the line. But then I suppose that one of the reasons people always come to see us and always came to see us in the past is that we try our hardest, we've never ever gone out there and chewed gum and sort of messed about, we've always played our bollocks off. Whether you like it or not is another issue altogether. We've always tried our hardest, on records and everything, that's all you can do, then you're happy with what you're doing and you're not compromising.

"And I'm not contradicting myself when I say 'compromising' when I say we sort our numbers accordingly in the program because in fact we're enjoying doing them. If we weren't enjoying doing them, or doing a number, we'd throw it out, and that would be it. If it were 'Whole Lotta Love' that everyone were sick to death of then it would probably go but as it is everyone still gets a big kick out of doing it 'cause we always change these things around every night. That's another thing I know a lot of groups don't do—they've got everything worked out note for note. But a number like 'Dazed and Confused' I defy anyone to come around and hear that the same way twice, it never would be."

And being on the short end of the establishment rock press' stick for the course of their first three albums could've shocked any band into oblivion, but Led Zeppelin took the opposite tactic and refused to compromise themselves on a fourth and fifth LP. "I know that there were originally quite a few people who picked up on the fourth LP and gave it a good write-up, but there were the usuals who gave it a good slam-off, in England was where we got a major slamming on the LP. But 'Stairway to Heaven' was just *there*.

"You see up to that point we'd been aware of all the crap that had gone on more than anybody, obviously, 'cause we were right on the end of it, and we knew there was this huge enigma that had blown up. As far as were concerned, whatever we did we always delivered the best we possibly could. So we said, 'alright, there's only one thing we can possibly do here and that's put out an LP with no title, no information, or anything.' And people would buy it because they like it. And it proved to be the best seller of all just purely because 'Stairway' was in there, but these reviewers must've heard it when they reviewed the LP, but they just couldn't *hear* it. They were too busy being messed up with all their pre-conceived ideas of what they expected to hear and outraged because there wasn't heavier rock or outraged because there wasn't enough—they didn't know what to write."

Led Zeppelin and Jimmy Page continue to define the art of Rock 'n' Roll, just as their albums have always defined their place in the Rock hierarchy over the last five years. While the shortsighted opportunists may rant and rave about the "Limp Blimp," Led Zeppelin continue to be accessible, continue to explore new musical directions—sometimes naively and with questionable results—but always with the idea in mind not to stagnate over time and not to bow to the trendy froth that surrounds them on the Superlevel they operate from. In the pantheon of Rock they are perennials who don't dare to live on their laurels and they are the essence of change, form, and function.

COMMUNICATION BREAKDOWN

LED ZEPPELIN AND PETER GRANT FORM RECORD COMPANY: SWAN SONG INC.
  –Danny Goldberg's Cullderstead, Ltd press release headline, May 9, 1974

COMMUNICATION BREAKDOWN

"Let's hope this will be different from other record companies . . . [b]ecause it would be awful if it was like . . . Oh, the Stones label or something like that. That's why we didn't call it Zeppelin Records . . . or Stairway, as someone suggested."
  –Jimmy Page to Lisa Robinson, *Hit Parader*, October 1974

COMMUNICATION BREAKDOWN

"It would be really nice to get a company together where it's run by people who really feel. I mean you can't get any closer to the artist than being a fellow artist and we had people around us who were getting semi-raw dealings—so why not? Instead of just having a Led Zeppelin label with L.Z. on it . . . Led Zeppelin means a failure. Swan Song means a last gasp, so why not call our label that? . . . There's gonna be more headaches, I should imagine, by taking the responsibilities but there's more satisfaction in the end because you only got yourself to answer to and you've only got your own idea of how far and how good and how hard one must try to reach—well perfection or the smoothness, fluidity. So you're totally your own master which is what it should be."

– Robert Plant to Loraine Alterman, *Rolling Stone*, June 1974

COMMUNICATION BREAKDOWN

"Albums are the true statement of a group's work. You have time in an album to show or to indicate exactly what you've been up to over a period of time creatively . . . I should say altogether the new stuff [*Houses of the Holy*] took about four or five months but there was no continuous work employed at all. We worked so long and then suddenly we feel maybe we should take a rest for a bit. That's Led Zeppelin really."

–Robert Plant to Bob Harris, BBC2 *The Old Grey Whistle Test*, January 17, 1975

ROBERT PLANT: RECORDING'S NO RACE FOR US

Chris Charlesworth | February 8, 1975, *Melody Maker*

Led Zeppelin spent 1974 in and out of the recording studio, preparing their Swan Song debut. Sessions were separated by breaks during which Plant and Page began their explorations in Asia and the Middle East. The epic "Kashmir" was conceived during these adventures. Even before *Physical Graffiti* came out, the band was back on the road. After the two European warm-up gigs, the mighty Zeppelin was cruising the States, including three (nonconcurrent) nights at Madison Square Garden and a show across the East River in Long Island. —Ed.

With weeks of the current Led Zeppelin tour under his belt, Robert Plant is feeling the strain. One show has been cancelled because he caught the flu and he's still sniffing and talking like he's wearing a nose-clip.

Robert blames it partly on his particularly enjoyable Christmas festivities and the changes in climate involved in traversing the Atlantic.

We're talking in his suite at the Plaza Hotel in New York, the same suite just left by the Chairman of Sonesta Hotels, the chain that owns this particular chunk of Americana.

Love's *Forever Changes* album is playing on a tiny portable record player and Plant spreads out on a couch, bare chested as always, golden hair curling everywhere, and sipping a fruit drink (he needs his Vitamin C) between assaults on a paper handkerchief.

We begin by talking about the new album, *Physical Graffiti*, due to be released anytime. It's Zep's first double album.

"I suppose it was about a year ago when we started if I can cast my mind that far back," he says. "It's always a case of getting together and feeling out the moods of each of us when we meet with instruments for the first time in six months.

"We began as always, playing around and fooling about for two days, playing anything we want, like standards, our own material, or anything that comes to us, and slowly but surely we develop a feel that takes us on to the new material. Some of the new stuff came directly from this approach, like 'Trampled Under Foot' which was just blowing out, and some comes from Jonesy or Pagey or myself—seldom myself—bringing along some structure which needs working on. Then the four of us inflict our own venom on it to develop the idea.

"We intended to record as much new stuff as we could before we started losing the fire, because we've always believed in not prolonging periods of recording or composition to such a degree where we know we are not up to our best. So we recorded as much fresh stuff as we could before looking back at some things we hadn't recorded. Then we saw that there was a lot of stuff we'd put down and we thought 'Why not put a double album out.' There's a lot of variation of material so it gives people a whole spectrum of style which is contained in one package and I think that's very good.

"It goes from one extreme to the other but at the same time it's very evident that it's Zeppelin. You could play a track on the radio that you'd think would never ever be us, but then when you listened you'd hear little things that couldn't be anyone else."

Recording took about four months which was strung out over a much longer period. "It sounds a long time but the whole essence of the band is that we do what we want to do when we want to do it. It's no race for us. We've got no deadlines to meet and when we finally do give something then it's got to be just dead right. We have a stride, a gait, that, if it was adjusted, would be very detrimental to the way we are."

Robert agrees that 1974 was a year of little public activity for the group, but maintains that setting up their own label, Swan Song [Records], took up much of their time.

"After the last American tour I was so relieved to be home again because I'd missed a season and I really need each season as it comes. I like to feel spring and I got back in August after that tour and realized I'd missed spring going into summer that year. I don't want to lose these perspectives in what I consider to be important for the lyrical content of what I write. I want to take stock of everything instead of going on the road until I don't know where the f*** I am and end up like a poached egg three days old.

"But the time comes, as it does in recording and the record company and every move that we make, when we know it's time to go out on the road again. We all met and thought 'what have we been doing?' We all needed that time off but we cursed each other for having it and agreed at the same time that we'd been physically idle."

The group hates rehearsing, says Robert, but they realize they have to limber up to approach playing in the way they want. "The first hour is usually great, but then we think how much better it would be if there was an audience there. A lot of the construction that we do on stage is fired by the atmosphere of the actual instant.

"Obviously we had to rehearse the stuff from the new album to get it into some viable shape. We played all the new songs at the rehearsal but some of them take such a direction that it would be difficult to employ them live after being off the road for 18 months.

"We do 'Sick Again' which is about ourselves and what we see in Los Angeles, but it's a pity you can't hear the lyrics properly live. The lyrics say: 'From the window of a rented limousine, I saw your pretty blue eyes. / One day soon, you're gonna reach sixteen, painted lady in the city of lies.' As much as it's pretty, it's sour really. That's exactly what L.A. stands for. Joni Mitchell summed it up best when she called it 'City of the Fallen Angels.'

"We do 'In My Time of Dying' which is a really old, old standard thing. 'Gallows Pole' was an old traditional thing too, and 'When the Levee Breaks' is something I have on an old album by Kansas Joe McCoy and Memphis Minnie in 1928*. There are so many classics from way, way back which we can give a little of ourselves to take them through the years."

---

*"When the Levee Breaks" was actually recorded in 1929.

It's now over two years since Zeppelin have appeared in Britain. Well Robert . . . "We shall definitely play England by hook or by crook before Midsummer Day this year. To say where and when at the moment is impossible as we haven't found out anything. All being well we shall definitely be in England soon during the summer.

"I play guitar now and again around Worcestershire but it isn't met by such tremendous outcries as it is when we all get together on stage.

"I've been 75 percent pleased with the shows we've done so far even though we've got a new stage set-up to get used to. It's quite hard to go out and confront thousands of people with a new stage, so we have to compensate for these new things.

"At the beginning of the tour I always feel nervous because I've got a lot to stand up for over here. If ever I've given all that I've got to give, it's been to an audience and the audiences here can really drain you until you're almost in tears.

"It's not as if these kids are all 17 or 18 and going barmy. These people have been going along with us for seven or eight years. Now I know there's people in England who'll say they've been standing with us for seven or eight years, but over here the whole motion is like a seven year trek that's charged with the energy that these people give. My nerves are really through hoping that I can re-establish the contact that I had before.

"The English promotion side of things has always been archaic. They didn't want to know us as the New Yardbirds in the early days, so we had to come over here and make a statement that no-one else had made before. Then everybody wanted to know.

"I can see this happening again with the Pretty Things who have achieved so much ability with their writing and playing. They get much more coverage here than in England, but how much coverage can you get in England, anyway? It's not too hot, and the promoters are a little reserved in what they can promote."

Zeppelin have always maintained a reputation as outlaws of the road in the US. Talk of their excesses in hotel rooms ranges far and wide, and the faint of heart have been known to cower when they approach with the twinkle in their eyes that spells havoc.

"Like the music, the legend grows too," said Robert. "There are times when people need outlets. We don't rehearse them and, let's face it, everybody's the same. Over the last few years we've spent some of our time at the Edgewater Inn in Seattle where Bonzo fishes for sharks in the sea from his bedroom window. Hence the mudshark thing on the Zappa album.

"No, we're not calming down yet. Calming down doesn't exist until you're dead. You just do whatever you want to do when you want to do it, provided there's no nastiness involved then the karma isn't so good."

Moving on to more serious topics, I asked whether Robert thought "Stairway to Heaven" was becoming heavily identified as the group's signature tune. "I don't know about that. We've always intended to try and create a spectrum of music that captures as many aspects of us as we could, although we never realized it at the beginning. We try and do this on stage, too. We start off like songs of thunder and then we take it down with a song like 'Rain Song' so you tend to develop a rapport rather than just a blatant musical statement. It ebbs and flows through two and a half hours or so, and we feel it would be unfair for the climax to be 'Whole Lotta Love' now, because that isn't where we climax anymore.

"It's quite a moving thing. I remember doing it at the Garden last year and I sang well away from the mike and I could hear 20,000 people singing it. I mean . . . 20,000 people singing 'High Heeled Sneakers' is one thing, but 20,000 people singing 'Stairway to Heaven' is another. People leave satisfied after that, and I don't think they leave satisfied because of the violent aspects of the music, which I don't think exists anyway, but because they feel a satisfaction with the music they've heard."

COMMUNICATION BREAKDOWN

"Oh heavens, there's so much to do. As diverse as the first album is from the second, and the second from the third, and the third from the fourth, and the fourth to *Houses of the Holy*, and *Houses of the Holy* again to *Physical Graffiti*, there is just a universe. There, I used one of Jimmy's terms. We should probably spin off into the whirling vortex."

— Robert Plant to J.J. Johnson,
NBC *Midnight Special*, March 30, 1975

ROCK MAGIC: JIMMY PAGE, LED ZEPPELIN, AND A SEARCH FOR THE ELUSIVE STAIRWAY TO HEAVEN

William S. Burroughs | June 1975, *Crawdaddy*

Where Robert Plant and John Bonham bought farms with the early receipts of their newfound fame, Jimmy Page had more esoteric digs in mind. He bought Boleskine House, the Loch Ness home of Aleister Crowley, the infamous early twentieth Century occultist, religious/cult leader, philosopher, and poet. Page's interest in Crowley became a major topic of discussion in the media, especially when things went wrong with the band. It also piqued the interest of legendary Beat writer William S. Burroughs, whose interest in, if not the occult then at least the arcane, was also acute. And so the two men got together, probably around the same time as Plant and Charlesworth for *Melody Maker*, though the article ran somewhat later in the venerable rock 'n' roll periodical *Crawdaddy*. –Ed.

When I was first asked to write an article on the Led Zeppelin group, to be based on attending a concert and talking with Jimmy Page, I was not sure I could do it, not being sufficiently knowledgeable about music to attempt anything in the way of musical criticism or even evaluation. I decided simply to attend the concert and talk with Jimmy Page and let the article develop. If you consider any set of data without a preconceived viewpoint, then a viewpoint will emerge from the data.

My first impression was of the audience, as we streamed through one security line after another—a river of youth looking curiously like a single organism: one well-behaved clean-looking middle-class kid. The security guards seemed to be cool and well-trained, ushering gate-crashers out with a minimum of fuss. We were channeled smoothly into our seats in the thirteenth row. Over a relaxed dinner before the concert, a *Crawdaddy* companion had said he had a feeling that something bad could happen at this concert. I pointed out that it always can when you get that many people together—like bullfights where you buy a straw hat at the door to protect you from bottles and other missiles. I was displacing possible danger to a Mexican border town where the matador barely escaped with his life and several spectators were killed. It's known as "clearing the path."

So there we sat. I decline earplugs; I am used to loud drum and horn music from Morocco, and it always has, if skillfully performed, an exhilarating and energizing effect on me. As the performance got underway I experienced this musical exhilaration, which was all the more pleasant for being easily controlled, and I knew then that nothing bad was going to happen. This was a safe, friendly area—but at the same time highly charged. There was a palpable interchange of energy between the performers and the audience which was never frantic or jagged. The special effects were handled well and not overdone.

A few special effects are much better than too many. I can see the laser beams cutting dry ice smoke, which drew an appreciative cheer from the audience. Jimmy Page's number with the broken guitar strings came across with a real impact, as did John Bonham's drum solo, and the lyrics delivered with unfailing vitality by Robert Plant. The performers were doing their best, and it was very good. The last number, "Stairway to Heaven," where the audience all lit matches and there was a scattering of sparklers here and there, found the audience well-behaved and joyous, creating the atmosphere of a high school Christmas play. All in all a good show; neither low nor insipid. Leaving the concert hall was like getting off a jet plane.

I summarized my impressions after the concert in a few notes to serve as a basis for my talk with Jimmy Page: "The essential ingredient for any successful rock group is energy—the ability to give out energy, to receive energy from the audience, and to give it back to the audience. A rock concert is in fact a rite involving the evocation and transmutation of energy. Rock stars may be compared to priests, a theme that was treated in Peter Watkins's film *Privilege*. In that film a rock star was manipulated by reactionary forces to set up a state religion; this scenario seems unlikely. I think a rock group singing political slogans would leave its audience at the door.

"The Led Zeppelin show depends heavily on volume, repetition, and drums. It bears some resemblance to the trance music found in Morocco, which is magical in origin and purpose—that is, concerned with the evocation and control of spiritual forces. In Morocco, musicians are also magicians. Gnaoua music is used to drive out evil spirits. The music of Joujouka evokes the God Pan, Pan God of Panic, representing the real magical forces that sweep away the spurious. It is to be remembered that the origin of all the arts—music, painting, and writing—is magical and evocative; and that magic is always used to obtain some definite result. In the Led Zeppelin concert, the result aimed at would seem to be the creation of energy in the performers and in the audience. For such magic to succeed, it must tap the sources of magical energy, and this can be dangerous."

The Interview

I felt that these considerations could form the basis of my talk with Jimmy Page, which I hoped would not take the form of an interview. There is something just basically *wrong* about the whole interview format. Someone sticks a mike in your face and says, "Mr. Page, would you care to talk about your interest in occult practices? Would you describe yourself as a believer in this sort of thing?" Even an intelligent mike-in-the-face question tends to evoke a guarded mike-in-the-face answer. As soon as Jimmy Page walked into my loft downtown, I saw that it wasn't going to be that way.

We started talking over a cup of tea and found we have friends in common: the real estate agent who negotiated Jimmy Page's purchase of the Aleister Crowley house on Loch Ness; John Michell, the flying saucer and pyramid expert; Donald Cammell, who worked on *Performance*; Kenneth Anger, and the Jaggers, Mick and Chris. The subject of magic came up in connection with Aleister Crowley and Kenneth Anger's film *Lucifer Rising*, for which Jimmy Page did the sound track.

Since the word "magic" tends to cause confused thinking, I would like to say exactly what I mean by "magic" and the magical interpretation of so-called reality. The underlying assumption of magic is the assertion of *will* as the primary moving force in this universe—the deep conviction that nothing happens unless somebody or some being wills it to happen. To me this has always seemed self-evident. A chair does not move unless someone moves it. Neither does your physical body, which is composed of much the same materials, move unless you will it to move. Walking across the room is a magical operation. From the viewpoint of magic, no death, no illness, no misfortune, accident, war, or riot is accidental. There are no accidents in the world of magic. And will is another word for animate energy. Rock stars are juggling fissionable material that could blow up at any time . . . "The soccer scores are coming in from the Capital . . . one must pretend an interest," drawled the dandified Commandante, safe in the pages of my book; and as another rock star said to me, "*You* sit on your ass writing—*I* could be torn to pieces by my fans, like Orpheus."

I found Jimmy Page equally aware of the risks involved in handling the fissionable material of the mass unconscious. I took on a valence I learned years ago from two *Life-Time* [sic] reporters—one keeps telling you these horrific stories: "Now old Burns was dragged out of the truck and skinned alive by the mob, and when we got there with the cameras the bloody thing was still squirming there like a worm . . ." while the other half of the team is snapping pictures CLICK CLICK CLICK to record your reactions—so over dinner at Mexican Gardens I told Jimmy the story of the big soccer riot in Lima, Peru in 1964.

We are ushered into the arena as VIP's, in the style made famous by *Triumph of the Will*. Martial music—long vistas—the statuesque police with their dogs on leads—the crowd surging in a sultry menacing electricity palpable in the air—grey clouds over Lima—people glance up uneasily . . . the last time it rained in Lima was the year of the great earthquake, when whole towns were swallowed by landslides. A cop is beating and kicking someone as he shoves him back towards the exit. Oh lucky man. The dogs growl ominously. The game is tense. Tied until the end of the last quarter, and then the stunning decision: a goal that would have won the game for Peru is disqualified by the Uruguayan referee. A howl of rage from the crowd, and then a huge black known as La Bomba, who has started three previous soccer riots and already has twenty-three notches on his bomb, vaults down into the arena. A wave of fans follows The Bomb—the Uruguayan referee scrambles off with the agility of a rat or an evil spirit—the police release tear gas and unleash their snarling dogs, hysterical with fear and rage and maddened by the tear gas. And then a sound like falling mountains, as a few drops of rain begins to fall.

The crowd tears an Alsatian dog to pieces—a policeman is strangled with his tie, another hurled fifty feet down from the top of the stadium ... bodies piled up ten feet deep at the exits. The soccer scores are coming in from the Capital ... 306 ... 318 ... 352 ... "I didn't know how bad it was until rain started to fall," said a survivor. You see, it never rains in Lima, or almost never, and when it does it's worse than seeing mules foaling in the public street ... trampled ruptured bodies piled in heaps ...

"*You* know, Jimmy," I said: "The crowd surges forward, a heavy piece of equipment falls on the crowd, security goes mad, and then ... a sound like falling mountains ..." CLICK CLICK CLICK: Jimmy Page did not bat an eye.

"Yes, I've thought about that. We all have. The important thing is maintain a balance. The kids come to get far out with the music. It's our job to see they have a good time and no trouble."

And remember the rock group called Storm? Playing a dance hall in Switzerland ... fire ... exits locked ... thirty-seven people dead including all the performers. Now any performer who has never thought about fire and panic just doesn't think. The best way to keep something bad from happening is to see it ahead of time, and you can't see it if you refuse to face the possibility. The bad vibes in that dance hall must have been really heavy. If the performers had been sensitive and alert, they would have checked to be sure the exits were unlocked.

Previously, over two fingers of whiskey in my Franklin Street digs, I had told Page about Major Bruce MacManaway, a healer and psychic who lives in Scotland. The Major discovered his healing abilities in World War II when his regiment was cut off without medical supplies and the Major started laying on his hands . . . "Well Major, I think it's a load of ballocks but I'll try anything." And it turns out the Major is a walking hypo. His psychic abilities were so highly regarded by the Admiralty that he was called in to locate sunken submarines, and he never once missed.

I attended a group meditation seminar with the Major. It turned out to be the Indian rope trick. Before the session the Major told us something of the potential power in group meditation. He had seen it lift a six-hundred-pound church organ five feet in the air. I had no reason to doubt this, since he was obviously incapable of falsification. In the session, after some preliminary relaxation exercises, the Major asked us to see a column of light in the center of the room and then took us up through the light to a plateau where we met nice friendly people: the stairway to heaven in fact. I mean we were really *there*.

I turned to Jimmy Page: "Of course we are dealing here with meditation—the deliberate induction of a trance state in a few people under the hands of an old master. This would seem on the surface to have little in common with a rock concert, but the underlying force is the same: human energy and its potential concentration." I pointed out that the moment when the stairway to heaven becomes something actually *possible* for the audience, would also be the moment of greatest danger. Jimmy expressed himself as well aware of the power in mass concentration, aware of the dangers involved, and of the skill and balance needed to avoid them . . . rather like driving a load of nitroglycerine.

"There *is* a responsibility to the audience," he said. "We don't want anything bad to happen to these kids—we don't want to release anything we can't handle." We talked about magic and Aleister Crowley. Jimmy said that Crowley has been maligned as a black magician, whereas magic is neither white nor black, good nor bad—it is simply alive with what it is: the real thing, what people really feel and want and are. I pointed out that this "either/or" straitjacket had been imposed by Christianity when all magic became black magic; that scientists took over from the Church, and Western man has been stifled in a non-magical universe known as "the way things are." Rock music can be seen as one attempt to break out of this dead soulless universe and reassert the universe of magic.

Jimmy told me that Aleister Crowley's house has very good vibes for anyone who is relaxed and receptive. At one time the house had also been the scene of a vast chicken swindle indirectly involving George Sanders, the movie actor, who was able to clear himself of any criminal charges. Sanders committed suicide in Barcelona, and we both remembered his farewell note to the world: "I'll leave you to this sweet cesspool."

I told Jimmy he was lucky to have that house with a monster in the front yard. What about the Loch Ness monster? Jimmy Page thinks it exists. I wondered if it could find enough to eat, and thought this unlikely—it's not the improbability but the upkeep on monsters that worries me. Did Aleister Crowley have opinions on the subject? He apparently had not expressed himself.

We talked about trance music. He had heard the Brian Jones record from recordings made at Joujouka. We discussed the possibility of synthesizing rock music with some of the older forms of trance music that have been developed over centuries to produce powerful, sometimes hypnotic effects on the audience. Such a synthesis would enable the older forms to escape from the mould of folk lore and provide new techniques to rock groups.

We talked about the special effects used in the concert. "Sure," he said, "lights, lasers, dry ice are fine—but you have to keep some balance. The show must carry itself and not rely too heavily on special effects, however spectacular." I brought up the subject of infra-sound, that is, sound pitched below 16 Hertz, the level of human hearing; as ultra-sound is above the level. Professor Gavreau of France developed infra-sound as a military weapon. A powerful infra-sound installation can, he claims, kill everyone in a five-mile radius, knock down walls, and break windows. Infra-sound kills by setting vibrations within the body so that, as Gavreau puts it, "You can feel all the organs in your body rubbing together." The plans for this device can be obtained from the French Patent Office; and, infra-sound generators constructed from inexpensive materials. Needless to say, one is not concerned with military applications however unlimited, but with more interesting and useful possibilities, reaching much further than five miles.

Infra-sound sets up vibrations in the body and nervous system. Need these vibrations necessarily be harmful or unpleasant? All music played at any volume sets up vibrations in the body and nervous system of the listener. That's why people listen to it. [Enrico] Caruso as you will remember could break a champagne glass across the room. Especially interesting is the possibility of rhythmic pulses of infra-sound; that is, *music in infra-sound*. You can't hear it, but you can feel it.

Jimmy was interested, and I gave him a copy of a newspaper article on infra-sound. It seems that the most deadly range is around 7 Hertz, and when this is turned on even at a low volume, anyone within range is affected. They feel anxious, ill, depressed, and finally exclaim with one voice, "I feel TERRIBLE!" . . . last thing you want at a rock concert. However, around the borders of infra-sound perhaps a safe range can be found. Buddhist mantras act by setting up vibrations in the body. Could this be done in a much more powerful yet safe manner by the use of infra-sound rhythms which could of course be combined with audible music? Perhaps infra-sound could add a new dimension to rock music.

Could something be developed comparable to the sonar communication of dolphins, conveying an immediate sonar experience that requires no symbolic translation? I mentioned to Jimmy that I had talked with Dr. Truby, who worked with John Lilly recording dolphins. Dr. Truby is a specialist in interspecies communication, working on a grant from the government—so that when all our kids are born Venusians we will understand them when they start to talk. I suggested to him that all communication, as we know it, is actually inter-species communication, and that it is kept that way by the nature of verbal and symbolic communication, which must be indirect.

Do dolphins have a language? What is a language? I define a language as a communication system in which data are represented by verbal or written symbols—symbols that *are not the objects* to which they refer. The word "chair" is not the object itself, the chair. So any such system of communication is always second-hand and symbolic, whereas we *can* conceive of a form of communication that would be immediate and direct, undercutting the need for symbols. And music certainly comes closer to such direct communication than language.

Could musical communication be rendered more precise with infra-sound, thus bringing the whole of music a second radical step forward? The first step was made when music came out of the dance halls, roadhouses, and night clubs, into Madison Square Garden and Shea Stadium. Rock music appeals to a mass audience, instead of being the province of a relatively few aficionados. Can rock music make another step forward, or is it a self-limiting form, confined by the demands of a mass audience? How much that is radically new can a mass audience safely absorb? We came back to the question of balance. How much new material will be accepted by a mass audience? Can rock music go forward without leaving its fans behind?

We talked about Wilhelm Reich's orgone accumulator, and I showed him plans for making this device, which were passed along to me by Reich's daughter. Basically the device is very simple, consisting of iron or steel wool on the inside and organic material on the outside. I think this was a highly important discovery. Recently a scientist with the National Aeronautics and Space Administration announced an "electrical cell" theory of cancer that is almost identical to Reich's cancer theory put forth 25 years ago. He does not acknowledge any indebtedness to Reich. I showed Jimmy the orgone box I have here, and we agreed that orgone accumulators in pyramid form and/or using magnetized iron could be much more powerful.

We talked about the film *Performance* and the use of cut-up techniques in this film. Now the cut-up method was applied to writing by Brion Gysin in 1959; he said that writing was fifty years behind painting, and applied the montage method to writing. Actually, montage is much closer to the facts of perception than representational painting. If, for example, you walked through Times Square, and then put on canvas what you had seen, the result would be a montage . . . half a person cut in two by a car, reflections from shop windows, fragments of street signs. Antony Balch and I collaborated on a film called *Cut-Ups*, in which the film was cut into segments and rearranged at random. Nicolas Roeg and

Donald Cammell saw a screening of the film not long before they made *Performance*.

Musical cut-ups have been used by Earle Brown and other modern composers. What distinguishes a cut-up from, say, an edited medley, is that the cut-up is at some point random. For example, if you made a medley by taking thirty seconds from a number of scores and assembling these arbitrary units—that would be a cut-up. Cut-ups often result in more succinct meanings, rather than nonsense. Here for example is a phrase taken from a cut-up of this article: "I can see the laser gate crashers with an appreciative cheer from the 13th row." (Actually a gate crasher was extricated by security from the row in front of us; an incident I had forgotten until I saw this cut-up.)

Over dinner at the Mexican Gardens, I was surprised to hear that Jimmy Page had never heard of [James] Petrillo, who started the first musicians' union and perhaps did more than any other one man to improve the financial position of musicians by protecting copyrights. One wonders whether rock music could have gotten off the ground without Petrillo and the Union, which put musicians in the big money bracket, thereby attracting managers, publicity, and the mass audience.

Music, like all the arts, is magical and ceremonial in origin. Can rock music return to these ceremonial roots and take its fans with it? Can rock music use older forms like Moroccan trance music? There is at present a wide interest among young people in the occult and all means of expanding consciousness. Can rock music appeal directly to this interest? In short, there are a number of disparate tendencies waiting to be synthesized. Can rock music serve as a vehicle for this synthesis?

The broken guitar strings, John Bonham's drum solo, vitality by Robert Plant—when you get that many people to get it, very good. Buy a straw hat at the door—the audience all light matches. Cool well-trained laser beams channeled the audience smoothly. A scattering of sparklers. Danger to a Mexican border town. We start talking over a cup of the mass unconscious—cut to a soccer riot photo in Lima. The Uruguayan referee as another rock star. Sound like falling mountains of the risks involved. It's our job to see trouble and plateau the center of the room—remember the stairway to Switzerland? Fire really there. You can't see it if you refuse—

underlying force the same. I mean we were playing a dance hall in heaven at the moment when the stairway actually possible for the audience was unlocked.

Word for Word

William Burroughs: I really, really enjoyed the concert. I think it has quite a lot, really, in common with Moroccan trance music.

Jimmy Page: Yes, yes.

WB: I wonder if you consciously were using any of that . . .

JP: Well, yes, there is a little on that particular track, "Kashmir"—a lead bass on that—even though none of us have been to Kashmir. It's just that we've all been very involved in that sort of music. I'm very involved in ethnic music from all over the world.

WB: Have you been to Morocco?

JP: No, I haven't, and it's a very sad admission to make. I've only been to, you know, India and Bangkok and places like that through the Southeast.

WB: Well, I've never been east of Athens.

JP: Because during the period when everybody was going through trips over to, you know, Morocco, going down, way down, making their own journeys to Istanbul, I was at art college during that period and then I eventually went straight into music. So I really missed out on all that sort of traveling. But I know musicians that have gone there and actually sat in with the Arabs and played with them.

WB: Yeah, well, they think of music entirely in magical terms.

JP: Yes.

WB: And their music is definitely used for magical purposes. For example, the Gnaoua music is to drive out evil spirits and Joujouka music is invoking the God Pan. Musicians there are all magicians, quite consciously.

WB: I was thinking of the concentration of mass energy that you get in a pop concert, and if that were, say, channeled in some magical way . . . a stairway to heaven . . . it could become quite actual.

JP: Yes, I know. One is so aware of the energies that you are going for, and you could so easily . . . I mean, for instance, the other night we played in the Philadelphia Spectrum, which really is a black hole as a concert hall . . . . The security there is the most ugly of anywhere in the States. I saw this incident happen and I was almost physically sick. In fact, if I hadn't been playing the guitar I was playing it would've been over somebody's head. It was a double-neck, which is irreplaceable, really, unless you wait another nine months for them to make another one at Gibson's.

What had happened, somebody came to the front of the stage to take a picture or something and obviously somebody said, "Be off with you." And he wouldn't go. And then one chap went over the barrier, and then another, and then another and then another, and they all piled on top of . . . you could see the fists coming out . . . on this one solitary person. And they dragged him by his hair and they were kicking him. It was just sickening. Now, what I'm saying is this. . . . Our crowds, the people that come to see us are very orderly. It's not the sort of Alice Cooper style, where you actually *try* to get them into a state where they've got to go like that, so that you can get reports of this, that, and the other. And the wrong word said at that time could've just sparked off the whole thing.

WB: Yes, there's sort of a balance to be maintained there.

JP: Yeah, that's right.

WB: The audience the other night was very well behaved.

———

WB: Have you used the lasers in all of the concerts?

JP: Over here, yes.

WB: Very effective.

JP: I think we should have more of them, don't you? About 30 of them! Do you know they bounced that one off the moon? But it's been condensed

... it's the very one that they used for the moon. I was quite impressed by that.

WB: That isn't the kind of machine that would cause any damage . . .

JP: Uh, if you look straight into it, yes.

WB: Yes, but I mean . . . it doesn't burn a hole in . . .

JP: No . . . It's been taken right down. I'm just waiting for the day when you can get the holograms . . . get three-dimensional. The other thing I wanted to do was the Van de Graaff Generator. You used to see them in the old horror films . . .

WB: Oh yes . . . Frankenstein, and all that.

———

JP: When we first came over here . . . when the draft was really hot and everything . . . if you stayed in the country for more than six months, you were eligible for it, they'd drag you straight into the draft.

WB: I didn't realize that.

JP: Yeah.

WB: Oh. I thought you had to be an American citizen.

JP: Noo. No, no. We almost overstayed our welcome. I was producing and having to work in studios here and the days coming up to the six month period were just about . . . it was just about neck and neck. And I still had a couple more days left and a couple more days to work on this LP.

WB: Were they right there with the papers?

JP: Well, not quite. I mean obviously it would have taken some time, but somebody would've been there . . . You know, they try to keep an eye on people.

———

WB: Did you ever hear about something called infra-sound?

JP: Uh, carry on.

WB: Well, infra-sound is sound below the level of hearing. And it was developed by someone named Professor Gavreau in France as a military weapon. He had an infra-sound installation that he could turn on and kill everything within five miles. It can also knock down walls and break windows. But it kills by setting up vibrations within the body. Well, what I was wondering was, whether rhythmical music at sort of the borderline of infra-sound could be used to produce rhythms in the audience—because, of course, any music with volume will set up these vibrations. That is part of the way the effect is achieved.

JP: Hmm.

WB: It's apparently . . . it's not complicated to build these infra-sound things.

JP: I've heard of this, actually, but not in such a detailed explanation. I've heard that certain frequencies can make you physically ill.

WB: Yes. Well, this can be fatal. That's not what you're looking for. But it could be used just to set up vibrations . . .

JP: Ah hah . . . A death ray machine! Of course, when radio first came out they were picketing all the radio stations, weren't they, saying "We don't want these poisonous rays" [laughter] . . . Yes, well . . . certain notes can break glasses. I mean, opera singers can break glasses with sound, this is true?

WB: That was one of Caruso's tricks.

JP: But it is true?

WB: Of course.

JP: I've never seen it done.

WB: I've never seen it done, but I know that you can do it.

JP: I want laser *notes*, that's what I'm after! Cut right through.

WB: Apparently you can make one of these things out of parts you can buy in a junk yard. It's not a complicated machine to make. And actually the patent . . . it's patented in France, and according to French law, you can obtain a copy of the patent for a very small fee.

JP: Well, you see the thing is, it's hard to know just exactly what is going on, from the stage to the audience . . . You can only . . . I mean I've never seen the group play, obviously. Because I'm part of it . . . I can only see it on celluloid, or hear it. But I know what I see. And this thing about rhythms within the audience, I would say yes. Yes, definitely. And it is . . . Music which involves riffs, anyway, will have a trance-like effect, and it's really like a mantra. . . . And we've been attacked for that.

WB: What a mantra does is set up certain vibrations within the body, and this, obviously, does the same thing. Of course, it goes . . . it comes out too far. But I was wondering if on the borderline of infra-sound that possibly some interesting things could be done.

JP: Ah.

———

JP: Last year we were playing [sets] for three hours solid, and physically that was a real. . . . I mean, when I came back from the last tour I didn't know where I was. I didn't even know where I was going. We ended up in New York and the only thing that I could relate to was the instrument onstage. I just couldn't . . . I was just totally and completely spaced out.

WB: How long was that you played recently? That was two hours and a half.

JP: That was two and a half hours, yes. It used to go for three hours.

WB: I'd hate to give a three hour reading . . .

JOHN BONHAM: OVER THE HILLS AND FAR AWAY . . .

Chris Welch | June 21, 1975, *Melody Maker*

Page and Plant, as you can tell, became the voices of the group as far as the press was concerned (it took Nick Kent enduring an Edward G. Robinson film festival to get some face time with John Paul Jones in 1973). This is not for John Bonham lacking in affability, just his lack of desire to deal with the press on any extended basis (with the possible exception of Roy Carr). Yet, as they settled into some fallow time between touring and recording (and touring again), Plant and Page decided to spend some time in North Africa exploring for new sounds (perhaps William Burroughs' power of suggestion). John Bonham settled into his bucolic homestead to await the arrival of his new child. Here, he takes *Melody Maker*'s Chris Welch on a walking tour of his life. –Ed.

Gossip in the village was running riot. John up at the farm was going to buy The Chequers. The American in the bar of another pub a few miles distant was adamant. So was the landlord, and a few grizzled farmers, as they downed pints of the finest beer known to men of science and agriculture.

But the object of the debate emitted a stentorian bellow that scotched the rumors once and for all. "No I'm not buying the bloody Chequers! Mind you . . . I was interested."

John Bonham, farmer, stockbreeder, and drummer with the world's heaviest rock band, was supping in a Worcestershire haven of low beams and convivial company.

The day before, his wife Pat had given birth to a baby daughter, Zoe, and there was plenty of cause for celebration. And apart from a small matter of being banned from driving for six months (no rumours here—it was all in the local paper), John was feeling that contentment and satisfaction most enjoyed by a self-made man.

A few weeks before, he had been pounding his massive drum kit in another world again. The world of thousands of admiring rock fans, enormous record sales, and marathon, sell-out concerts. He seems equally at home in both, and he applies the same direct, furious energy.

At the historic Earls Court concerts, Bonham's bombastic, metronomic drumming was an essential factor in a band that needs a regular supply of adrenalin. Bonham summons his reserves of strength from a tough, well-built body that was honed in the building, as much as the music, industry.

John pours out his ideas, opinions, and thoughts in a tone that brooks no argument, and yet he has a fearless warmth and humor that commands respect. He looks the world straight in the eye, and expects the same treatment. No shrinking violet then, this man who was once told there was no call for his kind of loud, aggressive drumming.

And yet it's hardly a coincidence that when the men of rock, who deal in volume, flash, and fame, reap the rich rewards of their craft, they head for the hills and vales, far from the stink of the city, there to enjoy the animals, earth, and silence.

Bonham's spread is a bit like the Ponderosa in *Bonanza*. After driving on stilted motorways through the smog of Birmingham (a living memorial to Sixties "planning"), the country's scars gradually heal, and the Worcestershire countryside blossoms.

A ranch style nameboard appears around a bend in a B-road, and twin white fences accompany a long, straight driveway to the modern brick farmhouse, where the gaffer and his family are ensconced.

Had John always intended to go into farming? "Never, I was never into farming at all. I wasn't even looking for a farm, just a house with some land. But when I saw this place, something clicked, and I bought it back in '72."

John seems to have been cheerfully accepted into the farming community, and is anyway guaranteed of one friendly neighbor.

Robert Plant lives just a few miles away, surrounded by goats that John avers "eat everything, old boots, you name it."

John gave a great guffaw that could probably be heard halfway round the hundred acres of sheep and cattle that surround the house.

We set off for a stump round the fields. The view was breathtaking, apart from a line of recently constructed electricity pylons.

One of the old barns has been converted to the needs of the modern rock and roll farmer.

"This is the hot car shop," said John with a chuckle, leading the way past a coven of cats who had been following us at a discreet distance. And there, squashed together in the darkness, stood a trio of highly improbable vehicles.

An elaborately painted contraption that resembled a pre-war taxicab, mounted on wheels a yard wide, was, John explained: "a show car. I bought her in L.A. She can do 150 mph. And that one is a '67 Corvette with a seven litre engine.

"This one is a 1954 two door Ford with an eight litre engine. You get guys coming past in a sports car who think it's an old banger, until I put my foot down.

"It's an amazing car, look at all the chrome inside. She'd only done 10,000 when I bought her."

Like many enjoying success for the first time, John once bought himself a Rolls-Royce.

"It was a white one. I went to a wedding reception in Birmingham. When I came out it looked like a bomb had hit it. All these skinheads had jumped on it. They kicked in the windscreen, smashed everything. If it had been any other car they would have left it alone."

Red rags to the bull obviously. But John has worked and still works hard for his seven-litre crust.

Back in the house we talked about his early days and the drumming career that has earned him world renown.

"This used to be just a three-bedroomed house. My father did all the wood panelling, and I did a lot of the work with my brother and sub-contractors.

"If you have builders in they'll make excuse after excuse about delays during the summer so that they can have work inside during the bad weather.

"I know, because when I left school I went into the trade with my dad. He had a building business and I used to like it.

"But drumming was the only thing I was any good at, and I stuck at that for three or four years. If things got bad I could always go back to building.

"I had a group with Nicky James, an incredible lead singer. But we had so much of the equipment on hire purchase, we'd get stopped at night on the way back from a gig and they'd take back all the PA.

"Nicky had a big following then, and he could sing any style, but he couldn't write his own material.

"We used to have *so* many clubs we could play around Birmingham in those days. Lots of ballrooms too. All those places have gone to the dogs—or bingo.

"I was so keen to play when I quit school. I'd have played for nothing. In fact I did for a long time. But my parents stuck by me.

"No, I never had any drum lessons. But I remember Carl [Palmer] went, he had a lot of lessons. I just played the way I wanted, and got black-listed in Birmingham. 'You're too loud!' they used to say. 'There's no future in it.'

"But nowadays you can't play loud enough. I just wish there was a way of wiring a drum kit to get the natural sound through the PA. I've tried so many different ways, but when you're playing with a band like ours you get so many problems with sound.

"With Jimmy and John Paul on either side playing lead, they can leak into the drum mikes, and if you have too many monitors you start to get feedback. I never get it the way I want."

And yet Bonham's drum sound was fairly fantastic at Earls Court I thought.

"I enjoyed those concerts," said John. "I thought they were the best shows that we've ever put on in England. I always get tense before a show, and we were expecting trouble with such a huge audience.

"But everything went really well and although we couldn't have the laser beams at full power, I thought the video screen was well worth doing. It cost a lot of bread, but you could see close-ups you'd never be able to see normally at a concert. It was worth every penny."

———

Did the band rehearse for weeks before the concerts?

"Nah, three days. Mind you, it was only a few weeks before we got back from the States. We just needed a bit of rust remover.

"We had already done a lot of planning for that States tour, because we like to change the show each year. There's nothing worse than playing the old numbers over and over again.

"You've got to keep in some of the old songs of course. I don't know what would happen if we didn't play 'Stairway to Heaven,' because it's become one of the biggest things we've ever done.

"When Jimmy plays the first chord in the States, it's like instant bedlam, until Robert comes in with the first line.

"And we always play 'Whole Lotta Love' because people want to hear it, and I still get a great kick out of 'Dazed and Confused.'

"I always enjoy the number because we never play it the same. With the other stuff, we'll put one in, or take one out.

"On the last night at Earls Court we played 'Heartbreaker', 'Black Dog,' and a bit from 'Out on the Tiles'. With the songs from *Physical Graffiti* we've got such a wide range of material.

"It wasn't done on purpose. It's just that we went through a stage where we were very conscious of everything we played. We felt it had to be a certain kind of thing for Zeppelin.

"Now we record everything that comes up and, of course, in the States they play it on the radio so the people know what we're doing.

"In Britain we never get any airplay except from John Peel and Alan Freeman. In the States they'll play 'Trampled Under Foot,' all day.

"When we first ran through it, John Paul and Jimmy started off the riff, but then we thought it was a bit souly for us. Then we changed it around a bit. It's great for me. Great rhythm for a drummer. It's just at the right pace and you can do a lot of frills.

"But compare that to 'Dazed and Confused'. The speed of the thing! While we're playing, I think 'Christ if I drop one, knit one, and purl one— that's it.' You've gotta be fit to play that one, and if I don't feel too good, it's very hard.

"We keep tapes of every show, and it's very useful afterwards, especially for my drum solo, because then I can hear what works best."

Despite John's burly appearance and confident mien, it's a fact that he suffers from doubt and worry just before every Zeppelin concert. He'll sit backstage, nervously tapping sticks, anxious to get on stage and stuck into their exhausting three hour show.

"I've got worse—terribly bad nerves all the time.

"Once we start into 'Rock and Roll' I'm fine. I just can't stand sitting around, and I worry about playing badly, and if I do, then I'm really p—— off. If I play well, I feel great.

"Everybody in the band is the same, and each has some little thing they do before we go on, just like pacing about, or lighting a cigarette. It used to be worse at festivals.

"You might have to sit around for a whole day, and you daren't drink, because you'll get tired out and blow it. So you sit drinking tea in a caravan, with everybody saying 'far out man.'

"We don't do festivals so much now because of the amount of equipment we have. There's all the PA and lights and the black floor for the stage. Imagine the changeover between us and the Floyd? It would take hours! The Bath festivals were the only ones we ever played here, and they went really well."

One of the features of Bonham's marathon drum solos during the Earls Court concerts was the special effects employed on the tympani. Had he been using a synthesizer?

"No, it was just phasing on the pedal tymps. I was using them in '73. It's just a different sound.

"Not everybody likes or understands a drum solo, so I like to bring in effects and sounds to keep their interest. I've been doing the hand drum solo for a long time—before I joined Zeppelin.

"I remember playing a solo on 'Caravan' when I was 16. Sometimes you can take a chunk out of your knuckles on the hi-hat or you can catch your hand on the tension rods.

"I try to play something different every night on the solo, but the basic plan is the same, from sticks to hands and then the tymps, and the final build up.

"It would be really boring to play on the straight kit all the time. On the last States tour I was really chuffed when I had some good reviews from people who don't even like drum solos.

"I usually play for twenty minutes, and the longest I've even done was under thirty. It's a long time, but when I'm playing it seems to fly by.

"Sometimes you come up against a blank and you think 'how am I going to get out of this one?' Or sometimes you go into a fill and you know halfway through it's going to be disastrous.

"There have been times when I've blundered, and got the dreaded look from the lads. But that's a good sign. It shows you're attempting something you've not tried before."

Was there any danger of John losing power in time in view of his arduous years on the road? "I'm not losing strength. I'm less tired after a solo than I used to get in the early days. Of course we didn't have a break for the acoustic numbers then.

"But it was so cold at Earls Court, we had to have an electric fire in the dressing room. The unions wouldn't let us use blow heaters. I had a run through on the Friday night before the first show, and I was playing in an overcoat."

One of the mysteries of Zeppelin is that they have never put themselves out for a hit single, and [Physical] Graffiti had obvious singles chart potential. Didn't they want one?

"No, not really. It's because of the length of a piece like 'Trampled Under Foot.' It's not worth cutting something out just for the sake of a single. And if people like Led Zeppelin they would have bought the LP anyway. No—it would be pointless to put a single out from the album."

After a sojourn at the pub, we returned to the farmhouse to sample some brandy and the delights of a quad sound system that threatened to stampede the sleeping herd of Herefords.

"Listen to this. It's great." John put on the Pretty Things' new single "I'm Keeping." They're a band who seem to be enjoying a whole new lease of life since they signed to Swan Song, Zeppelin's own label. He was also raving about Supertramp's album and admitted a new interest in country music.

"I wish there were some more live bands around here I could have a blow with," sighed John, tossing back a brandy, and barely audible above the thunder of speakers.

"There's nowhere for them to play—now it's all discos. God, I hate those places, all those flashing lights. It's all right if you're out for a night on the tiles. But I like to hear a good live group. You've gotta remember—they're the backbone of the business."

But in case the rock business does start to dry up, John is setting his nine-year-old son Jason on the right path. He has a junior drum kit set up in front of dad's juke box, and pounds away to Gary Glitter.

But John is not sure if he'll take the right path to becoming another drumming rock superstar. He came home from the Cubs during the afternoon clutching his latest single, "Whispering Grass" by Windsor Davies.

"You can't teach him anything," warned John. "He's got a terrible temper."

LED ZEPPELIN TO RECORD NEW ALBUM IN MUNICH THIS NOVEMBER: NO TOUR PLANS UNTIL PLANT'S ANKLE FULLY HEALS

Danny Goldberg | November 13, 1975, Swan Song Records Press Release

It was probably a good thing that the group played the series of five shows at Earls Court that Welch and Bonham discussed, or else they probably would have had to renege on Robert's promise to play England by midsummer. After chasing around for more rock 'n' roll in Morocco, Robert Plant met his family in Greece for a proper holiday. While driving around the islands, he and his family were in a terrible but nonfatal automobile accident that left Robert with a badly broken ankle as the most serious of his injuries (more on this anon). At first, no one was sure if he would ever walk, let alone perform, again. However, after three months of recuperation, he felt well enough to record (sitting down). So rather than hitting the road again, Led Zeppelin went back into the studio. –Ed.

November 13, 1975—Led Zeppelin are recording a new album this month in Munich, Germany at Musicland Studios. The album is expected to be released sometime in the early part of 1976. The group has been rehearsing material for the new album over the summer at Studio Instrument Rentals rehearsal studio in Los Angeles.

Meanwhile, it has been announced that while Robert Plant's ankle has healed substantially since its multiple fracture in a car crash on August

6th, he still is unable to perform and no Led Zeppelin tour anywhere in the world is currently scheduled. The cast on Plant's right ankle has been removed, but he still cannot put any weight on it. Another medical report on Plant's ankle is expected in February—but under no circumstances would any Zeppelin tour be scheduled before the summer, and no plans or arrangements of any kind will be made until Plant's ankle is fully healed. Plant's left elbow, which was also fractured at the time of the accident, is almost completely healed now, and he was seen throughout the summer at various concerts in L.A. and was universally considered to be in very good spirits. Plant said just before leaving, "Staying in California helped me to recover months earlier than I otherwise might have—in coming from the old world to the new world, I felt renewed." Plant wrote the lyrics for the new Zeppelin album in Malibu this summer.

COMMUNICATION BREAKDOWN

"There is a lot of urgency about [*Presence*]. There's a lot of attack to the music. I think that's reflecting a state of mind of actually being constantly on the move. You know, no base, because of the situation then. That definitely is reflected. I know it's talking in a pretty nebulous fashion, but I think people will know what I mean when they hear it . . . There's a hell of a lot of spontaneity about it. I think that's the element, really. That aspect of it has to be taken into account when you start talking about the actual development of it, because that's the whole key to the theme of it, the level of spontaneity . . . We've done a lot of constructive work in the period off the road. It's not as if we've retired."

— Jimmy Page to Harry Doherty, *Melody Maker*, March 20, 1976

COMMUNICATION BREAKDOWN

"I was sitting at rehearsals . . . in a big, soft fuckin' armchair, rocking along-facing the group in a fuckin' soft armchair! I mean, if you want to really feel stupid or totally out of it, sing with Led Zeppelin sitting in an armchair. In the end, they got me a large stool and every time I really started hitting the notes, I'd sort of raise myself off the stool on one leg and do a Rudolf Nureyev."

— Robert Plant to Jim Jerome, *Crawdaddy*, April 1976

PLANTATIONS: SHOULD RALPH NADER JOIN LED ZEPPELIN?

Chris Charlesworth | May 1976, *CREEM*

In interviews, Page was somewhat reluctant to discuss Plant's injuries except in relation to how they impacted the group. Plant was not nearly so reticent. Here, he and Chris Charlesworth discuss the accident, his North African sojourn, the tour that wasn't, and the making of *Presence*. –Ed.

The ever-elusive Led Zeppelin surfaced in New York in January at the Park Lane Hotel on Central Park South. Jimmy Page was accounted for, his mission being to finish mixing the soundtrack of the long-awaited Led Zep movie. The rest of the boys were just in town for "social reasons", according to Swan Song. Who should know.

Of the four, Robert Plant was by far the most "social," stopping off at bars uptown and downtown, always in the company of English sound engineer Benjie LeFevre, and an English bodyguard named David. Plant still walks with a crutch, a wincing reminder of last August's car crash on the Greek island of Rhodes. Although the plaster has now been removed, his usual hurried shuffle has been replaced by a deliberate, careful plod. He doesn't think he'll be able to dance until the beginning of next soccer season, which is tantamount to saying that Led Zeppelin won't be able to perform live until that time also.

Indestructible? Obviously not. The fractured foot has stymied Plant's usual punk arrogance. Temporarily, at any rate, he can't run with the pack and this compulsory moderation to the pace of his life seems to have brought about a certain sympathy that wasn't always apparent in his personality. He might look like the proverbial Greek god rock vocalist as he struts magnificently across stages with the studlike hauteur of the rock idiom, but he's human just like the rest of us, broken bones and all.

Plant has always seemed rather divorced from reality, often giving the impression of being a leftover from the days of flower power, with his golden curls and brightly-coloured stage tops. That image has been perpetrated by interviews that are both vague and filled with scattered references to peace, love, and world understanding—topics which have tarnished considerably in the reality of the Seventies.

It was something of a relief then, that the Robert Plant of 1976, with his crutch and newly curled hair, seemed to have come to terms with his public image on a more evenly-balanced level. Goddammit—*he* phoned me to arrange the time of the following interview, and if that isn't a turn up for the book, then I don't know what is!

He had much to talk about: the accident and its consequent effects on the band, his travels to Northern Africa which preceded the crash, the new Led Zeppelin album, and, lastly, some thoughts on the eight-year career of the group.

Initially Plant seemed reluctant to discuss the accident, but as the interview progressed he warmed to the subject.

"The memory is very vivid, but it's like spilt milk and there's no time to cry over it when there's another bottle around the corner . . . you know what I mean?

"I had the normal instant reaction of anybody and that was for my family who were in the car with me. I didn't know what the implications and the final outcome of the wounds or whatever would turn out to be, but they were of minimal importance at the time.

"I didn't think about the possible consequences for the band but as I had plenty of time to lie back—not even sit back—I started gaining a new perspective on the situation.

"After I'd been pieced back together I had to think about it all because I didn't really know whether things were going to be the same as they were before . . . uh, physically."

There was a chance, then, that you might be crippled forever? "Mmm, yes. I had to, not so much grow up very quickly, as be prepared to face odds that I never thought I would come up against.

"I haven't come out of it too scarred, either physically and mentally, and, in fact, once I knew Maureen [Plant's wife] and the kids were OK I really threw myself back into my work. By engrossing myself more and more in the work we had on hand, the time passed by quicker.

"If I stop and brood, which is a very bad thing to do, then time moves with a lead weight around it, but the time between August 4 [the date of the accident] and now has gone by quickly because I applied myself to what I do best. I mean . . . I can do 99 percent of what I could do before, so we sat down and had a meeting.

"We obviously couldn't tour, so we decided to make an album which wouldn't have happened if it hadn't been for me.

"It was quite remarkable that I found myself sitting in an armchair facing the band with my leg in the air. We were planning to tour right around the world and back to England, playing possibly in South America, Hawaii, Japan, and Asia Minor and ending up doing dates in Europe, especially Scandinavia, before dropping anchor in Albion."

Far from being frustrated at the necessity for inactivity, the rest of Led Zeppelin were merely relieved when they heard that Plant would not be limping for life. In the weeks before the accident—the time between Zep's Earls Court concerts and August 4—Plant and Page had covered thousands of miles together, travelling in desolate Arab countries by Range Rover, visiting Southern Morocco, and, incidentally, introducing Bob Marley and the Wailers' music to those regions.

"I was idly researching the possibility of recording various ethnic groups of different tribes in Morocco, just checking out how hard it would be, not so much the actual recording, but cutting through the ridiculous bureaucracy in Morocco. They were governed by the French for so long that they have a lot of the French traits on efficiency which, of course, are absolutely nil. The Morroccan version of that is even sillier.

"On the Monday morning after the last gig at Earls Court I was on my way to Agadir with Maureen, and three weeks later Jimmy flew out to meet me in Marrakesh where we spent several nights at the folk festival. That gave us a little peep into the colour of Moroccan music and the music of the hill tribes. Once you get off the normal tourist path and have the right vehicle, so long as you know a little bit of Arabic, which I do, then you discover they are quite fine people. They're very warm people and they're overjoyed when they find you have taken the trouble to learn their language."

Plant and Page's journeys took them on pretty dangerous routes, especially in view of the growing tension between Spain and Morocco which was bubbling-up at the time. "One day we had lunch with a local police chief and received his blessing before travelling on, and we showed him on an old map where we wanted to go.

"He called round one of his friends who was a tourist guide and the guide told me and Jimmy he had been that route once in his life but wouldn't go again because he was a married man. We still went, driving for hours and hours and the further south we went, the more it seemed like a different country. Gone are the people who can take the back pocket off your Levi's without you knowing it, and you're into a land of nice, honest people who find a Range Rover with Bob Marley music very strange.

"We tried to get down as far as the Spanish Sahara at the time when the war was just breaking out. There was a distinct possibly that we could have got very, very lost, going round in circles and taking ages to get out. It's such a vast country with no landmarks and no people apart from the odd tent and a camel.

"We kept reaching these army road blocks where we'd get machine guns pointed at us and we'd have to wave our passports furiously and say we were going to bathe at the next beach. Then we'd go on thirty miles to another road block and claim we were going along to the next beach again.

"We wanted to get down to a place called Tafia which is not very far from the border of the Spanish Sahara. We got as far as we could but eventually the road got so bad we had to turn back."

From Africa, Page and Plant journeyed to Switzerland for a pre-arranged group meeting, travelling by car up through Casablanca and Tangier. "It was devastating leaving Morocco behind and suddenly finding ourselves in Europe. For two months I'd lived at a Moroccan speed which is no speed at all, and then suddenly I was in Spain being frisked.

"We saw the jazz festival in Montreux, living on top of a mountain in a total extreme of climate from what we'd had for the past two months. After a while I started pining for the sun again, not just the sun but the happy, haphazard way of life that goes with it, and Rhodes seemed a good idea.

"I knew Phil May was going to be there so down we went. Jimmy came down with me but he left to go to Italy the morning before the accident, and we started rehearsing. Then there was the accident and . . . well, we were just stopped in our tracks."

Plant was taken to a Greek hospital where, with the aid of an interpreter, he tried to explain that he was who he was.

"I had to share a room with a drunken soldier who had fallen over and banged his head and as he was coming around he kept focusing on me, uttering my name.

"I was lying there in some pain trying to get cockroaches off the bed and he started singing 'The Ocean' from *Houses of the Holy*. I can remember a doctor working on us for 36 hours nonstop because there was no one else there. My brother-in-law and Maureen's sister *were* there, so he managed to get things together pretty fast. As soon as the news got through I was whisked out of there quick.

"The doctor in London told me I wouldn't walk for at least six months and he gave me some odds of various possibilities about the future, so we had another group meeting, cancelled all the tour plans, and decided to make an album instead. We've always taken so much time making albums, but we thought that this time we'd take a totally different attitude and cut one as quickly as possible."

Plant likens the new album to Zeppelin's second album in that it was made in a short time and retains an immediacy that has not been so apparent on later efforts. "It's so adamantly positive, so affirmative for us. Everybody was aware that there was a crisis in the band so we got together and went forward as if nothing had happened, like turning into a storm instead of running from it."

"In L.A. we just rehearsed and rehearsed. It was so strange for me the first time because, as I said, I was sitting in an armchair, singing, and I found myself wiggling inside my cast. The whole band really wanted to play and had wanted to do that tour, so the same effort was put into the album. It was a unique situation where we rehearsed for three weeks— on and off in true Zeppelin style because we're not the greatest band for rehearsing. We've always felt that too much rehearsing on a song can spoil it for us . . . sort of take the edge off the excitement, but this time it worked in the opposite way because the enthusiasm was contained in such a small space of time.

"Then we went to Munich to record and it took us just 18 days to finish it. That's ridiculous for us because we usually take an eternity to finish an album."

The 18 days, in fact, included a black hour when Plant tripped in the studio and narrowly avoided re-opening his fractured foot. The cast had been removed in Los Angeles and he was rashly rushing around the studio when . . . "half way through the recording I fell.

"Now I can play soccer all day and run and swim and I still love to be very active, but here I was hobbling around in the middle of this great track when suddenly my enthusiasm got the better of me. I was running to the vocal booth with this orthopedic crutch when down I went, right on the bad foot. There was an almighty crack and a great flash of light and pain and I folded up in agony.

"I'd never known Jimmy to move so quickly. He was out of the mixing booth and holding me up, fragile as he might be, within a second. He became quite Germanic in his organization of things and instantly I was rushed off to hospital again in case I'd re-opened the fracture, and if I had I would never have walked properly again. It was a bit rash of me to bop around but . . . well, the track is brilliant."

So when would Plant be recovered enough to tour again? He became very serious. "Already I've surprised the doctors by recovering as much as I have in such a short time. They've called me a model patient and that surprises me because hospitals are really not my cup of tea. I mean, I was faced with a situation that dented every single thing I had going for me. My usual . . . er . . . sort of leonine arrogance was instantly punctured by having to hobble around, so I'm having to take my time. I don't want to rush. Every day I walk more and more without the stick and I'm going to need physiotherapy so I should think it'll be the beginning of the next soccer season before I'm running about again."

Plant had said his piece, and with the obvious questions about current affairs all answered, I suggested he look back and record the highlight of eight years with Zeppelin. He looked puzzled, "There have been so many amazing things, things that were once beyond my wildest dreams. I mean, basically I wanted to sing, and sing and sing.

"I mean, heavens, how could I ever have envisaged anything like this? Me and Bonzo had just come down from the Midlands to join a band. Jimmy was the experienced man and he'd been over here on the *Dick Clark Show* or whatever, so he knew we would end up at least on that level. I don't think Jonesy had been to the States before, but Bonzo and I had no idea. We even got lost in London.

"I remember when we played the Fillmore West in San Francisco, Bonzo and I looked at each other during the set and thought 'Christ, we've got something.' That was the first time we realized that Led Zeppelin might mean something; there was so much intimacy with the audience, and if you could crack San Francisco at the height of the [Jefferson] Airplane, Grateful Dead period then it meant something. Mind you, we went on with Country Joe and the Fish so we didn't have that much of a problem . . . how could we fail? But we knew the chemistry was there when we recorded the first album."

It wasn't until after the first album that Plant began writing the band's lyrics; he logically surmised that as he had to sing them, he might as well sing words he wrote himself. "You've got to live with them so it's a very personal thing. I did some of the lyrics on 'Whole Lotta Love' and some of the broader things like 'Ramble On,' but it wasn't until later that I really worked hard on them.

"I think that songs, like 'Kashmir' and 'Stairway' are far more relevant to the band now than songs like 'Whole Lotta Love' which we don't really do now anyway. Ever since it came out, 'Stairway' has been the most requested track on FM radio here in America which is amazing because it's so old now. That song was astoundingly well accepted and personally

I'm very proud of it, but I think 'Kashmir' is just as good, and so is the one that I fell over on when we recorded this new album."

The long-awaited Led Zeppelin film is now ready, according to Plant. "Yes, we're as happy with it as we could possibly be. It's been mixed in quad, and I'm not sure whether the Futurist Cinema in Birmingham is going to be able to handle that, but I would say it will be released about the same time as the opening of next soccer season, probably in August.

"The film features more than just us on stage. It has a few tastes of spice from everybody's imagination, sort of humorous in parts. It ain't all music, anyway, it touches on some of the things that make up the personalities in the group, Peter [Grant, manager] and Richard Cole [the band's ever-present tour manager] too."

Finally, I mentioned that of all the bands of their stature (and many, also, beneath them) Zeppelin seemed to be the only group whose members had not, at some time, veered off the rails to produce a solo album. Plant seemed horrified at the thought. "I think to want to do that, you've obviously got to be dissatisfied with the set-up as it stands.

"If you can't bring out everything that comes to mind musically with the group you are working with, then to go away and do a solo album and then come back, is an admission that what you really want to do is not playing with your band.

"If you have to depart from the unit to satisfy your soul, then why go back afterwards? I know I couldn't find anybody as musically imaginative as Jimmy, anybody who could play the drums as hard as Bonzo, and anybody who could play as steadily as Jonesy. It's as simple as, that."

JIMMY PAGE RADIO INTERVIEW

Alan Freeman | 1976, Capital Radio/DIR

One of the things that took up Page's time during Plant's recovery was tackling the movie, *The Song Remains the Same*, they had been making for nearly half a decade. Rather than making it a documentary as such and using live footage from throughout their career, the group decided to make it more of a "musical," a live performance with other elements. The film was shot primarily during a show in Baltimore and three nights at Madison Square Garden during the 1973 tour. That it took three more years to see the light of day is a story worthy of a movie of its own. Here, Page sits for an extensive interview with Alan Freeman—one of the first BBC announcers who played the band's music early on—talking about the film and the band in general circa 1976. —Ed.

Alan Freeman: Jimmy, this is your seventh album, is that right?

Jimmy Page: Mmhm, sure.

AF: And a live album, how do you feel primarily about—

JP: Wait a minute! Eighth!

AF: It's your eighth album?

JP: Yes, eighth.

AF: If you take . . . yes, this is your eighth album.

JP: Eighth album, yeah.

AF: This is your first live album, isn't it?

JP: Sure, yeah.

AF: Was there any kind of particular courage needed by yourself or Robert or Bonzo or John in putting out a live album as against—

JP: Well, let's say this: it is a live album primarily, but it is a soundtrack as well—

AF: Mm.

JP: Because we've got live recordings of concerts going back to '69.

AF: Mm.

JP: And Albert Hall and Madison Square Garden again, Forum in Los Angeles . . . and yet we haven't put them out before. In fact that there was a plan at one point to put out a chronological live LP which would've been fun, you know?

AF: Yeah.

JP: But what happened was the film came to be and obviously a sound track was needed so that's why it's come out.

[*"Rock and Roll" live version plays.*]

AF: Jimmy, as apart from being a rock musician, how do you feel about almost primarily being a film star virtually overnight?

JP: Oh! [*Laughs.*] I haven't even thought of it in that way at all. Just this sort of an appearance every now and again, really, because to me the whole thing's basically a musical.

AF: Mm.

JP: And there are different sequences, that make-up montage or whatever, but it's not acting as such, is it really? It's just appearing and showing your face, y'know?

AF: Tremendous, tremendous things have happened to you since 1968, really, haven't they?

JP: Oh did you, did you hear?

AF: Are there any, are there any particular moments between 1968 and '76 that you qualify as being the highs of your total career at this particular stage?

JP: Well, there seems to have been a build all the way through really, which sort of overwhelmed one. But I do remember one particular point that sort of knocked me flat on the backside, so to speak. We went to the States after not having put out an album for, oh, 15 months or something, and not having *been* there for a year and the very first two concerts—the first one being Atlanta, had like fifty three thousand people there, and the next one Tampa, Florida, fifty seven—and suddenly I thought, "My goodness, what's going on?" You know, it's crazy.

AF: Mm.

JP: You know, it's the way that people would really just flocking to us, this great royalty. And the promoters that were saying, 'Oh, they'll never do it. Nobody's gonna turn up because they haven't put out any product.' And then suddenly it occurred to me that we had a different sort of following to most people. That sort of thing is obviously very warming to the heart and soul.

AF: Were you very happy initially of having a very different following from the usual following that follows rock musicians?

JP: I think really, it's—as far as groups and audiences go, groups—especially on live shows—they're as good as the audience, really. I've seen some shows were the audience has been better than the group. They're fun to see sometimes.

[*"Whole Lotta Love" LP version plays.*]

Let's put it this way: pacing the history of the group, so to speak, an album will come out say its the third LP, and there was a lot of more acoustic numbers, there's more of a total mellow mood than, say, on the second LP which is like a rock 'n' roll one, really. And the critics gave it a bad time because they expected us to be in sort of groove that they could relate to, and it was too much of a shock. But we'd gone through changes within our own lives and it reflected in the music, as it has up to now, sort of thing. It's very encouraging to find that the audience as such can relate to those changes and still be with you, you know that's really great.

AF: Do you ever worry about an image that you have of being extremely heavy?

JP: What, that sort of heavy metal thing? I think we managed to erase that sort of tag and cliché that got put on us, round about the fourth LP, to anybody that was still doubtful about us and wondering, really, where we were at and everything. When "Stairway to Heaven" came out, they realized that we were a group that was intent on change, and there was far more of a dramatic quality within our particular brand of music then say the, so to speak, heavy metal groups. You know, there was more going on within it, within the framework.

[*"Stairway to Heaven" plays.*]

AF: At the advent of Led Zeppelin, did you feel that it was—that in fact when you developed some kind of musical policy that it was very important that your audiences came along to identify with the particular thing that they thought Led Zeppelin was? Was that a worry at all?

JP: Well no, no. In putting the group together in the early days, you know, I had an idea of what I thought was right within those days. And it didn't really matter whether it was going to happen or not within one's mind because it was so enjoyable to be playing. One could feel the chemistry was there even from the very first day of rehearsal, that there was something there that was definitely gonna be really good and really enjoyable to be part of. We never really bothered to purposefully engineer situations which we knew would be acceptable to audiences.

AF: Yeah, surely.

JP: In fact, it's been quite the reverse, because we've come under the hammer a number of times just by sticking to one's guns, and I mean, if one is to compose a certain amount of songs at one time and they've gone on an LP—because basically an LP is only where you've been, collected at that time—obviously one knows if it's got a change of direction or something. Maybe a group could say, "Well wait a minute. Wouldn't it be better to sort of stick to the usual policy?" To keep it—keep the identity and everything there. But we've never done this. It's obvious we've been very highly critical of what we do. But, as I say, the band is a band highly intent on change and ever onward pressing as far through the boundaries as one can possibly go.

AF: Yeah, sure. Jimmy, do you think there was any kind of reason why audiences developed almost overnight for Led Zeppelin, particularly in America? And America happened first, didn't it really?

JP: Well, yeah. I think the fact was, we were a really, really a very earthy group and as I've said, there was this exploratory thing going on within music and at that time there was a lot of apathy setting in. And—

AF: What kind of apathy actually?

JP: Well, it was just at the end of the San Francisco phase, *well* at the end of that. And I remember that's in fact where we really took off, in San Francisco and Country Joe was on the bill and one of the other San Francisco groups. But they'd been like a sort of—almost like a brotherhood of groups over there and they just knew these people inside out and suddenly somebody was there *really* laying it down and of course they just reacted to it. The news of that particular night just spread like wildfire over the States and suddenly we'd made our mark.

AF: Did you have any particular plan of attack—of musical attack or musical structure?

JP: No.

AF: On your very first night in America, before an American audience?

JP: Well no, only the amount of stuff that we'd written. I mean, to be quite honest, I'd been in the Yardbirds before and obviously I had a lot of ideas that I'd built within the Yardbirds that hadn't gone down on record or anything. And I worked on those a little bit as a framework, 'cause obviously when you start a group, you've got to have a certain amount of framework unless you're going to do other people's numbers.

AF: That's right.

JP: And there was obviously overtones of *that*. And of course that erased itself as we continued.

AF: As a member of the Yardbirds, were there burning musical policies within you, itching to get out that you that you couldn't fulfill with the Yardbirds?

JP: Only at the end. Keith Relf, bless his soul now, he got so . . . just generally brought down with things. I don't know what it was, really, underlying everything. I remember him saying one day that the magic of that group left him, or it had disappeared, when Eric Clapton left the group, and that had been many, many years before I joined. Obviously that was the way he saw it, the band, and it was just very, very difficult. It was an uphill struggle to keep the message and they just didn't want to know anymore. So, eventually that band split.

AF: Yeah, sure. How did you actually physically go about the formation of Led Zeppelin? The finding of them?

JP: Well, I wanted to carry on, for sure, because I had a certain amount of faith in what—there were certain reactions that we had experienced in the States, with the Yardbirds—and other places: Australia, too. And England, too. Terry Reid was a singer that I remember having worked with on a bill—the same bill, I should say.

AF: And an enormous singer, too.

JP: Yeah. It was the Rolling Stones' tour. When you think about the bill now, it's amazing. There was Ike and Tina Turner Revue, Terry Reid with a band then called Peter Jay, Yardbirds, and Rolling Stones! I mean you just don't get bills like that.

AF: You're right.

JP: But anyhow I tried to track him down and lo and behold he'd just signed with Mickie Most! But he suggested Robert, so I tracked up to Birmingham and saw him and I was amazed! Then suddenly it all started to come together in a very short time. It wasn't like a year's process of getting it all together, which seems to be the usual thing. I mean, the whole thing came together within a matter of weeks.

AF: When you—when you first saw Robert, can you remember your immediate reactions?

JP: Yes, I do! I do! It's very strange actually. I thought there must be something wrong with this chap because if he hasn't got on, because the quality of his voice was really striking. I thought it must just be a personality thing, you know what I mean? He'd made records, and this, that, and the other in Birmingham, and I just couldn't understand what it was that had held him back.

[*"Good Times, Bad Times" LP version plays.*]

AF: When you actually first approached Robert Plant, and spoke to him, can you remember what you said to him?

JP: Well, I made reference to Terry Reid and I said, "you know, I think we should get together. If you're interested come down and spend some time at my place. We'll go through some sounds and records, see if we've got the same idea, if we're sympathetic, and take it off from there."

AF: He was very aware of you of course, was he?

JP: Yeah, yeah, he knew . . . that there was this thing of forming a group. And then, well, we seemed to get on pretty well. He was very blues orientated and of course I'd been through that as well. And then I played him a lot of other things which I planned to sort of attempt. Like "Babe, I'm Going to Leave You," and things like that, which, you know, had a totally different approach to the way that it had been originally done by Joan Baez. And he seemed to be into all of these things, so it was definitely on.

AF: It was a real jelling of—

JP: Yes, it was, for sure.

AF: Apart from his ability as a singer and obviously as a musician, did your personalities jel? I mean, did you like each other, or—

JP: Yeah, it was that. The only thing was I remember is he was doing a lot of West Coast music which I had an aversion to, [*laughs*] a lot of Buffalo Springfield . . .

AF: What didn't you like about it?

JP: Well I just—you see, there was an image over here of the West Coast scene and actually, a lot of the bands were very, very poor. The quality was terrible. I could understand how he'd become involved in the whole—you know, this great sort of family image of groups, all together and everything. But I wasn't about to tell him that in fact the music was awful—

AF: [*Laughs loudly.*]

JP: —when you actually heard it live.

AF: When you had this feeling yourself about the quality of West Coast music—

JP: Ah, now what you're saying, you see, what you're saying is broadcasting an opinion where I wouldn't normally do that. I'm only doing that [*laughs*] within conversation here. For instance, say—I'll give you two examples: Buffalo Springfield; I saw them and they had this sort of balance, obviously the musical content was totally different. But say, the Hollies, if one of us saw those in the old days, perfect balance, perfect harmonies. Everything was completely routine, right down to the line, and that's how they were.

AF: Yeah.

JP: Now I went to see Jefferson Airplane, and they began their set with a bass solo which was absolutely phenomenal and these were in the days of the whole apex of the San Francisco scene and I thought, "Oh my God, this is going to be just the end of the world when they start!" And then they began playing and I couldn't believe it! They couldn't keep time and it was awful.

AF: [*Laughs.*]

JP: It was just a great shock, you know. It was only a personal opinion. You see, as far as the social importance of it, the social attitude, it was very important, and so I'll really only speak to you on the musical point . . .

AF: Yeah, sure. After Robert, you gathered . . . ? For Led Zeppelin, for the completion of Led Zeppelin?

JP: Well, John Paul Jones is somebody that I've worked with many times before—

AF: Yes.

JP: —on studio dates, and John Bonham, Robert had played with . . . and fought with, in the past and he was playing with Tim Rose at the time. So we went to see him. He was—well there were *two* people, actually. It was B. J. Thomas* from Procol Harum and Bonzo. Those were the two possible drummers, you see. But when I saw Bonzo, I knew it was definitely on, you know.

AF: When you think back . . . when you think back to your very beginning of a thinking human being, [*laughs*] which is sometimes very hard, and sometimes—

JP: Yesterday.

AF: —sometimes, yes, sometimes very clear, and very easy, to assimilate almost immediately. I mean, I remember you being musically sparked off by Chuck Berry, etc. Is there something even before that?

JP: Yeah, yeah, "Baby Let's Play House" by [Elvis] Presley.

AF: Yeah.

JP: That was the record.

AF: Even before Elvis Presley? Can you remember the musical thing—

JP: Oh, what, the first sounds that I ever heard?

AF: Yes, exactly.

JP: Oh, um . . .

AF: Do you get upset (inaudible question)?

JP: Well, obviously I feel for the people that who have made the music [*indecipherable*]. It's just a shame because you know that those people got

---

*Actually, Page is referring to B. J. Wilson, not the "Raindrops Keep Falling On My Head" guy.

something going for them and sooner or later it's gonna die out because they cannot sustain themselves. I mean, I liked, still do in fact, Bert Jansch. At a particular point of time, he was such an innovator and unsurpassable. But he just didn't get that general acceptance that you needed to really fire imagination and creative stability that can keep you really going. He took the backseat. That happens many times. I was a bit disappointed in the group Kaleidoscope in the States. They were brilliant, probably the best band I ever saw in the States. And another one, Spirit. They just didn't get as big an audience. Sooner or later, it's just going to filter out. [*Inaudible.*] Stan Kenton, I should think.

AF: Yeah.

JP: Those sort of things. But the . . . but the first rock 'n' roll thing that really turned me on, when I went, "Wait a minute, what was that?" was "Baby Let's Play House."

AF: It was the very first time you'd heard it—

JP: Yeah, and that's when I wanted to play, after hearing that. I thought, "I want to be part of this."

AF: What did it do to you and—

JP: It just sent shivers up my spine.

AF: And how did you devise in your own mind, how were you going to become a part of this?

JP: Well I didn't know. I didn't know at all. But I was just determined to sort of be part of it, y'know?

AF: Yeah.

JP: Because in those days, there just wasn't anybody playing.

AF: That's right.

JP: You know, you may find one other guitarist, but he'd live about thirty miles away somewhere.

AF: Had you at that particular—

JP: There was no textbook, let's put it that way.

AF: There was what?

JP: No textbook, which there is now.

AF: Sure. And you at that stage picked up any kind of instrument?

JP: No, no, not really. No.

AF: And you had been—

JP: Not at all. I would say no, not at all, no. And I think somebody had given a guitar to the family, just soon after hearing that record and then I . . . you know . . . it just sort of happened, this obvious sort of process, of one day finding somebody who knew how to tune it and then one was away. And then went through the rock 'n' roll phase, you know, Rick Nelson's guitarist James Burton being a great influence, Chuck Berry, and then B. B. King . . .

[*Twelve-bar blues montage, ending with Led Zeppelin's "You Shook Me" plays.*]

JP: All these things started to unfold. The different styles of guitar, electric styles anyway, and then becoming involved in classical music and really seeing the guitar as such an important instrument and the so many different approaches and styles that could be employed upon it.

AF: When you got your first guitar how did you go about developing some kind of style?

JP: Well, I don't know 'cause I wasn't really doing very much at that time.

AF: Did you buy a book with chords on it or did you figure out runs and work things out for yourself?

JP: I don't know! I think I probably just used to take all my frustrations out on it, like some people smash plates against walls you know—

AF: Yeah.

JP: Uh, it mainly it was just trading things with other people. And then once one got an ear, you could hear it from records. You heard a record and you think, "Well, [I'll] try and play that solo." And that's really how it started, and I think all the other guitarists are the same way too. You started to try and emulate what you heard and before long you could play those solos note perfect. So then you started to follow these good guitars so to speak, that could play, in your own mind, well—

AF: Yeah.

JP: And each time that next record came out, you'd buy it, and a day later you'd have the solo off. So bit by bit, that's the way one taught themselves.

AF: Can you remember some of the frustrations that made you want to play the guitar?

JP: All I remember about it was taking it in school and having it taken away every time it was seen.

[*Both laugh.*]

JP: Yeah, I tried to hide in the corner of the field to practice. I used to try to play the thing all the time, to improve. It was sort of confiscated and given back at the end of the day. [*Laughs.*]

AF: Do you, do you think it detracted from, let us say, your possible academic skill?

JP: No, no not really. Certainly not to the degree that obviously that the staff would have thought. Nevertheless, I would've thought one of the most important things about this music is the fact that it wasn't taught, that it is self-taught, almost like a craft, and it has evolved through the young folk in the street and it's been a social statement, and so it should really go hand in hand with any academic subject.

AF: When you started playing a guitar, when you first heard Presley, was it the start of a personal rebellion against society? Against rules laid down as to what you should—

JP: No, no. No, no. It didn't really occur to me at that point that that's what they were—that's what was going on within the lyrics and everything.

That became evident to me through Chuck Berry, and what he was singing about. And . . . suddenly the coin dropped and I thought wait a minute, this is what he's saying on "No Money Down" and things like that.
Incredible, incredible stuff.

AF: When you heard "No Money Down," when you heard your first
rebellious lyric—

[*Jimmy laughs.*]

AF:—as against all you'd been taught to accept—

JP: "Oh baby let's play house, come on come on move in with me." I
mean that was 1956 or '57 or something. You just didn't do those sort
of things—live in sin. You would almost be excommunicated, won't you,
from society! [*Chuckles.*]

AF: Right. And you thought what?

JP: Well I—more so than actually the lyrical content, which hit me later,
it was the whole the musical thing, the fact that it was so vibrant and that
you could feel that they were . . . I can't just say they were enjoying what
they were doing. It was just a total commitment and involvement.

AF: At a cost—

JP: I mean I'll tell you one thing—at the end of "Mystery Train," of Presley's, you can hear him laughing, just on the fader. And it's just things like
that where you—it's like they know that they're doing something which is
revolutionary, almost, within musical fields, and they're just so into it and
committed to it. That sort of dedication and conviction, I can sympathize
with it. Especially when I viewed what was going on around me in *other*
sort of music. The Guy Mitchell days and things like that. It was just—it
just had nothing going for it at all.

AF: Because it is quite amazing, you know, when I interviewed Robert
at one particular stage of my career, I asked Robert about music and the
initial spark that made him go "What hey? What?" He talked about Rosemary Clooney and "Where Will the Baby's Dimple Be," which, I think
that if you actually played to a public in 1976, and people associate with

it being in the initial spark for Robert Plant, they would be absolutely, totally blown away. I couldn't believe it!

JP: I'm blown away, too, to be honest.

[*Alan laughs loudly.*]

JP: Yeah, that's incredible. [*Laughs.*]

AF: It really is very odd indeed. Do you ever look back upon old records that in fact you liked, say, in your very early childhood—do you listen to them now and say to yourself "My God, what was that all about?"

JP: No, I don't actually.

AF: Or do you—do you still find validity in them?

JP: Yes I do, especially in Jerry Lee Lewis and people like that, Eddie Cochran. You've gotta remember how young they were at the time and you, say a record like "Mean Woman Blues," something like that by Jerry Lee Lewis, seventeen, eighteen years of age. Who's doing anything as good as that nowadays at eighteen years of age? No one! That's the point. And they were innovators, they were doing something new. They weren't relying on a whole textbook that's been laid down for them. Now these people, something just happened to that particular point of time. This whole thing blossomed within a whole collective number of people, and it just came out. And that that's the thing that knocks me out: when you think that the ones that we sadly lost, like Eddie Cochran, Buddy Holly, died before they were, what were they twenty-two when they died?

AF: Yes. Very young.

JP: I mean the amount of stuff that they laid down! And then when you think of the music that, say, has been laid down in the time between, and you look at the younger ones, say the pre-twenties, there's not that much there that hasn't—that hasn't really been really cribbed right from blues or from rock and that's the thing that impresses me.

AF: Jimmy, is there a danger, let's say in 1976, of trying to be, or in fact not even trying but being overcreative?

JP: No, I don't think so, no. I think that from this point on there's gonna be some amazing composers coming through, which will be on a par with Wagner and Stravinsky. It's going to come, but the thing is we needed this breakthrough to take away the confines of what is being laid down as this discipline that must go with the . . . I call it the intellectual classical music.

AF: Yeah sure.

JP: And there's a great point that's been forgotten that, before the Victorian times, when the copyist, who wrote the music down, chopped out these very important parts there, there were basic steps for improvisation [*inaudible*]—

AF: Yeah.

JP: But as we know it now, classical musicians don't improvise. They lay down as the textbook. Well this is it, these barriers are being broken down and I think you know we're ready now to see some really fine, superb, lyrical composers coming through.

AF: And in fact, I think in—in the coming years very important major works.

JP: Well, this is what I mean.

[*Modern classical montage plays.*]

JP: Well, this is what I mean. It's scratching the surface, *almost* at the moment. I reckon another five years it's gonna be—the younger people are gonna be coming through, and then it's really all gonna happen you see. Obviously it's gonna be an exciting musical heritage to be looking forward to.

AF: Yes, um—

JP: And it's needed, all this sort of this great fight that went on in the '50s and the '60s and everything else to open up the doors, almost, to let the flood come through. To break down the barriers.

AF: Right. How much influence do you think that the Beatles exert on today's breakout of rock music generally?

JP: Um, I don't know about today. Certainly at the time that, you know, the social question posed by the Beatles, the long hair and stuff . . . it was called long hair then, um . . .

AF: But of course, with long hair we've only recycled again, haven't we, in fashion?

JP: Well exactly, yeah—

AF: Yeah, sure.

JP: And it got cut off because of the wars and lice and things like that—

AF: That's right, yeah.

JP: But I think at the time, certainly a lot of change went down, a lot of social barriers . . . again, they broke down and crossed barriers even though it may have been resented afterwards. But nevertheless, they helped to do that and over the years that they were very musically prominent and productive—and I think there's a classic example of a group who shows so much development and maturity within their music within the years that they were together. I mean, let's face it, the early records aren't, you know, they're nothing to really write home about. But by the time they were at *Magical Mystery Tour*, I mean it was really going somewhere. Really.

[*"I Am the Walrus" (by the Beatles) plays.*]

AF: Would you, as an eminent musician of the '60s and the '70s, advocate that in fact there is possibly room in our educational structure where people who are gifted, immensely, musically, have no need to go through all the academic studies that they may never use? Stick and tie to the music, really from the moment it's discovered that they have ability?

JP: Well, you see, now you're posing your own question of education, the whole system of education—and let's face it, as it is, it's pretty much a waste of time. As far as my own education went, I didn't really receive *any* education, as far as I'm concerned, until I went to an art college. Then somebody sort of started to talk to me as an individual, as opposed to a number in a room. And—

AF: What did that do for you, Jimmy?

JP: Well the point was, you see, at that time, within art college, there was debates and people could discuss between themselves and with the staff certain aspects of what you were doing. Whereas in the classroom or school, you shut up! That was the sort of thing that was just totally hopeless and it wasn't long before you realize that the people that were supposed to be teaching you were fools. However, in these times now, I know it's changed quite considerably. You've got some damn good people within the education system. But as I said, as far as my own education, that's how it was. And as far as just concentrating on one particular thing, no, I don't think it's a good thing. I think that one should be versed within all subjects but not necessarily to the degree where it's almost a specialist degree. Like I've said, trigonometry, calculus, I've never used any of that since I left of school, nowhere at all.

AF: Do you—do you feel, though, it was a waste of time learning? Has it helped you at all musically?

JP: Well, no, not in the way that it was taught, though I have in fact become familiar with Pythagoras' approach to music and scale which relates to mathematics. But that, I mean, I could've approached that with possibly two or three years of school tuition in mathematics—

AF: Yeah.

JP: The whole thing was just a silly status game to get as many G. C. subjects as you could, and if you were a bright spark you'd get on to university at the end. It's difficult. Obviously this is the sort of thing that can be debated, somebody could raise or throw a lot of points at me to pooh-pooh the argument. I'm just thinking about friends of mine who were at school and the ones that carried on through university, most of them carried on through a very, very heavy academic system and went through the whole bit but at the end of it, they ended up doing something entirely different that didn't relate at *all*, in one possible way to any of the education that they'd received.

AF: When you think back on going into music, do you feel that you've missed anything else by being so preoccupied with it?

JP: Well, no. I've been too lazy, that's the only thing, the honest thing. [*Laughs.*] I should've been more dedicated to it. I mean it would've helped a lot if I learned to read music in the early days—so that I could write it down and tabulate it, so that when one started to explore, say, Indian music, which has a totally different concept of tabulation to Western music, one could have been able to relate to that instead of having to fight one's way through it.

AF: Jimmy, in relation to our previous talking about the composers of today and, in fact, the sprint towards, in the future, major works that will be acknowledged by the public at large right around the world, what kind of part do you think Led Zeppelin can take in this in the future?

JP: Well I don't know that they can take any at all!

AF: You don't?

JP: No, but I'm only thinking of the sort of experience that they must've felt the first time of seeing or experiencing like, uh, the Ring Trilogy*, you know, Wagner, or [*The Rite of Spring*] or the Ballet Russe and all these sort of things all tied up together. You know it's a whole environmental experience. I mean let's face it, we've lost a lot that we're not really aware of. In the old silent picture days, it wasn't a jangly piano, it was an orchestra in the big cinemas and there were sound effects. Now if you imagine some of those old Cecil B. DeMille epics, with orchestras and sound effects, it must've been amazing! But we just think that they had jangly pianos, but that was when it reached, you know, the suburbs. Hay-on-Wye. [*Laughs.*] What I mean to say that is this environmental experience with group musicians, this needs some sort of tablature and yet again it also needs a freeform expression of the individual where he can improvise, which has come through from jazz in the old days. As I say, it's gonna be coming, these major works. There's only a few us. There's only four of us.

AF: That's right.

JP: I'm talking about like orchestras.

---

*Jimmy Page is presumably referring to the *Ring Cycle* by Richard Wagner.

AF: What caused me to ask you that: can you see an enlarging of even the Led Zeppelin complement in order to take part, in the future, in major works that may be written by yourself or Robert?

JP: Well, I'm not so sure that's it's gonna be coming from us, I wouldn't imagine. If we can make any dent within that road that would be very rewarding. But the sort of scene that I'm thinking of is on the scale of great composers, and the way that I view the musical situation at the moment, I just don't think that there's anybody that's capable of doing it right now. But I think that it will be coming from the ones who are doing their dues at the moment.

AF: Do you have any idea how long duration this may take?

JP: Ah, I'd say about five years!

AF: About five years?

JP: Yeah! I might be totally wrong—

AF: And you may well be totally right because . . .

JP: I mean you found the jazz greats, Miles Davis, people like that, have used basically rock 'n' roll soul rhythm sections.

[*Miles Davis fusion plays.*]

JP: —Bernstein was getting very, very close to being very involved with rock musicians, and Stockhausen . . . It's all there it is this fusion going on . . .

AF: That's right.

JP: . . . and it just needs those sort of people, like we've been talking about, the ones that can really crystallize things and comes through those fields, [Leonardo] DaVinci, [*indecipherable audio*]. But take somebody like [Jimi] Hendrix, for instance, who tied up all the loose ends of, say, the different approaches of rock guitar, at least, and blues, and recording too, recording facilities and what could be done, and really, really laid it down. There's somebody that it's very sad we lost as far as I can see, because he was really doing some amazing work. Not ahead of his time, but intellectually way ahead of the others.

[*"Purple Haze" by Jimi Hendrix plays.*]

AF: Very ahead of his time, yes. I think that when the people view the film, *The Song Remains the Same*, there'll be many things they'll want to ask themselves. And the one that I'd like to ask you, and I hope you can answer in some degree, is what you think about whilst you're onstage playing incredible, intricate guitar.

JP: I don't.

AF: You don't?

JP: No. It sounds really pretentious—

AF: No, it doesn't sound pretentious.

JP: It's like a trance state. You don't think. The more you try and plan something, the more you're likely to make a mess of it. It's just like, you almost have to cleanse yourself almost of all thought and everything and then you start playing and it starts to jell with everybody else.

There is obviously certain amounts of direction that go on, but the more programmed it becomes, *before* going on especially, that the more plastic it would appear. There's so much improvisation that goes on and so many times where you'll just be playing something and the staccato rhythms will just fit . . . in total synchronization. And you'd have no idea that it was ever going to be doing. You'd look at each other and wink and you know that it'd never going to come again, but there it was. It's just one of those things.

AF: It's amazing that watching you visually in a performance, it is amazing that you are all so totally obsessed with the performance, and as you say, you seem to be in another world and then all of a sudden there's the sly wink and the sly smile and . . .

JP: Yeah. But don't you think that most actors themselves, when they're— I mean, I've always had the impression that an actor, when he takes on the part within a play, he becomes that person. I mean, it's just a total involvement within it. That's just how it is with your instrument, you're just totally involved in it. It's just a part of you, an extension of you and yet sometimes maybe you're an extension of *it*. It's like driving a car, you're part of the machine.

AF: Um-hm.

JP: You know, it depends on how you look at it.

AF: Outside of music, Jimmy, what are the issues that most worry you about humanity?

JP: Oh gosh, now we're getting to that. [*Chuckles.*]

AF: Are there many?

JP: Oh well it's—it's countless. I shouldn't really get into it.

AF: Do you think that the world has become a little overintellectual, collectively?

JP: No. I've sort of been rambling on here. It's basically having curiosity, questioning certain things within the classification of the group. As far as the world, it's hard to say what we're going through right at the moment. The fact is, this whole century has been documented. This is unique! It's difficult to know what kind of reaction the people are going to have to all of this. I mean they wise up much quicker. They can see corruption. It's exposed through the media and they know within a day as opposed to ten years in the past.

AF: It's almost a collective. . .

JP: So it's hard to know how things will go, and what incentive people would take from this sort of thing.

AF: Jimmy, the film *The Song Remains the Same*: it isn't just a documentary. It really is a feature film, isn't it?

JP: A musical. [*Chuckles.*]

AF: Is it a musical?

JP: Yeah it's a musical really.

AF: How about these sequences? Outside of the actual documentation of being onstage at Madison Square Garden, were they easy to devise, to get together?

JP: You mean the fantasy sequences?

AF: The fantasy sequences, yes.

JP: Well, each chap within the group had his own concept of what he wanted to do. It was like free license. And I'd like to do my fantasy, and that's how it came across.

AF: I thought there was a very poignant moment in the film when you reach the top of the cliff and looked up and see your face, which was very aged, very old.

JP: Well, at that point, it's just an anonymous person.

AF: Does the aging process worry you at all?

JP: Not at all.

AF: Not at all?

JP: Not at all! Provided I don't get senile. I will say, the one thing that worries me is arthritis—

AF: Because of your fingers . . . and your body in general. Jimmy, supposing that [at] some stage you develop arthritis, rather critically—and I pray God that never happens—and the Jimmy Page fingers could no longer work their magic, do you have an alternative in your mind?

JP: I haven't, no. It's amazing how one can adapt under circumstances. One of the greats of all time, Django Reinhardt, his gypsy caravan burned and he lost, what, three fingers? No, no, he was left with two fingers and a thumb. He carried on playing and probably produced his most important work after that. So, if it's just adapting to certain things—well, I don't know if I got that much will power, you know. [*Chuckles.*]

AF: Would you find it very hard, as a person, to be apart in your life, perpetually, from Robert, Bonzo, and John?

JP: I would be very disappointed because of the amount of—the alchemical quality that seems to be with us, and the sheer excitement it's generated within—even in rehearsal. It would be a great shame. It's a great energy source.

AF: What is the tremendous thing, for you, personally, and collectively as a group, appearing in front of American audiences?

JP: Well, the feedback.

AF: What is the difference, Jimmy, in the feedback? Say, from, America and Australia and England—

JP: Well, I think the American audiences, and it has to be said, they are far more involved in the musical scene. And by that I don't mean the image, but the creative side of it, what's being said lyrically. And what sort of barriers are being broken down, and boundaries: ones that are being smashed by the music. They're really more interested in that, I think, than some other countries.

AF: Yeah.

JP: And they really are totally, you know, involved—on an intellectual scale anyway—

AF: Yeah, surely.

JP: And that's how they sort of mark the people that they sort of can relate to, by what they're actually saying in their music and lyrics. Obviously a prime example of that is [Bob] Dylan.

AF: Yeah.

JP: You know, he just captured the imagination of an age.

AF: Would you be disappointed if an audience overreacted voluminously to "Whole Lotta Love," yet not—

JP: Well no, because you see the whole thing is, we don't do that anymore, that number. Obviously there comes a time when . . . obviously you put out so many LPs that you want to give a taste of this, that, and the other, and give as much contrast and light and shade within a performance, especially if you've been playing for a long time. Otherwise people will just get up and walk out, if it's all the same sort of stuff. And at this particular point, well, the last tour, so to speak, we weren't doing that. We just did a few bars of it and it went into something else; we didn't even sing one verse.

AF: Jimmy, when you come back to England from an American tour, or a tour in the world somewhere, and you come back to the tranquility of your family life, is there a void in your life at all?

JP: Well, it never stops. I never stop being involved, I'm always writing it or playing or doing something . . . it's there all the time. There's no escape.

AF: I'm very reluctant to use the word "image" because I didn't believe it is image oddly enough, I think there is an enormous reality with Led Zeppelin, the monumental impregnable thing that is Led Zeppelin. Do you think the public feel this way although they love your music?

JP: Well, first of all this whole thing about images goes, I think the star thing really doesn't mean anything. Nothing would make me choose to be associated with, say, the film stars in the '30s. Because it is more a part of the people's music. Everybody knows how you do it, and plays guitar, and can make music, and probably make music well. You can't currently see the "star quality," it doesn't have the ring to it as it relates to image.

As far as the public's vision of us, it would be mainly related to the dedication to what you're doing you know whether you're a dilettante, somebody on the periphery of the thing, or whether you have a total involvement in the thing, when the music is your life. And that they can tell by the output of what people do. And I think it probably took a couple of years in the early days, after that people realized that we were for real. Whether they like us or not, they couldn't deny the fact that we were there. It was definitely a presence of some description, you know.

AF: That's right.

JP: If you loved it or hated it, you knew that we were going to keep going and keep striving onwards, and that's the way it's been and always will be.

COMMUNICATION BREAKDOWN

"The last day of rehearsal was pure magic, and I thought, 'Right. We're going to have a go. We've got the stamina to play ten straight hours.' And then, all of a sudden, Robert gets tonsillitis!"

– Jimmy Page to Wesley Strick, *Circus Weekly*, June 1977

COMMUNICATION BREAKDOWN

First Plant's tonsillitis delayed Led Zeppelin's tour, then Page came down with an intestinal disorder that cut one of their Chicago shows short. But despite these setbacks, the come-back tour through the US (the first in two years) was going off very well. Then, a week before the tour was going to end, Plant's wife Maureen called to tell Robert that their son, Karac, was in the hospital with some mysterious ailment. By the end of the day, his condition was critical. Within another day, he was dead. The final shows of the tour, already rescheduled because of the tonsillitis, were cancelled, Plant caught the next flight home, and mourned his child. Though he had performed very few shows, the readers of *Circus Weekly* voted Plant the Male Vocalist of the Year in the 1977 Modern Music Makers Awards, perhaps in part out of sympathy for his loss, but also because he and the band were in the studio, preparing to once again "come back."

"By sitting down and taking up the challenge and realizing that we were, are, and will be capable of expanding, *that* can be the only hope for the future, and that's how we want to make our impression and be remembered. . . . A lot hangs in the balance struck, the relationship between the guy at the front of the microphone and 20,000 people, and we learned to soft pedal it carefully . . . We're not going to take the easy way out."

–Robert Smith interview with Robert Plant, *Circus Weekly*, February 1978

COMMUNICATION BREAKDOWN

"There's no question of the thing splitting up. I know Robert wants to work again . . . Everybody in the band is really determined to do the best for themselves and the people that have followed us up to now without bullshitting around. I just don't see how there could be a bad karma or whatever . . . I think it's just bad coincidence. Okay, one may say there's no such thing as coincidence, but I really feel that . . . I get such a charge from playing with everybody. It became so apparent on the last tour that it was something which I really needed."

— Jimmy Page to Angie Errigo, *CREEM*, February 1978

COMMUNICATION BREAKDOWN

Plant: Bonzo came over and worked on me a few times with the aid of a bottle of gin. He was the only guy that actually hugged me, that helped me at all. And he said, "C'mon, we're gonna go down to Clearwell and try some writing." But it had changed so much . . .

Jones: I think Robert was interested, but he was seeing things in a different light. He was wondering whether it was all worth it.

—Barney Hoskyns interview with Robert Plant and John Paul Jones, *MOJO*, June 2003

LED ZEPPELIN: SMILING MEN WITH BAD REPUTATIONS

Chris Salewicz | August 4, 1979, *NME*

Robert Plant and his family took close to two years to mourn Karac. By the late fall of 1978, the band got together in ABBA's Polar Studios to record. Though Plant had achieved some clarity, and the ever-taciturn Jones maintained his equilibrium, Bonham's drinking had become a problem, as had Page's dalliances with drugs. Where Page had been the linchpin of all the previous Led Zeppelin recordings, Plant and Jones found themselves alone in the studio with Jones' new synthesizer. The resulting album, *In Through the Out Door*, featured the first hit Jimmy Page had not written or cowritten for the band: "All My Love." It was a ballad awash in synthesizers that sounded like Led Zeppelin mostly because of Plant's unmistakable voice. By the summer of 1979, they were ready to play live again. They played two shows in Denmark towards the end of July in preparation for headlining a massive festival gathering at Knebworth, England during the early days of August. –Ed.

Of all the old superfart bands it is certainly Led Zeppelin who have been and still are the most reviled by the New Wave.

Whatever jerk-off socialite absurdities Jagger may have got himself into, The Rolling Stones have at least always had one of the prime punk archetypes in Keith Richards. The Who, meanwhile, have the ever perceptive Townshend, a man who appears to have gone through something of a personal rejuvenation that seems to be a direct result of his encounters with Punk.

For whatever reasons, though, the manner in which Led Zeppelin have consistently presented themselves has made the band's name synonymous with gratuitous excess. Even the almost equally guilty Pink Floyd have at least had the decency and sensitivity not to quit these shores just for the sake of saving money.

Don't sell your soul for silver and gold, as Lee Perry once said. If rock 'n' roll is essentially an all-encompassing roots culture, then obviously any musician who isolates himself away in some anal retentive tax exile life-style is neither responding to his obligations nor in harmony with those roots. Also, his initial purpose and motivation must be doubted.

The Clash's Paul Simonon summed up pretty well the total lack of respect that the new bands feel towards Zeppelin. "*Led Zeppelin???* I don't need to hear the music—all I have to do is look at one of their album covers and I feel like throwing up!"

In some ways part of the reason for the venomous loathing directed at the band is not just because they've let themselves down, but also because you know damn well that Jimmy Page at least—like many of the new Punk icons a former art student—certainly knows better.

"I've read about many records which are supposed to have turned me on to play rock 'n' roll," the guitarist told *Trouser Press* in September, 1977, "but it was 'Baby, Let's Play House' by Presley . . . I heard that record and I wanted to be part of it; I knew something was going on. I heard the acoustic guitar, slap bass, and electric guitar—three instruments and a voice—and they generated so much energy I had to be part of it. That's when I started."

Yet, in the same way that the death of the original, classic rock 'n' roll punk the previous month to the publication of that article could have been seen as a serious warning of the false paths and box canyons into which Babylon could misroute rock 'n' rollers, it also appeared at the time that perhaps the whole mighty edifice which Led Zeppelin had created itself to be was starting to crumble away as inevitably as the Malibu Beach Colony will one day slide into the Pacific Ocean.

By the middle of the year when the two sevens clashed, the belief that the whole Led Zeppelin operation had got it all more than a little bit wrong appeared to be being backed up by concrete facts. The band appeared to be in a state of crisis. In artistic terms they seemed to have reached an absolute nadir. Following the turgid *Presence* LP released in the Spring of the previous year there'd then been, six months later, the critically lambasted *The Song Remains the Same* film and double soundtrack album. Even this emphasis on double records—two out of the three LPs the band had put out since they'd formed their own Swan Song label had been two-record sets when none had been released before—suggested attempts to milk their market for all it was worth while fighting a rearguard action to forestall an inevitable end.

Perhaps more to the point, though, a general atmosphere of personal doom and gloom appeared to surround the once invincible Zeppelin. The lengthy US tour undertaken by the outfit in the Spring of '77 seemed ill-fated from the outset. It was to have been the band's first live work since 1975 when vocalist Robert Plant had been severely injured in a car smash on the Greek island of Rhodes during a year of British tax exile. It was ominous then that the first dates were cancelled when Plant developed a throat infection.

Jimmy Page himself was also believed not to be in a good state, an assumption fuelled by the news that the full time services of a doctor were being employed to care for the guitar hero. Now Page denies that the medic was there to look after him alone—"We had a doctor to look after all of us, period. It was a bloody long tour"—with the same ease that he dismisses reports of his having been wheeled around between gigs in a wheel chair—"I may have done that for a laugh—not seriously. No, no. That wasn't happening at all."

In addition, manager Peter Grant was said to be severely depressed following a divorce. Matters appeared to reach what seemed to be an inevitably unpleasant culmination when, following a Bill Graham–promoted San Francisco gig, one of the promoter's security men was badly beaten up by Grant, drummer John Bonham, and one John Bindon, a Zeppelin employee.

If some form of near-tragedy during the tour had seemed unavoidable, however, it was yet to wreak its worst toll. This happened some two weeks later when Robert Plant's five-year-old son died of a sudden mystery virus infection and the tour was abandoned while the grief-stricken singer flew home.

Now, of course, all these incidents may be seen as random happenings, as the chance intervention of fate. However, if you believe that you create your own fate and that human beings do not exist in isolation from one another and from the universe but are part of a far greater, interacting scheme in which actions and activities of the past create those of the future, then all this begins to look rather different.

Certainly, Jimmy Page's interests in the occult suggest that he should believe in such a cosmic overview. Indeed, there are those who would claim that it is solely down to Page's interests in these matters that such a tragic atmosphere has surrounded Led Zeppelin in its latter years. Personally, though, I don't think that Jimmy Page has inked a pact with Satan. To think like that is mere superstition—and that's taking into account certain rumors which have floated about the music business the past 18 months or so that there are even certain members of the Zeppelin entourage themselves who lay blame for these assorted misfortunes on Page's fascination with Aleister Crowley.

When it comes down to it, though, I don't really think that there's been some clear-cut metaphysical holy war of good and evil waged on the rock 'n' roll boards the band has been treading the past ten years. In fact, it's probably that outside interest which has kept the guitarist's head relatively together during the most successful years of the band. The occult, after all, is concerned with knowledge and plumbing one's own mystic depths for certain truths that are beneficial to the whole of humanity. Yes, of course, it can be used in a malevolent manner, but to view all occult activity as the work of the Devil is a red herring laid down by Babylon and therefore is the work of the tricky Devil himself.

I think, though, that Jimmy Page is very confused. His confusion doesn't spring from his occult interests but, I feel, from the very nature of Led Zeppelin itself and his position with regard to the band of which he is indubitably the leader. Indeed, when we met in Swan Song's London office on the hottest day of the year, it became glaringly obvious that

Jimmy Page was totally comfortable and, at times, positively exhilarated when talking about these extra-curricular activities.

It was noticeable, however, that when the conversation changed to the subject of his band he appeared frequently to find eye contact exceptionally awkward. Now, it's quite possible to blame that on the fact that in the isolated, self-enclosed existence in which Jimmy Page dwells he probably doesn't have that much verbal interchange with people outside his own sphere. Also, like many musicians who're far more at ease when living out their fantasies onstage, he may well be slightly nervous. Mind you, although a hermetic, fairly newsless lifestyle is part of the whole Led Zeppelin problem anyway, Page's behavior does suggest that he is not always totally convinced by his arguments—and Page is an adept in the art of being a media salesman for his band while at the same time revealing little about himself; check how many times the word "Knebworth" gets mentioned in this piece.

It's the very nature of Led Zeppelin itself that is the problem. Let's not mince words, it's always been regarded as a "heavy" operation. There has been a slightly odd vibe about it.

Now, of course, part of the nature of rock 'n' roll is the manner in which it allows people involved with it to live out their childhood Cowboy & Indian fantasies. So I don't know whether Peter Grant really is a figure from the fringes of the underworld or whether he just enjoys people thinking that he is. I suppose it doesn't really matter (though in a way it does) because I've no doubt, as Page himself comments later on, that certain of the behind-the-scenes music industry figures with whom he has to deal, particularly in the States, actually are dodgy characters. So maybe it gives him an edge over them. (Unless they're also all just living out their fantasies—in which case it all gets a bit complicated and self-perpetuating, and a bit pointless too.)

"The whole point of the bit in *The Song Remains the Same* film," Page tells me when I ask him about this, "where Peter plays a gangster, was just to send up all that and show how it was just a joke anyway."

Nevertheless, I counter, there was the slight problem with the security guy in San Francisco. There's certainly concern in his voice when he replies, "I didn't see it, you know, so I can't say exactly what happened. There were no million dollar law-suits put out on me, y'know.

"But," he continues, "you must remember that Bill Graham has a very heavy reputation, that all his security people have a reputation for heaviness. As for Peter . . . well, he's a very big guy and, if people are coming up to him all the time and calling him a bastard and telling him to piss off to his face, then he's probably going to react accordingly."

Alright, fair enough. But let's not forget that John Bindon is currently in Brixton either awaiting or serving a sentence for a subsequently committed manslaughter—an incident which wasn't connected in any way with Led Zeppelin. Once again, judging from his reply to being reminded of this, there's no doubt that this genuinely troubles Page, much more out of real concern for Bindon, I feel, than for any unhappiness about him being linked with Zeppelin. It's a pity I forgot at the time, but I'd like to have also got his reaction to Nick Kent's claim that John Bonham once threw a drink over the hapless writer for a negative review.

But that's by the by, I suppose. It seems more important to tell the guitarist that, whether he's aware of this or not, an oft-expressed opinion on Led Zeppelin has been that the problems Robert Plant has faced have been something of a karmic backlash that Plant, as the most accessible and open band member, has had directed towards him.

Page seems very shocked by this. "I don't think that's so," he replies slowly, almost as though slightly dazed, "if what we were doing was really evil then . . . then I suppose we'd just put out lots of records and try and make loads of money . . . I hope that's not so."

Sometime about the middle of last Friday morning I'd had a call from the Swan Song press office. Could I arrive maybe an hour before the interview was due to begin? That way I could be given an earful of the new Zep waxing. I can't pretend the idea exactly thrilled me to the bones, especially in the light of the last studio album, *Presence*, which I find utterly unenjoyable. If I felt the same way about the new, as yet untitled, LP, it could mean a chilly start to an interview.

By lunchtime, however, this potentially awkward situation had been resolved by Jimmy Page himself. A further phone call passed on the information that the guitarist felt it pointless for me to hear the record as it was, apparently, "a separate entity"—from what I'm not certain. Obviously it did cross my mind that maybe he was thinking the same way as myself and saw a little gain in the songs being numbered some time before the record was even released.

Perhaps predictably, when the record did come to be mentioned he was full of enthusiasm for it. The titles of the new numbers are: Side 1—"In the Evening," "South Bound Suarez," "Hot Dog"; Side 2-"Carouselambra," "All My Love," "I'm Gonna Crawl." The Knebworth bashes will feature "at least two songs from the new album plus several numbers from previous LPs that haven't been performed live in the past. What can I say?"

I was also asked for some idea of the sort of questions I'd be asking. As I was at that time deciding on these for myself I couldn't really help out there. Besides, would this not have detracted from the natural spontaneity of the occasion? I was, however, informed that questions about the death of Plant's son and about Aleister Crowley were strictly taboo. This did not augur particularly well, especially when, while waiting for the assistant editor chap from the *Melody Maker* to finish his rap with Jim, photographer Adrian Boot emerged from that session to inform Pennie and myself that Page was "doing a Chuck Berry" and ignoring most of [Michael] Watts' questions. The guitarist was also apparently none too happy about Boot's snapping needs.

In the event, of course, Page gave Pennie plenty of pix-taking time prior to our encounter. Also, as far as our interview went, Page and I just started talking conversationally (but not before he made a rapid attempt to flog Knebworth) rather than adhering to any strict question and answer form. This situation lasted for much of the interview.

Page was drinking pints of lager from a straight plastic glass and chain smoking Marlboros. So was I. It was probably down to a combination of the booze and the hot weather, but the conversation quickly became very speedy. Maybe we were also blocked on the carbon monoxide fumes wafting through the open window from the early evening rush-hour traffic three floors below on the Kings Road.

What with the roar of London Transport Roadmasters stopping just past the offices and the constant rumble of jets on their way to Heathrow overhead, it was often hard for either of us to make out what the other was saying. Though his enunciation is very clear indeed, Jimmy Page's soft Surrey accent—the family business is Page Motors in Epsom—makes him perhaps the most quietly spoken interviewee I've ever come across. Even so, I was pleased that he didn't pull the slumped-out whispering wimp number that I'm told is one of his favorite interview techniques. Not once, I think, did he lean back on the couch on which he was seated next to the window.

No doubt exacerbated by the booze intake—Jim is fond of the odd tipple, I'm told—perspiration poured off of his forehead in large drops, frequently lodging for a few moments in his close-to-shoulder-length hair. Coupled with the collarless striped shirt he wore, he didn't look very different at all from when in the late '60s he laid down the ground rules for the classic pre-Raphaelite, faintly androgynous British rock star. He actually looked younger than when I'd encountered him a couple of years back. Only the lines around his sometimes troubled eyes gave any indication of age.

The Selling of Knebworth began right from the very outset. I don't think you really like doing interviews, do you, I ask?

"Well [laughs] it depends. I don't mind if the questions are alright."

You look incredibly well.

"Well, I was looking forward to . . . to Knebworth, actually. We've done a lot of rehearsing and checked things out. We've actually been down there and worked things out relative to the actual site."

It must seem odd with it being such a long time since you've played onstage . . .

"Well, it did at first . . . But then again it's like a natural amphitheatre, so I should imagine it's actually quite a good gig to be at. I went to Blackbushe, but that was a bit of a sea of bodies. But it was great to see Dylan."

Phew, that was close. The Zim to the rescue. At least we can talk about Bob Dylan for a while. This might be handy. Maybe if I mention to Jim that I met Dylan last year when he went to an Alton Ellis gig at the 100 Club and that he told me how he preferred the vibe in England to that in the States, and also in Germany from where he'd just returned then we can get on to this matter of Punk and The New Wave without too much discomfort.

Instead, though, Page mentions his surprise that Dylan had played in Nuremberg. "I couldn't believe him doing that. They played the place where they had all the big rallies. He must have come out of there feeling very strange. I know I would and I'm not even Jewish."

He hasn't heard of Dylan's conversion to Christianity. "Oh, that's very interesting. Especially after that Nuremberg thing. When did that happen? Quite recently?"

Oh, about six months or so ago, I think.

"We met his mum once, actually," Page tells me, "it was about the third tour and we were in Miami and this typical Miami woman comes up with the spectacles and tinted hair bit and she says, 'Oh, I hear you're a group. My son's a singer. You've probably heard of him—Bobby Dylan. He's a good lad,' she said.

"The strangest thing she said of all was that he always goes back to his . . . you know, the school turn-out when they got their degrees and things. He always goes back to that . . . Which is obviously a side of Dylan that many people would be actually shocked about. He's probably very orthodox in some areas where you expect him to be very bizarre and anarchistic."

Logically, I suppose, the matter of meeting Dylan at a reggae gig leads to discussion of matters Rastafarian. Jimmy Page is far more au fait with it than I would have expected.

"Yeah, it's very interesting: the Lost Tribes of Israel and all that. It was at the time when Haile Selassie died that I wondered 'What's going to happen now?' because there is this big thing that he's invincible and that he would never die but obviously," he chuckles, "he could give up his bodily form if he wanted to, that was the loophole.

"But it *is* fascinating."

We talk about Egypt for a minute or two. Page's trip to Cairo had, indeed, been the subject of some quite splendid rumors. On the first leg, I think it was, of that last ill fated Led Zeppelin US tour it was said; that one night he'd been watching TV when the screen became filled with flashing lines. Immediately, so the tale went, he cancelled the next dates and flew off to Egypt. The conversation didn't lead into my mentioning that and, besides, I'm fairly certain I once read a fairly thorough refutation by the guitarist of that story.

Thoughts of Cairo seem to make Page feel very happy. "I didn't want to come home," he smiles, "it was so good. I didn't go for long enough, though. I went at the end of an American tour and with every day I was there family ties in England were pulling more strongly. I just thought 'Oh, I'll be back soon' and haven't made it yet. I'd certainly like to see The Valley of the Kings near Luxor.

"I haven't been to many Arab countries, but I've been to Morocco and there and in other hot countries there's this constant hub-bub, but in Egypt it's just so tranquil. It really is quite an experience. Let alone the pyramids."

Equinox, the Kensington occult bookshop that Page owned and which specialized in the works of Aleister Crowley, is closed these days. The lease expired and besides, "It obviously wasn't going to run the way it should without some drastic business changes and I didn't really want to have to agree to all that. I basically just wanted the shop to be the nucleus, that's all."

His interests in the occult haven't in any way diminished, however. "I'm still very interested. I still read a lot of literature on it."

I mention the last time I'd gone past Equinox a small sticker that someone had placed on the door had attracted my attention. "For the real truth about the changes in the Church of Rome," it had read, "write to the following address." The name and address of a priest in Mexico was given. We talk about the Rasta belief that it was at the Pope's insistence that Mussolini invaded Ethiopia in order to prevent Haile Selassie organizing the Christian church in such a way that would have reduced the Catholic Church to the second largest Christian church in the world.

"I know the Pope definitely blessed the bombers going to Ethiopia," says Page, "that's a fact. My lady went to the Vatican. She said it's like Fort Knox, a completely separate state. A highly guarded treasury. And they have all these links with suspect organizations . . .

"The whole image of the Pope being borne around St. Peter's on a throne doesn't even bear thinking about. They had some program on TV about the Vatican and they got through to one of the heads of the business division. And he was asked if it wouldn't be an act of faith to give all this wealth away—if your faith was sufficiently high and strong then obviously this wouldn't really affect the church. But he was dumbstruck. So obviously," he laughs, "he didn't have the faith."

Jimmy Page has had some involvement with the community politics up in Scotland where he owns Crowley's former home, Boleskine, on the shores of Loch Ness. After, against much opposition on the local council, a harbor wall utilizing raw materials had been built under the guidance of the local job recreation scheme. Page, largely as a result of previous similar activities within the community, was involved in the final unveiling ceremony. The local Labour man, he said, jumped on the platform at this event in a predictable attempt to make political mileage.

"I just got up and said 'I'm not here for any political reasons whatsoever but just from my own endeavors as an untrained musician. And it's just sheer determination that's been employed here against a good eighty per cent of the council who wished them to have no encouragement whatsoever.'"

One is not particularly surprised that the politician appeared to milk the event for his personal aggrandizement; it is the nature of such a breed of people to behave in that manner, no matter what political party they belong to. It does seem interesting for a moment, though, that, when I inquire as to whether the council members were operating in a truly reactionary manner, Page seems a little uncomfortable when he realized that I regard "Reactionary" as being synonymous with "Tory."

Maybe that's by the bye. Page has, after all, been involved up there in other battles with officialdom. "The Hydro board in Scotland were putting in this scheme which wasn't of benefit to anyone except for a small percentage of local laborers—although, in fact, most of them were being brought in from places like Manchester and Liverpool.

"What it was going to do was pump power at peak times to the South. It wasn't going to benefit the Scots at all. And for this they were going to put pylons up all over the place and mess up the loch. There were no pylons there whatsoever before. And I just didn't think it was on. For them, of course it was purely a financial investment. It was really a revelation to see how these things go on. So corrupt.

"But we managed to force a public inquiry whereby it was put under the Secretary of State. They really put you through it at those things. It's like a court of law. They try and throw so much mud at you. Although it does seem that in London these days if they're pulling down buildings to put up new ones they are trying to keep the old facades. It makes it much more palatable. At least you don't get things like that too much," he waves in the direction of the World's End council housing project.

"But," he continues, "so often people just get apathetic and think there's nothing they can do. At least sometimes you can uncover a bit of unsavory business that's going on. I do really care about these things. I don't particularly go around doing a load of public campaigning, but both those things were there on my doorstep. On the other hand it can help if it is on your doorstep because it gives your protest much more credibility."

By now I'm feeling a bit confused by Page. I rather like him. Even though I have the reservation that when he pointed out of the window at the housing development he was perhaps more concerned with aesthetic niceties than with the bureaucratic contempt and condescension with which it is decided that human beings should have to live in such monstrosities, it still seems that his spirit is very definitely in the right direction. Yet how is this compatible with the lumbering dinosaur that his rock band has become?

Well Jimmy Page is essentially a conservative person. He is also a Conservative person. A Capricorn, he has much of the rather hidebound love of tradition and status that can be a characteristic of that sign. He could do with a bit of overstanding of things. He voted Tory at the last election, he says. "Not just for lighter taxes—I just couldn't vote Labor. They actually stated that they wanted to nationalize the media—so what possible criticism of them would you be able to have?"

Although I believe all politicians of whatever creed to be largely self-seeking egotists, I point out that, as the City already has effective control of both Fleet Street and ITV, then the Tories already control the media. Page doesn't seem that convinced.

He voted Tory at the previous election too, he tells me. "I voted Conservative then because I believed in Heath. And I still believe that Edward Heath was a very honest man. He was too honest to be a politician. But I suppose that's politics."

Actually, I'm not surprised Page rates Heath, a man who was certainly superior to the deplorable [Margaret] Thatcher. Page has much of that same laissez-faire mercantilist attitude to life that Heath favored. The only problem with espousing that particular political philosophy is that it can permit you to piss on a lot of people in the name of freedom. I'm not suggesting that Page necessarily behaves in such a manner, of course. A better clue to his attitude to such matters comes in the same series of *Trouser Press* articles from which I took the Presley quotation.

He's talking about the song "Hats Off to Harper," on the third Zeppelin album:

"[Roy](Harper's) *Stormcock* was a fabulous album which didn't sell anything. Also, they wouldn't release his albums in America for quite a long time. For that I just thought, 'Well, hats off to you.' As far as I'm concerned, though, hats off to anybody who does what they think is right and refuses to sell out."

In the light of this quote, and another, more ambivalent one relating to the New Wave, I ask him if he'd ever in younger days inclined more to anarchy.

"Well," he replies with due deliberation, "anarchy's alright if you can see where you're going afterwards. Although I don't see any point in destroying things just for the sake of it. It's the easiest way out. It's hard to have an optimistic goal and strive towards it—that's really hard work. But, yes, anarchy can certainly be an answer to a situation if there's no other answer."

Quite understandably the Establishment always presents anarchy as being very negative when, in fact, it's more concerned with a positive spirit . . .

"It's difficult," Page nods, "at the time when Hitler came into power in Germany during the '30s, he appeared to be stabilizing the economy and giving people more work and was emerging as a very patriarchal figure. The Germans felt that everything was going to be alright. Yet underneath was this fundamental plan—be it evil or whatever.

"And at the time when Hitler came in there'd been a form of anarchy existing. So, yes, you just have to see at the end of the day what's really gone down."

And so, boys and girls, we come to that section of the interview when we talk to Jimmy Page about New Wave music. Even though he seems to consider Dire Straits a New Wave band, Page is perfectly aware that there are punk bands and punk bands who aren't really punk bands. He has heard The Clash and appears to rather like them. He warms very much to the mention of Ian Dury. "Yeah, he really imparts such a great feeling, doesn't he? Makes you feel so good. That was certainly the first thing that struck me about New Wave music—that it was sheer adrenalin pouring out. Real energy just tearing to get out."

But how did the beat group Led Zeppelin relate to it? They were presumably aware of what was going on. I remember Page and Plant going down to the Roxy to check out The Damned once.

"We were aware of it," he nods, "but it's not . . . I mean, music is like a 360 degree circle from which some people may drop out to let others come in. And there are obvious examples of that—say, the feeling that Free generated and which was replaced by Bad Company. Also, the raw blues, going back to the early Fleetwood Mac days. Well, now you have George Thorogood. And Herman's Hermits are replaced by The Bay City Rollers.

"Bands like us and—I hate to say it but . . . The Floyd . . . we're off in our own little bits. It's always open for anybody who's really raw and earthy and who makes sheer rock 'n' roll music. Even though much of the New Wave had the political content . . . I mean, The Damned—I was absolutely amazed by the power that was coming out of them. Though they didn't really fit into the New Wave movement, as such.

"Nevertheless, there are categories. But it's all relative; anyone who plays good music and is expressing themselves with an instrument or on vocals has got something to say. It just depends whether you can relate to them or not. And that also depends on whether your musical tastes are narrow or very broad."

And certainly from what you're saying you would claim to be able to relate to New Wave . . .

"But I can also relate to classical music—and you wouldn't find *them* saying that . . ."

Oh, don't count on it. I'd think you'd be very surprised.

"Oh . . . well . . . good . . . well, they ought to."

I think if you went round to the places of a few punk musicians you'd be very surprised by the width of listening material you'd come across . . .

But equally, and I think this must be said, of all the Old Fart bands certainly Led Zeppelin, for whatever reasons, are the most loathed . . .

"*Really????*" Jimmy Page sounds quite startled.

'Fraid so . . .

"*We-e-ell* . . ." he pauses for several moments, ". . . people write to us, you know, and a lot of younger people who I'd never have expected to have got into us have said that they got really fired up by the energy of New Wave bands—and they still like New Wave bands—but they got interested in the actual musical content and wanted to go one step further which is how they discovered bands like us . . .

"And . . . uhh . . . I'm not sure whether that's going to last or not," he laughs, not altogether confidently, "but it's quite good if you can keep turning people on."

Didn't you ever worry, though, over the past months while you were making the new record and planning the Knebworth thingy that it might be like throwing a party for which no one turns up?

"Yeah," he laughs again, more confidently this time, "but no—because when we'd finished our album I knew at the time that it didn't matter if it didn't come out for nine months afterwards because I knew that I could rely on the fact that Led Zeppelin *hadn't* dated—the actual identity of the band is still there. There's a fresh approach which can still give it an edge.

"I had my reservations at one point about playing a date like Knebworth. But in the end it all went hand-in-hand with the LP. When that was finished I did actually stop and take a breath and I thought 'No, it's alright. We've moved on sufficiently to be able to see the next horizon' . . .

"We're not sounding complacent, I hope. There's a lot of hard work still to come obviously. It's not like we've felt we had to change the music to relate to any of the developments that've been going on. There's no tracks with disco beats or anything. But I think some of the numbers are some of the most immediate we've done anyway.

"Like I say it's not a new musical form but there is still something very fresh about it."

But, prior to doing it, were you not perhaps apprehensive? I'm not talking about how you'd do in the States, where obviously you're still going to sell loads of records. Presumably it still does mean something to be still respected in your own country . . .

"No, sure. We were concerned about it being good. And we were pleased to hear that the actual environmental area of the stage was good. But if the playing hadn't been feeling right, I would've worried. But that feels alright so I'm pretty sure it'll be good . . . "

But I wasn't really talking about Led Zeppelin To Play Gig Shock Horror. I was actually wondering whether maybe you were concerned you might make this platter and no one would buy it in Blighty . . .

"Well, we were worrying about too many other things at the time. I was worried more about whether we were still going to jell. Having felt something special towards the band for that amount of time and still wanting that feeling to be there without . . . without being quite sure it would be. But then we got together a few times to play and could see that it still was . . . well, it was a very good feeling.

"The LP really is a bit of a by-product. To me Knebworth is far more important . . . Because people can buy the LP and we won't see how they're reacting to it. But, he laughs, "I will at Knebworth. The LP's a frozen statement which can be always referred to, but Knebworth's going to be different."

Do you actually see much of each other?

"No, not really."

Robert Plant and John Bonham don't live in London, do they? They live up in the Midlands, yeah?

"Yeah, they live pretty close to each other. No, I mean, we don't have monthly get-togethers for the sake of it."

Now look, you've been involved in community politics up in Scotland, but should it necessarily stop there? For whatever reasons, Knebworth is a huge gig. But a couple of weeks back The Clash—who are quite a big band these days; their last LP entered the charts at number two—did a couple of gigs for orphans. Have you ever thought of doing something like that?

"We did that—about the third year of the band. And we got fucked for it. Previously we'd played places like Manchester Free Trade Hall and the

[Royal] Albert Hall and we'd had all these letters saying 'Why do they let their fans down? Why don't they play the clubs anymore?'

"So we said 'Yeah, let's play clubs!' And it was chaos because people couldn't get in. So the next barrage was 'Why are they so selfish doing small clubs?' So the supply-and-demand thing becomes a problem. So from then on we were faced with a sort of dilemma. But then again it became a challenge to see if we could try and make it work on a large scale.

"Don't get me wrong. I'm the first to admit it can get too large, but something like Knebworth can be a challenge because you know it's worked in the past. But we couldn't do that. We tried—when we'd done the LP, we were trying to work out where we could get in and play. But then we thought, 'Are we running away from something?' And we weren't.

"It was almost like denying what you were. And you've got to be true to yourself."

Hmmm . . .

"I know what you mean, but it just gets impossible to do unless you play four weeks at the Marquee."

But you're supposed to be a rock 'n' roll band. Why don't you just *play*? Look, it's not that hard: The Clash did two dates at the Notre Dame off Leicester Square. It wasn't publicized—only by word of mouth. They played new songs, tried out new sets, made money for charity. So it obviously is feasible . . .

"I'll give you an example of a band that I don't think could play the Marquee: Status Quo."

What an odd thing to say. I'd rather have hoped that Page would consider Zeppelin to have a slightly different awareness to the dandruffy riffers. But of course, I counter, they *could* play it if it wasn't announced as such . . .

This is ignored. "And I know they've played Wembley—so, if fifteen percent of those people tried to get in, it would be chaos. So you see the problem."

Not really . . .

My next question is inter-related with a lot of things about which we're talking—just how important is the institution of the music business to you? Do you feel that Led Zeppelin is part of the great corporate conglomerate?

"Obviously. Yeah. But to them you're only a matrix number. We sweat the songs out, though."

But is it down to just letting the shareholders have bigger dividends? You're a musician, right? I think that's what you feel you are . . .

"Yeah, but don't you see that we're only as good as whatever we come up with? Say we didn't put out another LP . . . Well, we've probably done really well for our record company but, if we did that, they'd probably come right down on us. I think it's probably really ruthless behind the scenes. It comes down to things like Kinney owning car-parks and things."

You imply, I suggest to Page, you don't care about the record company. But, by acceding to those demands to play those huge venues—and in a way they're just perpetuating the whole thing . . .

"I see what you mean—though I'm not sure you see what I mean. The problem is trying to supply the demand of the people who want to see you. You can only gauge that. I mean, it is a rather nice feeling deciding on this huge date and not being quite certain that there's enough demand and then finding you can play a second one the same size.

"Anyway, at this point in time we just want to get back into playing music. And we will be doing other dates. I don't know where: not necessarily in England. We've been talking about playing Ibiza—just getting in there and playing. Just so we've got a chance of trying out new ideas and new riffs and arrangements and songs."

So do you not think that Led Zeppelin has become part of some huge thing that's got totally out of hand?

"Well, if it has it certainly won't in the future because we'll be playing places like Ibiza."

Was there a stage that you reached with Led Zeppelin when it became important just to make money?

"No. Never. No, because we've been our own worst enemies over that. But you wouldn't see it like that now. But at the time we put out our fourth LP we had the worst reviews of anybody. And to put out an untitled LP at that time was considered professional suicide. It probably doesn't seem it now. But then . . ."

Are you very materialistic?

"Well, I dunno. Yeah, I suppose I am a bit. But on the other hand, even though I have material possessions, the most important things are books, studios, and records. If I had to get up and run that's what I'd try and take," he laughs.

Do you think that you personally have perhaps unavoidably become caught up in the Whole Great Swell?

"I don't think I have. No, no. I haven't. Otherwise I wouldn't have opened up a bookshop. I'd have opened a boutique or something where I could really make money. Equinox was never designed to make lots of money but just to tick over so it could publish books."

Do you think people have ever taken advantage of your having such desires?

"Quite probably. Yes," he replies in a certain tone.

But you're a reasonably happy human being?

"Well," he seems momentarily uncertain now, "as happy as the next one." Then he gives a spirited chuckle. "I think I'm pretty fortunate in that I'm able to do what I'm best at. It's a pretty fortunate position to be doing what you really want to do and turning people on."

But you've made tapes with people like Keith Richards. Obviously you must have wanted to make records with other people . . .

"Yes, I did. But in the end it comes down to playing with the people who I really like to play with."

Jim now tells me that he must leave in a few minutes as he has to meet Charlotte, the lady with whom he lives and by whom he has a five-year-old daughter, Scarlet. This is unfortunate. We were just getting going, it seemed to me. It's a pity also that interviews with members of Led Zeppelin are inevitably set in the anonymous Swan Song offices, thus providing writers, and therefore readers, with little comprehension as to how the band members actually live. Even the Stones seem to have woken up to the fact that both journalist and band benefit from less clinically set-up situations. But I suppose that's all part of the Led Zeppelin problem anyway.

There were many other things I'd like to have asked Page: what have he and the other three band-members done for the last eighteen months or so, for example? Whose records has Page been playing recently? Why doesn't Swan Song sign any hot new acts?

As it is, though, I only have time to touch on some of the more, uhh, "controversial" topics that are raised in the first section of this piece.

A large part of the original strength of Led Zeppelin surely stemmed from the energies and ideas Page derived from his lengthy session work in the '60s. Now, though, it seems that all that has been exhausted and there is little new creative input to replace it. Page's views on the music business show a startling lack of original thought and clarity. Mainly, though, they suggest, as I mentioned earlier, confusion. And it's by perpetrating that state of chaos and confusion that the music business is able to persist in its Babylonian and fatuous desire to be part of the vast dehumanized, cynical corporate state. Grrrrr . . .

On the other hand, compared with certain of his contemporaries, maybe he's not faring too badly. I ask him if he feels isolated and cut-off. He claims not to feel that now, though admits to having been in a pretty weird state round about the time of the band's fourth LP.

"Of course," he adds, "it can do very odd things to you, the whole guitar hero bit. Look at Eric Clapton. Peter Green . . . Well, that's the obvious example. Jimmy Page: well, I don't think I'm doing too badly," he laughs, with a fair amount of confidence.

COMMUNICATION BREAKDOWN

"We did nothing for a year and a half. . . . I tinkered on the village piano and grew so obese drinking beer that nobody knew who I was . . . With what happened to me, I thought I might not have anything left to give . . . But I found out I've still got it—from here to the moon."
— Robert Plant to Jerene Jones, *People*, August 27, 1979

COMMUNICATION BREAKDOWN

[The pre-Knebworth articles were the last any member of Led Zeppelin did for a long while. On September 25, 1980, as the band prepared for their first extended tour of the US in three years (after a summer tour through Europe), the lead zeppelin dropped suddenly from the sky. As the music critic for the *New York Times* reported:]

"John Bonham, drummer for the rock group Led Zeppelin, was found dead in bed yesterday in Windsor, England, near London. He was 32 years old."
—John Rockwell, *New York Times*, September 26, 1980

COMMUNICATION BREAKDOWN

"We wish it to be known that the loss of our dear friend and the deep sense of undivided harmony felt by ourselves and our manager, have led us to decide that we could not continue as we were."
—Swan Song press release, December 4, 1980*

---

*Since a lot of hard rock magazines had three-month lead times, Led Zeppelin reportedly remained on tour in several publications. News items about how well the tour was going appeared in publications like *Hit Parader* as late as spring 1981.

PART III

RAMBLE ON

"When Led Zeppelin expired, I was left petrified—alone—thinking, 'What on earth should I do? Is there even a need to do anything, and can I work being inspired by only those guys?' ... [The first tour] was the ultimate boost, not so much to my confidence as to my raison d'être. It made me see I could now carry on."

— Robert Plant to Philip Bashe, *International Musician and Recording World*, September 1985

PLANT BACK ON TRACK

Liam Lacey | June 26, 1982, *Globe and Mail*

For the two years following John Bonham's death, all that existed in the press about Led Zeppelin was speculation. The band members remained silent, even to the point of discussing whether Led Zeppelin would disband or remain together. By December 1981, Page began working with former Yes-men Chris Squire and Alan White in a project they called the XYZ band. Initially, Plant was supposed to sing in it, but he only lasted one rehearsal—he was still too distraught about Bonham's death to embark on a new musical project. About midway through the summer of 1982, however, public sightings of Page and Plant became more frequent. Page released the soundtrack he wrote and recorded for the sequel to the movie *Death Wish*, called (appropriately enough) *Death Wish II*. However, he didn't seem to want to talk about it. Meanwhile, Plant was reportedly recording with folks like Phil Collins and Cozy Powell, among others. —Ed.

As the elevator slides open, the group of journalists, photographers, disc jockeys, and hangers-on steps out into the hotel hallway looking both directions at once in an effort to figure out the numbering systems. A door to the left swings open, and a head, blond hair neatly trimmed at shoulder length, appears. "Come straight through gentlemen," says the newly-coiffed Robert Plant, in an English circus barker voice. "Come see how many people it takes to run a record company." He waves them into the room, then retires into the bedroom, while about a dozen and a half record people mill about, sipping at green Perrier and Heineken bottles, introducing themselves to each other and sending small teams of journalists into the bedroom for interviews at half-hour intervals.

Curiosity is naturally high. The Led Zeppelin singer has not offered interviews promiscuously in the past, and the Toronto visit is only one of two stops in North America; the other was in New York; and before this, he has given only one previous interview to the British heavy metal fanzine, *Kerrang!*

The four members of Led Zeppelin, probably the biggest selling rock group of the seventies, were the founding fathers of the still flourishing heavy-metal movement, and the originators of every nuance of the heavy-metal style—not only Plant's stratospheric vocals and Jimmy Page's self-parodying excesses on lead guitar, but also their habit of trashing hotel rooms as well.

Led Zeppelin's 12-year existence came to an abrupt end in September, 1980, though, when drummer and wild man, John (Bonzo) Bonham was found dead in Jimmy Page's home, killed by a massive drinking bout. The remaining members of the band have been in seclusion since, except for an ambiguously worded statement released in December, 1980, which explained that, out of respect for the group and for Bonham's family, "we can no longer continue as we were."

Plant, who is in his early thirties, sits crossed-legged on his bed, looking tensely bemused and tautly fit in his white T-shirt, ready to fill in the answer a little further. "Come a little closer," he suggests. "I don't have a very loud voice," which, as ridiculous as it sounds, happens to be true.

The first question, of course, is about the future of Led Zeppelin and Plant answers in a tone of patient weariness: "I think I've gone through this before. Led Zeppelin was a four-man band, we played as a four-man band, and recorded as a four-man band. And now that's over."

He acknowledges that there may be "scraps of tape" around, but "Led Zeppelin will never play or record again."

The point of his current talks with the press, after "eight or nine years of not talking to anyone," is to promote his first solo album, *Pictures At 11* [sic]. The title, he says, "is about information—as in the news."

He is also concerned about "clearing up the image we had over the past few years," and, he adds, "I kept in the closet because I was overweight. Now I'm feeling fit again."

At the other inevitable question—about the recent accusations from California evangelists that secret "satanic messages" were subliminally buried in the music of a number of rock songs, including Led Zeppelin's "Stairway to Heaven," Plant looks even more pained: "Negativity of any kind is best to be avoided. Even asking that question encourages this kind of negative speculation.

"How could anyone sing backwards? It's complete bunkum. It can't be done. It's like one of those Superman-Bizarro comics you used to read as a kid where everyone did everything backwards and said 'thank-you' when they meant 'please.' Only Americans could come up with something that ridiculous. Nobody in Europe would understand the point of doing anything backwards; it's hard enough to do it forwards.

"I didn't mind for us so much," he adds magnanimously, "but why on earth did they pick on poor bands like Styx? Next it will be ABBA, Pat Boone, and Rosemary Clooney. Why don't people take up swimming or squash if they're bored?"

When someone mentions the Moral Majority movement, Plant responds: "I have nothing against the Moral Majority. I have no loose morals; I'm clean in my body and my mind, if you like. Do I sound like Billy Graham? Well, I don't mind."

He skirts over his reaction to Bonham's death, only saying that he kept to his home for a while, playing his rockabilly tapes and avoiding performing. But eventually, a rag-tag collection of musical friends convinced him to go back to the stage, playing other people's songs in bars and travelling in a van, under the name The Honeydrippers. After two or three months of playing, and recording bits of songs with guitarist Ronnie* Blunt in his spare time, Plant decided to do his first solo album, using mostly unknown musicians, with the exceptions of his drummers, Phil Collins and Cozy Powell.

"When I started, I was like this weak-kneed, pale-faced, scared kid, but Phil and Cozy insisted on making it fun."

Asked if he was ready to leave Led Zeppelin's Swan Song label at the time, he quips. "I was ready to change everything in my life, but I ended up just changing my socks . . . I think it's worked out. It sounds like record liner hype to say it, but I'm proud of what I've done. I still view myself as competitive—I'm not an icon. I don't accept this attitude of 'Oh yes, he

---

*Actually, Robbie Blunt.

was from the Led Zeppelin era, but that day's gone though he can still play a few sports and get about.'"

Plant also mentions that his 13-year-old daughter has recently adopted his fascination with rockabilly. "She kissed Brian (Setzer) of The Stray Cats right on the lips after a concert, so she's been gone on it ever since. She makes me feel like I've spent this last 12 or 13 years just wasting my time. We've reversed roles; I steal her Human League singles and she steals my old Sun rockabilly records."

If such a domestic picture seems a little tame for one of the seventies' high priests of excess, Plant has plenty other of other disappointments in store for the Led Zeppelin faithful. Nowadays, he plays on a local soccer team to keep fit and has recently taken up squash.

"I like doing things that are healthy," he says, fondly patting his stomach. "It seems that everybody I know these days is doing sit-ups."

COMMUNICATION BREAKDOWN

"It was extremely hard for me to even consider working with other people. I know that might—sound corny, but it really was. Initially, I didn't want to play with anyone. And then the Honeydrippers got me at it again . . . Robbie (Blunt) and I had been playing in a band called the Honeydrippers for quite a while, playing out our fantasies with Rhythm and Blues with a horn section. It was enjoyable, and we went around the country appearing in small clubs."

–Robert Plant, *Kerrang!*, 1982

COMMUNICATION BREAKDOWN

"I'm just dying to get out there. It'll need some time to get it together, because I don't want to do anything that isn't 100% terrific. It would be silly to even think about going on with Zeppelin: it would have been a total insult to John. I couldn't have played the numbers and looked 'round and seen someone else on the drums. It wouldn't have been an honest thing to do. No, it'll be new ideas, new material, and I'm ready to do it. Music is more than just notes and chords. To me it's an ongoing process that can never die."

– Jimmy Page to Andy Secher, *Hit Parader*, July 1982

——— COMMUNICATION BREAKDOWN ———

"I thought it would be a misdemeanor to put out *Pictures At Eleven* and then whoosh out on the road with eight or nine songs, because the way it is now about for me and for Jimmy if you like, is that if Jimmy decides to work shortly, which I think he probably will, then neither of us are in the position where we should try out and bring some more life out of "Communication Breakdown," and "A Whole Lot of Love [sic]" and "Stairway to Heaven." So it had to be, for me as an artist if you like—I can be roughly called that, or a rough artist—I really got to do it all over again and that is the challenge. I mean, without that challenge, I might as well go to Vegas and do cabaret, you know, and there are a lot of rock-and-rollers doing that. I've just been there."

— Robert Plant to Mark Goodman, MTV, July 1983

ROBERT PLANT WITH DENNY SOMACH, FIRST US SOLO TOUR

Denny Somach | August 1983, NBC *Friday Night Videos*

About a year after Robert Plant released *Pictures at Eleven*, he released a second solo album, entitled *The Principle of Moments*. Although recording was not a race for him, as he had told Chris Charlesworth years earlier, he did have incentive: with two albums' worth of material, he could do a serviceable live show. To blow the cobwebs out of his voice, he warmed up onstage during the December 29, 1979, benefit Concert for Kampuchea. In anticipation of his 1983 tour, Robert spoke with *Friday Night Videos'* Denny Somach; this portion of the interview ran on the program. −Ed.

Robert Plant: I've been very fortunate. I have quite a reputation which allows me to please myself whether I want to talk to the media or be a part of the whole circus or not. I don't think I ever tried either to make myself a public figure or to avoid the publicity. I think my philosophy, for what it's worth, and I'm not particularly a wise or versed character, is that my true worth to anybody at all or even to myself as far as anybody knowing who I am, or where I am, or what I do, is really only relevant when I am onstage singing.

[*Photograph montage of Plant performing in concert plays.*]

People have often said that my voice sounds, or has been made to mimic instruments and to sympathize with instruments and in fact extend the art of singing on that level. I've found personally that I had to do that because there was so many instrumental sections with Led Zeppelin that I might easily have taken a break and had a can of Mountain Dew while some of the solos were going on, so I guess to remain part of the band I used to extend the vocal, in as much as I could.

I started playing R&B and singing R&B in clubs and bars and stuff which most English people did who were in their midtwenties like me. And then, it was only a matter of time before I was a member of different blues bands and stuff or playing the American black R&B.

[Photograph montage of Plant performing in concert rolls while "You Shook Me" plays.]

All of a sudden I teamed up with Jimmy and Jonsey and Bonzo and just kept playing the sort of stuff that had always influenced me. I came over to America and found that it was like bringing coals to Newcastle really, as we say. It was like taking the goods and taking them back again.

My involvement in the Kampuchea concerts was completely out of the blue, really. I just went along to see the show, had a chat with Dave Edmunds, and was seduced into singing "Little Sister."

[Footage of Plant performing "Little Sister" at the Concert at Kampuchea plays.]

It was also funny to come off stage and Elvis Costello turned to me and he said, "I never, ever thought I'd hear Dave Edmunds do 'Stairway to Heaven,'" which was quite funny.

I was going to say there was a conscious sort of pattern of thought to incorporate video as you actually write the song, but it would be sacrilegious to do that because the song is all powerful whereas the video is a delicacy.

[Footage of Plant's video for "Big Love" plays.]

If I were to think back to all the antics and the sort of good times I've had and all the experiences that I've gone through, and try and compare myself in 1968, when I first came to the States, to now, in 1983, I would say that right now, I'm probably a lot calmer and a lot easier going. A little more studious, but equally as eager to make my point.

FROM HOT DOG TO BIG LOG: ROBERT PLANT HITS THE ROAD

Dave DiMartino | October 1983, *CREEM*

Robert Plant hit the road and people hoping to see him perform Led Zeppelin songs were sorely disappointed, but people who just wanted to hear what he was up to were thrilled. Not that it seemed to matter much to Plant, who just wanted to rock 'n' roll. —Ed.

"Why don't you take off your *clothes*?" asks Robert Plant, grinning, clutching at the bare white towel wrapped around his waist.

Sheesh.

It didn't seem so funny at the time, but Plant's polite query, addressed to the three of us—one interviewer and two record company VIPs—seemed very logical, considering that we were soaked to the skin by a late afternoon downpour. The Scene: a super-swank hotel suite at the Plaza, in Manhattan, the sort of room where three "Magic" Johnsons might stand on each other's shoulders and still not touch the ceiling. Plant, himself soaked by the same sudden shower, grinned at the irony as he went to the room attached to change.

When Big Guns like Robert Plant come around, you can bet it isn't just to make funny jokes. Our rendezvous signaled just one more stage in Robert Plant's re-emergence since the demise of Led Zeppelin—the point somewhere in the chain of events between where he starts recording again (as he did with last year's *Pictures At Eleven* comeback), begins a massive international tour, and finally—who knows?—maybe goes off and lays low again for a while. It's a cliched cycle perhaps, and certainly one his former band had no small part in establishing, but nevertheless *de rigueur* for Robert Plant circa 1983, veritably part of the gameplan.

Yet it isn't all bullshit. Plant's new career as a solo artist has none of the air of desperation, of floundering, one might expect from an artist of his stature who's trying to start all over again because of, say, financial necessity. Whatever need Robert Plant has to go it alone, it reflects instead the finest and noblest sort of motivation: the man simply wants to *create*. From him you'll get none of the pathetic last-tour-*ever* spiel that's indelibly marred the Who's continuing "career"; you can also bet that Hal Ashby won't be making a movie of his current tour, or that we'll be seeing Robert Plant *designer jeans* in 1984. Say what you will about Led Zeppelin and the excesses of the '70s, but Plant's contributions and intentions have never been less than of-the-highest-order since that very first Zep LP emerged back in 1969.

Think about it: of all bands, Zeppelin could have exploited their audience much more than any other—yet in retrospect there really hasn't been that album they'd just as soon forget about, that tour undertaken (or album released) for purely financial gain so screw the fans. Last year's *Coda* seemed more an interesting artifact than a grapple for dollars and, personally, left me admiring the band for not milking their audience dry with other, more sub-standard material, many years earlier. Zep—and obviously Robert Plant—maintain a dignity and pride that very few of their contemporaries can still decently claim. They have yet to compromise their name.

In speaking of his new solo career, Plant attaches importance to the concept of "carrying on." He apparently means it on a personal level more than in carrying on the "Zep tradition"—in fact, says he, he initially worried *Pictures At Eleven* leaned "too heavily" on Zeppelin, until many things, not least his bringing it around to Jimmy Page to hear, convinced him he was very much his own man.

Most important is his current songwriting partner, guitarist Robbie Blunt, an integral part of that album and *The Principle Of Moments*, the newest.

Blunt's rise to prominence with Plant is interesting, in theory, because on paper he's basically just another British blueser. He spent some time with Jess Roden's Bronco (their second album, *Ace of Sunlight*, is an unsung '70s classic), flirted with Silverhead, and went off with Chicken Shack's Stan Webb to form the short-lived Broken Glass (one LP, Capitol), which also featured the Keef Hartley Band's guitarist/vocalist, Miller Anderson. I bring all these dire Anglo connections up for a reason: there are more British bluesers than I'd care to count who've marked time in bands, both bad and good, that ultimately *didn't make it* like Led Zeppelin did. The Hartley Band, Colosseum, Chicken Shack, Savoy Brown, oodles more related to John Mayall and thus Fleetwood Mac, etc., all of them deriving their music from American blues and R&B and attempting to forge "new" music, some of which is remembered, most of which isn't. Plant, obviously, shares all these roots—yet for him something *clicked*, something he's been able to share with Jimmy Page and now Robbie Blunt—who might've just as well languished in obscurity until the Plant connection. It's this tradition Plant is ultimately carrying on, taking his British blues boom roots of the '60s and making them relevant in the '80s; Eric Clapton, Jeff Beck, Fleetwood Mac, and very few others have managed to make viable music in the '80s, yet of them all, Plant—without ever really changing direction, or winding down, or taking that one hit and recycling it to death—has managed to stay relevant almost 20 years on.

He's been very lucky.

Motivation?

"Well," says Plant, "you do it to please yourself. This . . ." he gestures at me, at the hotel room, "this is a forced situation, which you go through all the time and I go through very seldom. But with *Pictures At Eleven* and *Principle Of Moments,*" he grins, "these are new days. This is a new approach, and I'm really proud that the things are really that *good*, you know? So I'm prepared to do this, to gain some communication with some people."

Confidence?

"I didn't know if I was leaning too heavily on Zeppelin the first time around. I didn't think so, but . . . I didn't know. I hear my voice—I mean

I've heard it for *years*, right?—I hear my voice and I always listen to see if there's the right amount of *top*, whether the graphic equalizers and limiters sound right. I listen to it in a *technical*, as well as a sort of . . . soulful manner. And after Robbie puts on the tenth or eleventh guitar part, say, I no longer hear it as a song. I hear it as you might when you take an X-ray. You can see *bones*, you know?" He laughs.

"So it was a boon to take it to Jimmy. It was also very emotional. This one," says he, referring to the new LP, "I haven't had *time* to knock on the big gates. This time I just kept going. My self-confidence is on a different level. I *know* I can do it. Before, I didn't know if anything was going to happen."

Something does happen on *The Principle Of Moments*. Robert Plant has, for better or worse, demonstrated that he has no real need of Led Zeppelin to make the inspired music his former band made. It's a surprisingly good album, the sort that sounds better with each hearing. Like Zeppelin's, it's got a "timeless" air about it, making it difficult to pin down any sort of realistic time-frame about it—it might've been recorded 10 years ago, and that's meant as a compliment.

Don't know about you, but I don't think Zeppelin have gotten just recognition for the really spectacular production work on their albums. To non-fans, "Led Zeppelin" is a two-word cliché basically signifying what the band sounded like on two historic tracks—"Communication Breakdown" and "Whole Lotta Love"—yet this remains the fault of those hundreds of HM bands who took that sound and based entire careers around it. Zeppelin rarely descended into cliché; they were witty, caustic, and *always* striving for new paths of expression. It showed from the beginning, became increasingly clearer on *Physical Graffiti*, and probably came to a head on the underrated *Presence*, on which may be the band's finest moment: "Achilles' Last Stand," 10 minutes and 26 seconds of Plant, Page, and John Bonham using the HM cliché they almost singlehandedly devised and taking every screeching excess and tension to new, sometimes ridiculous, heights. From that point onward it became ridiculous to speak of Led Zeppelin as sounding "like" anything at all. And, to make it as concise as possible, this quality has carried through to *The Principle of Moments*, and that's pretty much it.

Though the Zep albums weren't exactly received with open arms by the press—isn't it almost the cliché of clichés?—*Eleven* got a surprisingly warm reception. Plant himself feels he was treated fairly: "In Britain, I got *one* bad review, from one paper that takes pride in, um, a sort of building-and-destroying style, you know? Everybody else said, 'Well, we've had solo albums from so-and-so and so-and-so, but they've all gone under the carpet, so we're naturally gonna expect Plant's album to do the same thing. But we're here to tell you otherwise.' And when I read that, I cut it out and my old lady's still got it hanging up. It meant," he says proudly, "that I was *carrying on.*"

Plant's polite reference to that "one paper" is significant. Zep's career was rarely shaped by anything ever written about them—it was the music, first and foremost, the audience, and the relationship between both that made his former band the phenomenon they remain today. If anyone might be living in a dream world of hippie success—where it's still peace 'n' love because, hey, the money's here and where did everybody go?—you might expect it to be Robert Plant. But it isn't. I remark that he still sounds like he's trying to break new ground.

"Well," he grins, '80s-aware, "I wouldn't like to think I've sort of dropped into the AOR [album-oriented rock] bracket *completely,* you know? Where you mix, in the studio, along certain predestined paths . . ."

Oh yeah. What do you think about that stuff?

"I think it's . . ." he pauses, searching for the word. "Comfortable. *Too* comfortable. And boring. That's why the Human League are good. That's why the English Beat are good, you know? That's why the Stray Cats are good, why Heaven 17 are OK."

Who *do* you think is good nowadays?

"All those artists I just mentioned. Because they all sound different. Yazoo [Yaz in America] are *excellent*—I mean, they just split up, right?— but her voice, combined with those modern techniques . . . The B-side of their latest single is incredible, it's brilliant," he enthuses. "It's a masterpiece of modern technology *with* a voice that's *singing*. It's not deadpan, not a real boring, semi-suicidal vocal—which, well, there's a lot of that about, you know? It's got all those incredible swirls and the brassy, cutting edge of the blues voice."

Zep weren't exactly conservative in their own arrangements; how much synthesizer is floating around on *those* records?

"Zeppelin didn't," he says—almost too fast—and then thinks again, reconsidering. "Jonesy was actually far ahead of his time, using synthesizers in 'The Crunge' way back on *Houses of the Holy*. And there were synths on things like 'All My Love' and 'Carouselambra.' But it was a different approach than the sort of . . . *mathematical* synth approaches, though nonetheless very good in its time."

And what's *he* doing today?

"Synthing himself into paradise," he laughs.

Oh? Is there a record due?

"I believe so, yeah," Plant says. He looks away. "I don't hear from him. Very much."

Yeah. Well, I know you guys never really hung out with each other.

"Yeah," he says. "Well, you can saturate relationships, if you're not careful."

In case you haven't figured it out, Robert Plant is an entirely affable, very positive personality. He doesn't *have* to be, he just is. It's nice. In the short time I'm with him, it's the little things, those not worthy of discussion, that most impress. Like when after the interview, when I'm in the next room while a woman from the Associated Press grills Plant, and I dutifully peek into the suitcase lying on the ground. It's Plant's. Inside are the personal things which, I suppose, he doesn't want anybody to see. The cassettes he's listening to on these trips to the States: the best of Marvin Gaye, a Gene Vincent reissue, even Soft Cell. Pretty neat. I mention seeing Stan Webb with Chicken Shack, long ago, he of the 30-foot guitar cord. "Yeah," Plant says as an aside. "Yeah, well of course Buddy Guy used to do that." And you must know Plant sang "Little Sister" with Dave Edmunds on that *Kampuchea* album; I mention I'd just spoken with Edmunds in Detroit that week. "Yeah?" he wonders, genuinely curious. "What does he have to say about it all?"

There's a respect that Robert Plant has for the music—all forms of the music—that maybe a lot of people wouldn't think he'd still have. Maybe that a lot of people have even forgotten about, these days. Like I said: It's nice.

Robert Plant knows enough about Biz '83 to have wrapped up a brand new video—in this case the very nifty "Big Log" put together by the biggies at—where else?—Hipgnosis. "Old habits die hard," says Plant. I wonder if he thinks his appearance in *The Song Remains the Same*—you know, Plant as mythological folk hero aside from the Zep concert pizazz—might be viewed as a veritable first in rock video ancestry.

"Well," he says, very reluctantly. "Maybe."

How do you look back on that?

"With a great deal of *humility*." He clears his throat. "And some embarrassment. It was a moment in time, and we tried to capture the moment, and I think we did, more or less. I find the actual mood of the film good, but"—here he digs in his rock-crit bag—"from my point of view, I find it overindulgent."

Plant's willingness to speak about the past may, in part, be due to the fact that he hasn't had a whole lot of pressfolk asking him about it. But, I find, he'll pretty much answer anything you ask him. When I nabbed him for a quote he once made about Zep being simply "the best" there was, he doesn't hedge: "I think what's happened over the years is that what sense of humor I've got has passed over the top of most people's heads. So when I'm stating things, maybe at a time when I've been fooling around, it's been taken quite seriously."

You mean talking about Led Zep?

"Oh, no, no, no," he protests. "Because actually they [interesting choice of words, no?] were a brilliant band—and, I mean, why not *brag* when you're surrounded by mediocrity?"

OK. Robert Plant 1983, confronted with a question inspired by one too many *Super Session* albums—a musician who's been around long enough to actually answer the question without a quick, flip answer. *If Robert Plant were God* (his eyes widen) *and everyone in his current band was*

*busy, and he wanted to put together the best band he could, bar none, is
there anyone he'd like to have play with him he couldn't ordinarily have, due
to "other" commitments?*

"Oh *God*," he sighs, eyes leaning upward at the too-tall ceiling. "I
couldn't *start* to think about it, really. It's not so much a question of how
good these people are, it's a question of how easy it is to get *on* with 'em—
wherever they are, whatever they've come from, or wherever they've gone
to. I mean, primarily, my nature as an individual is changing, and, I suppose, it would be nice to think that as long as I can have a nice time, working with no idiots around me, I think by working with *anybody* we can
reach a reasonably good sound.

"So," he says, playing the game, "... I'll start with Brian Setzer. I dunno,
I mean the sky's the limit, really. I don't think I'd feel uncomfortable working with anybody. I mean, I'd never like to take the 'famous musician' and
make a band, because that's the very thing I avoided doing in the first
place. I always think that everybody's got their styles, and I think that I
was able to dictate to these people, in," he stresses, "a very righteous and
friendly way—that I also brought across the mood and dynamics that you
might find it very hard to do with, say, Jerry Lee Lewis or someone like
that."

He laughs. "Or Willie Nelson. So, whatever the circumstances, I'd like
to find people that are good, but who aren't in the Hall of Fame."

What you don't realize, of course, is that at this point, the very moist tape
recorder I borrowed from Atlantic Records, that I innocently marched
over to the interview, actually *ate the tape,* and thus 20 minutes I spent
with Robert Plant, at which time he screamed like a banshee, jumped
around the hotel room nude, declared that yes, he and Jimmy spent *hours*
sneaking those little satanic messages on all the good parts of his records
and that, in fact, he thought all he stood for was a total waste and that
his favorite band was Uriah Heep, that his plan was to eventually *buy
the world* and leave all his earthly possessions to me—all of this can only
remain a shared experience between the former lead singer of Led Zeppelin and myself, which of course would never hold up in a court of law,
so why I even bring it up is beyond me. Nonetheless, it would help me

carry over to you, the reader, that despite all the bullshit you read here or in other mags, USA or otherwise, Robert Plant and Led Zeppelin have already left a legacy that, as far as I'm concerned, would've left them legendary had they never recorded a second album. But they have, of course, and a third, and a fourth, and they haven't been together in many years, but if you were to put one of their many albums on the stereo you wouldn't even notice.

And Robert Plant's new album is more of the same, in a way, but it's 1983 and maybe now, more than in a very long time, these few years will make a difference. "There has to be a sense of humor in all this," insists Plant. "That's why all the titles are so stupid and don't have any relevance at all."

Like "Hot Dog?"

"*Yeah*," he says, thinking. "She *was* a dog," he mumbles, and if I didn't get it then I don't get it now—but I'm glad Robert Plant gets it, and I think he'll be getting it for a very long time, and if you *don't*, you probably haven't been listening.

JIMMY PAGE ON STAGE '85

Chris Welch | April 1985, *CREEM*

Plant predicted Page would not go out with his first record post–Led Zeppelin, and he was partially right. Jimmy had done the sound track to *Death Wish II*. His next recording was with Paul Rodgers from Bad Company, the first band signed to Swan Song all those years ago. Together, they merged into the Firm, its name a shot at anyone who dared call them a corporate entity. And so, a year and a half after Plant made his post-Zeppelin debut, it was Page's turn, and like Plant, he did it without evoking Led Zeppelin-or at least their songs. –Ed.

A green pyramid of laser light forms around the figure in white. A violin bow is held aloft and then swishes wand-like across the guitar, its strings howling in protest. It is the moment rock fans around the world have been awaiting. An emotional, historic moment that marks the return to the rock battlefields of one of its most heroic figures . . . Jimmy Page.

All the years of crisis, rumor, and anticipation roll away, and Jimmy, master guitarist and rock 'n' roll legend is back where he belongs, playing for the people! He is back with a great new band, the Firm, and teamed with a singer worthy of the same respect, Paul Rodgers.

The launch of the Firm with concerts in Europe marked the end of months of speculation, and the boys will be going around the world, hopefully in the summer. The Firm swiftly proved itself a vital force as it barnstormed around Stockholm, Frankfurt, and London. Says Jimmy: "The main aim is to play some rock 'n' roll and have some fun." And he achieved that with a mix of fine new songs and the sort of showmanship many thought they would never see again from the man who launched Led Zeppelin on the world.

It's been difficult for Jimmy in the years that followed the sad end of the old group. "How do you follow *that*?" is the obvious question—and Jimmy admits it was a long time before he could even contemplate finding an answer. But the cheers of the crowds and easy acceptance of the new band brought Jimmy a delight and renewed confidence that cynics could not dent. I saw the Firm in action on their fourth gig, in Frankfurt, which was an exclusive preview.

Jimmy told me how he formed the Firm, talked about the making of their album, and about his crisis in confidence until fans helped him back to playing in public. He paid tribute to folk singer Roy Harper and the work they had done together. Jimmy, who appeared so uncertain on the ARMS [Action into Research for Multiple Sclerosis] charity concerts, is now positive, together, and playing a storm.

I arrived in Frankfurt under grey, cloudy skies on a cold Monday morning. Something about the mission and its potential pitfalls had put me on edge. What would the Firm be like? Would it be a rambling jam band or something, literally, to write home about? And would Jimmy be willing to talk about the project after so many years of silence?

Phil Carson of Atlantic Records in London has been looking after the Firm. An old friend of Jimmy's from Zeppelin days, he once played bass with Zep at a concert in Japan, and was booed offstage! Phil told me that the Firm had been socking it to the Euros. "Obviously we didn't want to play up in the promotion that it was ex–Led Zeppelin and ex–Bad Company, and of course a lot of the kids didn't know who was in the Firm. Then the word spread. Ticket sales were slow at first, but the walk-up at Copenhagen was three times the pre-sales. The shows have been great and they are a really exciting band."

Later it was said that some promoters doubted the drawing power of the band and wanted to switch shows to smaller venues, which would have been a great blow to morale. But the Firm held firm and the fans turned up on the night in thousands. Astonishingly—and much to the band's delight—there was no insistent shouting for old numbers. Instead they listened and accepted the new material as it came up.

That night's show was at the Kongresshalle. Jimmy was in a white satin suit, but he soon took off the jacket to get down to work. Gone was the tentative Page who emerged earlier this year in charity shows and sit-in sessions with friends. He plays with all his old zest and command, as the band opened up with "Closer," a cut off the new album, followed by "City Sirens"—a tune from the *Death Wish II* soundtrack Jimmy wrote in 1982. The Firm's material was divided between songs from *The Firm* album, some of Paul's recent solo LP, and a couple of unexpected standards.

Paul's voice caressed the lyrics with that honeyed, understated restraint that sounds so much more melodic than endless screaming. Paul's role in the Firm serves to remind us just what a fine singer he is. Already Jimmy is blending his guitar with Paul in the way he used to with Robert Plant. Jimmy stuck a cigarette between his lips and stripped down to a white T-shirt. He rocked back on his heels as he stomped into riff sequences or constructed brief solos in that extraordinary, cliff-hanging way that often defies logic and always follows an unpredictable path, even on the most basic blues.

"Do you feel alright?" demanded Paul. The answering roar showed that the Firm were winning over audiences probably too young to have known Bad Co. or Led Zep in their touring days. Jimmy Page stamped both feet to count in the tempo to "Make or Break" and "Together." Tony [Franklin] played some keyboard while Jimmy picked out some simple notes that sent shivers down the spine, ankles, and kneecaps. This was during "Prelude" from *Death Wish II*, which moved into another new song, "Money Can't Buy."

"Radioactive" came next, which will be their first single release. It was a fast, simple, stomping tune, with Jimmy stoking up a powerful beat while Paul strummed his blue acoustic. The band caught fire—showing how they have fused together as a tight unit in a remarkably short time.

Next came Paul's song, "Live In Peace," on which he played a keyboard wheeled out on rollers and bathed in the first laser light of the night. A slow ballad, it gave Paul a chance to wring forth every drop of emotion. Jimmy soloed next on a piece called "Midnight Moonlight" with Chris's sizzling gong heralding more impassioned vocals. It was a magic piece and one of the high spots.

To provide contrast, Paul next chose to sing the Righteous Brothers' hit "You've Lost That Loving Feeling" with some doomy bass work from Tony underpinning Paul's moody, almost sinister treatment of the lyric

Onwards now the major work of the night—"The Chase," first composed for *Death Wish II* and now turned into a 20-minute vehicle for the band's full instrumental power. The Firm had taken pains not to stand accused of being long-winded, one of the criticisms leveled at the great virtuosos of their generation. But on "The Chase" they cast restraint to the winds. Tony began proceedings with an amazing solo which showed the youngest member of the band doesn't have much to learn. "A new star is born," muttered someone in the balcony, as Tony started playing first a few desultory notes. This was a subtle way to establish credentials. Suddenly he let fly with myriad hammering notes and chunky, funky licks that brought roars from the crowd. They loved every minute, as Tony—his blond hair flying over the strings—created a crescendo of excitement. Jimmy patted him on the back. Now it was *his* turn, and it was obvious nobody in the band was going to lay back and give anybody else an easy ride.

This was Page getting down to business and exerting all his powers. Chris Slade played a blinding drum solo and Jimmy watched with approval. He had found a worthy successor to John Bonham. The instrumentals were very welcome, although Paul must have felt a bit out of things. "Hello there," he said, bouncing back on stage after a long absence. He led into "Found Someone To Love" off *The Firm*—and when Jimmy's guitar broke down for a few minutes, Tony covered on bass. The crowd cheered anyway. Above the roar Paul could be heard shouting, "We haven't got any more tunes, what can we do?" The band disappeared to think about it, then returned for a slow blues, "Mama Boogie,"—with sizzling interplay between Paul and Jimmy. No, it wasn't Led Zep, but it was a whole lotta fun and feeling. And it was just great to see them again.

"I'm so glad to be here tonight," exclaimed Paul as the Firm grooved into the stomping old soul riff "Everybody Needs Somebody to Love," the Solomon Burke hit from 1964, once covered by the Stones and every other group you could remember. It was a good humored way to end the show. Tony grinned at the front rows as they sang along. The band faded out on a chant of "You, you, you," as they lined up, abandoning their instruments to point Jagger-style at the crowds. The Frankfurters danced and sang. I spotted a pair of legs waving in the air as one German kid danced on his head, with a little help from his friends. The Firm threw their arms around each other as the house lights went up. It was a gesture of togetherness that spoke volumes. The success of the band meant a lot to all of them for any number of reasons. And they could all feel . . . it was working!

A few days later the band played a concert in Middlesbrough, Paul's home town, then two nights at the Hammersmith Odeon in London.

The day after the gig I waited for Jimmy in the hotel bar. Suddenly he appeared, chatting to some fans. "You want to talk?" he said. "Right, let's sit over here away from all the noise." I wondered what mood he was in. After all, he hadn't talked to the press for four years and he was supposed to be a recluse. Instead of being monosyllabic, he was charming, cheerful, and anxious to talk. Occasionally, he betrayed signs of impatience—but he gradually thawed out as he sipped iced whiskey with a beer chaser. I congratulated him on his new band. "Well, they *are* all good musicians, aren't they? If you've got them, you've got no problems," he rejoined.

When did Jimmy start piecing his band together? "Well, I tried to get together with Paul earlier, but it was difficult because he was doing a solo LP. But when the ARMS charity shows came up in America, Paul came with us. Stevie Winwood—who sang in London—had pulled out. So we went to the States and had a very good tour, singing songs like "Bird on the Wing" which we did on the album. At the end of the tour I asked if he fancied carrying on and doing something else, because I really love his singing. He's such a brilliant singer. If I do a guitar solo I have to warm up and do three takes. He does it in one take. Note perfect. No problem! He's an amazing man."

Jimmy didn't want to lose the momentum gained by doing the ARMS concerts. These had been arranged to raise money for research into Multiple Sclerosis, the wasting disease that has stricken singer Ronnie Lane. The concerts brought together the cream of the '70s brigade—including Jeff Beck, Eric Clapton, and Jimmy, the [last] making his first public appearance since the demise of Zep.

"I thought if I stop now, I'm just a bloody fool. I had to carry on—but the only vehicle I had was playing with Roy Harper, and also with Ian Stewart [Stu of the Stones]. Those were the only things I'd done. I really wanted to get a band together with Paul, and thought some fantastic things could happen. I played on some Alexis Korner cancer benefits with Ian, and there were the ARMS things, which I hope we'll be doing again." Jimmy agreed with Paul he would get the rhythm section together for the new band, and rehearsals began at London's Nomis Studio. Rumors spread, and it was thought the band would be called the Mac. Jimmy had been appearing with Roy under the pseudonym of Jimmy McGregor. "There WERE a lot of rumors, but I didn't want it to come out until it was really together," explained Jimmy.

"People would have said 'Oh, Paul and Jimmy are getting a group together,' but it wouldn't have BEEN a group. There was nothing concrete. Paul came down and sang and he really liked Chris. Tony came in after that. It got together very quickly actually. We just wanted to have to go and play on stage." One of the first numbers they played was a new ballad they wrote called "Bird on the Wing." Said Jim: "That was a bit of a test. If anybody can handle that, they can play!"

Jimmy was on tenterhooks for three months while he waited for Slade to finish touring with Floyd man Dave Gilmour. "I kept playing with lots of people, just to keep myself going. Am I rambling? I'm trying to remember what happened! The main thing was, after ARMS I thought 'I'm not going to stop playing now. I want a *group*.' At the back of my mind, I wanted to engineer it so that Paul would want to come in. For a while I did a lot of jams. Everyone was invited. On drums I had Rat Scabies, who is absolutely *brilliant*, by the way. He handled everything beautifully, and he's got a lot of heart, that man. I used to love the Damned—and I wanted a real rock 'n' roll drummer. From Rat it went to Bill Bruford from King Crimson. One extreme to the other! Then Chris came back and was absolutely brilliant. So I said to him 'What are you doing?'

"Tony was on the dole. He'd been playing on Roy's album. Maybe that's *why* he was on the dole! I called Roy and asked him if Tony would like to come and have a play with us. Then we said, 'Right, Tony is the bass player.' The amazing thing is, prior to this tour Tony has never played a solo onstage. Now he's a star!"

How committed was Jimmy to the long term future of the Firm? "Well, it started out as one-off project, but now we've seen how it has gone down, who knows? I've got an idea anyway," he added mysteriously. "I've got so many projects. That Ronnie Lane thing did me the world of good. You can't imagine. It gave me so much confidence. I realized people DID want to see me play again. So I thought, 'Blow it, I'm not gonna let things slip now. I wanna get out there." At the moment, it's fun. The business aspect is a bloody bore, but yeah, it's fun. That's the main thing we want out of it."

The sad end of Led Zeppelin following the death of John Bonham in 1980 is still a sensitive subject for Jimmy—and his signals warned not to probe too deep too soon. But in the aftermath, how did he feel?

"I just felt really insecure. Absolutely. I was terrified. I guess that's why I played with Roy whenever I could, because I knew his stuff and I knew him well. After the split, I just didn't know what to do. I lived in a total vacuum. I didn't know what I was doing. In the end, I went to Bali and just thought about things. And I wasn't sitting on the beach because it was the rainy season! I sat in my room thinking. Then I thought, dammit, I'm going to do the Firm and see if it works. At my time of life I should just do what I enjoy.

"This will be the first of many projects. Some of them are going to be pretty bizarre. But at least I can still rock 'n' roll, even if everyone thinks the other things are a load of shit. I used the violin bow again with the Firm because it's *fun*—and I know everyone in the audience enjoys it. They're not thinking, 'What's that wally doing?' It's all right. A light-hearted, tongue-in-cheek thing. Showmanship? It's great. I've always gone to concerts to be entertained. So lasers and the violin bow all help out."

The concert I saw in Frankfurt presented a total contrast to the Page I saw with Harper at Cambridge Folk Festival, when they strummed gentle songs in the sunshine. "Yeah, this *is* rock 'n' roll, isn't it? I love rocking and having a dance. It's just good fun, and that's the way it should be viewed. The rock music I learned from was always exhilarating stuff. Whenever I feel miserable, I put on old rock records on my jukebox. You feel so much better. It makes the adrenalin rush. Roots music always has that effect on me. When I play a gig to an audience, it's there only for the moment, a thrill lost in time . . . unless it's bootlegged!

"I thought last night was a good gig, because it was only our fourth and every night has got better.

"All I remember was raw nerves and shaking arms and legs. But it got to the point where I could relax and actually remember what the set was supposed to be. I remember we finished the first number and the stage blacked out. I shouted, 'Paul, what's the next number?' the next night I actually remembered the set."

Couldn't Jimmy have taken a list with him?

"I couldn't remember where mine was—ha ha! That's how bad it was. The set is actually a mix of the new album, some of *Death Wish II* AND Paul's solo album, plus some things that didn't go on our album. The LP is all ready and finished and ready to go. It was done in November, and should be out soon. We're gonna put 'Radioactive' out as a single—which is new territory for me."

Jimmy wants to make a video of the single and tour America and Japan. But releasing a single is a new departure. He wouldn't touch them in Zeppelin days. Times have changed. "It's all down to supply and demand," said Jimmy. "I don't know what will happen in America, if people will come and see us. I hope things go well, but the problem is . . . OK . . . the band is called the Firm. But no one knows who's in it! So Paul and I have agreed to do a 'live' video of us doing 'Radioactive.' I know Zeppelin wouldn't do a single, and now I am, and a video too. People will say 'Well, there's the hypocrite.' It's not that. The idea is to go out and have a play and show people who have had a lot of faith in me that I'm ready to work.

"Believe me, some of the fans touch your heart. Especially on the ARMS tour of America. I realize then the fans wanted me back. And I don't want them to see me playing in an empty hall! So I'll do a video and everyone can see this band is having a go."

"I don't want to pretend to be an actor—because I'm not. I remember in *The Song Remains the Same*, when we did all our fantasy sequences.

Nobody was allowed to be around the others while we did them, because they'd all take the piss. All you can do is be what you are."

The Song Remains the Same is now available on video—and Jimmy is not pleased, because of certain deficiencies in the soundtrack. "In the violin bow piece, it's supposed to repeat and come back. There's no coming back! I screamed about that, because on the original soundtrack it was done on four tacks for cinema speakers. I insisted they went back to the original negative if they were going to put out a video. Actually we *are* in a bit of a hole over that, because Swan Song [Zep's record label] went bust, and the film was one of its assets. I haven't got the time to sort it out, because I am involved with this."

So Swan Song is no more?

"No. It's a shame. The idea behind it was good. Peter Grant was not as much a part of the vitality of it as one would have hoped. Because of that, and he was the one delegated to make major commitments and decisions about getting artists in, he wasn't following things through and it was a shame. At one point it had the momentum to do a lot, and it didn't. I know Robert feels bad about it, and I feel bad about it, because it wasn't just a pipe dream. It could have been a reality."

Robert has his own label now and Jimmy did some work on Plant's *Honeydrippers* album. "Yeah, I overdubbed guitar solos on a couple of tracks. Then I heard Beck's solo on 'Rockin' At Midnight' and thought bloody hell, that's good. It's beautiful, his solo. I was happy with my 'Sea of Love' solo, but I didn't get the other one together. I felt it was a bit labored. I can't remember the title."

ROCKIN' ROBERT LIKES 'A BIT OF GRIT BELOW THE WAIST'

Liam Lacey | June 8, 1985, *Globe and Mail*

As a solo artist, Robert Plant did not feel the need to play arenas anymore. He could probably live comfortably for the rest of his life on royalties from "Stairway to Heaven" alone. So, like he did in Zeppelin, he recorded and played the music he wanted to play, with mixed sales results. *Pictures at Eleven* peaked at #5 in *Billboard*; *The Principle of Moments* hit the teens. It took a toss-off recording ostensibly made during a weekend with a bunch of friends and cronies playing a half dozen pre-'60s R&B tunes to earn him a top-five album and single, a hit record. The irony was not lost on Robert. —Ed.

Robert Plant is sitting cross-legged on his bed, talking about his latest album. This is the third year in a row he has visited Toronto to promote a new release, and the third year in a row he has sat the same way at the same hotel. Some things never change.

And other things change in unpredictable ways. Last fall, under the direction of Atlantic Records chief, Arif Mardin, Plant spent the weekend in the studio with a handful of famous musicians, including Jeff Beck, Nile Rodgers, and *Late Night with David Letterman*'s Paul Shaffer. They released an album of old rhythm and blues and pop standards under the name, the Honeydrippers. It went to the number one spot in the country, and Robert Plant found himself with an unexpected new audience. He says he accepts all the criticism people want to throw at him for the project because, from his own viewpoint, it never really meant much more than a way to spend the weekend.

"What do you do on weekends?" he asks. "Other people have ways of turning off from their regular jobs. I can't, so I do something that's less creatively intense, and that's how the Honeydrippers came about."

The Honeydrippers' success has been disconcerting:

"I had mixed feelings—to say the least. That record reached radio audiences that Led Zeppelin had never reached. Lots and lots of people, including those in the radio industry, never had any idea that I was involved with it, and they probably wouldn't have known who it was if they did.

"Today on the plane, a little girl—well, not really little, but a fairly young teen-ager—came up to me and started talking. I asked, 'Do you know who I am?' and she said, 'Yeah, you're the guy from the Honeydrippers' video.' So I said, 'But do you know me from anywhere else?' She obviously had no idea what I was talking about."

As for his third solo album, *Shaken 'n' Stirred*, Plant doesn't expect it to be nearly as successful: "I doubt if my own albums could ever reach number one, not the way I make them. They're not that accessible, and I'm not willing to make the compromises to make them that accessible."

Occasionally, he admits, he has fretted about trying to write a hit—and others, including Eurythmics and Phil Collins—have offered him material, but he refuses to do it. He thinks the new album is his strongest, and most free. "The second one (*Principle of Moments*) means a lot to me because it reflects my emotional state at the time. You've probably talked to Leonard Cohen; do I sound like him? But I think this one is more alive. It rides an edge that has something to do with the different tastes of me and Jen* (Woodroffe), who plays keyboards. Whenever he hears sequencers and electronic drums on the radio, he wants them turned up. He's at home with the sort of Nik Kershaw or Howard Jones type of synthesizer pop. When I hear anything that sounds like an old Gretsch, semi-acoustic guitar, rockabilly sound, that's when I want the radio turned up.

---

*Jezz Woodroffe

"We deliberately crossed techniques and styles: on the song 'Kallalou, Kallalou,' I told him I wanted him to use all his thousands of dollars of equipment to make this early sixties, keyboard sound—like a cheap $200 Farfisa organ on Dave (Baby) Cortez doing 'Rinky Dink,' or the Kingsmen playing 'Louie Louie.'"

Plant is an avid record collector. He makes frequent references to fifties and sixties pop hits, but some of his musical tastes are surprising. When an interviewer from radio station Q-107 asked him for his three "desert island" albums, two of Plant's choices were reasonably predictable: Eddie Cochran's *Greatest Hits* and former partner Jimmy Page's soundtrack to *Death Wish II*. His third choice was an album by This Mortal Coil, a collection of dark mood pieces featuring the Cocteau Twins and other generally obscure young musicians, released earlier this year and listed on England's independent charts.

"I'm definitely interested in creating soundscapes, in using modern sounds. The difficulty is in using the right sounds, from whatever period, that convey the mood you want. If you can take those modern sounds, and give them a bit of grit below the waistline, then you have something different, don't you?"

ROBERT PLANT: GUILTY!

Tom Hibbert | March 1988, _Q_ magazine

If nothing else, Robert Plant proved prolific once he got his post-Zeppelin career under way—not quite as prolific as the first years of Led Zeppelin, but he put out an impressive four solo albums and the one-off _Honeydrippers_ album between 1982 and 1988. His fourth (and a half) album _Now and Zen_ had a sound like an unpolished version of the Cars at times, a precursor to Don Henley at others; with it, he continued to bring his roots into the future or at least keep them present tense. The album was a success, based largely on the hit "Tall Cool One," which topped the Mainstream Rock charts. This interview is not as much about the new album as it is incredibly revealing about how Plant put his past into personal perspective and deals with the good, the bad, and the ugly about his Led legacy. –Ed.

"I can't blame anybody for hating Led Zeppelin. If you absolutely hated 'Stairway to Heaven,' nobody can blame you for that because it was, um . . . so pompous."

Robert Plant, the one-time writhing and mewling Adonis-figure who did the singing and the shrieking for the most monstrous, most celebrated, most infamous hard rock act of all times, leans back in the plump sofa in the offices of his new manager Bill Curbishley (who managed the Who) and enters confession. The famous locks that once shook in the spots of the grandest stadiums on earth are just near shoulder-length now—respectable; the face is lined with the sins of the ages but alive and amicable. Robert Plant owns up: "Those accusations that were leveled at Zeppelin at the end, during punk, those accusations of remoteness, of playing blind, of having no idea about people or circumstances or reality, of having no idea about what we were talking about or what we were feeling, of being deep and meaningless and having vapid thoughts—there was a lot of substance in what was being said. People were quite right to say all that. It hurt at the time but I'd have to plead guilty."

Robert Plant pleads guilty. He is only now coming to terms with his history, becoming able to sort the Good Times from the Bad. Led Zeppelin at their best is something he'll always be proud of. At their worst, most self-indulgent? Well . . .

On the wall some feet away, there's a poster of Judas Priest. Plant springs to his feet, strides purposefully towards it and points a scornful finger at this gargantuan photo of the heavy metal chaps dressed in their leather and their chains, and festooned, naturally, with sundry Diabolic tokens. "If I'm responsible for *this* in any way (which, of course, he is—the influence of Led Zeppelin on heavy metal can never be overestimated), then I am really, *really* embarrassed. It's so orderly and preconceived and *bleuurghh*. Hard rock, heavy metal these days is just saying 'Come and buy me. I'm in league with the Devil—but only in this picture because after that I'm going to be quite nice and one day I'm going to grow up and be the manager of a pop group,' or whatever. Zeppelin was *never* saying that. When I see something like *this* (the finger wags sternly like some demonstrative prosecuting counsel at a murderous defendant), it's then that I wish I could materialize Page at my side. And the two of us would steam up on stage and take their names for being absurd. It's like a bunch of Arabian eunuchs—there's no balls. We'd have them reported to a higher authority for taking the good name of Zeppelin in vain. Zeppelin, for all their mistakes and wicked ways, were bigger and greater than any of *that* kind of nonsense . . ."

Robert Plant has spent seven years—since the death of John "Bonzo" Bonham and the demise of the group—attempting to lay the ghost of Led Zeppelin. His four solo LPs to date—*Pictures At Eleven* (1982), *The Principle of Moments* (1983), *Shaken 'n' Stirred* (1985), and the new *Now and Zen*—have hinted but fleetingly at the black sound and fury of old—this new music is polished and relatively modern, with proper choruses to prove it. In his (few) interviews he has mentioned *that* band sparingly,

only in passing, preferring to discuss current projects and musical pre-
occupations. ("I hate pop. In a fair world Let's Active should be Number 1, R.E.M. should be Number 2, and I should be in there somewhere
behind them at Number 5 . . .") He has stripped those horny squealings
of old from the vocal repertoire and ironed the voice into a more round
and orthodox rock 'n' roll implement. He has had annual telephone calls
from John Paul Jones (whom he never sees) suggesting that Led Zeppelin
reform ("Jonesy always was a breadhead"), and he has treated these with
contempt—Live Aid, at which Page, Jones, and Plant were reunited for 14
minutes (we'll come to that later) was most definitely a one-off. And he
has always steadfastly ignored, when on stage with his own band, the constant cries of the audience for Percy—as Planty was known to his friends
and admirers—to do a "Stairway to Heaven" or a "Whole Lotta Love" or a
"Dazed and Confused" or a . . . ("Where's Jimmy? That's what they always
shout. Where's Jimmy? In fact, that should have been the name of the new
album: Where's Jimmy?"). A sturdy refusal to comply with audience's nos-
talgic wishes—until, that is, last night, when, at a secret gig in Folkestone
to test *Now and Zen's* material with his new young band (billed as the
Band of Joy, Plant and Bonham's Midlands group of 1967/8 whose set was
full of songs by Moby Grape, Jefferson Airplane, and other West Coast
entities) he encored with 'Misty Mountain Hop' (from Led Zeppelin's
untitled fourth album, the one with the Zoso "runes") and found himself
"up there, eating my words furiously." The Zeppelin Beast (the number
of which may or may not have been 666) is finally slaughtered and buried as far as Plant is concerned. Jimmy Page makes a Zeppelin-like guest
appearance on *Now and Zen* and, finally, Robert Plant feels himself able to
discuss those old and spooky days. He can talk about it now.

He can talk about how hard he found it to make the decision to leave
all thoughts of Zeppelin behind and re-invent himself as a modern rock
item after the (fatal) collapse of stout party Bonham in September 1980:

"It was a very hard and difficult process to re-evaluate myself after
that. I did nothing for as long as was respectful to Bonzo, really. Because
he and I *were* best mates. Page and Jones obviously became friends but
they were never *mates* like Bonzo was because we'd started out with that
age and experience gap that was never totally bridged. But Bonzo and me

were so close that all the kind of insinuations of carrying on and all that were just totally unacceptable to me.

"Because I knew how much Bonzo loved what he did and I thought it would be terrible to just fob the whole thing off and say, Well, that's it. We'd better get someone else now so that we can carry on this incredible sort of amoebic carnage game, you know. So rather than take the whole Zeppelin thing and try and do it myself, I rejected the whole thing. Anything to do with the enormity of the success and the attraction and the *oddness* of Led Zeppelin, I didn't want to have anything to do with. So I cut my hair off and I never played or listened to a Zeppelin record for two years. It would have been longer but my daughter's boyfriend who was in a psychobilly band started telling me that part of 'Black Dog' (from the "runes" album) was a mistake because there's a bar of 5/4 in the middle of some 4/4. Well, my dander was up at *that* so I pulled the record out and plonked it on and said, Listen you little runt, that's no mistake, that's what we were *good* at! And having done that, I listened to the whole record and got really drunk and went, *Right!* I knew what I wanted to do. Not Zeppelin but I still wanted to sing. I knew I had to carry on because I love what I do. I love to be anxious and I love to nurture this thing like some kind of new woman every two or three years . . ."

He can talk about how hard he found it to approach the notion of assembling a band of his own:

"We had always led a very cloistered existence in Zeppelin. We really didn't know anybody else. We knew each other and we knew the entourage but that was about it. And a lot of people were very frightened of us and avoided us like the plague. It was only the Stones that we really ever had anything to do with because we used to take the piss out of everybody else. So it was hard for me getting to know other musicians for the first time. But once I'd met some—people like Phil Collins (who played drums on Plant's first two LPs)—it was good because I could see them thinking, Oh, he's not so frightening. He's quite *dumb* but he's not frightening. And I'd go back and see Jimmy now and again and I'd try and say, Now, come on. It's quite *nice* out there, you know. And so he started stepping out as well, leaving his great shell at home. It was like the metamorphosis; he'd step out a bit and then go home and climb back into his shell and the shell would grow. It's like Kafka. Kafka could have been writing about Page. He's still Jimmy Page, you see. I'm sure he's still got dragons on his jeans. And if he *hasn't* got them on his jeans, they're on his skin by now . . ."

He can talk about how hard it was, after 14 years in a songwriting partnership with Jimmy Page, to start writing with someone else (guitarist Robbie Blunt):

"It was so uncomfortable to begin with that I wasn't sure I could handle it. Because Page and I had known each other back to front in that area. We had had a rather self-congratulatory partnership for years and it had been comfortable—a bit twitchy at times because of all the drugs but basically comfortable. And so to start with anyone else was a very, very odd feeling. Unnerving. Because I started getting so many flashbacks of the night Page and I wrote bits of 'Stairway to Heaven' or of doing the lyrics of 'Trampled Underfoot' or whatever. I found myself getting all these great swirls out of the mist and at first I couldn't cope. But I got used to it. And once I'd done it once, I realized I could do it a million times . . . "

And Robert Plant can even talk about *Hammer of the Gods*, Stephen Davis's unauthorized Led Zeppelin biography, published in 1985, that told us things we'd suspected for years—tales of grand debauchery, of Page cavorting naked on tea trolleys before roomfuls of groupies, of Bonham's bottle binges that would end in near rape, of the girl in the hotel room being made "love" to by a red snapper fish, about the aggressive, gangster-like tendencies of manager Peter Grant, and more, much more.

"*Hammer of the Gods*. Well there *was* some truth"—(the snapper episode, it seems, really did happen, though Plant was not a party to it, nor to any of the other grosser outrages in the tale) "and a *tiny* bit of insight in that book. But, basically, it was compilation of Richard Cole's clearer moments of recollection in between smack and God knows what else." (Cole was Zeppelin's tour manager and lieutenant to Grant; or sergeant—"Cole was the ultimate sergeant—big, nasty, a natural leader, an Anglo-Irish pirate who would have been at home with the notorious White Companies, looting France during the Hundred Years War" runs Davis's descriptive introductory passage on the man.) "But a lot of what he remembered about Zeppelin wasn't about Zeppelin at all. I think a lot of his recollections were confused with memories from when he was with Vanilla Fudge or the Young Rascals or Hendrix. Of course, Zeppelin had *many* moments of outrage too sordid to mention but somebody else would write a better book, I think. A *funnier* book, because 90 per cent of what we got up to was just *funny*. Richard just possesses an inherent bitterness because he was in a constant position of absorbing and reflecting glory without ever being given the reins of authority because he was always second in command to Peter Grant. So when it all ended he decided to get his own back on a bunch of guys who were just shambling their way through the universe. It's sad, in a way, because underneath all that fighting and kicking and wrecking, he's a really nice man . . . "

Cole doesn't come across as a "nice man" in the Stephen Davis book. He comes across more as an unsavory leech, an opportunist, and a pervert. Peter Grant, meanwhile, comes across as a gangster and a monster. Either the book lies or Plant has a forgiving/naive/diplomatic nature. He still loves Grant, this man who, all evidence tells us, was not averse to beating a man unconscious if his path were crossed, however innocently.

"You have to understand the kind of man Peter Grant was . . . *is*," says Plant. "An ex-wrestler who'd have been on the road with Wee Willie Harris and Gene Vincent in the bad old days. He had his own way of getting things done. Since Zeppelin . . . well, I have no idea what's happened to him. But *he's* the man who should write the book. He maneuvered Richard Cole into every circumstance going and if we were The Gods, Grant was The Hammer. And Grant was the one who kept us cloistered from the world. Well, that's not quite true. I still knew how to use money, how to shop and how to drive, how to shit and walk, I still saw my family and I still spoke to the milkman, but we didn't see too many people in *our* world—rock 'n' roll. We were kept remote. But what that book doesn't tell you is that Peter Grant was one of the most witty and intelligent men. He smashed through so many of the remnants of the old regime of business in America. Like all the old road shows in America, which I was too young to have gone on, thank God: Page used to travel in a bus in the Yardbirds with Gary Puckett and the Union Gap and the Shirelles and Bobby Vinton and nobody got a cent apart from the promoter. Then we came along and Grant would say to promoters, Okay, you want these guys but we're not taking what *you* say, we'll tell you what *we* want and when you're ready to discuss it you can call *us*. And of course, they *would* call us and do things on our terms, on Grant's terms, because otherwise they'd be stuck with Iron Butterfly. Peter Grant changed the rules. He rewrote the book. And he did so much for us that in 1975 he had to turn around and say, 'Look, there's nothing else I can do for you guys. We've had performing pigs and high-wire acts, we've had mud sharks and all the wah, but there's no more I can do. Because you really now *can* go to Saturn.'

"We had twitchy times at the end, me and Peter Grant, but I owe so much of my confidence and my pig-headedness to him because of the way he calmed and nurtured and pushed and cajoled all of us to make us what we were. There were so many times I wanted to wring his neck but I wish him well and I wish he'd get off his fat arse and *do* something because I happen to love him a lot. Funny chap . . . "

Hammer of the Gods suggests another charge, one well known to all fans of Led Zeppelin and to those who grew up with the myth and the legend of this peculiarly successful group. It is this: for fame and fortune, Led Zeppelin made a pact with Satan himself. Thus: play 'Stairway to Heaven' (the song that is *still* the most requested song on American FM radio; the song that *still* makes it into those listeners' Top-Of-All-Time polls just behind 10cc's "I'm Not In Love" on Capital Radio and other stations) backwards and you will, it is said, hear a witchy, "twitchy" message in Beelzebub-styled code. "Here's to my sweet Satan!" the tones of Lucifer proclaim. Or is it "I live for Satan!"? The Evangelists of America, who have spent many years searching for hell-fire and brimstone in the works of Led Zeppelin, are divided. But of one thing they (and many a gullible Zeppelin fan) are certain: Led Zeppelin dwelled within the bosom of the Prince of Darkness. So where, pray, are Robert Plant's spiky little horns?

"Oh, I cut those off with the hair, hahaha. No, all that crap came from Page collecting all the Crowley stuff. Page had a kind of fascination with the absurd, and Page could afford to invest in his fascination with the absurd, and that was it. But we decided years ago that it would be prudent to say nothing to people about all that because the people we'd have had to talk to were pretty lame. There was just no point in going along and bleating and saying, Listen, this is fucked, if you believe this Devil stuff, you'll believe anything. So we just let it go. But it did infuriate. I mean, 'Stairway to Heaven,' as much as I find it intolerable to even consider that song now, at the time it was important and it was something I was immensely proud of. Page and I had a moment when we wrote something incredibly pompous but at the time it was alright and the idea of the Moral Majority stomping around doing circuit tours of American campuses and making money from saying that song is Satanist and preaching their bullshit infuriated me to hell. You can't find anything if you play that song backwards. I know, because I've tried. There's nothing there. In fact, I was thinking of putting some back-tracking on my last album saying 'What did you miss from *before*? in Latin. It's all crap, that Devil stuff, but the less you said to people, the more they'd speculate. The only way to let people know where you're coming from is to talk to the press, and we never said fuck all to anybody. We never made a pact with the Devil. The only deal I think we ever made was with some of the girls' high schools in San Fernando Valley."

Satan's finest played their last ever show on English soil at Knebworth in 1979—two nights before 380,000 people. Plant remembers the occasion with mixed feelings.

"The punks hated us for Knebworth, and quite rightly so. But we couldn't go playing Nottingham Boat Club just to prove to people in long overcoats that we were OK. But although we were supposed to be the arch criminals and the real philanderers of debauchery and Sodomy and Gomorrah-y, our feet were much more firmly on the ground than a lot of other people around. But you wouldn't have believed that to see us swaggering about at Knebworth, because Knebworth was an enormous, incredible thing. I patrolled the grounds the night of the first gig—I went out with some people in a jeep—and people pushed the stone pillars down, with the metal gates attached, because they wanted to get in early. Those gates had been there since 1732 and they just pushed them over. It was a phenomenally powerful thing."

The following year Led Zeppelin toured Europe (a tour on which, Plant claims, the band showed they'd "learned a hell of a lot from XTC and people like that. I was really keen to stop the self-importance and the guitar solos that lasted an hour. We cut everything down and we didn't play any song for more than four and a half minutes.") and on their return, John Bonham passed on, a surfeit of vodka in his belly, and Plant vowed that he'd never perform as part of Led Zeppelin again. Five years later and the promise he'd made himself was broken when, in Philadelphia, he and Page and Jones assembled on stage to play their 14 minutes—"Stairway to Heaven" included—for Ethiopia. Mixed feelings here, too.

"Live Aid was a very odd thing to do, really. It was the old trap. It was like George Harrison was saying in Q recently that he always had to be careful in case Paul and Ringo were both invited to do the same show and it would be, Oh, as the three of you are all here, why don't you get together and give us "Love Me Do" or something? And that's exactly what happened to us at Live Aid. I'd been asked and Jimmy had been asked to play separately and the emotional onus swung round to whether or not I'd eat my own words because I'd always said 'No, I don't want to play with them again. I just don't want to rest on my own laurels for the sake of some glory that's out of time.' But there it was. I found myself saying, 'Yeah, what a great idea, let's have a rehearsal' and we rehearsed with Tony Thompson and then Phil Collins came on his plane and we virtually ruined the whole thing because we sounded so awful. I was hoarse and couldn't sing and Page was out of tune and couldn't hear his guitar. But on the other hand it was a wondrous thing because it was a wing and a prayer gone wrong again—it was so much like a lot of Led Zeppelin gigs. Jonesy stood there serene as hell and the two drummers proved that . . . well, you know, that's why Led Zeppelin didn't carry on. But through all that and through the rejection of ever having anything to do with *that* song again, through facing all these compromises, I stood there smiling. The rush I got from that size of audience, I'd forgotten what it was like. I'd forgotten how much I missed it. And I'd forgotten how Led Zeppelin and Bonzo could never, ever be replaced. I'd be lying if I said I wasn't really drunk on the whole event. The fact that they were still chanting for us 15 minutes later and the fact that there were people crying all over the place . . . odd stuff. It was something far more powerful than words can convey . . . It's just filled me up with tears thinking about the whole thing . . . "

By the time of Live Aid, Robert Plant had already recorded his first three solo albums (as well as the Honeydrippers' set, a collection of old rock 'n' roll standards featuring Page and Jeff Beck on guitars). It's taken him another two and a half years to record his fourth (and best) and to get the specter of Led Zeppelin finally out of his system. But can you ever truly lay the ghost of a Devil? Last night in Folkestone, Robert Plant found himself getting up to old tricks:

"I don't know where it came from, my style. I must have been pretty insecure when Zeppelin started to want to run around puffing my chest out and pursing my lips and throwing my hair back like some West Midlands giraffe. But I did it again last night. And when I did it, I laughed so much. It was like self-parody; I was wiggling around like some ageing big girl's blouse and I realise how stupid it all looks. I mean, last night while I was crouching and leaping up in the air and doing a spiral as I came down again, I thought 'I wonder if David Coverdale does that yet?' But that's what I'm good at. That's what I know. What else am I going to do? Sleep with the board of directors of Coca-Cola and make an ad? I don't know. I don't want to end up playing in the back room of some pub in Wolverhampton waiting for the night match at Molyneux to end. It's a bit of a naff old game, life . . ."

COMMUNICATION BREAKDOWN

"'Tall Cool One' is like tipping my hat to the original song, and that whole Ralph Nielsen kind of approach . . . I think I retain the attitude that got me into rock 'n' roll in the first place—I haven't fallen for the way rock has deteriorated over the years, the way it's become so corporate again, just like in the early '60s, this situation where David Coverdale's mainly concerned with how he wears his sunglasses or whatever . . . I'm trying to do something that's not been done before, even at the risk of not making that extra buck . . . For now, I wanna get into something you can really put your arms around, something that kicks ass. *Shaken 'n' Stirred* is a record I'm very proud of, but you gotta remember that you and I love music—we pay attention to details. But I want people to still have a handle on what I'm doing. I mean, my daughter is so happy that I'm finally making songs she can sing along to!"

– Robert Plant to Chuck Eddy, *CREEM*, June 1988

EMERGING FROM THE SHADOWS: JIMMY PAGE

Patrick McDonald | July 7, 1988, *Advertiser*

In 1988, Jimmy Page returned to center stage. The Firm never caught the creative or commercial fire that Page had in mind for the group and it fell by the wayside. For his new project, Page went back to one of his older ideas (see the BBC Radio interview from 1976 on page 183): the guitar orchestra. The resulting solo album, *Outrider*, was thick with riffs and textured guitars, with Chris Farlowe doing his best Robert Plant impression except on "The Only One," which featured Robert himself. Also playing on the album was Jason Bonham, making good on his father's assertions (see the 1975 piece by Chris Welch on page 165) about his prowess as a drummer. –Ed.

He was the master axeman who redefined music in the 1970s; a guitarist whose power chords and riffs were so distinctive that, a decade on, they have resurfaced as the most influential force in popular music today.

For the first time since his heavy rock supergroup, Led Zeppelin, disbanded eight years ago, guitarist Jimmy Page has emerged from the shadows with a solo album.

Page has been anything but inactive since the group's untimely dissolution, recording two albums with the Firm, a band he co-founded with Paul Rodgers, and writing and recording the soundtrack for *Death Wish II*.

However, both projects lacked the wild drive of his previous work and met with less-than-favorable critical and commercial reception.

Now Page has burst back on to the scene with a collection of hooks and licks which will not only delight fans new and old, but show those newcomers like Kingdom Come (which he nicknames "Kingdom Clone"), which look to Led Zeppelin as a blueprint for success, a trick or 10.

To promote the new album *Outrider*, Page's new record company, Geffen, issued an imaginative promotional mini-briefcase, containing video and compact-disc interviews with the legend, as well as the music cassette.

Outrider was recorded over a nine-month period and was originally intended to be a double offering.

"It was going to be a double album, and that, I s'pose, also took up some of the nine-month period because I recorded enough tracks to make it a double album," Page said in the interview.

"But it was just too much of a grueling task coming up with all of these ideas for the guitar overlays."

The album is divided into two distinct sides, the first a ferocious offering of Zeppelin-style rock, while the flip delves deeper into Page's blues roots.

"There is a heavy blues content in it," he said. "I wanted to try and incorporate it as well as electric guitar playing. You know . . . acoustic guitar playing and blues playing just to give an overall sort of spectrum there," Page said.

"It's all guitars. There's some synthesizer on it, but that's guitar synthesizer as well. That was the sort of master plan of it, to make an album which was primarily a guitar album—as I don't sing, you see."

Page uses three different vocalists, who contribute their own lyrics on five of the nine tracks: former Led Zeppelin singer Robert Plant on "The Only One," John Miles on the first single "Wasting My Time" and "Wanna Make Love," and Chis Farlowe on the blues tracks "Prison Blues," "Blues Anthem," and Leon Russell's classic "Hummingbird," the only cover.

"I wanted to use Chris Farlowe because he has such a strong identity to his voice and after working with somebody as immediately identifiable as Robert, I needed somebody with that strength of vocal character of their own," Page said.

Page had jammed with John Miles, who most recently performed in Tina Turner's band, and asked him to join on the album.

"The way he's singing on this album is completely different to the work he did with the Alan Parsons Project and even on his own album—I mean, he's really stretching out on this," Page said.

Plant's presence was partially in return for work Page did on his latest solo album.

"I played on a couple of tracks on his album, and I guess it's this temperate thing of working together—I mean, we're really good mates anyway and when I had the track, I thought this would be perfect for Robert if he wanted to do it," Page said.

"He was really enthused about it. I gave him a cassette copy of the tape and he came down with reams of lyrics and we had a great time."

Also joining Page on seven tracks is drummer Jason Bonham, son of Zeppelin drummer, John Bonham, whose untimely death precipitated the band's break-up.

Jason astounded audiences when he performed with the briefly reformed Zeppelin for Atlantic Record's recent 40th anniversary concert. "He's certainly got the sort of power within his drumming which is, I think, just right for me anyway," Page said.

"He's got the same approach with his bass drum. Mind you, his father taught him to play drums. He encouraged him virtually from the point where he could sit on a drum stool—literally, I'm sure.

"There was one amusing story, really, when we (Led Zeppelin) were playing our last British gig, and we were doing a sound check, doing 'Trampled Underfoot.'

"We were playing along, concentrating on the guitar, and I looked around and Jason was on the drums. It was so John could go out the front and listen to his sound balance. So in other words, that's the approach Jason (who was about 10 at the time) had.

"I didn't know it was him playing until I looked around; it was quite a shock."

Jason Bonham, John Miles, and bass player Durban Laverde will join Page on his planned August/September tour. The show will include a complete retrospective of Page's work, including the Yardbirds era, and Page said he would "definitely" do the Zeppelin classic "Stairway to Heaven," "but as an instrumental."

"I think the audience will probably sing it if Robert's (Plant) not there," he said. "I think that's the way it should be."

Page said that, despite the lack of international success for the Firm, it was basically put together so that he and Rogers could perform live together, and he did not regret putting his solo career on hold.

"I think the time was right for me to do a solo album now. I plucked up courage, finally, to do one," he said.

He also said he believed that if it had not been for John Bonham's death, Led Zeppelin would be together and flourishing today—and he did not dismiss the possibility of a future reunion, replacing John with Jason.

"From the sort of discussions we were having just prior to John's death, because we were going to go to the States on tour anyway, we would have been revitalized after getting on the road because that would have been the first really big tour we'd have had for quite a while," Page said.

"Every album was so different from the previous one. That's one of the best things about the band; that it was always in a state of change."

Page said he was at a loss to explain the resurgence in popularity and critical reappraisal of Led Zeppelin. Clearly, he holds some contempt for the new generation of copycat bands.

"Obviously the thing that we were doing, the energy that we were putting out, touched a lot of people, and it is wonderful to have been part of something like that," he said.

"It's quite interesting really. All these bands that are using it as a text book. I must admit there were a few moments when there were sort of ghosts walking around, the ghosts of myself so many years back."

Much has been written about Led Zeppelin, but Page hesitates to put his own memoirs down in print.

"I don't know—it would probably get banned before it even got on the shelves. It would probably be too controversial," he said.

"We'll put it in a time capsule. Then, when everyone's forgotten about Led Zeppelin, we'll bring it out."

ROBERT PLANT KEEPS THE FAITH

John Swenson | October 14, 1988, *UPI*

When he hit the road with *Now and Zen*, Plant was forced to confront his past. Like so many artists who went solo after earning their reputation with a previous band, Plant had initially sworn to let Led Zeppelin lie sleeping. And like many of them, after a time he added "his legacy" back into the mix. Here he meditates on the situation of being an aging rock star, and why no one should hope to die before getting old. –Ed.

If guitarist Jimmy Page was the heart and mind of the legendary band Led Zeppelin, lead vocalist Robert Plant was its soul.

The dynamic frontman was the most influential vocalist and rock's dominant sex symbol of the '70s. When Zeppelin disbanded at the end of the decade, Plant went on to continued success as a solo artist.

While Page contemplated his creative future, Plant set himself up as the logical heir to the Zeppelin legacy.

Plant's first solo album in 1982, *Pictures at Eleven*, hit big and the next year's platinum-selling follow up, *The Principle of Moments*, showed the vocalist expanding his stylistic range and musical context.

Instead of sticking to the hard rock formula that kept him at the top of the charts, Plant switched gears on his next effort, the Honeydrippers, singing roots-rock and rhythm and blues tunes dating back to the '40s.

Though the record was designed to be a tribute to some of Plant's favorite old tunes, it became a huge hit to the surprise of record company officials who'd given Plant the chance to make what they considered an indulgence.

Plant's next record, 1985's *Shaken 'n' Stirred*, was eclipsed by speculation that Led Zeppelin would reunite following an emotional performance at the Live Aid concert.

The rumors continued to circulate despite Plant's solo success and Page's work with the Firm, culminating in the dramatic show-closing Led Zeppelin reunion earlier this year at the Atlantic Records 40th anniversary celebration.

Meanwhile, Plant had put together his hottest post-Zeppelin release, the chart-topping *Now and Zen*. The very Zep-oriented "Tall Cool One" has become one of the most popular tracks of the year, and Plant's band has been scorching audiences across the country on the most extensive tour of his career.

"I've tried to maintain some kind of self-esteem," said Plant during a break in rehearsals for the current leg of the *Now and Zen* tour, "without ending up in the corporate whorehouse."

Unlike performers who stick to a stock show each tour, Plant has prepared a different show from the one he performed earlier this year. "Some of the mainstays are still there, of course," he said, "but we have a new stage, new lights, and a lot of new material. We've changed the Led Zeppelin stuff around."

Plant promises several Zeppelin tunes, including "Immigrant Song." "There's quite a lot of stuff to choose from," he pointed out, "but you've got to be reverential. You can't do 'Stairway to Heaven,' for example.

"I think one of the contributing factors to Led Zeppelin's success was the fact that we never tried to emulate the same thing twice," said Plant. "You get more musical stimulation if you try to change things around as much as you can."

Plant conceded that the first steps in his post-Zeppelin career were a bit shaky. "At first I was kind of shy, I didn't think that I had a great deal to offer on my own in the stark reality of 1981. Then again, maybe confidence isn't the best thing to have when you're writing.

"It was a most peculiar time trying to croon ideas from a stool to people you are kind of hiring. I need the feedback because I can't write the musical structures, I can only sing them."

Plant is getting tremendous feedback from his current partner, guitarist Phil Johnstone, and the band backing him up. The Zeppelin days are over, and nobody knows it better than Plant.

"My physical appearance is changing," he said. "Nothing we can do about that. I don't stick my chest out in such an audacious fashion as I used to, although I'm still sticking a few things out.

"Some things change. They've got to or you look like a turkey. Sixty percent of the audience at my shows is female, age 18 to 24, which is very encouraging.

"I think the musicians around me are guarding my identity as much as developing their own. There are bands who are hugely successful who are running out of steam. That's a sad thing for a musician. Some things that are painfully obvious have a short life span. If you start playing because you want to play but end up just doing it for the money, why prolong the agony?"

Though his youthful days are behind him, his talent is still very much in evidence. Always a sterling screamer, his singing has improved over the years as the approach has toned down. "I stopped smoking cigarettes about a year ago," he noted, "and my voice definitely sounds better for it."

A DECADE LATER, PLANT REFUSES TO LIVE HIS PAST

Thor Christensen | July 22, 1990, *Milwaukee Journal Sentinel*

No matter how far forward he moved, the specter of Led Zeppelin rarely strayed from any consideration of Robert Plant. As he continued to create, anytime he got within hailing distance of Jimmy Page, rumors started to spew like volcanic ash. Yet he sounded as diverse as ever in his solo work, which continued in the trend of how he once described In *Through the Out Door*: "more conscientious and less animal." –Ed.

Robert Plant has spent his entire solo career trying to prove he isn't a creature of the past. But when your past involves a band as legendary as Led Zeppelin, it's a tough specter to elude.

Last month, Plant joined former Zeppelin guitarist Jimmy Page onstage at a charity concert in Knebworth, England. The duo played just three songs together, but it set off a flurry of rumors and questions, including the one Plant dreads the most: When is Led Zeppelin going to re-form?

"All I did was play Knebworth with Pagey, and now I should think I'll pay for that for about a year," Plant said with a hearty laugh, speaking by phone from his Washington, DC, hotel room.

"It's OK to quote from your past. But I'm more interested in quoting from my present and pointing toward the future."

He has achieved that goal. Since Led Zeppelin disbanded in 1980 after the alcohol-related death of drummer John Bonham, the singer has toned down his wildcat scream and forged a sound that is both more restrained and modern than his old band's atomic hard rock.

At first, Plant refused to sing any Zep songs onstage. "I wanted to develop success with my own music before I could go back and recite from my past," he said. "And now I've done that."

So when Plant, 41, plays Saturday night at Alpine Valley Music Theatre, he'll mix three or four Zeppelin tunes in with songs from his five solo albums. (His current band comprises guitarist Doug Boyle, bassist Charlie Jones, keyboardist Phil Johnstone, and drummer Chris Blackwell.)

But the show will emphasize *Manic Nirvana*, a montage of folk, metal, hip-hop, and psychedelic rock that is perhaps his most innovative solo album yet.

"It's not for me to say how innovative I am," Plant said. "But I am always wiggling around, both physically and emotionally, trying to drag the next phase of exploration out of the whole thing.

"I try to stay away from the obvious flailings of hard rock, and you could describe [*Manic Nirvana*] as being a little more extreme and a little less mainstream than my other albums. It's the same as Zep really. Zep touched on folk and Eastern music, and with songs like 'The Crunge,' we even got near James Brown."

In 1988, Plant finally came to grips with his past and injected his *Now and Zen* album with computer samples of such Zeppelin gems as "Dazed and Confused" and "Whole Lotta Love."

On his new album, he even quotes a few lyrics from "Black Dog" in his remake of the obscure 1961 Kenny Dino hit, "Your Ma Said You Cried in Your Sleep Last Night."

"I'm tipping my hat and looking back," he explained to an interviewer in 1988. Today, however, Plant bristles when it is suggested he is paying tribute to Zeppelin's legacy.

"No, no, no, no," he said. "It has nothing to do with paying tribute. I'm the guy who wrote the lyrics, and I'm just sending myself up. I mean, when I'm singing the lyrics from 'Black Dog' in 'Your Ma Said You Cried,' it's a tease. It doesn't fit, therefore it works. I don't do it to insult the great legend, or whatever it is. I just do it for a bit of laugh."

Plant isn't the only one sampling his old band these days. Two rap groups, the Beastie Boys and De La Soul, have used snippets of Zep's songs in their music. The avant-garde New York band the Ordinaires recorded a classical remake of "Kashmir" last year, and the list of hard-rock bands stealing Zeppelin's sound is endless (Whitesnake, the Cult, the Mission U.K., to name a few).

Twenty-two years after it formed and a decade after its swan song, Led Zeppelin continues to shape the sound of pop music.

In its heyday, however, the group was a punching bag for punk rockers and critics.

Lumped together with Elton John, Rod Stewart, and other rich English superstars, Zeppelin was criticized, in Plant's words, "for being remote and conceited and missing the plot."

"To a large degree, the punks were right. Groups like Deep Purple and Black Sabbath had lost the point, if they ever had it, and I thought Led Zeppelin had lost the point, too, around the time of *In Through the Out Door*," he said, referring to the quartet's last album.

Yet the group made vital music up until the end. For proof, you need only listen to "Wearing and Tearing," a devastating hard-rock piece that Plant likely will play Saturday.

The tune (which appears on *Coda*, a 1982 LP of outtakes) came about while the band was preparing *In Through the Out Door* in late 1978. The punk band Generation X happened to be rehearsing next door, and the group's singer, Billy Idol, yelled taunts at Zeppelin's members whenever he saw them.

"We wrote 'Wearing and Tearing' because of the punks, to say we could make challenging, crashing music just as well as they could," Plant said. "We struggled near the end of Zeppelin as far as the personalities in the band. But creatively, our potential was still huge."

Inspired by the same punk movement that loathed Zeppelin, Plant listens to quite a bit of alternative rock these days. He lists the metal-punk bands Faith No More and Soundgarden as current favorites, and calls the Zep parody band Dread Zeppelin "absolutely excellent."

Jimmy Page, by comparison, has spent his post-Zeppelin career mining traditional hard rock. The subject of Plant's former band mate is a prickly one.

"I'm not in a position to comment, really," Plant said when asked about Page's 1988 solo album, *Outrider*. "If it was good enough for him, it was good enough for me. How'd you like that? Tactful enough?"

Despite their uneasy relationship, the two have teamed publicly on several occasions. They reunited Zeppelin for Live Aid in 1985 and again in 1988 for the Atlantic Records' 40th anniversary celebration. At Knebworth, they played Zep's "Rock and Roll," "Immigrant Song," and "Wearing and Tearing" backed by Plant's current band.

Although Plant calls their Live Aid set "a shambles," six months later he met with Page, bassist John Paul Jones, and ex-Chic drummer Tony Thompson for a week of secret rehearsals in Bath, England. The reunion attempt quickly disintegrated, but in later interviews Plant still seemed open to the idea of launching a new Zeppelin.

Now, however, he's changed his tune.

"Led Zeppelin was a really wonderful thing, but it lives as a part of people's memories," he said.

"It's not something in the present tense and neither will it ever be in the present tense. It's not going to exist again."

COMMUNICATION BREAKDOWN

"The prime motivation was to write challenging songs and enjoy ourselves while playing them . . . I believe touring is the only way to see and experience the things you write about. I still believe the way one illuminates his life is through humor and hard work, and touring has equal parts of all of that."

– Robert Plant to Bruce Britt, *Telegram and Gazette*, August 19, 1990

COMMUNICATION BREAKDOWN

"I was fully aware the work that I did during the '80s certainly wasn't of the quality of Zeppelin, but that wasn't necessarily my own fault. The other components weren't there. I didn't feel I had the right pieces. But working with David [Coverdale] was a totally different thing. It was suddenly right back to that original spark of creativity and ideas flowing. I feel I have my heart in it again."

– Jimmy Page to Robert Hilburn, *Los Angeles Times*, March 17, 1993

COVERDALE/PAGE
ELECTRONIC PRESS KIT VIDEO

March 1993 | Geffen Records Public Relations

Page's next move, hooking up with former Whitesnake and Deep Purple frontman David Coverdale to create an album simply titled *Coverdale/Page*, was at once unexpected, ironic (considering Plant's attitude toward the man), and entirely logical. In its time, the album was a hit, going gold and—considering the way things had changed since the heyday of both men—garnering a fair bit of airplay and attention. Ultimately, however, the odd-coupling faded, with both men ultimately going back to their strongholds: Coverdale reforming a variety of Whitesnakes and Page evolving and doing something even more remarkable. –Ed.

Jimmy Page: I had a call from my manager. I guess this came in a roundabout fashion. I think we both received individual calls, but the essence of it was, "How would you like to work with David?" And I said I would give it some thought. And anyway, it came to be that we decided to meet up in New York. I'll pass you off to David here, because his situation is slightly different.

David Coverdale: Well, I was languishing in the Bastille for a period of time, of all of the peripherals of the rock business, coming towards the end of—going into 1990 with Whitesnake. I'd had quite enough, thank you! The mousse abuse had actually gotten to me, and there was an assortment of reasons that I wanted to take a reflective period away from what is called "the music business."

We met in March, the end of March in New York, where we actually stopped traffic when we went for a walk, which was a blast, and got on terrifically well. Agreed on . . . really we covered a great deal in a short space of time. And the most important agreement would be that we would take everything one step at a time. It was obvious we got on very well together, the next step was to find out whether we could actually *write* together.

JP: At that point in time I was certainly looking to work with a—in a—collaboration. This became a partnership, as such, rather than just a casual thing.

DC: Jimmy and I have a great deal in common in terms of the library of music which has influenced us, and we can still draw upon, particularly the blues, and obviously a passion for rock.

JP: We had bumped into each other in the past on possibly almost a handful of occasions—

DC: *Literally.* [*Laughs.*]

JP: Yes. Usually in the club here and there in the town where both our respective bands may have been. At no point did we ever appear on the same bill at a festival or anything like that, or jammed together. So it was just really casual meetings. Totally informal.

DC: All of the demos for the songs that we made together, I think it was the extravagant cost of 50 dollars from Radio Shack. It was a little, what they call a "ghetto blaster" or whatever. In essence, we sat down with acoustic guitars and this extravagant recording device and literally just teased tunes out of each other, worked on things . . . one thing led to another in terms of riffs or chord sequences and stuff. It was an absolute bonding of two . . . well, I'd like to think, craftsmen.

JP: There are a lot of acoustic guitars demos without any doubt, but the very first one that we did was through an amp, an electric guitar through an amp. And we had a tape with some drums—it wasn't even a drum machine. This is real primitive stuff we're talking about.

DC: The original—

JP: But the first number to come out from this collusion between the two of us was on the very first day. It was "Absolution Blues." And we pretty much got the whole structure of that together in the first day, plus some other ideas that were coming out. These ideas were just pouring out over that first day.

DC: It was terrific.

JP: They were just coming so fast, we'd say "well, let's get this down, let's get this down" and then we came back and we finessed them, and rearranged them.

We didn't go in with any preconceived notions or anything. As I was describing previously, "Absolution Blues" was just a lick that just came out of thin air, as did the many of the subsequent licks which followed and caused sequences and those . . . I did have a few bits and pieces tucked away from the past, but I only really plundered a couple of those, you know, from my old demos, I'm talking about. Because most of it was just coming up fresh. There was no necessity to scratch one's head and think, "Oh what are we going to be doing next?" It was just pouring out.

DC: Absolutely, absolutely no frustrating times. The song "Pride and Joy," which is the first video from the *Coverdale/Page* album, I came up—I had an introductory riff which I thought would be rather jolly to present to "His Royal Darkness." After he'd paid me the compliment of visiting Tahoe, I said, "Okay, it's up to you to pick a place for us to go." Because I mean, I think we'd pulled all the vibes out of Mother Nature up there. And we'd run out of movies, as well, I think at the time.

[*Page laughs.*]

DC: So, he who shall be obeyed picked Barbados! So initially that song was called "Barbados Boogie." And, of course, instead of this lovely, charming, lilting, hoedown, toe-tapping piece, he puts in this riff from hell and changed the whole new coloratura of it and had me screaming again, at my age.

[*Page laughs.*]

JP: David's vocal approaches . . . he has many different timbres to his voice, many textures. And as far as we've been talking about the real high, stratosphere vocals, he's a total vocal gymnast in this area, and the sensitivity, almost caressing quality of his ballad approach.

DC: When Jimmy first played the introductory guitar riff to "Shake My Tree"—apart from the fact it was "What's he doing?"—it was this blur of fantastic fingers. *That's* what he rejoices in that I can't copy. Because I play a bit—I play a little guitar, but only for composition. But I do like to think I'm a guitar stud, don't I now and again? I'll go into flights of fancy, right when he slaps me around heartlessly and totally . . .

JP: Something I rarely do is let somebody play guitar on an album, but I did with David! I did with David!

DC: He encouraged me, in fact. He encouraged me to play guitar on the record. And apart from it being a singular honor, it was an absolute pleasure.

JP: We started in Vancouver, laying down tracks, basically going for the drum tracks because the studio up there, Little Mountain, was exceptionally good. It has a reputation for getting good drum tracks, and of course that's the backbone of the whole thing. After that, you're going to be layering on the instruments and voices. But we actually went from Vancouver to Miami and employed some of the local musicians down there, a local bass player, a studio musician, and also a keyboard player. We just layered guitars. We got to the point where we were working 72 track, with these different instruments plus David's vocals, etcetera.

DC: The verse ideas and stuff for the song "Waiting on You" were a double. I'm just a meat-and-potatoes, nuts-and-bolts singer, other than the chest beating, the . . . *bravado*. But it came to the—what I would feel, if we could call a chorus line or potential hook line—there were all these weird ascending, descending . . . and I'm going, "Oh, dear. That's the guitar solo, is it? That's a bit quick." Unfortunately not, that was the hook line, and that completely and thoroughly evaded me for a while, quite seriously. And then one morning, I just received a signal from God, and he said, "Just sing straight through it." And I called [Jimmy] up and confused him by saying, "I think I've got this great Motown lick for 'Waiting on You.'"

JP: He numbers himself with this Motown lick. This has nothing to do with Motown.

[*Page and Coverdale bicker and talk over one other.*]

JP: Okay, go on.

DC: It was [*sings*] "No matter what you say, no matter what you do, this heart is dedicated . . . " All that stuff. I was just singing Diana Ross! Honest to God! I want a pearl necklace and a wiggling butt! An assortment of wigs!

JP: Honestly, when we were working on this, David came up with the melody for the verse almost immediately, you know, it was just there. Yes, the chorus had hung around for a little while. I actually had a melody for it, which I was holding back unless we *really* got stuck. But when he came out—

DC: You were just making me suffer.

JP: That's right. Absolutely! But when he came through with this melody, it beat my one, hands down, so that was really good. No contest.

DC: Jimmy is a sonic architect, in terms of his structure. It's the most interesting—he is without a shadow of a doubt, regardless of his legacy—the most interesting musician I've worked with because he looks at the song as a song, and how he can complement the theme of the song as a musician, as a guitarist. Whereas a lot of musicians use it as an excuse for showing off, technical expertise and whatever.

JP: "Take a Look at Yourself" came out of a chord sequence which I—which we'd worked on the guitar . . . It was more of a reflective feel, of "Take Me For a Little While."

DC: And we had one of them, didn't we? [*Laughs loudly.*]

JP: We had one of those already. And it was during that period we had in Barbados that David came up with another section to it, and we tried it in a different tempo, and that's the way it went.

From the beginning of this project, David and I were partners, total 50/50, and we were going to produce the record ourselves, between just the two of us. But Mike Fraser, the engineer who'd worked on Aerosmith projects in the past, produced such a fine sound to what we were doing, and also was helpful as far as a barometer in certain aspects, as well, that we decided, at the end of the day, to give him coproduction credit along with us. But it was right at the end that we decided that, but it was certainly on merit.

DC: "Over Now" started off as one of Jimmy's crunchy, malevolent, dark, chord sequences, and a particular groove and tempo that is *very* appealing to me. And I just felt the mood of the song was dark. So I took a chapter out of my particular life, and we actually discussed it because he's had the same kind of experience, when your actual partner isn't all they're meant to be and it takes a little bit of time for you to actually realize that. And afterwards, it's kind of an exorcism just to dispose of it by putting this—by actually writing that kind of lyric. So now that's . . . it's over now, but this is a testament to a particular time.

JP: "Feeling Hot" is one of those really fun rock 'n' roll numbers. It's got all the energy that was really there buzzing away within the writing period in those early stages. It's got all of that . . . adrenaline pump. And all the way through—well once we'd finished putting it together, we were saying to each other, we said, "This is the opening track when we do live shows." It's got all that energy. It's a damn good track as well.

DC: Particularly for the style of music that we enjoy, analog seems to be able to handle the crunch, the real dirty, grungy stuff at the bottom end. Which is no disrespect to digital equipment, I mean it's magnificent, and the advent of CD has been a blessing for any musician, really, because the last time you hear your work how it ought to be heard, is the last playback of the mix in the studio. Unless, of course, like him [*gestures to Page*] you've got your own studio. It's wonderful technology, it's just that the particular approach that we enjoy, analog lends itself much more as a *pow*, isn't it, than—

JP: It's really for recording. If you were going to be recording a classical session, for instance, with a huge orchestra, then you would go straight into digital. But with all the overdubs that we were doing, we just felt [analog] was better.

DC: We do have a secret there, which we're not going to share, how we keep the signal so fresh, of course.

JP: Absolutely.

DC: And that is our secret for us to know and you to ponder.

JP: That's why we produced this.

DC: In terms of in concert, Jimmy and I have actually jammed in various blues clubs whenever the mood has taken us, without any kind of announcement or whatever. Just the adrenaline, and the rush has been incredible. All we do is suck that in and send it back. It's indescribable, the rush that you can get from an audience. When you're a *part* of an audience, you're focused towards the stage, but when you're on the stage, you're on the receiving end of this *enormous* wave of emotion and adrenaline. It's the most energizing experience I've ever had in my life.

I think both of us feel that this has to be taken live. It really does. From the very beginning, we shook hands in New York—this was before we'd even sat down to see whether we could compose together—and agreed that if indeed everything did work out positively, that we would take it to the street and feature slices of our careers. We will most definitely be featuring Zeppelin and Whitesnake, and certainly, as we're so very proud of the *Coverdale/Page* album.

JP: I was just thinking about this, "Let's make a really, really good record," one that deserved to be made by the two of us, and we got the best out of each other without any denying of that. It's a fact.

DC: There isn't anything on the record that can't walk off the disc and into the arena.

JP: Sure.

DC: We were a great inspiration to each other and very encouraging. A lot of people, I would imagine with Jimmy or myself, are somewhat intimidated because of whatever we've done. We settled with each other immediately. For me, it was an enormous inspiration to work with somebody I'd admired for so long, and certainly learned from—and copped from, too. It was a treat. It was the most refreshing experience I've had for a long, long time.

COMMUNICATION BREAKDOWN

"I want Jimmy to do whatever he can to have a groove—it's his career. He's a fantastic guitar player. Whatever he wants to do, he should do and enjoy it. . . . On his record, his playing sounds great . . . It's quite a quizzical situation, really. Having worked with Jimmy for so long, it makes me wonder whether or not he could have tried a little bit harder (to sound like Led Zeppelin) or a little bit less hard."

—Robert Plant to Peter Howell, *Toronto Star*, May 26, 1993

PLANT'S NEW WORK HARKS BACK TO LED ZEPPELIN'S ACOUSTIC FOLK

Neil Spencer | May 5, 1993, Observer News Service / _Guardian_

For the first time in their careers Plant and Page were, if not competing, not cooperating. Plant knew Page had hooked up with David Coverdale, the person that he saw as his antithesis, and many in the press recognized it, as well. But comparing _Coverdale/Page_ with Plant's _Fate of Nations_ shows just how much Plant had changed as an artist after the passing of John Bonham. —Ed.

The long shadow of Led Zeppelin still falls over so much contemporary music, and over the flaxen head of Robert Plant in particular, so that it's something of a shock to realize that the singer has now been a solo act for longer than he played the strutting frontman for the most infamous band of the '70s.

"I know!" says Plant, 44. "I think about that sometimes in the morning, when I'm studying the effects of time in the bathroom mirror and saying, 'Ah my boy, shall we do the [Royal] Albert Hall with the orchestra yet?'"

Unlike many of his contemporaries, Plant has never succumbed to such temptations; never taken the proffered pots of gold for a Zep reunion. Instead, since Zeppelin's demise in 1980 following the death of drummer John Bonham, Plant has held to his own course with quiet conviction, through five solo albums and a brace of hit singles in 1983's "Big Log" and 1988's "Tall Cool One." By his own admission "it hasn't been the most resounding of solo careers, but I feel good about the way things have gone for me."

Currently, the singer has good cause to feel satisfied. His new album, *The Fate of Nations*, is his most accomplished solo work to date, a convincing mixture of thundering, wide-screen rock and catchy FM ballads like the newly released single, "29 Palms."

"I think it stands comfortably alongside most things going on," he says with satisfaction.

If Plant's previous two albums, *Now and Zen* and *Manic Nirvana*, borrowed freely from Zeppelin's oeuvre, then *Fate of Nations* harks back to the less-acknowledged strand of acoustic folk that ran through their music. Guitarist Richard Thompson and Clannad's Máire Brennan show up on "Come Into My Life," uilleann pipes warble on "Down to the Sea." Several other songs illustrate Plant's interest in travel, landscape, and pre-history, including "Network News," which addresses the ecological aftermath of the Kuwait war.

"Musically I'd become a bit techno'd out," he says "and I had a real desire to make things more emotive, to write songs from the pre-techno heart, forgetting the public's usual view of me. I wanted to be the other RP, the one who sits up in the Welsh mountains and waits for Arthur."

One could arguably retrace heavy metal's love affair with Viking warriors, broadswords, and pillage, evident in band names like Saxon, Slayer, and Megadeth, to Plant's fixation with Celtic and Saxon Britain, along with his ululating battle cries on Zeppelin classics like "The Battle of Nevermore" and "The Immigrant Song."

Plant's interests in the past are no superficial flirtation with death or glory imagery, however. Alongside his enthusiasm for rock trivia and forgotten B-sides he will wax lyrical about the Welsh borders—"where the last real nationalist spirit thunders around aimlessly up in the hills"—and about Raymond Williams' epic history of the region, *The People of the Black Mountains*.

"My two major loves, apart from the human and the animal, are the virgin desert and the history of the post-Roman Celtic state in (Britain)," he gushes. "It sounds sublimely stupid, the old rock king sitting here holding forth, but it provides a good balance to the rock world, it's good stuff to sing about."

It would seem so, to judge by the enduring appeal of that old Zeppelin anthem, "Stairway to Heaven," which still crops up in radio listener surveys as the most popular pop number ever.

"It was written with absolute sincerity as a piece of optimism. The trouble is you can only have that frame of mind in the good moments. After you'd stopped a Led Zeppelin show several times to prevent people kicking the s—— out of each other, to bring it to some kind of sanctimonious finale with 'Stairway' seemed absurd."

COMMUNICATION BREAKDOWN

"As you can imagine, I get lots of bands that want me to get them to sound like Zeppelin, which doesn't really interest me. [Producing the Butthole Surfers] was very strange and somewhat subversive . . . I try and do a lot of different things so as not to end up doing rock band after rock band. Fortunately, I'm in a position to pick whatever looks interesting."

– John Paul Jones to Jason Cohen, *Rolling Stone*, June 24, 1993

MUSICIAN ROBERT PLANT DISCUSSES HIS LATEST ALBUM

Mark McEwan | October 25, 1993, *CBS This Morning*

Once upon a time, Mark McEwen spun and announced records on New York's venerable (and sadly deceased) AOR Pioneer WNEW FM. Which meant he should have known better . . . —Ed.

From the very beginning, rock musician Robert Plant was a superstar as the heart and soul of Led Zeppelin. Yet, after twenty-five years in the business and continuing success, he still doesn't do a lot of interviews. We pinned him down at Manhattan's Anarchy Cafe—good title there—to talk about his latest album, *Fate of Nations*.

[Excerpt of Robert Plant's music video for "I Believe" plays.]

Mark McEwen: Let's talk about a song on the album, "I Believe." It's the latest single. And it's a song written, that you said, about your son who passed away in the '70s. Tell me, why now? Why did you come to that song now?

Robert Plant: I ain't got the slightest. Good TV, eh?

MM: Yeah.

RP: I don't carry the whole situation around like some huge emotional disaster in my life. Life is life. All those things come and go, you know. It's fate. But it just was appropriate. The mood of the music was there.

[*Excerpt of "I Believe" plays.*]

MM: Critics like this record. Do you care?

RP: Yeah.

MM: Why?

RP: This is the ego game, too, you know. There aren't many people around who've been around for this length of time and actually still give something that is refreshing. There's a lot of people around who—they lose the fire in their bellies that was there originally and they—it becomes something else, cabaret.

[*Excerpt of a Warner Home Video of Led Zeppelin's "Stairway to Heaven" plays.*]

MM: The fire in Plant's belly carved him a place in rock 'n' roll history as a member of Led Zeppelin, who released nine hugely successful albums from 1969 to 1979.

[*Excerpt of Plant's video for "I'm in the Mood" plays.*]

MM: Plant followed up his Zeppelin years with a solo career that's lasted over a decade.

RP: When I began after Zeppelin finished, I was always looking behind, going, "Oh, no, here it comes, my past." I, you know, I don't care about anything now. I just care about what I do which gets me to this point.

MM: Were you nervous when you started as a solo—Robert Plant as opposed to Led Zeppelin with Robert Plant as a lead vocalist?

RP: When you're in something that's so successful—when you're a part of something that is nurtured and fed and pampered and, you know, idolized to such a degree, it's insane, absurd, and ridiculous. In a way it's quite ref—it was quite refreshing to stand there and go, "Oh, OK."

[*Excerpt of Plant's video to "Heaven Knows" plays.*]

RP: I play the pop game. And the artistry and the desire for success sometimes have collisions, you know?

MM: Tell me about that line "I play the pop game." What do you mean?

RP: Well, what are we doing here? Look, look, what does this mean? We, you know, you're talking to me about my career, and there are moves that you can make that are part of the game and there are things that you do for yourself.

[*Excerpt of "I Believe" plays.*]

MM: Robert, one thing. What you do—you make music, you tour, you write. This part of it, how much of a pain is this part of it?

RP: It's a really big pain.

MM: Why do you do it?

RP: Because there are three people from the record company over there and they've got the story of my early days in Led Zeppelin and they'll publish it if I don't do this.

MM: I mean, because you get asked a lot of the same things over and over, picking meat off of the bones.

RP: If I've got any dignity at all, I can maintain it by—through my music. And you're not a bad guy, you know? And it's this time of day when you have to have a—a drink.

MM: Not that Robert Plant needed a drink after our interview. He just happened to be a few feet from the bar at the Anarchy Cafe when our chat ended.

COMMUNICATION BREAKDOWN

"I don't think happiness is a permanent state; it's some kind of treaty you make with your circumstances at the time . . . I've been chiseling at it for years. I find that when I try to echo this thing in the bottom of my soul, that's when I do my best. It satiates this little flickering flame that won't go away. If it were to go away, I'd lose my gift. It's a remarkable condition, really. I'm glad I've got it."
— Robert Plant to Kim Neely, *Rolling Stone*, July 8, 1993

COMMUNICATION BREAKDOWN

"I became aware of Diamanda [Galás] in 1983 with her album *Wild Women with Steak Knives*. It was different from anything I'd ever heard before."

– John Paul Jones to Sam Wood, *Ottawa Citizen*, November 10, 1994

PAGE AND PLANT

Mat Snow | December 1994, *MOJO*

Inevitably (or so it seems in hindsight), Plant and Page decided that maybe they were better together than apart. This far ranging interview is equal parts informative and hysterical, which just shows that, at the behest of MTV, Page and Plant were able to hit their old Led Zeppelin balance running. The resulting live album, *No Quarter: Jimmy Page and Robert Plant Unledded*, sounded like they had grown massively musically but never lost a step in the interim. Yet it was not meant to be a Led Zeppelin album. Page and Plant sought to work with two kinds of musical capital instead: the classic material fused with their new chops and interests acquired in the decade plus since the band broke up. They did not want to sound like Led Zeppelin, which is why they didn't invite John Paul Jones to the party. —Ed.

THE DATE: Thursday, September 29, 1994. THE PLACE: a table outside a café in Tottenham Street, London W1. THE CAST: Robert Plant, Jimmy Page, Mat Snow.

Mat Snow: Is this the first time you've been interviewed together since talking to *Rolling Stone*'s Cameron Crowe in 1975?

Robert Plant: It probably is, isn't it?

Jimmy Page: Yeah.

RP: If I'd known that last night I probably wouldn't have got any sleep, like on *A Question of Sport**. We've never had anything new . . .

**A Question of Sport* is a long-running quiz show on the BBC.

JP: Since 1975?

RP: We had nothing to talk about—

JP: We must have had something.

RP: We didn't have anything that—

JP: —was futuristic to discuss.

RP: If you say so. So this is it—quite an important moment, I suppose. Especially for the waiter.

MS: Who was it who actually popped the question?

[*Meaningful looks are exchanged. A pause.*]

RP: Well, Jimmy had been sending me signals through various publications. Ha ha ha ha.

JP: People were always asking me what the story was, and all I had to say was, "I guess the time is not right at the moment."

RP: The thing to avoid was us being gotten into the wrong hands and manipulated into ending up like a sort of animated Pink Floyd, if you like, roll out the barrel, the same old shit.

JP: That worry surmounted the possibilities of how good it might be if we got back together. Once we got back together we started vibing each other up into getting on with what we really ought to be doing, which is making music and writing new stuff, back to square one. And it all started coming into place, which became very apparent. A new focus on our old stuff and everything.

RP: The pressures that I wanted to avoid we've been able to. Like a Rolling Stones situation where the lads get back together and it's like, "Well, I remember back in so-and-so, and they're still pretty good . . ." Just being candyfloss for some total retro occasion.

JP: Once you do that you're caught, aren't you? Because that's what everyone is always going to expect.

RP: What we have is four new songs. Admittedly, they're totally out of context with how people would have expected us to write and present new songs.

JP: Not necessarily "Yallah," Robert . . .

RP: "Yallah" is a loop put together by Martin Meissonnier. He's married to Amina, the Tunisian singer, and he worked with Khaled and Youssou N'Dour and so on. I met him when I played in Paris last year and I told him that Jimmy and I were thinking of working together, and could he come up with some drum loops from stuff that he's recorded in Mauritania? He's got access to all sorts of stuff, and I said, "Let's get some real slinky loops which are coming from an African or a desert sound." He did, and that gave us the opportunity to have rhythms which we could slow down, so it's got real sleaze, and all the drums open up so it has much more of a hangover sonically. And we just started writing around loops. We started kicking into this guitar/vocal talk against these Arab loops, and that was it.

MS: Would you start off with a rhythm groove back in the days of Led Zeppelin?

JP: We've never done anything like that before. Well, I certainly haven't but maybe you have . . .

RP: I've done a bit, but not with such fluidity.

MS: Did the MTV offer to do *Unledded* concentrate the mind or was it irrelevant to the decision to work together again?

JP: It might have been a catalyst in such a way that it was presented from their end: it would be nice to have Led Zeppelin in an intimate situation. That's the way it was presented to us. But, of course, being us, it was, "Well, how shall we really do it?" The acoustic versions of songs, after so many of them, you'd start to lose the character of things . . .

RP: A compromise.

JP: So we just thought we'd rethink everything and do it properly and show people we'd really thought about this whole thing.

RP: Really, the cuteness of having a whole acoustic program wears quite thin. There are certain people who can pull it off because their music is totally acoustic . . .

JP: We could have done it! But this was far more of a challenge to try and go over the horizons again.

RP: I wanted to call it "Unhinged" . . .

JP: Yeah, haha.

RP: Because I felt we should begin to open up our whole account again as two guys. As soon as we started working on Meissonnier's loops we knew that it was a good blend and nothing had really changed. In fact we'd gained quite a bit of experience from doing all the other things, obviously, and that would give us some focus on working together again. I'm certainly a lot different to the guy who sang on *In Through the Out Door*. So it meant that we would be working together in a different form of partnership. The whole idea of being able to brandish the Arab link was so important to me, and really crucial because, outside of Raï music and the whole WOMAD [World of Music, Arts, and Dance] politeness, there's something round the corner that we're just touching on now and we're going to expand on, where if you bring these two musics, these two cultures, these two—well, I don't know about our side—aesthetics, on the Arab/Berber/Gnaoua thing, and you don't modify it, you don't present it in hushed tones in the Royal Festival Hall—you mix it with the way we are, a pair of questionable characters of ill-repute, you make a totally different form. Do you know Dimi Mint Abba, a Mauritanian singer? She's amazing. Her band has just started using electric guitars and stuff. It's so reckless! It's got nothing to do with Youssou N'Dour and that sort of smooth, Senegalese, polite African thing. It's, like, really radical.

MS: Africa is a big place.

JP: Yeah, hahaha.

RP: Haha. I'm glad you said that. So, the idea was MTV calling and us saying, "Unplugged? Sure," then leaving it another couple of weeks and then saying, "If we're going to do it, we're going to do it electric with all sorts of different things . . ."

JP: It's really totally plugged. Even the acoustic guitars are plugged in.

RP: It would be silly to linger on the terminology too long because it's worked for them for a period of time and is working for us in its antithesis.

MS: The new approach is a shorter step for Robert from his last album, *Fate of Nations*, than for Jimmy with *Coverdale/Page*—true?

JP: It certainly was an adventure. But I've been looking forward to working with Robert for so long, and have been looking in that interim period for someone I could have the same rapport with as I had with Robert. And it's certainly come back.

RP: If anything I was frightened off from working with Jimmy for the reason that we'd instantly get manipulated into a compromise in the general tone, and people's general will—"Aaah. Why isn't John Paul Jones playing? Aaaaah. Will they do 'Stairway'?" All that crap. If we're going to have a life together musically, creatively—which we have, more than we've had for twenty years, I think— then we've got to do it this way. I knew at the end of *Fate of Nations* that even if I ended up busking on street corners in Rabat, that I'd have to go and work on a much more Arabic level . . .

JP: Plus, putting it in context on my behalf, we went to Bombay in the '70s, around '72, and we did some early recordings then with Indian musicians to see how that would go. That was really successful for what it was over the course of an evening . . .

RP: There's a great bootleg out of it. [*The March 1972 version of Friends with Plant, Page and the Bombay Symphony Orchestra.*]

JP: The bootleg does really well, apparently. It was quite an historic occasion. So we knew it could work. There was a reasonable amount of danger, though.

RP: Yeah, and I think that was a good thing.

MS: What's the worst that could have happened? The musical partnership might not have worked after all?

RP: If we hadn't started with the loops, then we'd have had to have started as a four-piece, which would have been a bit "roll out the barrel" for me.

MS: Is that why John Paul Jones was not asked? It would have thrown out the chemistry?

RP: Apart from the fact that it would be virtually Led Zeppelin and the next person you start talking about is Jason Bonham, which is just so cheesy and ridiculous, the fact is that our thread was this North African thing, was India, was the Howlin' Wolf riffs. We focused together on those mutual points, so rather than confuse the issue let's see what we've still got. So it's nothing at all personal. It's just that at this point in time you've got to get a result quickly to know if it's worth it.

JP: We were gaining so much momentum from the loops and working with Charlie [Jones, bass] and Michael [Lee, drums], that quite honestly I for one wasn't thinking John Paul Jones. I was thinking about what we were getting together between the two of us and the rest of the band. It was its own thing before all of that started to become an issue.

RP: Jonesy, I really like what he does and the angles he employs and the projects he works on, which are far from the mainstream, and he has a great career in that respect. But I didn't think it necessary for us to . . . This is the pressure thing again.

JP: We're working together and all of a sudden everyone's saying John Paul Jones ought to be there.

RP: So anyway, it's good luck John, and maybe we'll all get together again somewhere down the line.

JP: Yeah, in the future.

RP: But right now this thing is growing so much. We've about another nine songs written from a four-piece angle.

MS: Where will this momentum take you?

RP: We write songs, record them, get intimidated by management and record company, we have stormy marriages then we go on the road. Then we go round and round and do that until smoke comes out of the chimney and the ashes are spread at the centre spot at Molineux. [The home of Wolverhampton Wanderers, the football team Robert supports.]

JP: Hahahaha!

RP: So we can take Nigel Eaton, the hurdy-gurdy player, and Jim [Sutherland], the bodhran player, and Charlie and Michael, and Hossam Ramzy, and three drummers . . .

JP: And the amazing violin player.

RP: We've got work permits already under way for the Egyptians and we can go, and we can play for ten people or ten thousand.

MS: Given language barriers and so on, how will that work as a band on the road?

RP: We've been rehearsing with them so much and had such a laugh with the Egyptians. They are wicked in the real sense of the word. They're so funny, so kind of surreptitious, and it's great fun! Even getting a cup of tea you have to haggle!

JP: They've really got into the spirit. You can tell that they play from the heart.

MS: Will you be playing in North Africa?

RP: Hopefully in Rabat and maybe Fez. Western pop music in North Africa—although Morocco out of the whole of North Africa is the most cosmopolitan and has the most access to MTV and stuff like that—is still a bit like us reading Sufi sayings: we think we know it, but our translation of what's going on is probably two leagues away from what the intention was originally. The only person who's successful in the psyche of Moroccans is Bob Marley. Bob Marley is huge, and I can understand why, because of his link with Africa and Haile Selassie. There is no room really for Western pop music in North Africa, and neither should there be. The great thing about the music there is that it isn't part of this shit. People sing in the marketplace, make cassettes, do a few gigs: it's much more like it always has been, before Tin Pan Alley.

MS: Jimmy, did you embark on each new partnership after the dissolution of Led Zeppelin hoping that it might be long-term?

JP: No, I never thought of anything being a long-term thing. Do you mean with, like, Paul Rodgers?

MS: Paul Rodgers, John Miles, Chris Farlowe, David Coverdale.

JP: Everything was supposed to be a one-album thing so I could move on to something else. The fact that the Firm even went on and did two albums really wasn't at all what was planned. I didn't want to get locked into anything at all.

MS: So is Page Plant like Burton Taylor, the marriage that always should have been, back on track?

RP: The main thing is we haven't had to compromise anything to make it exciting, exhilarating, and very refreshing. I've found as I've gone along I've denied Led Zeppelin's existence because I didn't want to end up like a fucking fat mouse in a trap. I'm still denying Led Zeppelin as coinage on which to feast, but this situation, mentally and physically, is the best thing that could possibly happen. I haven't got to keep shouting at guitarists about why don't you go listen to Otis Rush's version of fucking "Double Trouble" with Ike Turner, one of *Spin*'s Top 50 guitar solos of all time, and get the vibe, or whatever. We've got so much we already know, where we meet with other music.

MS: In the months back together, when the tapes stop rolling on the Arabic material, do you surreptitiously plug in and rock out again?

JP: How long did it take to get the melody line and guitar of "Yallah" together?

RP: Seven minutes?

JP: I'd say fifteen at the most. OK. That's us. Put the loop on, he goes out and has a beer, I've got a guitar and he comes back with the melody. Boom, like that. That's what we're about.

RP: We played it in the middle of the Djemma el Fna in Marrakech along-side snake-charmers. We just went there, set the gear up, and played it to the Moroccans. Depending on which Moroccan you're talking to, the Djemma el Fna means either "the square of the dead," because up until the 1920s the Pasha used to bring the people he'd defeated there and put their heads on stakes all around; or it means "the holocaust," because it's so chaotic. With all the fire-eaters and jugglers it's one of the most filmed spots in North Africa.

MS: Yes, indeed. But you haven't quite answered my question. Do you ever now plug in and play such original rock 'n' roll inspiration for your earlier career as "Train Kept A-Rollin'" or "Baby Let's Play House," for example?

RP: I suppose so, yeah. But not because that's where we come from.

JP: Yeah, we have, like when we did those rehearsals for Buxton [Opera House]. I can't remember which numbers we did, but we must have done those sort of things.

RP: It's funny because Charlie doesn't know where the chords change.

JP: We did "Train Kept A-Rollin."

RP: It's good to do "Train Kept A-Rollin." It's great, that Rock 'N' Roll Trio album with Paul Burlison. When we used to do it in '72, it was almost a constituent part of the next album, if you like, along with "Boogie with Stu" and "Candy Store Rock" from *Presence*, that sort of thing. They were actually lifts—or salutes. Salute to Ral Donner or a salute to Johnny Burnette. This was just fucking about, really. We'd do "Season of the Witch" as well, so we're all right!

JP: That's great!

MS: Has this project, along with the now completed Led Zeppelin remasters, lifted the shadow of the '70s and tempted you back to the huge stash of archive material for possible release?

JP: We've got tapes and we've got footage from along the way, starting with the [Royal] Albert Hall whenever that was [1969] . . .

RP: I don't like that as an idea. I think *The Song Remains the Same* is such a load of old bollocks.

JP: Yeah, but it's a shame that that's the only document there was. I tell you, some of that later stuff . . .

RP: Yeah, playing-wise it was great.

JP: Not Knebworth, but Seattle really was incredible . . .

RP: The playing is great, but the whole idea of studying it as a piece of history . . . I'd rather just get on with this . . .

JP: Yeah, absolutely.

RP: And not fog the issue at all. Not because it ain't any good, but because it's another deal.

JP: It's just better to have it done properly than see it on a bootleg. There's something for maybe down the line.

MS: So is it just a matter of timing?

JP: Probably. It's nothing that would even surface in the next five years. Who knows? We've got more important things to do at the moment. That's what it really comes down to.

RP: And personally I don't want to bring too much attention to the past, beyond the fact that we're a pair of old fuckers who can do it, and have a history. Rather than brandish old bits and pieces of twenty-five-year-old footage around the place, let's get on and do this. And no matter where it sticks or doesn't stick, it's stuck for us, and that's what counts. And that's what dispels all my fears about the grand reunion and all that fawning and groveling from all the yuppie magazines, because this isn't quite what everybody wanted—but it's more than anybody could ever expect.

MS: People will indeed be excited by what's new in the MTV *Unledded*.

RP: It's a big coiffure, the MTV element of it. It had to be filmed the way it was—there are only certain camera angles and stuff. The songs demanded a bit more recklessness in the way they were put across, because if you put them onstage it won't be such a sedate rendition. But it was done like that because you have to have fixed points or else everything goes nuts. But you can't knock "Four Sticks" and "Kashmir," no matter what, with 30 or 40 people playing on it.

JP: We jammed a section on the end of "Kashmir" that was made up on the spot. It was so live and exciting all the way through.

RP: When we worked with the Egyptians before we brought an orchestra in, the drum/vocal/guitar interplay and phrasing was out of this world. The Egyptians would start counter phrasing and the whole insinuation of the song moved right round, 45 degrees, 90 degrees, the song slanted off somewhere. That's not something that happens a lot. That's when you bring in Egyptian hired guns who play in the Bayswater Road till seven in the morning.

MS: What do you know of this mooted Malcolm McLaren film about Peter Grant?

RP: Nothing. He's trying to raise some interest to get the money to make the film, I think. It's been the most publicized non-event of the latter part of this century. McLaren—you know what he's like. What do they call it? Throwing a sprat to catch a mackerel.

JP: I thought he was taking the piss to begin with. John Paul Jones was going to be Jason Donovan. Or was Jason Donovan going to be you? And Gary Oldman was going to be me, just after the Dracula film.

RP: I met Jason Donovan at RAK studios. He had jodhpurs on and small riding boots as he jumped out of the cab. He looked just like me! I'd rather have Steve Bull [Wolverhampton Wanderers and former England striker] do the job; he'd do it much better.

MS: Did the invention of the term "heavy metal" and its early application to Led Zeppelin restrict how people perceived you?

JP: Yeah, because it hones in on just one element of what we were doing. We were so multifaceted it's a shame we got lumped in with any of those . . .

RP: It's journalistic complacency and claptrap. It's a very easy thing to say: who were the most successful band around at that time? If it was us, and that period had a lot of people cavorting around using their manhood as the main weapon to sell records, then we have to be held responsible and used as a trademark for that period, when our better songs, apart from "Black Dog" and "Rock and Roll," were more or less acoustic-based or Eastern-based anyway. But who cares? Leave it to Deep Purple. They're a nice, imaginative, original band.

MS: Do you feel there's a story to be told which would set straight the public misconception?

RP: No. This is supposed to be entertainment, you know. It's not that bloody serious. Let people think what they like. It doesn't really matter so long as what we've got to be proud of we're proud of; that's all that matters. Otherwise we're wasting our time. And we've only got about forty, fifty years to live, each of us. And you. Pissing about, trying to set the record straight and all that sort of thing is a waste of time. We just get on and do what we do. And if we don't like it, then in a month's time clear off and do something else. That's the most logical way of thinking about it.

JP: I might send a book back by psychic communication after I've passed over.

RP: What? Telling the truth?

JP: Absolutely.

RP: Don't do that! It'll be a bestseller again and then . . .

JP: I shall bury my book with me in the coffin so that it gets raided . . .

RP: Hahahahahaha!

JP: . . . with the L-plate on the tombstone.

RP: I'd have my Patrick Keegan tops in there. They have green soles, you know. These are mid-'70s soccer boots—I've still got 'em. The dog nibbled the back where the ankle support is so I had to run in on a Sunday morning with this serrated rear on my soccer boot. But recently, in my 46th year, I've bought some new boots. I'll die with them and see if they can dig them up . . .

JP: Hahaha!

RP: See if they can chip a ball at the far post.

MS: So as far as you're concerned then, Led Zep road manager Richard Cole [the main source for Stephen Davis's bestselling book *Hammer of the Gods*, and author of his own account of life with Led Zeppelin, *Stairway to Heaven: Led Zeppelin Uncensored*,] can continue to circulate his lurid stories?

JP: No, he can't do that. It's totally inaccurate, and he's the sort of person who ought to know better, considering he's been in AA, and the whole thing about AA is that you keep things discreet. He went into AA as a chronic alcoholic and came out a chronic liar.

RP: Hahahaha!

JP: And apart from that, he just makes up stories which are totally untrue and which I'm extremely furious about. You'd have thought he'd have learned his lesson the first time round, but it's amazing what people do for a buck, isn't it?

RP: It was 12 hundred bucks, actually.

JP: It's the old Judas dollar.

RP: Not only did he give us a quick kiss but he got 12 hundred bucks, which doesn't buy you a lot of smack, really. But this is not what it's all about.

MS: No, but people will always believe the sensational story, because they want to believe.

RP: So do I! I once saw Kenny Hibbitt [Wolverhampton Wanderers hero of the '70s] pissed on a Friday night. I was furious. I went home and I couldn't sleep. Terrible. I want to believe *Hammer of the Gods* because it's done us huge favors in terms of aura.

JP: Wicked, wicked boys.

RP: Jimmy's always been the cause of all the problems.

JP: That's right. Of course. Naturally. Who that?

RP: Hahaha. What a great title for the piece: Who That?

MS: Is there a significance in titling the album *No Quarter*?

RP: Only the obvious ones.

MS: Try me.

RP: No, no. You're as bright as we are. It's just obvious, isn't it?

MS: Is there always the sense of the empty place at the table?

RP: No.

JP: Nah.

RP: I've lost too many people around me to even see any empty places. I know that there's emptiness in my heart but I fill up the places.

MS: Have your musical tastes diverged or grown in parallel in the 26 years since you first met?

RP: I don't think we've discussed it that much. I've played Jimmy pieces he hasn't heard, and he's done the same for me.

JP: We've probably remained consistent in our taste in music haven't we? Robert's always listened to a wide variety of things, and I certainly have as well, going way back—all these diverse roots that came together. One's tastes haven't changed, really. Ever onwards with the ears!

RP: I like to enquire all the time: what's that? That's Portishead. What's that? That's the new Massive Attack. Or the 4-Track Demos by P.J. Harvey or whatever. There's loads of stuff around, and if you're at all inventive, or even jackdaws as we are, you can learn a lot and steal a lot . . . The loops were the catalyst for us. How do you respond when you set the PA up in an old room in Kings Cross, whack up the loop real loud, and go, "Fuckin' 'ell—that's not a Western drummer." What do you do with that?

MS: Returning, briefly to the exchange of messages in the press before resuming your partnership, do you two gentlemen agree to disagree about Mr. Coverdale?

JP: I'll let you handle that.

RP: No, no. He's your mate. Hahaha!

JP: Well, I'm not going to answer that question.

RP: That's very, very well done. You've come on a bundle!

JP: Hahaha.

RP: And I'm not going to either.

MS: How nice that there's a diplomatic accord here.

RP: Well, I think he's a fucking idiot. Horses for courses: I've worked with Phil Johnstone [Robert's main musical collaborator in the late '80s]— nobody's perfect.

JP: See what happens when you're at a loose end for too long?

RP: You got a birdie this morning, hahaha! We'd be all right on talk shows after all.

MS: A double act?

RP: A bit like Mork and Mindy!

COMMUNICATION BREAKDOWN

Robert Plant: When I said I would never do this again, I couldn't see this set of circumstances happening. But as Jimmy and I started to discuss the whole thing it seemed that the least we could do was try it until such time as it became a no-no and then pull out.

Jimmy Page: We had only rubbed shoulders, really, over the past 14 years. So the most important thing was to see how we got on together. And at the end of recording, there was just a big beaming smile between us, and that said so much.

—Jancee Dunn interview with Robert Plant and Jimmy Page,
Rolling Stone, December 1994

LED ZEPPELIN:
THE BBC SESSIONS (ATLANTIC)

Mat Snow | December 1997, *MOJO*

Despite Page and Plant's new iteration together, people still wanted to hear Led Zeppelin, especially previously unreleased Led Zeppelin songs. The bootleg market for the band's music was robust, which in its way was a good thing, because there was no "legitimate" live Led Zeppelin album besides *The Song Remains the Same*. —Ed.

Led Zeppelin's first official all-live release since 1976's *The Song Remains the Same*. The 2-CD set is drawn from sessions recorded for the BBC before small invited audiences. CD 1 was recorded in mono on March 2, June 16, 24, and 27, 1969; CD 2 was recorded in stereo on April 1, 1971.

There are culture shocks and there are culture shocks. The one that struck London's Aeolian Hall on Monday June 16, 1969, when Led Zeppelin tore into "Communication Breakdown" will have kicked up some dust on the worn BBC plush of the stalls. The seismic force of the band's sonic storm erupts here with an air-quivering presence unimaginable to those who'd tuned in on the old cat's whisker the first time round on Chris Grant's *Tasty Pop Sundae*, *Top Gear* and the like. And so good is the sound quality that if you listen closely you might even be able to hear the commissionaire's medals jingle.

Yes, it was a different world, and no, I wasn't there either, but these irreproachably exciting CDs bring you very, very close.

Led Zeppelin hit the ground flying in September 1968. Seven months into their career together, as documented on the first tracks here, the four-way chemistry blending youthful hunger with only slightly less youthful experience had crystallized into a perfect balance of forces. There is no fumbling around: everyone knows exactly what they're doing, how far out to take it, when to rein it in, when to explode. No group has grasped so well rock's dynamics of tension and release. And, to this day, no group has packed such a punch, due partly to Jimmy Page's care in recording not just the instruments but the acoustic tremor they created (a phenomenon better heard than described), but mostly due to the band's natural inclination to hit very, very hard. Drums thunder like snorting Victorian steam engines; guitars bite.

Unlike such contemporaries as the Stones and the Who, Messrs Page, Plant, Bonham, and Jones approached the studio with all the rude vigor with which they hit the stage. Superficially, the songs here that haven't been elongated into jams sound like only slightly less tidy versions of the studio classics. But in the small differences of accent and timing, phrasing and timbre lie all the reasons a fan could need to buy with confidence and listen with renewed awe. Led Zeppelin, like movie explosions, never fail to get one going.

Oddly enough, the 1971 session is not quite so powerfully recorded as two years before. By then the biggest rock band on the planet with the possible exception of the Stones, they previewed four songs from their fourth album, which was not to be released for another seven months—a state of affairs which seems almost criminally relaxed today when it sometimes seems you can get sued for even talking about an act's new offering before its official release. And how quaint also to hear a rock band not only with the self-assurance to attempt 18 minute versions of songs better known at a third of that length, but also with the skill and instinct for the dramatic musical coup to keep the whole thing boiling—borrowed riffs, knowing quotes from Elvis [Presley], the Isley [Brother]s, and more, cheeky asides and all.

A timely reminder, then, that if you're crowning yourselves the Kings of Rock, then this is the standard you have to meet. And better still, the most rumbustious fun with a five-inch diameter to be had in this and almost any other year.

Jimmy Page and Robert Plant

Mat Snow: When you heard those tapes again, from 1969 and '71, it must have taken you back. But how did it take you back?

Robert Plant: The whole thing was very quaint: the politeness of the audience, the technicians fumbling about, proper, almost hallowed, low-key introductions—Pete Drummond, those sort of guys—like there was some kind of holy moment about to occur. Of course, as the years went on nobody gave a flying hoot if you just played and made a noise.

Back then the air of scrutiny, an air of study, really intimidated me. There was a sort of crispness and a formality about the whole deal of playing in a small theatre. I think the environment actually intimidated the audience to some degree. Guys with ribbons on their shoulders, the commissionaires.

Jimmy Page: You're shown to a certain area of the building and then —shh-shh!

RP: Lights off.

JP: And it's being recorded, and it's gonna be transmitted, as opposed to just doing a little small club where there are no repercussions. So you're much more under the spotlight. Those audiences are really very polite, plus they haven't heard some of the material. But when we're doing what I call a "proper" show, it's really organic between the audience and a band, and the vibe is building all the way through.

MS: Who was your audience at the BBC?

RP: They announced it the week before, didn't they?

JP: Yeah. Send in for tickets.

RP: Same old thing as *Round The Horne*. But not quite so gripping.

MS: There was one BBC daytime host in 1969 whose interview with you was edited out because it was such a disaster: Chris Grant and his *Tasty Pop Sundae* . . .

JP: There was a classic bit on one of those interviews where they said, "Let's get an atmosphere going here—Jimmy, if you stand over there and you play out some rolling blues guitar, we can conduct the interview over here." And he started to talk to Robert and John Paul Jones, and then he asked me a question. Of course I'm way off-mic and you can hear the engineer say, "He's off-mic!" and I said, "Of course I'm bloody off-mic— you asked me to be over here playing some rolling guitar!" It was terribly chaotic.

But concerts were just one day on your schedule: you'd go in there with a "you get what you get" sort of thing. We're doing a whole set, we're not stopping and doing the numbers again.

MS: But you were allowed to overdub parts on later.

JP: Within a band's very busy schedule at the time, you just went down to the Maida Vale Playhouse and did whatever you could. We were so organic at the time that we used to make stuff up in the studio while others would be very tentative about what they were doing.

MS: How much of the incredible sound quality, especially on the 1969 sessions, has to do with the BBC's original recording, or is it the magic of today's sound-restoration technology?

JP: They had a fantastic engineer there. But you'd go back a second time and that engineer had now been promoted to be a producer of a programme, and then you'd get an engineer who wasn't quite so good, so it was the luck of the draw. That reflects on the quality of the tapes. Some of the tapes sounded really fantastic and others were a bit muddy."

MS: You edited down one of the BBC "Whole Lotta Love" medleys for release. Was that just to fit the CD?

JP: The whole concert was 98 minutes; we had to leave some of it out. There was another "Communication Breakdown" that came as an encore—that had to go.

MS: We get three versions as it is.

JP: At the time it was a little bit of promotion of the album, and that's why "Communication Breakdown"—and "Dazed and Confused"—are in all those appearances we were making. If people were going to be in aware of what we were doing, those were the things on the albums which had a big cross-section.

RP: We came up with this really corny statement, or maybe Jimmy did, that we never put singles out because the album was the statement of what we were writing and stealing at the time . . .

JP: No, I don't like all this stealing bit. A lot of us were unaware that we were stealing . . .

RP: No, I was stealing, but you had no idea about that . . .

MS: Is it true you improvised "Travelling Riverside Blues" on the spot at the BBC?

JP: The BBC are not gonna allow you to make up music on the spot, so they didn't know we were making up music on the spot. I had a riff and that was it. It was, Try this, and Bonzo and Jonesy fit it in immediately— the riff was dead simple—and Robert just put singing on top. An overdub on the solo and that was it, thank you very much!

MS: You covered "Somethin' Else" here. The Move, the Who, Rod Stewart, and Blue Cheer also covered Eddie Cochran tunes in that period. Was Eddie the late '60s rockers' favorite late '50s rocker?

JP: It was that riff, wasn't it? Little Richard things, "Good Golly Miss Molly" and "Lucille," had a rhythm section that was swingin', but that particular Cochran thing, and things like "Completely Sweet" from *Sittin' in the Balcony*, his first album, it was really a tough riff and that was the whole deal.

RP: We used to do a lot of old Cochran things just for fun, didn't we?

JP: Yeah, "Weekend."

RP: The later stuff, "Pink Peg Slacks," is great; Cochran's view of rock 'n' roll had great humor, as well as his serious stuff like "Milk Cow Blues." But now when you listen to it, for me it's so corny. Now I'd rather we'd have been heard doing Love's "7 And 7 Is" or "August" from the *Four Sail* album, something like that.

JP: They were too hard to play, Robert.

RP: Anyway, you can play Eddie Cochran songs when you're pissed. We'd all played them since we were kids. The whole credibility of the song didn't matter, it was just the excitement of all knowing the song and actually drifting into it, which wasn't always that easy, 'cos not everybody in the band knew a lot of the sequences of various songs that we went into.

MS: Do you regret that you didn't do more acoustic stuff on the BBC?

JP: We had a set that we had worked out. We just did that set.

RP: On-stage proper, when we were playing for far too long, three hours or whatever it was, then you could do an acoustic set that was 45 minutes long.

MS: Do you really think that your sets were too long?

JP: He does.

RP: I do. I could have been selling matches and cigarettes with one of those strange little trays with a bit of a ribbon and a small black and white dress on, because there was so much instrumentation going on.

JP: It was called a rest, a hiatus for the vocal cords, Robert.

RP: Yeah, but I could have been doing card tricks.

JP: The vocalists always complain that their voices are getting strained 'cos they're having to sing too much.

RP: You were very considerate I must say, because it did give me time to learn a little bit of Moroccan Arabic on the side of the stage. Or invent the first Casio keyboard. But whatever was going on, to me it did go on a little bit. It's not it wasn't that good, it's just that I had to start thinking about things to do because after a while you can start to look a little bit of a jerk wobbling your head around like some sort of Indian tradesman.

JP: Yeah, but the whole point about the improvisation section is the interplay between us. It wasn't as though we were doing it like the Grateful Dead, the jam just going on perpetually. We were changing it all the time.

It was organic, and that's why it holds up. Some of them obviously do go on too long, but when it's happening . . .

RP: I'm not complaining about the musicality of it, it was just that I really had to invent things to do—mimicry and using my voice in a different way. Some of it works great and other bits are close but no cigar. Those bits really grate with me. I was really trying to get into the middle of the instrumentation of the whole thing without becoming Oscar Brown Jr. It's like a dodgy solo is a dodgy solo . . .

JP: Sure, well there's loads of those but I don't care because I know what I was trying to do and sometimes I pulled it off, other times I didn't.

MS: Did the BBC invite you back for any sessions after 1971?

RP: I think we went away so much, that by the time we came back we thought so much of ourselves that there was no way we were gonna go and deal with that. We didn't stop until I had that car crash [1976]. We were in Morocco, we were recording in India with that orchestra. I think when we came back, if we had had the opportunity, it would have seemed a bit of an anticlimax to grapple with that sort of white-coated phenomena.

MS: So when global success, including the UK, kicked in, you didn't need the BBC anymore?

RP: It wasn't like, We've had enough of that and we don't need you anymore, sort of bollocks. It was more a case of, We haven't got the time and if we did have, maybe we should just chill out a bit or get some more ideas. The ideas, creatively, were flowing thick and fast from every angle. The writing process was really strong. And I suppose when we got home, because we all lived in various parts of England, when we got off a plane the band said goodbye or sometimes didn't even do that—you'd leave each other at the carousel, thumbs up, and we'd be gone. So if we were offered things, Peter Grant probably thought, "Well, if they're back home now, let's just leave them alone for a bit."

MS: How much did the BBC pay you?

JP: Oh! I've got a BBC check which I framed, actually. It was about £5.50 a month, ordered not to pay.

RP: I think about eight quid, actually.

JP: Ordered not to pay. So they didn't necessarily pay you even though you played!

RP: Yeah, they stopped the check. The BBC's gone from that to the lofty heights of Radio 1? Amazing isn't it?

JP: But the BBC were doing live sessions with bands—the States had given up on all of that; by then it was just disc jockeys. It's pretty good that they keep that tradition going.

RP: They won't even play our stuff at all now, we're too old!

JP: No, that's it! And they haven't for years.

MS: Are you Radio 2 now?

RP: I think we're Radio 7. We should be on the surf station, really.

JP: We're radio unfriendly, aren't we? Whichever channel that is.

RP: Yeah, wherever they play Dick Dale, you'll find us.

John Paul Jones

MS: What is the current relationship between you and Plant and Page?

John Paul Jones: I see them for record business: artwork, covers, choosing songs, that sort of thing. And that's it. On the *BBC Sessions* I listened to the tracks and commented on what versions to use. Generally, we were all pretty much in agreement on everything.

MS: You and Jimmy had both done BBC sessions before Led Zeppelin. Did that help steady nerves for the performance?

JPJ: A session's a session, BBC or TV or anything, and we'd both done thousands of them. The two of us were full well used to walking into studios and being able to perform when the red stoplight goes on. Of course I knew never to plug my own amp in, which I did once on BBC TV, and nearly everybody walked out because of the union thing.

MS: Do you remember Zeppelin's first BBC audiences?

JPJ: There were people you would see at the gigs. We weren't much heard of except from the people that actually saw the gigs, and they all thought we were American when we played in England. It was all still a word of mouth thing for us in England. Which was nice. There was no hype at all at that time. The press weren't overboard on us.

MS: "Travelling Riverside Blues:" was it really a spur-of-the-moment creation?

JPJ: We may have jammed it around in rehearsal. Basically, I didn't know any blues at all. Obviously I knew how it went—twelve bars. But Bonzo and I weren't into the blues at all. I'd never heard of Robert Johnson or Willie Dixon before I joined Zeppelin, but it became an easy thing to jam around on. Jimmy and Robert used to come in with licks and words; they'd start things and we'd follow on. Bonzo and I liked James Brown, Motown, rhythm and blues, Philadelphia—black music generally. Although he didn't like jazz; I used to like jazz—I listened to it for relaxation, recreation. When starting Zeppelin, I was listening exclusively to soul music. That's what I was as a bassist in the session world. Nobody else listened to the records, knew the parts, knew what to play. They used to give me the chords and say, "Get on with it." I never used to listen to rock at all apart from Jimi Hendrix—about the only rock record I had, I think.

MS: Robert says he wished the band had dabbled with the hip West Coast sound of the time, Love and so forth.

JPJ: I wasn't into that. Nor was Bonzo, I don't think. It was a Robert thing. He used to like the Doors, haha. I'm beginning to appreciate the Doors a bit more now, but I didn't then, I tell you.

MS: Were there tensions about different tastes?

JPJ: Not really. I've always said Zeppelin was the space in between us all. It was because of the different tastes that Zeppelin was what it was. The trouble with bands who quote Zeppelin as an influence is that they usually quote one song as an influence, "Whole Lotta Love" or something, and that's it. I get the impression that a lot of bands all listen to the same sort of music now. Between us we listened to pretty much everything. I liked Indian and Celtic music, like Page, and I think Robert liked jazz as well, so there was plenty in common.

MS: Does the high sound quality of the BBC material deter you from examining other live recordings taken off soundboards from later in the band's career?

JPJ: It might deter us from releasing it, but not from looking at it, providing it has enough of the feeling and it's not marred by hums or over-loud bass, the things that bootlegs classically suffer from.

MS: Are there any bootlegs of a quality to target on the civilian population?

JPJ: You hear the odd little bit of the odd one. And I've always noticed the band sound really tight. But I don't really listen to Zeppelin music, to be honest. I tend to be one of those musicians who, once you've made a record, moves on. I've only listened to this stuff because I had to participate in the release. Not that I don't think it's any good, haha. That youthful energy was there, it stands, and I'm proud of it. But I want to go on—my musical curiosity is nowhere near satisfied.

Thanks to Dave Lewis for background information. Zeppelin: The Concert File by Dave Lewis and Simon Pallett is published by Omnibus Press.

COMMUNICATION BREAKDOWN

"[The BBC Recordings album] is a very interesting testament in its own way; it goes to show . . . just how organic the group was. Led Zeppelin was a band that would change things around substantially each time it performed . . . What we have done for [Walking into Clarksdale] is reverted to how we started out before we got into that sort of 'unledded' thing to what we did back in Led Zeppelin just working with bass, drums, guitar, and vocal."
– Jimmy Page to Ed Christman, Billboard, November 10, 1997

JIMMY PAGE INTERVIEW: BRING IT ON HOME

HP Newquist | August 1998, *GUITAR* magazine

Jimmy Page is, of course, a guitar legend, and is the focal point of many an issue of the guitar magazines. Since not everyone is a guitarist, and most of the interviews in them didn't really move the story forward, such pieces are not included in this book. However, this interview deals with some of the technical aspects of the guitar in context of the *Walking Into Clarksdale* album, and it shows the evolution of both Page and Plant as performers and songwriters. –Ed.

Jimmy Page is the only rock guitar icon from the blues-based British Invasion who still matters. Think about it.

As the blues-rock of the late '60s hurtled towards the hard rock of the '70s, four men were pushing the limits: Jimi Hendrix, and the Yardbird triumvirate of Jeff Beck, Eric Clapton, and Page. Jimi Hendrix is gone. This apparently doesn't affect his legacy, but it does affect his ability to create new music that still matters, regardless of how many "lost" recordings are posthumously released. Jeff Beck, who continues to be an amazing and inventive guitarist—and has the edge over Hendrix in the still-alive-and-well department—tends to prefer spending time with cars instead of guitars. These days he appears on record and on stage with less frequency than Elvis. Eric Clapton, meanwhile, has all but forsaken the driving blues-rock music that propelled him to early fame, opting instead for his current grandfatherly white-bluesmaster persona. One needs to look no further than what he did to "Layla" on his MTV *Unplugged* special to see that rock and roll is indeed a distant memory for Slowhand.

That, of course, leaves Mr. Page. The man who poured concrete into the throat of rock and roll has never stopped working his brand of musical genius on the form. With the release of *Walking Into Clarksdale*, Page and Robert Plant have revisited the styles that made Led Zeppelin the preeminent purveyors of innovative hard rock. Whether it was reinterpreting decades-old gritty blues numbers or fusing Middle Eastern drones with searing guitar riffs, Page and Zeppelin always had a tight grasp on, and full understanding of, their influences.

Walking Into Clarksdale is the latest example of Page extending the language of those influences. Indeed, the title of the new record takes its cue from a tiny town in the middle of Nowhere, U.S.A. called Clarksdale, Mississippi. It may seem like an obscure locale, but Clarksdale lies in the heart of the region that gave birth to the blues: the Mississippi Delta. For Page and Plant, walking into Clarksdale could just as easily be construed as "walking back."

The record is vintage Page, easily recognizable but fresh enough in its construction to show how Page and Plant have managed to refresh and reinvent the music they make together. The blues roots are still here, but the cultural impact of other points on the globe have been even more deeply explored. For Page, it was simply a matter of stripping it all back to what he grew up with. Sitting in his hotel in Manhattan, seemingly a million miles from Clarksdale or Cairo, Page reflects on this latest addition to his repertoire.

"The most obvious thing for us to do," he begins, "was to go back to the four-piece unit that we knew best and that has always worked best for us. A lot of people thought we were going to carry on with that big extravaganza from the last tour [behind 1995's fully orchestrated *No Quarter*], but for us it was more important to come to terms with the songs."

Page started by writing most of the songs on an old Harmony Sovereign guitar, one that he has used ever since the making of *Led Zeppelin III*. Then Page, Plant, bassist Charlie Jones, and drummer Michael Lee headed to a most unlikely location to record: Abbey Road Studios in London. Gone was the farmhouse in Bron-yr-Aur or the privacy of his Sol

Studios. "I sold Sol because it was 10 minutes down the road, and when I moved there was no point in keeping it," says Page. "I'd recorded in Abbey Road in the '60s and I'd worked with George Martin there as well. We all call it the Beatles' studio, but it was really his studio, wasn't it? Or EMI's studio, anyway."

Page laughs at the irony. "In fact, I remember doing sessions there in the daytime and you'd see all the Beatles' equipment pushed up against the wall because they only went in there at night—and they spent all night. So the studio could safely put in afternoon sessions and know the Beatles wouldn't be there. I'd never had the freedom to turn up an amp in there before. This time I had the freedom in their huge room, and I just took full advantage of it." He laughs again.

"Poor Robert, he couldn't sing in there with us because there was so much leakage. He had to stand in between the double doors and sing with his notebook and mic stand. We had a great time in there."

The *Clarksdale* sessions lasted barely a month, which seems to be an abbreviated amount of time for a modern-day record. But Zeppelin often recorded quickly, sometimes even on the run. "We did *Presence* in three weeks and *In Through the Out Door* in three and a half. The main thing is that we can work fast, and we enjoy working fast. We've always been about spontaneity."

The finished recording hints at the music Zeppelin was producing when it disbanded after the death of John Bonham. "When the World Was Young" has tones and melancholy riffs that easily could have been found on *In Through The Our Door*, as does "Upon a Golden Horse," which recalls "Carouselambra" with its minor-chord drones into the verse. But there are sounds and passages that come from other ventures of Page's. "Please Read the Letter" shares the roiling riffs that were the foundation of *Outrider*, while "House of Love" resonates with the snarling attack of the Firm's *Mean Business*. Tracks like "Most High," however, break the more exotic ground that was first explored with "Kashmir," as Page explains. "'Most High' is an alternate tuning, the only one on the record. It's in a C tuning: the bottom string is C, the fifth string is G, the fourth string is C, the third string is G, the second is C, and the top string is E. I haven't used that particular tuning before. I had it set in my

TransPerformance guitar, but I've only used it occasionally to make a big open chord. I had a tuning close to it which I used for 'Bron-Yr-Aur' and on 'Friends' [low to high: C–A–C–G–C–E], but actually for those songs the A string remains the same. So," he laughs, "in that case, the string remains the same."

Even though Page has long been one of the most visible employers of alternate tunings, especially for some of his original blues and slide compositions like "Hats Off To (Roy) Harper" [C–G–C–G–C–E] and "Bron Y-Aur Stomp" [C–F–C–F–A–C], the determination not to agonize over the recording process preempted their use. "It's really the sort of thing I do more at home," he muses. "A lot of this record was written on the spot—apart from going away and thinking about a section and bringing it back in. That's not the most ideal time to be fiddling around with a tuning that you don't know, because ideas are coming out fast and furious."

Those fast and furious ideas manifest the spectrum of music Page has absorbed over the last five decades. "My roots go back to when I was at school. Today, everybody keeps going on about bloody 'world music'" he says with a touch of disdain. "It isn't new music at all. It's the fact that communications are better and people are more open to hearing stuff today. I was listening to that music back then, and I've listened to it all through my life. There's so much in me that's relevant to all that, and I can still put a new slant on it."

Does this constant exploration of non-traditional music affect his playing style? "When it comes to other techniques, like tapping, that's not my bag, and I don't listen to it for hours on end because I'm not going to get that much from it. But if there's a street musician from Morocco or a country-blues player, I'm going to get far more exhilaration out of that because it's where I'm coming from."

Page settled into *Clarksdale* with a relatively stripped-down setup, mirroring the song-writing approach. He used his trademark Les Paul, the Harmony Sovereign, a Gretsch Chet Atkins, and a Fender Tonemaster amp for the majority of the songs.

Since the sparseness here comes consciously, there are surprisingly few swaths of his "guitar army," the dizzying multiple layers of guitar over-dubs that defined tracks like "Achilles' Last Stand."

"Well, 'Achilles' is the ultimate example of that," he recalls. "When you're doing an overdub, you've got to shape the sound in your head. That's where I guess I'm lucky; it's part of what I can do without a struggle, almost immediately. It's probably experience, really, isn't it? I've got a lot of experience," he grins.

"But 'Achilles' began as a bit that had come out of 'Dazed and Confused,' a live bit that we did. And I said to John Paul Jones that I'm going to put a rising scale over this. At the time, he said 'Well, it can't be done,' and I said, 'Oh yes it can. I know what it is.' I didn't even bother to play it but it was in my head from the point when we were first rehearsing it in Los Angeles. I remember the day it happened, and I knew what it was; I could just feel it. And then when I got in the studio I did it in harmony!"

Page laughs at the recollection. "I knew the scale and how the rest of it should go; or, rather, what I call a progression. I've never been into practicing scales, though I shouldn't say that because I don't want to discourage anyone from doing them, but I just did progressions. I mean, it could be a scale, but I think of them as progressions."

"The only time I did practice scales was when I was playing sitar, and then you have scales in the classic Indian sense of ascending and descending. You have to practice them to become familiar with the music. For instance, when you have two different sets of notes in one particular raga, if you're ascending you mustn't touch any of the notes in the descending scale."

The mention of "Achilles' Last Stand" brings about more of Page's thoughts on his playing over the years. For a time, he thought of the epic as the pinnacle of his playing, but his blues solos have come to have singular importance to him. "I was always happy with my playing on 'Achilles,' but then I thought the solo on 'Tea for One' was really good."

"But other people have pointed out the solo on 'Since I've Been Loving You.' And you know, 'Tea for One' was about the only time we consciously tried to do something in Zeppelin that we'd done before. Really, it was the only time; we set out to do a more laid-back version of 'Since I've Been Loving You.'"

Page is looking forward these days, not back. He is in the middle of a new tour, and has little time to think about anything other than his current collaboration with Plant.

But the question has to be asked: Is there anything he hasn't done, or anyone he would like to try working with? After all, he's worked with and guested on albums by artists from the Rolling Stones (*Dirty Work*) to Tom Jones (uncredited sessions) to John Paul Jones (the latter's *Scream for Help* soundtrack). It takes him a moment to answer.

"Well if I was to work with anybody, it would be in an instrumental capacity. I've been spoiled as far as singers go, if you think about it. Working with Robert and Paul Rodgers, David Coverdale . . . . David Myles [who sang on *Outrider*] was an excellent singer. But the one thing that Robert and I had, that he was missing all the time that he wasn't working with me and I was missing all the time I wasn't working with him, was the fact that we can spark off of each other. If I have an idea, he knows exactly where I'm coming from. It's really good—*really* good—and it's a really healthy package at the moment.

"I was thinking about it the other day. We've both been away, and now we're coming home."

ROBERT PLANT AND JIMMY PAGE OF THE FORMER LED ZEPPELIN DISCUSS THEIR UPCOMING TOUR

Mark McEwen | May 11, 1998, *CBS This Morning*

The late rapper DJ Jam Master Jay recalled that in the early days of rap, Led Zeppelin were the kings of the turntable for their durable, heavy beats. While working together on *Walking Into Clarksdale*, Page took some time to do a long-distance session with rapper Sean "Puffy / Puff Daddy / P-Diddy" Combs for the sound track to the film *Godzilla*. Then he and Plant hit the road. —Ed.

Mark McEwen: Now, if I told you the Beatles have sold more albums than anybody, you probably wouldn't be surprised. But what if I told you the group in second place was Led Zeppelin? Well, they are moving past Garth Brooks, for now, with more than 63 million albums sold. With a new album and an upcoming tour, former Zeppelin front men Jimmy Page and Robert Plant are serving notice to the rock 'n' roll world that they are back.

[*Excerpt from* The Song Remains the Same *plays.*]

MM: What's the muse that sort of strikes you, that gets the two of you to come together to begin the process of writing?

Robert Plant: I suppose agitation, for me. You know, you do something for a while, then you leave it alone. And then one morning you wake up and go, "We've gotta do something, quick." It's—there's too many days gone by without actually being challenged to get into the creative zone again.

[*Excerpt from "Most High" plays.*]

MM: What emerged from that creative zone is *Walking Into Clarksdale*, Page and Plant's first collection of all-new material since Led Zeppelin's last album in 1979.

Over the years, Led Zeppelin built a reputation for wild hotel parties and living to excess. But Plant and Page have come a long way since those days. By the way, these rock 'n' roll bad boys are now in their fifties.

It's always interesting playing. How is it interestingly different now at the age that you're at now?

RPL: Well, the Zimmer frame, we have to keep it very neatly tucked away behind the curtains. It's very . . .

MM: What's the Zimmer frame?

RP: It's what you have to—when you're walking you have to have a lot . . .

MM: Oh, a walker!

RP: I don't know, it's a different time, you know. I mean, we're still essentially writers, trying to get out on some kind of edge. We—we write for ourselves. We entertain for ourselves. The differences, I guess, are that this is a very clean organization. A lot of the excesses of the past have gone. So we see everything with a lot of clarity now, and a lot of experience.

[*Excerpt from videotape plays.*]

MM: They recently ended a European tour in support of their new album, where they play to a predominantly younger audience.

What's it feel like to you to have people who are fifteen, sixteen, and seventeen, still into the music that you put together?

RP: Interesting, really. Because, you know, it depends on which country you play in. In South America, audiences are predominantly—it's all youth. Spain, youth; Italy, youth. And it's—it's cool, 'cause it means it still works.

MM: Jimmy Page recently collaborated with rap superstar Sean "Puffy" Combs on a remake of a classic Zeppelin favorite for one this summer's blockbuster movies. I hear he's putting together something for the movie *Godzilla* with "Kashmir."

RP: So he's named, Sean, really?

MM: You didn't know it was Sean "Puffy" Combs?

Jimmy Page: I didn't know that.

RP: Well, I say; he's just the boy next door.

MM: Tell me about that project.

RP: Yeah, I was aware of the *Godzilla* film, because I'd seen the—the—the trailer for it. What they were talking about doing was having, like, a media first, whereby I'd be in London, he'd be in L.A. and we'd have the—we'd have the tapes rolling at the same time in each studio, you know? And have a satellite linkup. And I thought, "Yeah, this sounds fun."

MM: Now that you look back on it, ten, fifteen, twenty years later, what's the pride that comes out when you hear a good riff, a good lyric?

RP: I don't really think about pride. But I do look in the front row. You know, but—I mean, Billy Joel taught me a little about that.

MM: What'd he teach you?

RP: He said, "Never sell the front row. Always hold it back, and find everybody in the auditorium who really wants the show to happen and put them in the front row." The Golden Circle. It's a good name for the tour, isn't it?

MM: Golden Circle Tour. The US leg of their tour begins on May 19th; the new album *Walking Into Clarksdale* debuted at number eight on the charts. Jimmy Page is on *Saturday Night Live* with Sean "Puff Daddy" Combs singing that *Godzilla* song—playing it; Sean rapped it this Sun—Saturday night.

Jane Robelot [Cohost]: Classic rock.

MM: Mm-hmm.

JR: It's all back.

COMMUNICATION BREAKDOWN

"What Puff Daddy did, as he is wont to do, was be 'inspired' by 'Kashmir' . . . The whole thing relies very heavily on the riff, because that's the thing that inspired him to write new words for it. But Puffy decided he didn't want to do it with a sample, he wanted to work with me on it . . . My son lives over here in New Orleans, and I thought it would give him something to latch onto at school, because when parents say to their children, 'You go to school with Jimmy Page's son,' that doesn't mean anything to most kids. But they understand if something's in a *Godzilla* film!"

– Jimmy Page to Richard Harrington, *Washington Post*, July 3, 1998

JOHN PAUL JONES: LIFE AFTER LED ZEPPELIN

Steven P. Wheeler | October 1999, *Happening*

"There's been a great deal about Jimmy Page and Robert Plant here, but wasn't there another surviving member of the band? Played bass and keyboards?" John Paul Jones fell off the radar for two reasons: after the group broke up, he decided, as he puts it, "I had been working for eighteen solid years by the time Zeppelin had finished, so I decided that it would be a good time to take a break anyway." Also, he certainly could afford it. While it became the unspoken subtext of every interview after 1972 or so, the fact was that none of the band members (or their heirs) would really be hurting for money. Jones, however, was the first to really spell it out: "I've done fine out of the whole thing. It's bought me endless studios and the freedom to do what I want, so I really have no complaints." Over the post-Zep years, Jones taught electronic music at college, wrote classical works on commission, produced artists ranging from Heart to the Butthole Surfers to Stefan Grossman, worked with Brian Eno, Diamanda Galás (with whom he toured and recorded), and Peter Gabriel. However, he never had a great deal to say about his post-Zeppelin life until he finally came around to put out his own solo album, *Zooma*, in 1999. –Ed.

While John Paul Jones will forever be known as the bassist and keyboardist of Led Zeppelin, his musical legacy extends far beyond the boundaries of his work with Jimmy Page, Robert Plant, and the late, great John Bonham. In fact, prior to joining Zeppelin, the soft-spoken Jones had already established himself as one of the top arrangers, session players, and producers in pop music. A point that is rammed home by the fact that he had already been involved with three Number One hits by the time he reached the tender age of seventeen.

During his pre-Zeppelin days, Jones arranged for the likes of the Rolling Stones ("She's a Rainbow") and Donovan ("Hurdy Gurdy Man"), while also working as one of London's top session musicians, including work as an organist on Jeff Beck's *Truth* album. His studio prowess brought him into contact with another session guru, Jimmy Page, who was forming a new band from the ashes of the Yardbirds in 1968. It was actually during the Donovan sessions, in which both men were involved, that Jones asked Page for the bassist gig in what was then being called the New Yardbirds. And within a year, rock & roll history would be rewritten as the band—now called Led Zeppelin—would go on to become the most influential and popular rock band of the Seventies, if not all-time.

With the untimely death of drummer John Bonham, Zeppelin officially broke up on December 4, 1980, and, suddenly, Jones was at a professional crossroads. Today, Jones says, "When Led Zeppelin ended, I realized that I had been working solidly for eighteen years, and so I decided to stop. When I decided to start working again, I didn't want to be in another band, having already been in the world's best, so I immersed myself into composing, producing, and then arranging again."

As vocalist Robert Plant went on to achieve success on his own, and Page went to work on movie soundtracks, various unsuccessful solo ventures, and short-lived collaborations with former Free/Bad Company vocalist Paul Rodgers in the Firm and former Deep Purple/Whitesnake vocalist David Coverdale in *Coverdale/Page*, Jones went straight back to the shadows of his earlier career. Whether supplying his trademark lush arrangements to R.E.M.'s smash album, *Automatic for the People*, or lending his arranging and production magic to everyone from Heart and Peter Gabriel to the Butthole Surfers and Brian Eno, Jones was once again an in-demand studio wizard.

Throughout the years since Zeppelin's demise, Page, Plant and Jones would reunite on occasion, First at Live Aid in 1985 and then at Atlantic Records's 40th Anniversary celebration at Madison Square Garden in 1988. These one-off, short reunion performances were less-than-stellar, but they only fueled the seemingly endless rumors of a full-blown

Zeppelin reunion that continue to this day, despite never having reached fruition.

Instead, Page and Plant went out on their own in 1994, without inviting Jones to participate, and released *No Quarter* (a live/studio hybrid focused on Zeppelin material); an ironic choice for an album title since that Zeppelin staple was co-written by Jones and had been strongly identified with him as it served as his concert showcase for years). Page and Plant would also release one full-blown studio album, the unsuccessful and disappointing *Walking Into Clarksdale* in 1998.

The decision by Page and Plant to go on without Jones was considered by many industry insiders to be very cavalier treatment for someone whose contributions were so vital to the Zeppelin legacy. This sentiment was not lost on Jones himself, who, at the band's induction ceremony into the Rock and Roll Hall of Fame*, quietly remarked from the podium, "I'd like to thank my friends for finally remembering my phone number."

In spite of this professional slight, Jones moved forward and with the recent release of his first solo album, *Zooma* (released on Discipline Global Mobile, the label owned by Robert Fripp of King Crimson fame), he has stepped back into the spotlight as a recording artist. And his brief US tour in October is only a taste of what's to come for this legendary figure, as plans for an ongoing solo career and world tour are inked for the future.

Happening recently spoke with the former charter member of Led Zeppelin to discuss his latest work and past glories, his various business ventures with his former band mates, and how one goes about maintaining a musical career after losing the world's most popular band.

Steven Wheeler: Let's start with the new album, your first solo album. What made you decide to do *Zooma* at this point in time?

John Paul Jones: I've always had a solo project in the back of my mind, but I think the final impetus was when I did an album with Diamanda Galás called *The Sporting Life* in 1994, and we took that out on the road and I basically got the "playing" bug again. I realized that of all

---

*The band was inducted into the Rock and Roll Hall of Fame in 1995.

the things I have done since the Zeppelin days—producing, arranging, and composition—playing live wasn't one of them and I found out that I really missed it.

SW: In terms of *Zooma*, what made you decide that an instrumental album was what you wanted to do, rather than hiring a vocalist and writing lyrics?

JPJ: Obviously I don't really sing myself and I don't write songs, per se. I also knew that if I got a singer involved, I would stop being an instrumentalist and a composer and that I'd quickly turn into a producer and an arranger. I knew that's what I'd do just by pure instinct and that my music would just fall by the wayside in that situation, and I just didn't want to do that. And, to be honest, I'm really not that interested in writing song-based rock. Also, right now, nobody else is doing instrumental rock at the moment, so I kind of have the field to myself [laughs].

SW: How did you get hooked up with Robert Fripp's label, and are the contractual terms with his label different than if you have gone with a major label?

JPJ: There's a big difference, because there aren't any contractual terms [laughs]. I really wasn't crazy about going with a major label, because I sent out some inquiries and everybody was asking the usual major label questions like, "What's the single going to be?" or "How about doing a video?" You know how people are in the music business. They know what's been successful, so they just try to go down that same road again. Not everybody of course, because there are the innovators who really do things because they just believe in a band or an artist. But I didn't really spend a lot of time trying to sell this project to any major labels, and it just so happens that I share management with Robert Fripp.

I knew that Robert is a bit of a maverick as far as the industry is concerned, so I asked my manager, "What exactly does Robert do?" And he said, "Well, he has a label called Digital Global Mobile, and, first of all, there are no contracts." And I said, "None? No contracts on either side?" And he said, "No, it's on trust. If you don't like them, leave. If they don't like you, they'll tell you."

SW: Did not working with a contract worry you at all?

JPJ: Actually, that really wasn't so strange for me, because in the early days of Led Zeppelin, we didn't have a contract with [band manager] Peter Grant for many years, until Atlantic Records found out and they drew something up. But it was all done on trust.

The other thing is that Digital Global Mobile has this very ethical policy, whereby they insist that the artists own all their copyrights and masters, and they pay a very good royalty rate and they have very good distribution with Rykodisc. They have very enthusiastic distributors all over the world and they have a very good Internet presence and a really good set-up with mail-order as well, because a lot of their stuff isn't wildly commercial, so they've built up all these other alternative methods of promotion and distribution. My album isn't going to be a big chart album, which is why I want to do a lot of press and promotion to make sure that everybody at least gets a chance to know about it, because they might like it.

SW: So you prefer to work this album in an alternative way?

JPJ: If you look back at the history of these things, nobody really knows what's going to sell or what's going to work. I always like to point to Tracy Chapman. I mean, could anybody have predicted that a black, female folk singer would take the charts by storm in the late Eighties? And in the days of Zeppelin, the record company was always telling us that we had to put out singles, but we never did.

There's a great Peter Grant story, where [Atlantic Records chief] Ahmet Ertegun said, "Peter, you guys have to put out a single. If you have a single, you'll sell 800,000 singles, easily." And Peter just stood his ground and said, "No, no single." And guess what, we sold 800,000 albums instead [laughs]. So nobody knows what is going to work or what isn't going to work in this business. I just want to give this album the best possible chance.

SW: Moving back in time to when Zeppelin officially disbanded. Aside from the sorrow of losing a close friend in John Bonham, did you have any fear of what to do professionally?

JPJ: I didn't have any fear. Although I did run into problems in the early going. I did try to get into film scoring, but everybody was saying, "He's a rock bass player. What does he know about scoring?" They'd forgotten that I had done arrangements and scores prior to Zeppelin. So I decided to move away from film scoring and I got more into the production side of things, but even that was hard.

At first I didn't realize that I'd be pigeon-holed, because before Zeppelin I did television, radio, films, all of that. So I never worried that I'd have to go get a real job, but it was kind of hard in the Eighties. You have to realize that I had been working for eighteen solid years by the time Zeppelin had finished, so I decided that it would be a good time to take a break anyway.

When I first decided to try and get some work, nobody took me seriously at first, and it was like, "Now wait a minute, I'm a professional musician and an arranger and a producer. I've worked with more people than you can possibly imagine." Once I did the production for the Mission U.K. it got better, but even then, it was tough. I remember wanting to produce a John Hiatt album and these record company people would say, "We really can't see your relevance to John Hiatt?" And I said, "Wait a minute, it's music. What relevance are you talking about?" I remember Sir George Martin telling me that he had the same problems after the Beatles, where these people said that he wouldn't be able to score a film because he needed to work with an American marching band and he wasn't American [laughs]. So you deal with things like that and work through it.

SW: In terms of your forays into production and arranging, how does the financial aspect work? Do you get a flat fee or points on an album?

JPJ: Both cases are different. A producer will get a fee plus points, usually a point or two or three. Arrangement is usually done as a flat fee, per title, with expenses and that sort of thing. But you learn as you go. In the early Sixties, I did arrangements for Herman's Hermits and there's one particular arrangement that I did for a song called "[There's] a Kind of Hush," which was a big hit for them and it was an even bigger hit for the Carpenters, who more or less used the same arrangement that I had written, note for note. And I think that I got paid $80 for that arrangement when I first did it [laughs]. So I learned from that experience and now my arrangement fees are a lot higher today [laughs], because they got a lot of value out of that $80.

SW: As an arranger and producer, what's the usual scenario for you?

JPJ: I like to do arrangements, because they're usually very quick projects and they're really a lot of fun. What usually happens is that they'll send me the tracks and they leave it up to me. The most I usually get in terms of instruction from the artist is something like what happened when I did the arrangements on *Automatic for the People* with R.E.M. Michael Stipe wrote me this little handwritten message saying, "We like what you're doing and if you could have the strings come in about halfway through 'Everybody Hurts,' that would be great." Or it might be things like, "Watch out for this guitar part, which we want to keep." And that's all they'll say.

Production, on the other hand, is much more time-consuming, especially the way that I produce. I tend to make sure that the band really knows what they're going to be recording, prior to going in the studio. I spend a lot of time in pre-production when I'm producing bands, before we even go into a studio, because it is the band's money that's being spent. They always tend to think that it's the record company's money, but it's not. It's the band's money being spent, so you really want to use the studio time responsibly. So I'll tend to work two or three months on a production and I work very hard in that field as any band that I've worked with will tell you.

SW: You mentioned film scoring. What was your experience like in that field?

JPJ: I did dabble in it, although the film [*Scream for Help*] wasn't very good, and I think it went straight to video [laughs]. Again, it's one of those decisions where if you want to make a career of something, you need to dedicate yourself to it. If I wanted a film scoring career, I should have probably moved to Hollywood and accepted pretty much anything that came along, which is what I did back in my session days. You accept everything that comes along, and then you can start to pick and choose. But I just didn't want to start that kind of career and that way of working.

SW: Many people, including myself, thought that Page and Plant not bringing you into the *No Quarter* project was really uncool. Were you upset about not being asked to be involved, and are there still wounds surrounding that whole situation?

JPJ: It wasn't so much that I felt that I should definitely be included or anything, but I just felt that I should have been informed. You have to understand that every year after the band broke up, there were rumors that Zeppelin was getting back together again. So at one point I called up a business associate of the band and said, "I hear the rumors are getting thick again," and this person said, "Oh, haven't they told you? They're working together again, but they're definitely not doing Zeppelin material or anything."

So I said, "Oh, okay, whatever." And then when I was on tour with Diamanda in Germany, I turned on the TV and I saw them playing this concert on MTV. And I'm thinking to myself, "That organ part sounds familiar," and then my bass parts came in, and then my strings parts came in, and I thought, "OK, so that's how it's going to be then." In the final analysis, though, they've done me a favor. I'm out here doing my solo stuff and they're doing well. I'm not sure what they're doing at the moment. I mean, we see each other for business purposes and meetings and stuff like that, and, it's, well, let's just say that it's "formal."

SW: I loved it when you took a well-deserved poke at them during your speech at the [Rock and Roll] Hall of Fame induction ceremony.

JPJ: [Laughs.] Yeah, well, I just never really understood why they just couldn't pick up the phone and call me about it, which is why I made that remark at the ceremony. I just felt that I should say something, and the noise of people falling on the floor with laughter at the press table after I said that made me feel a whole lot better [laughs].

SW: After the band broke up, there were various reunion appearances onstage and endless rumors of a full-blown reunion throughout the Eighties with everyone from Tony Thompson and Cozy Powell to Jason Bonham on drums. What kept them from becoming a reality?

JPJ: Basically, what always seemed to happen was that we'd end up together for a reunion of sorts, where we'd play concerts like Live Aid or the Atlantic Records anniversary show, and we'd immediately think of how good it felt and we would want to try to take it further. But for one reason or another the enthusiasm would eventually wane, so it never came off.

We tried various things, but we also knew that there would never be another Led Zeppelin. If there's no John Bonham, there'd be no Led Zeppelin, and it was always as simple as that. But the three of us—myself, Robert, and Jimmy—worked together for twelve years, so there was never a reason not to have another go at it, although Robert was always much more concerned with his solo career and really didn't want to get involved with Jimmy and I. But when he finally got back together with Page, without me, perhaps he was thinking that nobody would call it Zeppelin. But then the two of them started doing all Zeppelin songs [laughs].

I've never really understood why they did what they did. I remember one time when a journalist asked me, "What do you think about *No Quarter*," meaning Page and Plant's album title, and I said, "I always reckoned it was one of my best tunes" [laughs]. Robert once said that what he and Page are doing now would have been different if I was involved, which is damn right, and is probably why they didn't want me along.

SW: When you talk about current business meetings with Page and Plant, what are you referring to?

JPJ: Mainly for things like the *BBC Sessions* album or remastering projects and things like that. We all have to agree with something in order to make it happen, because that's how the band was always set up. It's funny, because when you think there's nothing else to be done with Zeppelin, someone will say, "I've heard that there's this tape." So you never know when or if more stuff will be coming out in the future.

SW: I saw a recent interview with Boz Burrell and Simon Kirke of Bad Company, who recalled the time that John Bonham sat down with them after they signed with Zeppelin's own label, Swan Song. And John apparently explained that this was a real business and that the guys in Bad Company would have to behave themselves . . .

JPJ: Well, Swan Song was really driven by our manager Peter Grant, although we all had some involvement with it, but it got kind of loose in those days. I don't know if we all should have been running a record company to be honest with you. It was one of those things that seems like a good idea at the time, but then suddenly everybody's doing something else. So it wasn't the most successful venture.

SW: As for the other business matters of Zeppelin, it's been said that as great as Led Zeppelin was in artistic terms, the band would never have reached the financial success that it did without the involvement of the late Peter Grant, who many believe revolutionized the business of artist management. Would you say that's an accurate statement?

JPJ: Oh yes, absolutely. I'd definitely agree with that. He was a brilliant manager. He certainly revolutionized the touring business for one thing. I mean, it was a 60-40 split between the artist and the promoters before Zeppelin came along. And Peter Grant stood up and said, "If you promoters want Zeppelin, it's 90-10 [laughs]." And that's kind of how it's been ever since, so Peter certainly changed all that.

He really and truly believed that the artists should get their due, because he believed that artists were getting pretty much ripped off by just about everybody in the business. And he wanted to change all that, and he did. He was a really fair man. If you were fair with him, he'd be fair with you. I know that there are a lot of concert promoters who probably hated his guts, but there are a lot of promoters who really respected him and knew that his word was very honorable.

What he did for us—as a band—was he kept everybody away. He said, "You take care of the music, I'll take care of the business." And that was how Zeppelin and Peter Grant worked. It was a simple division. He'd never say anything about the music, or he'd say, "That's great." He was just very good at keeping everyone away from us, and he allowed us to get on with what we needed to do.

SW: Is touring where Zeppelin made most of its money, or was Peter able to get the band higher royalty rates as well?

JPJ: Pretty much both of those things. We did very well with touring, but we also did very well with record sales. Zeppelin sold a lot of records over the years; we really did. The only thing we didn't really do in those days was merchandising, which was back in the days before anyone in the industry really understood merchandising. But between touring and good record sales, Zeppelin did very well.

SW: On the band's last true studio album, *In Through the Out Door*, you were much more involved in the writing and production than ever before. Does that album have special meaning for you?

JPJ: I was always involved with that stuff on all the albums, but I got more credits on that album because Page was less involved with it. Basically, I was at rehearsals earlier and Robert and I more or less wrote that album together. In all honesty, I'd say that I probably should have paid much more attention to the writing credits in the earlier days of Zeppelin. In those days, I'd just say, "Well, I wrote that, but it's part of the arrangement," or something like that, and I'd just let it go. Not realizing at the time that that part of the arrangement had more to do with the writing than just arranging something. I always thought that John Bonham's contribution was always much more than he ever received credit for. In fact, I know it was.

Zeppelin was really a partnership between four people, and sometimes when you see songs with "Page-Plant" on everything, it makes it seem like it was a "Lennon-McCartney" situation where they wrote everything and John and I just kind of learned the songs that Jimmy and Robert taught to us [laughs]. That's so far from the truth, it's ridiculous. For one thing, Robert usually used to write the lyrics last, after the track was recorded. Of course, he's credited on every one because there's lyrics in every song, but sometimes we'd send him back to rewrite them [laughs]. But I've done fine out of the whole thing. It's bought me endless studios and the freedom to do what I want, so I really have no complaints.

SW: Having been through virtually every creative aspect of the music industry, what advice would you have for a musician starting out?

JPJ: Musically, I always tell musicians to keep their ears open and to listen to everything. On the business side, I would say to probably make sure that the way your band determines writing credits is worked out very early on, and perhaps even put it down on paper. And you should also try to work with people that you really trust. But the most important thing for all musicians is to just get on with discovering your talents and your music.

COMMUNICATION BREAKDOWN

"I'd always promised myself to do a solo album, probably since I was a kid
... but I wasn't quite sure what to do which was partly why it took so long.
I wanted to use all my skills I suppose ... In my mind I'm halfway through
the next album. ... It will be rock-based. I can do a lot of different things
but I actually like playing rock 'n' roll. It's funny—my father thought that the
bass guitar would be a forgotten instrument in about two years. He thought
it was only a novelty instrument and told me: 'You should take up the saxo-
phone, it'll always work.' I proved him wrong!"
 – John Paul Jones to Fiona Shepherd, *Scotsman*, September 14, 1999

COMMUNICATION BREAKDOWN

" . . . we did 'Ten Years Gone,' and when I did that with Led Zeppelin, one
guitar was like an army of guitars on the recorded version. But it was so
good how the [Black] Crowes were playing it—and then all of a sudden
they started playing all of the harmonies too—and they got them right! I'd
thought, 'Well, there's bound to be bits here that we'll have to 'top and tail,'
but they'd done their homework amazingly well. It was sheer bliss for me,
hearing all this stuff 'living' round me, if you know what I mean. I'd only
heard it on the album when I did it, and now there it was, without me!"
 – Jimmy Page to Timothy White, *Billboard*, October 25, 1999

COMMUNICATION BREAKDOWN

"I recently went to Disney World where I put my hands in some concrete
in Orlando's Magic Kingdom, and so the name [the Priory of Brion] is a
send-up of that sort of majestic vacuum ... I haven't been able to sing like
this before because I haven't felt so inspired. It's lighter, springier, bouncier,
funnier, and there's no earth-shattering importance to any of it. You don't
have that flexibility if people have paid good money to hear you sing the
songs that were your contribution to their lives ... I've finally achieved my
freedom."
 – Robert Plant to Nigel Williamson, *Times of London*, July 28, 2000

ZEPPELIN RAIDER'S SOFT SIDE

Sue Williams | December 8, 2000, *Derby Evening Telegraph*

As John Paul Jones readily attests, one of the nicest things about having made his fortune in his youth is that he can do pretty much anything he wants now (see his remarks in "John Paul Jones Life After Led Zeppelin" on page 333). His experimentation led him to many interesting places that a musician concerned with earning his crust might not access, at least right away. Similarly, Robert Plant delved into various experiments in popular music, but by the turn of the millennium, he decided to look back to the music that originally inspired him. Plant started touring the UK with a group he called the Priory of Brion (a pun on the film *Monty Python's Life of Brian*). They played small venues throughout England, singing the songs of Plant's youth and having a grand old time doing it. Musically, it was a win/win: Plant had a lot of fun and his audiences got an up-close and personal look at one of the icons of contemporary music.

Now here's a quiz for you: Within the articles in this book, how many bands (or at least different named groups) was Plant playing in when Jimmy Page came calling in 1968? This article adds a new one to the list. —Ed.

As Lead Singer of Heavy Rock Legends Led Zeppelin, Robert Plant Had a Wildman Reputation. But It's a More Mellow Sound and Approach He's Bringing to Derby.

Legend has it that Led Zeppelin were paying the bill for yet another night of hotel room trashing, including the cost of a high-storey TV ejection, when the foyer receptionist remarked with envy: "You know, I've always wanted to throw a television through a hotel window."

The rock band's manager Peter Grant is alleged to have taken out his wallet, peeled off $200 and said: "Be our guest."

Such stories make it even harder to believe that the voice of a heavy rock generation is now hiding his light under an acoustic bushel, singing songs by Donovan and Stephen Stills.

But that's the path ex–Led Zeppelin wildman Robert Plant has chosen to tread.

Under the unlikely title of Priory of Brion, Plant's four-piece is currently playing pubs, clubs and small theatrical venues across the country.

And he doesn't even mind that he is following in the footsteps of ABBA impersonators and boy tribute bands.

"I don't really want it to get any bigger," he said in a recent interview. "In a way I'd like to move it on to the next level, but at the same time I can't do that without reintroducing all that rock 'n' roll hoopla."

Of course it's the rock 'n' roll hoopla which is paying for what some believe is his personal indulgence. Twenty years after they split, Led Zeppelin were still among the top five British rock star earners last year, grossing an awesome GBP 14.5m.

In fact, it's almost as if Plant wants to sneak in and out of venues before fans realise who he is. The Derby gig was such a last-minute booking that it was too late to include it in the Assembly Rooms brochure.

Like ex–Rolling Stone Bill Wyman who has taken to the road with a group of friends under the obscure title, the Rhythm Kings, Plant appears to be revelling in his low profile.

"I started off scratching around tiny basements in the bowels of buildings and to come full circle back to this might not seem much to a lot of people, but to me it's really exciting," he said.

The band's name, he admits, is partly a play on *Monty Python's Life of Brian* and partly a send-up of the "majestic vacuum" of his former career.

His current folksy stance could certainly not be further than those heady days of drink, drugs, groupies, and hotel trashing.

Plant (53) was frontman of a struggling Midlands act Hobbstweedle when he was introduced to Yardbirds guitarist Jimmy Page and bassist/keyboard player John Paul Jones. Plant in turn brought fellow "Brummy" John Bonham into the band.

It was the Who's Keith Moon who remarked they would probably go down like a lead Zeppelin which spawned the name.

After a tour of the States and the release of their first explosive album *Led Zeppelin*, they immediately became a headline act.

Plant's sexuality combined with his expressive, beseeching voice and Page's incredible dexterity saw them go from strength to strength.

But nothing lasts and the anthemic "Stairway to Heaven" on their fourth Runes album came to be viewed as their in-concert finale in 1975.

The same year Plant and his wife, Maureen, were seriously injured in a car crash. Two year's later their son Karac died suddenly from a stomach infection while Zeppelin were touring the States, and in September, 1980, John Bonham keeled over after a night of heavy drinking and died. On December 4, the band announced they were breaking up.

Plant now lives quietly in a 15th century farmhouse near Kidderminster and involves himself in campaigns to keep hospital services running. He also remains a lifelong Wolves fan and has even been seen watching Kidderminster Harriers.

Reflecting on his schizophrenic past, he said recently: "One day I'd be standing on a hotel balcony in Spain, raising my fists to heaven and declaring I was a golden god.

"The next, I'd be standing on the terraces in the rain with a meat pie and cup of Bovril watching Wolves get hammered. That sort of thing helps give you a sense of perspective."

Over 12 years, Led Zeppelin released 10 albums, sold 90 million records, and played to bigger concert audiences than either the Beatles or the Rolling Stones.

Now the almost self-effacing Plant says he's finally achieved freedom and is having fun. In a recent *Times* interview, he said: "If you want what I used to be you can get that off a CD. No matter how well Jimmy and I play we are not going to be what we were. I'm seeking out the nooks and crannies as far away from the main stage of rock 'n' roll as I can get. It's a long way from the king of cock rock, that's for sure."

Plant will be joined on stage by bassist Paul Whetton and drummer Andy Edwards with Paul Timothy on piano and hammond organ and Kevyn Gammond on guitars.

Kevyn played with Plant and Bonham in Band of Joy before the birth of Led Zeppelin and went on to work with Jimmy Cliff and Jimmy Witherspoon.

GETTING THE LED OUT: A JOHN PAUL JONES INTERVIEW

Gail Worley | April 1, 2002, KNAC-FM

While Plant was playing pubs in Putney, Jones took his album on the road. He enjoyed recording and touring so much that he made a second album, titled *The Thunderthief*. It sounded a bit like King Crimson (Mark II) meets the Incredible String Band in a cage match with Richard Thompson refereeing. More importantly, *The Thunderthief* had the same something that Led Zeppelin once had (though everyone had forgotten it): it was progressive. –Ed.

An Interview with Led Zeppelin

Besides the Beatles, who will, in my opinion, always be the greatest band of all time, my favorite hard rock band has been Led Zeppelin ever since I first heard "The Immigrant Song," when I was about 10 years old. I thought it was the most far out, wild song ever. When John Bonham died (I think I was 12 or 13 at the time) Led Zeppelin broke up and I never got a chance to see them in concert. I did see Robert Plant and Jimmy Page perform together at Madison Square Garden a couple of years ago and that was pretty close to the real thing, but I still get knots in my stomach when some of my friends talk about actually seeing the full band—Page, Plant, John Bonham, and bassist John Paul Jones—play live. One of the highlights of my Zeppelin worshipping happened at the South by Southwest [SXSW] music convention two years ago, when John Paul Jones participated in an interview panel: a one-on-one conversation with the bassist from the greatest heavy rock band ever! My personal Rock Critic Hero and Mentor, Jim DeRogatis, conducted the interview, so we all knew it would rock very hard. For over an hour, Jones held a capacity crowd spellbound as he rattled off "I remember when" stories and told his version of all the best Hammer-of-the-Gods style rumors—including that one about the Edgewater hotel, the groupie, and the shark—from his career with Led Zeppelin until I was giddy with excitement and actually became so overwhelmed and moved thinking about how "In the Light" and "The Battle of Evermore" shaped my youth that I actually got teary-eyed. Of course, I had to hang out after the interview ended to get my picture taken with Jonesy because, hey, this is Led-Fucking-Zeppelin we're talking about, and I'm a huge fan!

A couple of months ago, I got the word that Jones was going to be in town doing some press for his second solo album, the follow up to 1999's *Zooma*, and I wasted no time in securing a spot on his agenda. In this interview, conducted in his hotel room on Manhattan's Upper West Side, John Paul Jones spoke at length about his latest solo album *The Thunderthief*, reflected on his days with Led Zeppelin and his subsequent place in rock history, and explained how his work with avant garde vocalist, Diamanda Galás, inspired his own solo efforts. For Jones, one of rock's most influential living legends, the song, in no way, remains the same.

Gail Worley: I saw the interview you did with Jim DeRogatis at South by Southwest in 2000. In that interview you said—perhaps jokingly—that one of the reasons it took you so long to make your first solo album is that you don't sing. *The Thunderthief* has your first recorded vocals ever. Was singing on a record with no previous experience a scary thing for you?

John Paul Jones: Yes. I mean, I had to make sure I could sing well enough to put [the performance] on record, so it wasn't totally scary, you know what I mean? I sort of crept up on it [*laughs*]. The scary thing was actually doing it live on stage the first night, in Nashville (when Jones opened for King Crimson on their last tour). That was scary. What I wanted to do was do three songs from *Thunderthief*. We started with "Leafy Meadows" and then I did "Hoediddle" and then I did "Freedom Song"—which is scary enough. However, I suddenly thought, "I can't just sing one song" [two of these three songs are instrumentals]. So I thought, I need another vocal [*laughs*]. I didn't want to do anything else off *The Thunderthief*, so I, in my bravura, decided to sing "That's the Way." Singing a Zeppelin song was even scarier, I can tell you.

GW: I bet.

JPJ: What I used to do on the tour before, I played an instrumental version of "Going to California" on the mandolin, and I used to team [those two songs]. I would start with "That's the Way"—because I played those mandolin parts on the original record. [*Hums the tune.*] Then I said, "You didn't think I was going to sing, did you?" [*Laughs.*] But this time I did it and I sang it, so people who went to both concerts thought it was some kind of a trick [*laughs*]. But it went down alright. Nobody killed me for it, 'cause I can't possibly sing it like Robert Plant. I don't have that voice. But I did it in this other way, and it worked, but the first night I was terrified. Remembering words is the hard part. I put the lyrics on a music stand, so I couldn't fuck it up. But I'm learning, I'm getting better.

GW: How has working with a guy like Robert Fripp influenced your own writing and playing?

JPJ: Well, I haven't actually worked with him that much. The biggest connection is being on his label. [*Long pause.*] I mean, when Zeppelin first started in 1969, and people would say "What sort of band is it?" I used to say "Progressive rock," because in those days it meant rock that progressed [*laughs*]. You know, it was a very literal term; "Well you know, we're trying to advance the form of it, and this is what we're doing to make it go somewhere." But of course that title came to have all sorts of different meanings. When it started to mean "classic," that's when I stopped saying it was progressive rock. But then we'd say it's "Blues Rock," because people love to label things. I didn't really hear an awful lot of King Crimson [music] to be honest. But being on his label is great, mainly because of the fact that you get, obviously, total artistic freedom. There are no contracts either. He really hates the music industry with a passion, and he's not afraid of telling everybody [*a*] at every available opportunity, which is great. And the artist maintains the copyrights to all their material, so I just agree with him on that whole side, and I really like the way he approaches music, and musicians. He's so passionate about everything and has a definite way that he wants to do it. It's inspiring to know that people can say, "This is the way I want to do it!" and off he goes!

He's always kind of been around in the background, but the first time Fripp got my attention was when Brian Eno called me and asked if I knew a piano player who could do some avant-garde piano. He asked if I knew anybody who could do some spacey sort of piano, and I couldn't really think of anybody. I asked him to describe what he wanted and then I said "Well, I can do that" [*laughs*]. All right then, so I said, "What's the track?" and he said, "Fripp's doing a solo on it, and I want you to do the counterpart." So I went along, and it was just this rhythm track, and I played this sort of spacey piano. The next time I heard it, Fripp had put his guitar solo on afterwards, so there's this sort of alien spacey piano and suddenly this guitar comes in like [*makes sounds of cars crashing*], and I was like "Fuck! I wish I'd known he was doing that! Jesus Christ!" Like "Who is this guy?" [*Laughs.*] Then, when I met him he was like [*imitating Robert Fripp's gentlemanly nature*] "Oh, Hello, John. How are you?" I'm thinking, "Now, this isn't the same guy who was like [*makes car crash noises*] on that record?" But it was. And that's what he did on "Leafy Meadows." He walked in and he puttered about and set his pedals up and had tea and cake and then he went, "Whaaaahh!!!!" [*Laughs.*] I really like that. It's quite a paradox.

That's what I like about Diamanda [Galás] as well. When you meet her she's terribly nice and sweet. And then you see her sing and [*makes exaggerated face of terror*].

GW: I had to smile when I saw that Nick Beggs plays the Chapman stick on the album, because I remember him as the bassist for Kajagoogoo. How do you go about finding the various players who are involved with your solo projects?

JPJ: Well, on *Zooma* I had Pete Thomas on drums and Trey Gunn on stick. I wanted a stick player because they think differently. They're often bass players as well and they just approach it differently. Plus, from a very practical point of view, in a trio, it's great, because I'm a bass player and a keyboard player and I play quite a lot of lap steel in my show. If I'm doing bass, then [the stick player] can play all the lead parts. If I go to the keyboards, he can then switch to bass in mid-song, if necessary. So, it's very practical and it means I haven't got someone standing there with a guitar, who feels like, "Well, I should be playing something, because I'm standing here" [laughs]. There's loads of space in a trio—which is what was nice about Led Zeppelin, because when Robert wasn't singing we were a trio. There's loads of space and you can go anywhere you like.

So, Trey Gunn was on that album and originally I had asked him to come out with me on the road, because the idea, of course, with *Zooma* was to get out and play it. He was going to [come out with us], but then King Crimson had resurfaced and he said his first loyalty was to go with them. Then I asked Robert [Fripp] if he knew of another Chapman stick player, and he said [adopting Fripp's accent], "Well you won't believe it, but Nick Beggs is a really good player." I went, "Nick Beggs from Kajagoogoo? 'Too Shy'?" And he goes, "Yeah, try him out." So I did. Then I went through a few drummers and eventually Nick said, well, "Terl Bryant is a really good drummer." So he came on board and he was great, and their attitudes are just awesome. It's a happy family, they call me Pater [laughs]. But it really is just like a family on the road, it's really sweet. And they're just full-on, enthusiastic, 100 percent committed, and it's great.

GW: Will you be taking *Thunderthief* on the road now that your tour opening for Crimson has passed?

JPJ: Well, yes. We're trying to get some dates together at the moment, to do *The Thunderthief*. But the thing is, I'd like to headline again because then I can do my long show with the keyboards and things. But I may have to open for somebody else, again, because we really need to play to more people. It's just maddening. I mean, we can sell out Irving Plaza [midsize venue in NYC] but there comes a point where that's the biggest one we can sell out, because nobody knows us. Everybody comes to the show and goes away going [adopts American accent], "That was the greatest thing I've ever seen! It was fantastic!" and then they tell their friends and we get people going, "Wow, I wished I'd known he was playing there." We really just need to play to more people.

GW: Here's a quote from a review of *The Thunderthief:* "Since his days as a top sessioneer, his abilities as an arranger and multi-instrumentalist have equipped him to add musical finesse to any genre." That's a pretty nice compliment. Is that part of the reason you've been attracted to such genre-diverse projects? You know, from Cinderella to the Butthole Surfers?

JPJ: [Laughing] Cinderella . . .

GW: Oh come on, I love Cinderella.

JPJ: Yeah, they were all right. The drummer owns a bus company now. Yeah, it's all the same to me. As long as it's good [music] I don't care what it is. I mean, I've done classical composition and string quartets and [*sighs*] I don't really care what it is. If somebody asks me to do something and I don't know how to do it, I'll find out.

GW: In a criticism of the song "Angry Angry" one reviewer said that you were "Always too accomplished to achieve something so off the cuff." I guess you'd call that a backhanded compliment.

JPJ: Yeah, he didn't get it. The Brits don't like "Angry Angry." For a start, they understand the accent [I sing that song in], which they hate, 'cause it's music hall, basically, is what it is—like a vaudeville accent. And they don't like it because I think they think I'm taking the piss out of punk, which I'm not. I don't do parody at all. It's actually terribly prosaic, how it all happened, but music is just like that for me, basically. "Angry Angry" is at the speed it is because I heard Adam Bomb [Pink Gibson from NY based rock band, Get Animal, who plays guitar on this song] play at the Borderline in London and I immediately heard what I wanted him to do [on the record]. I went back into the studio and put a riff down, which was on bass, mandolin, and drum machine which was [*sings hyperspeed riff from song*], at that speed. I got it to play for three minutes, just that riff, and then I wrote the song and thought, "Now, what do I do with it?" It was at that tempo and had that intensity and the phrase "Angry Angry" just came to me, so I wrote the lyrics from there. And I had to do it in that voice because it sounds stupid any other way [*laughs*]. But the Brits hate it. They think I'm trying to be something that I'm not.

GW: Oh, those Brits are so serious about everything.

JPJ: Well, you haven't met the Germans. They'll go right into anything and find all the symbolism and the lot.

GW: "Ice Fishing at Night" is a really beautiful song with some dark lyrics. What inspired you to write that song?

JPJ: Well, I didn't write the lyrics. They came with *The Thunderthief.*

GW: What does that mean?

JPJ: What happened was, halfway through what was basically going to be an instrumental album, but was also a continuation from *Zooma,* I decided it'd be really nice to have voices [*laughs*]. As I've said before, I didn't want to get a guest vocalist in, for a couple of reasons actually. One is that I know that I'd forget what I was doing and work on producing them, whoever the vocalist was. I would immediately turn into a producer and it would go somewhere else. The other reason is that, being a bass player, I don't actually have a distinctive sound. I mean, some people will listen to a record and go, "Oh yeah, that's a John Paul Jones record," but if you just heard one song in isolation, [you couldn't tell]. Like, if you're [Carlos] Santana, that record he did, every time he hits that guitar you know that's Santana. It's what he does. He doesn't do anything else except for that sound. I don't have that, because of the instruments I play. I thought, guest vocalists will only dilute that and just diffuse it even more. I decided, "I'm going to try and sing myself." Then I thought, 'Well, I've got nothing to sing.' Then I was thinking that I don't want to become a singer and a songwriter all at the same time. One thing at a time, you know?

So, I knew Peter Blegvad, he's a singer/songwriter, and a cartoonist as well—he did the album cover. He's got a weird way of looking at things; just a strange, twisted sort of dark view. I thought he'd be the ideal person to write some lyrics. I asked him, "Have you got any lyrics that you haven't got music to? Any lyrics just laying around?" He had about four songs that he gave me and I picked up "The Thunderthief" and "Ice Fishing at Night" and set them to music and, basically, just experimented with singing to see whether I liked what I did. I thought I could work with these songs and I could sing enough to do what I wanted to do. I don't have a great technique or a great voice, but as long as I could convince myself that it sounded all right, then it would be OK . . . which is how I do everything [*laughs*]. You know, I'm not a great technician on any instrument, but as long as I can convince myself that is sounds real, then I'll do it.

I sang those two songs and then I thought, well I can't just sing two songs [*laughs*] . . . I think like this all the time . . . it's boring really. "You can't just have two songs . . . how about trying to do some more?" Now that I know I can sing, I'll try and write some lyrics and see how easy that is. So, I learned another trick. I discovered, like many people I'm sure have, that with the onset of the computer, I enjoyed writing e-mails. And since I enjoyed composing e-mails, I thought, "I wonder if it works for writing lyrics?" [*Laughs.*] I tried writing some lyrics on the computer and—sure enough—I wrote three songs in an hour . . . one of which was "Angry Angry." I thought, 'This is fun!' I could finally master the song form on the next album, 'cause there's no rules, you see? It's great!

GW: You make it up as you go along.

JPJ: Absolutely, you get away with it yet again. [*Laughing*] I've had a lot of encouragement, but at the beginning of *Zooma* I thought, "They're all going to go, 'It's boring!'"

GW: You've influenced so any modern rock bassists, from Tom Hamilton and John Deacon of Queen to Krist Novoselic and Flea. It's almost like, if you drew it all as a family tree, you'd be the father of rock bass playing. What's that like?

JPJ: Well, it's just that they haven't bothered to look further than me. I mean, I'm just lower down the food chain than somebody else is. It just depends on how far you want to go back, really. It's very nice, it's very flattering . . . but I'm imparting stuff that I probably learned from James Jamerson and [Donald] "Duck" Dunn and Charles Mingus. But it's very nice [to hear that I've influenced somebody]. I met some guy in New Orleans on the last tour and he says, "You probably don't remember me but I came to see you with my dad when I was 12 years old. You really influenced me and you got me playing the bass and you told me I should practice."

He was, like, in his twenties now. I asked him if he was still playing and he said yes, he was the principal bass for the New Orleans Philharmonic Symphony [*laughs*]. Right! Nice to meet you!

GW: How did it happen that "Rock and Roll" is now the theme music for a Cadillac commercial?

JPJ: Ah! Because they asked us if they could use it [*laughs*]. Cadillac's kind of a romantic thing—for Englishmen, especially. You think, "Pink Cadillac," and it was Elvis's car, and it's a limo and it just has this aura. I don't know whether it's the same in America; probably not, because you have them over here all the time—you've lived with them [*laughs*]. I can see a Cadillac now, and it's *big*, with big fins and whitewall tires. But they asked us if they could use the song, and they didn't get it for nothing. And why not?

GW: Do all three of you—you and Jimmy and Robert—all have to make a decision like that? It's not like Page did it when you weren't looking?

JPJ: No, all three of us make those decisions.

GW: Well, on one hand, you can think, "Classic car, classic song," but it does kind of bother me that I hear the Who's "Bargain" now and instantly think of a car commercial.

JPJ: Well, yeah . . . I haven't actually seen the commercial yet.

GW: Before Led Zeppelin ever came into being you had a successful career as a session musician and arranger. How much of Zeppelin's unique sound is owed to your work on the arrangements?

JPJ: Eh . . . some. But then it's equally the way Bonham approached the drums and it really was a group effort. Even if the original idea wasn't a group effort, the final thing was a group effort. It really was, more than any band I was involved in. It was never like the songwriter ruled the band. Robert wrote the lyrics last, usually.

GW: But there wasn't any other band that sounded like Led Zeppelin, and there never has been since. That's kind of a big deal when you think about it. Especially now, in this day of everybody sounding like everyone else.

JPJ: That's because people in bands these days always listen to the same music. They all start a band because they all like U2 or they all like Pearl Jam. Consequently, their field of reference is very narrow. Our field of reference was huge. Page and I were very hardworking session musicians and when you walk into a session it can be absolutely anything. Country and western, to Champion Jack Dupree, to Engelbert Humperdinck, to a big band session. You walk through that door and you don't know; it could really be anything [*laughs*]. You name it, I've done it. I played weddings, I've played bar mitzvahs, I've done Irish weddings, Jewish weddings, Greek weddings, Italian weddings. I can play it all. Musicians these days, they don't seem to do that anymore, and bring it all into the mix. Bonzo used to like soul music and knew the words to every Chi-Lites record, ever [*laughs*]. He was the biggest Smokey Robinson fan, he was into Motown, he loved the Beatles and James Brown. I was into all that soul music, jazz, and classical. Robert was really into blues and all the rock stuff and doo-wop. Page had all these other interests. It was just a huge range of influences, you could go here or there or this way or that. And that's what I do now, with this music.

GW: What was the dynamic like between you and John Bonham as a rock rhythm section?

JPJ: Well, we weren't like a lot of rock rhythm sections, we swung like a bastard [*laughs*]! Groove was extremely important in Zeppelin and it wasn't in a lot of those bands [that were popular at the same time]. It was extremely important, which is what, to me, made the band [so great]. We used to have a lot of women at our concerts—and I loved having women at our concerts because they'd dance. [*Laughing.*] It's great, because the guys stand there with their arms folded and the girls are dancing. Zeppelin was great because it was music you could dance to, and you can't say that about too many rock bands.

GW: How did your work with Diamanda Galás on her record *The Sporting Life* and its subsequent tour, end up affecting your own career?

JPJ: Oh, wow, she's my favorite piano player. She's just very inspiring as an artist, she's very passionate, very committed, always knows what she wants to do. I have several other things to thank her for; she got me playing steel guitar again, which I hadn't done for years. She saw it in the studio and said "What's that?" And I said, "Steel guitar," "I want to hear it." So we put it on one of her songs and we did two songs with it in her shows. It was good because it gave me some sort of high voice as well as being in the back playing bass. And I thought, this is a way I can work, this is a way I can actually do a solo show without being a bass player and having other people take over all the fun stuff.

GW: Didn't she also inspire you to start playing live again?

JPJ: Yes, she did. I mean . . . somebody actually said, I think this was a German interview, [the journalist] said that he thought that these records—this is interesting—that *The Thunderthief* was the third record in a trilogy, starting with Diamanda's record. And in fact, he's right in that way, because that was the first time I'd tried using that sort of riff, drums, and voice. A lot of people didn't like it, but to me it was blindingly obvious. I couldn't see why nobody had thought of it before, especially with her voice, because she has all that range and passion. Plus, her lyrics are great! These homicidal love songs are wonderful [*laughs*]. She came along with, "Hide the knives, baby's insane!" [*Laughs.*] "Skotoseme," that first track [on *The Sporting Life*], she did it in one take. Me and the engineer were shaking at the end of it, and she just went [*adopting a woman's voice*] "Is that OK? I'm going to get myself some coffee" [*laughing*]. When someone suggested we work together, I could hear it all in my head. I just went [*snaps fingers*], "I know what we're going to do as well." I sent her these riffs, to New York, and she sent back some ideas. Then she just turned up and stayed for two months, and we made the record. It was just brilliant. I thought, "This is great! We can do what we like again." I was just so inspired. Then she also told me—'cause she's collaborated with everybody as well—that she'd said in interviews, when they'd say, "Well, why don't you collaborate anymore?" She'd say, "Well, I've put effort into everybody else's music. If I'm going to put that much effort into music, it's going to be my own." And I went, "Yeah!" [*laughs*].

GW: She kinda scares me, to tell you the truth.

JPJ: She scares us all! That's the fun part. But she's so committed to her music. She's just having fun. She was great onstage one time, [*laughs*] there was that perfect moment in this theater in Chicago, she was there at the front of the stage and—you know how everybody shouts out song titles?—a little voice comes up in this slight lull between songs and goes "Song Remains the Same!" And she just looked at him and she goes [*makes malevolent face*], "No it doesn't, motherfucker." [*Laughing.*] You could see the crowd part.

GW: As a way of wrapping this up, I surely don't have to tell you this, but thinking about how Led Zeppelin always gets the nod as the greatest hard rock or metal band of all time—on VH1 shows or magazine polls, or radio countdowns or whatever—do you think the endurance and greatness of the Led Zeppelin legend has much to do with the fact that you guys called it quits after John Bonham died, while you were still a hot item?

JPJ: [*Pauses*] I suppose with hindsight, maybe that did have something to do with it. I mean, there was no point in carrying on, it would be a different band, because no John Bonham, no Led Zeppelin—it's as simple as that. He was so integral, to have gotten someone else would have made it more of a tribute band, if you were playing Led Zeppelin songs, because anyone else would have to be in his shadow all the time. However, he died at a time when there was like a new lease on life, a new awakening in Zeppelin. Punk had severely embarrassed us [*laughs*]. We'd stripped down and just went, [*shrugs*] "Oh, OK, right. This is over, off we go again." It was a very hopeful time, despite the darkness of having lost John. That was terrible. So, yes, [had he not died] we would have gone on and . . . who knows what would have happened?

PLANT RETURNS TO INTERPRETATION

Adam Howorth | July 20, 2002, *Billboard*

Even as Jones became more experimental, Plant turned the clock back a ways with *Dreamland*, an album of cover versions, perhaps inspired by his work with the Priory of Brion. Though it featured no new material, *Dreamland* was nominated for a Grammy in 2002. −Ed.

Led Zep Frontman Covers Buckley, Dylan, Hendrix on Universal Debut

LONDON—"My ability and vocal chords [sic] are all in good shape, but I haven't really felt substantially relevant as a lyricist for a long time." A stunning admission, but one characteristic of Robert Plant, the disarmingly honest voice of Led Zeppelin, whose new album, *Dreamland*, is essentially a set of covers.

In addition to delivering versions of Bob Dylan's "One More Cup of Coffee," Tim Buckley's "Song to the Siren," and Jimi Hendrix's "Hey Joe," *Dreamland* also includes "Skip's Song"—penned by troubled Moby Grape singer Skip Spence—and Arthur Crudup's "Win My Train [Fare Home]," in which Plant includes passages from Crudup's "That's Alright Mama," Robert Johnson's "Milk Cows Calf Blues," and John Lee Hooker's "Crawlin' King Snake."

"They were songs that I've always loved, and I didn't see them as covers because I was there when they were being written," Plant explains. "It was just this period in American music [that] I'd never really got near [to] vocally in my adventures up to now. So I thought, 'I'm dry as a bone, but these songs are still vibrant.'"

Following its June 24 international release on Mercury, *Dreamland* entered the UK sales chart at No. 20. The set is due Tuesday (16) in the US via Universal.

"The only question is, what are [they] going to put on the radio?" Plant says of the new record. "Will anybody play it? They have a little bit. But it's an ageist culture here [in the UK]."

The one national station to playlist the first cut—Tim Rose's "Morning Dew"—is the rock-formatted Virgin Radio, whose program controller, Paul Jackson, comments, "'Morning Dew' is a strong track, and the album is a good listen. That will please his core of fans."

After selling nearly 200 million albums with Led Zeppelin, Plant is now two albums into a solo stint with Mercury UK. In the US, *Dreamland* is his first project for Universal. It marks the end of his 34-year association with Atlantic that began when Ahmet Ertegun signed the young British rock band for the unprecedented sum of $200,000.

"I signed to Atlantic Records in 1968, and I left at the beginning of this year—and I still owe them a record," Plant says. "They said that they didn't want me to go, but there was nobody left who was there when I was there originally. As time's gone, even the guy who started the company selling vinyl from the trunk of his car—Ahmet Ertegun—had vanished almost. I felt like my associations had all dissolved." The label switches happened after Plant performed with his new outfit, Strange Sensation, in New York.

"Universal saw us play this set, and Doug Morris, who runs all the Universal labels, said, 'This is what you should do—you've got the gongs, how many more awards do you want?' That was fantastic. My manager, Bill Curbishley [of Trinifold Management in London], said, 'Don't tell him that! What about the blues album?' I said, 'Fuck off!' The first big encouragement came from the guy [Morris] who said, 'Look, if you've had enough and you're not getting the support, we'll put the record out.'"

Booked by Rod MacSween for ITB [International Talent Booking] in London, Plant is to open several shows for the Who this summer; he is to appear on *Late Night with David Letterman* shortly after the album's bow.

Derek Simon, senior director of marketing at Universal US, says the label is "enamored with *Dreamland*. The joy in working this record is the reaction we're getting when we're playing it for people. Robert only made this record for one reason—because he wanted to. The record lives and breathes through the arrangements created for these songs."

After the *Dreamland* campaign, Plant says, "I'll probably write an album," though he adds, "there are probably another three or four thousand albums in my house" that could fuel another set like *Dreamland*. "I rather like interpretation. Led Zeppelin's first album contained a lot of Howlin' Wolf, but they weren't called 'covers' then, because nobody knew they were covers."

So what of another collaboration with Jimmy Page? "I can't see any reason not to," Plant says. "He's found huge archives of really rare old Zeppelin stuff—live stuff from the States from 1969—and he's sifting through it with a view to putting it on DVD."

A reunion with Led Zep bassist John Paul Jones is unlikely. "My relationship with Jonesy is hampered by one misinterpreted word at the first press conference that Page and I did to go with the [MTV] *Unledded* stuff. The first question to me was, 'Where's John Paul Jones?' I said, 'He's parking the car'—and that was it. Fucked for life. I apologized, and I went to one meeting and got on one knee as he was walking out—to tie my shoelace as well—and said, 'John, surely now we're way too old for this?' But he just sidestepped me and walked out into the East London air."

COMMUNICATION BREAKDOWN

"[W]hen we lost John I was very keen to do a chronological live album at the time, because I knew we had the tapes that spanned these periods. And I was very keen because I felt that Led Zeppelin's live performance was so important to the sum of the parts. We'd go onstage, and if all four of us were really on top of it, it would just take on this fifth dimension, and that fifth dimension could go in any direction . . . There didn't seem to be any interest at that time, but now the sheer fact that the technology has moved to such a degree that you can have surround-sound cinema in your own home made the whole prospect very attractive and appealing."

– Jimmy Page to Barney Hoskyns, *Rock's Backpages*, March 2003

ROBERT PLANT, JIMMY PAGE, AND JOHN PAUL JONES DISCUSS THEIR LED ZEPPELIN CAREERS AND THEIR NEW TOUR FOOTAGE DVD

Matt Lauer | May 29, 2003, NBC *TODAY*

Even before the dissolution of Led Zeppelin—in fact as early as *The Song Remains the Same,* (see the 1976 interview with Alan Freeman on page 183)—Page had talked about a project featuring great live Led Zeppelin performances in chronological order. Just less than 30 years later, he finally did it. –Ed.

Want to feel old? 2003 marks the 35th anniversary of the beginning of the band Led Zeppelin. And to mark the occasion, a gift to fans, the Zeppelin DVD, five hours of previously unreleased live performances from four tours spanning 1970 to 1979, and a three-disc CD with more live concert material from concerts in California in 1972 called *How the West Was Won.* In a rare exclusive interview I had the opportunity to talk to the three surviving members of the legendary band Led Zeppelin: Jimmy Page, Robert Plant, and John Paul Jones.

[*Video clip of Led Zeppelin performing plays.*]

[**Matt Lauer, voiceover**] The music is legendary. The riffs considered some of the greatest of all time. With more than 200 million albums sold worldwide, Led Zeppelin is the biggest selling rock group in history.

[*Video clip of Led Zeppelin performing plays.*]

Jimmy Page [Led Zeppelin DVD]: When you look back and you measure up what the band was about, four very, very different people and personalities coming together and having this union onstage and taking on this sort of fifth element, which is something that's intangible but, you know, it's definitely something—it's very, very powerful.

[*Video clip of Led Zeppelin performing "Whole Lotta Love" plays.*]

[**ML voiceover**] From the groundbreaking early days of heavy metal to the power ballad, Led Zeppelin did it all.

[*Group interview.*]

ML: Take me through the process of getting ready for the live show because the live shows were legendary.

JP: I can—I think I can quite safely say here from the minute that you walked to the stage, the amount of time that was going to go on onstage and the time that you came back offstage, you never knew exactly what was going to be happening. Because of all this—the way—you know, this communication that went—went on musically. And the way that you would just go off on a tangent here and there. And, you know, there was no way that you couldn't be there. But just really throw yourself right into it.

[**ML voiceover**] Epitomizing the era of sex, drugs, and rock 'n' roll, they lost drummer John Bonham in 1980 from an alcohol overdose.

JP: Well, quite clearly, when we lost John in 1980, we'd been talking about this bond that we had, and it's almost like a musical ESP that we'd developed along the way. What were you going to do? People came to us and they—and I know they mention drummers not with a commercial mind there when they were saying it. It was purely for the best within the world. But there was—you know, you were saying, "Yeah, it's a great drummer," but what do you actually do here? Do you say, "Listen to this. This is what we improvised one night, now you learn it and we'll play it the same every night"? Of course not. So, you know . . .

ML: So it was really—this was—this was magic in a bottle.

JP: At that time it was—it was a measure of respect for John Bonham's part that he played. And plus what we—we felt amongst what Led Zeppelin was that—we—we could discontinue.

Robert Plant: But if you're going to talk about this, you should go to a clip from "Achilles' Last Stand" at Knebworth, because the—the unity between these guys was unbelievable. If you couldn't get near that, then it would be real a soulless, empty experience which nobody wanted.

[*Video clip of Led Zeppelin performing plays.*]

[**ML voiceover**] And while other bands of a similar generation continue to strut their stuff on stage, Led Zeppelin looks forward, by looking back, by letting the music speak for itself the way the band always wanted it to.

[*Group interview.*]

ML: Why did you decide to do this now?

JP: Well, the main reason is that if you think about Led Zeppelin's career, that was eleven years long, and that career was based really on the strength of its albums, and their live performances. There—there'd just been this missing aspect to Led Zeppelin.

ML: When it came time to gather this footage, and from all the sources, how do you go about communicating with the bootleggers? You call directory assistance and say, "Anybody who stole our music and—and our video in the '70s please contact" . . . how do you do that?

JP: It seemed a really good idea to try and get in touch with anybody who had anything, even though some of this stuff was out on what we call bootleg source, it really was a guy there with a Super 8 [mm] film in his—his day. The key to it was to get back to the—the original source, those Super 8s. So there had to be some delicate negotiations.

ML: What was it like, John, when you first looked at some of this footage that you hadn't seen in however many years?

[*Led Zeppelin DVD plays.*]

John Paul Jones [Led Zeppelin DVD]: How young we all looked, for a start! I mean, right from the—from the early album, you know, it was—it was a band with great sort of swagger and bravado. We had this huge attitude at the time and so it was great to see all that just searing off the screen.

[*Video clip of Led Zeppelin performing "Stairway to Heaven" plays.*]

ML: You have to know that when I walked through the office and I said "I'm going to interview the guys from Led Zeppelin," you know, the—more than a handful of people said "Stairway to Heaven." I mean, people always say that. Did you have any clue at the time that you recorded that song that it had the type of legs, or staying power, or quality, to become an anthem to an entire generation?

JP: Well, I think we all knew it—it—it was really—it was really a milestone for us when we recorded it. As far as it becoming an anthem or anything like that, of course we would be pretentious to tell you something like that. But we knew that it was really good. And for example, we were playing in L.A. and—and the fourth album hadn't come out. We did "Stairway" and—and we got something—we got a standing ovation. And I thought, "Wow, we're really transmitting something," you know? And that number was just really—it—it meant a lot—lot of things to many people.

ML: There are a lot of groups out there right now that started about the same time you guys got together. What is stopping Led Zeppelin from jumping onstage?

RP: We don't know how good you are on the drums.

ML: [*Laughs.*] That's the reason? You never could find anyone who could take John's place on drums?

JPJ: This band was performance-based and musician-based and everything came from within the band. And so if there was somebody else onstage but—other than Led Zeppelin it wouldn't be Led Zeppelin anymore. It's as simple as that.

ML: When people come up to you on the street these days, when they see you here or wherever and they say, "You know what, guys? This album, I remember that girl I was dating. And this album I remember I was living in Europe." Is it the same for you?

JP: Yeah, I've got those memories too, you know. And I think one of the things about that period was because we weren't given images. You—you made up your own images. You listened to the music and it just took you into another world.

[*Video clip of Led Zeppelin performing plays.*]

ML: What a pretty cool job. And we're back with more on a Thursday morning right after these messages.

COMMUNICATION BREAKDOWN

Jimmy Page: [Watching the Royal Albert Hall show] felt fantastic. Really exciting. We really had something going.

John Paul Jones: I loved it. Who wouldn't like looking at themselves when they're young, thin, and cute?

Robert Plant: It was an absolute shock when I first saw that Albert Hall stuff. It's so disarming—not unnerving but kind of cute and coy, and you see all that sort of naivete and the absolute wonder of what we were doing . . . and the freshness of it, because the whole sort of stereotypical rock-singer thing hadn't kicked in for me.

—Barney Hoskyns interview with Jimmy Page, John Paul Jones, and Robert Plant, *MOJO*, June 2003

ATLANTIC CAPTURES PLANT'S SOLO SIDE ON COMPILATION

Melinda Newman | October 11, 2003, *Billboard*

Although Plant had signed on with Mercury as a solo artist, Led Zeppelin was still at Atlantic and he owed them an album from his previous contract with them. As he was desultorily helping Page cull through the material that went into *How the West Was Won*, he thought, "Why can't I do this with my own stuff?" The result was *Sixty Six to Timbuktu*, an album that traced Plant's development from seventeen-year-old soul singer to world beatnik. −Ed.

Hoping to capitalize further on the summer success of Led Zeppelin's *How the West Was Won* CD and the accompanying DVD *Led Zeppelin*, Atlantic Records is releasing *Sixty Six to Timbuktu*, a two-CD solo collection from Zeppelin frontman Robert Plant.

Due Nov. 4, the 35-track set traces Plant's career, starting with his first solo single in 1966 through a live performance this year in Timbuktu.

The first disc features material from his solo albums, but it's the second disc that will grab fans' attention: It is full of rarities, bonus tracks, his work with pre-Zeppelin groups Listen and the Band of Joy and side projects like "Philadelphia Baby," recorded under the Crawling Kingsnake moniker, a one-off that included Dave Edmunds and Phil Collins.

The idea for the compilation was born as Plant was culling through tapes for the Zeppelin set, he tells *Billboard* in an exclusive interview.

"I was finding all this Led Zeppelin stuff, and I said, 'Wait a minute, this stuff of mine is really great. It's lively and springy and would tell people the kind of person that I am,'" Plant says. "This is not the God of Thunder—this is a guy who has a good time."

Indeed, the set reveals a side that those only familiar with his Zeppelin work wouldn't know or expect, including a dreamy, crooning Plant on 1967's "Our Song."

"Once upon a time when I was a boy, I found this gift of singing, and I did not know which way to take it," he says. "When I cut my first sides in 1966, I was 17 years old. I was so made up. I just couldn't believe my luck. I was telling all my friends I was going to be the greatest singer. It was a bit tongue-in-cheek, but perseverance counts for a lot."

Atlantic will tie the Plant title in with the two Zeppelin collections throughout the holiday season. The label has produced bin cards for retail that will cross-promote the three titles. Additionally, 30-second spots promoting the three projects will run on several networks in the Comcast system the week of Nov. 10 in conjunction with a Plant performance that is airing on "Comcast in Concert" Nov. 9 and Nov. 15.

The Zeppelin and Plant titles will also be part of a "Music That Changed Our Lives" promotion that FYE [For Your Entertainment] is running in 1,100 stores this fall.

Dave Alder, senior VP of product and marketing for Virgin Entertainment Group, says the 22-store chain plans to display the three titles together to maximize the excitement created from the Zeppelin releases.

Although the resurgence of interest in Zeppelin has reignited stories of Plant, Jimmy Page, and John Paul Jones being offered millions of dollars to reunite for a Led Zeppelin tour, Plant says, "I haven't been offered a dime." But then he adds, "That's because I've told the people who have the opportunity [to talk to me about it] that I don't want to hear anything about it. I told them ages ago: It's not an issue."

However, he doesn't rule out the three surviving members getting together again, as long as it is for something new. "If John Paul, Jimmy, and I play again, it has got to be a little more than 'Black Dog' every night. I left that big-time epicenter a long time ago."

As for the success of *West*, which debuted at No. 1 on The Billboard 200, and the DVD, Plant says, "it thrills me," but that the footage reminds him of the passage of time.

"[Led Zeppelin] was a young band," he says. "It was all over by the time I was 31. When I think about people who are 31 now, they're just learning to tie their shoelaces."

COMMUNICATION BREAKDOWN

"[T]he more I got drawn into the Led Zeppelin projects, the more I unearthed all kinds of one-off things I'd done—collaborations and various artists' albums. Because the whole chemistry of the Led Zep longevity—if eleven to twelve years is a long time—was the fact that it was constantly flying from pillar to post. So as I dug further into the tape stores, I found demos that I'd never used—probably another fifty or sixty pieces of music that are phenomenal moments of absolute insanity."
— Robert Plant to Barney Hoskyns, *Rock's Backpages*, October 2003

COMMUNICATION BREAKDOWN

"[*Sixty Six to Timbuktu* is] like a cathartic experience. My work before Led Zeppelin, when I was a kid. And then the slowly, slowly maturing time that I've had since. So it's a totally different world altogether. It's something absolutely infinitely removed, but the influences before Zeppelin are evident in Led Zeppelin from what we did in the Band of Joy with John Bonham and the work that I did afterwards is a continuation of my side of the coin."
— Robert Plant to David Haffenreffer, CNN, October 27, 2003

COMMUNICATION BREAKDOWN

Austin Scaggs: Why didn't you go to the Grammys, where ZEP got the Lifetime Achievement Award?
Robert Plant: I was in Milan, promoting the new record. I think it was a fantastic tribute, but . . .
AS: You wanted nothing to do with it.

RP: Oh, absolutely! I would have put my robes on and my crown, my scepter! With Jim [Page] and John Paul what a way to spend the weekend! It'd be nice to get together to see if we have anything to argue about!"
—Austin Scaggs interview with Robert Plant, *Rolling Stone*, May 19, 2005

COMMUNICATION BREAKDOWN

"I didn't want my new record to sound like a purist moment from 1967. It's edgy. It's fractured. The vocals have been fucked with. I just wanted to make music interesting for me now, so I can go off on my Granddad-on-the-warpath thing. I'm glad if you like my new record, but then again I know it's really fucking great or else I wouldn't be here. After all, there's a lot of tennis to play."

— Robert Plant to Scott Frampton, *Esquire*, June 2005

ROBERT PLANT: STARTING OVER AFTER LED ZEPPELIN

Ashley Kahn | June 22, 2006, NPR *Morning Edition*

Ashley Kahn sat down with Robert Plant to discuss the massive, nine-CD set of the complete Atlantic solo recordings, *Nine Lives*, as well as his most recent solo outing, *Mighty Rearranger*. Kahn ended up with one of most revealing and wide-ranging interviews in this book, a solid, introspective retrospective of Plant's solo career. –Ed.

Ashley Kahn: Just about two weeks ago I saw Foreigner.

Robert Plant: Oh yeah?

AK: And of course Jason Bonham was . . .

RP: Yeah, yeah.

AK: And there was that moment when I believe it was "Black Dog" that he was quoting. And to hear that and then to have this confirmed almost the next day, it just all came together really nicely.

RP: Yeah, Jason's doing good now. I mean, mind you, you would be doing good . . . if he was a woman he'd be too old for me to go out with. I mean he's like, he knows too much but he's doing good. He must be thirty-nine kind of forty years old.

AK: How old was he when you guys did that . . . was it an Atlantic celebration?

RP: That was twenty years ago because . . . yeah, I think that was the Atlantic fourtieth. And if I'm not mistaken, it's sixty years now. No, can it be? It must be thirty-eight years. I think Ahmet [Ertegun] and Jerry [Wexler] they put it together about 1948.

AK: I've interviewed Mr. Ertegun about fourteen times at this point.

RP: He's a gem.

AK: He really is. He's part of that little brotherhood of jazz collectors and from them came the future of the music industry.

RP: Yeah, it was interesting, I mean I have no real comprehension of how the jazz artists moved around from label to label. I guess they just had one-record deals with . . . That wouldn't be right though, would it? Because you see [John] Coltrane went to Atlantic. So many people went to Atlantic. But I think they went after the Riverside [Records] days with the Blue [Note Records] . . .

AK: Atlantic was the stepping stone towards the majors I think.

RP: Oh was it?

AK: By the '50s, yeah. Atlantic had grown to a certain . . .

RP: No, I mean later on, I mean later on when you get . . . Because I thought that the formative stuff came from Blue Note and Riverside and then later on people went with Atlantic when the post bebop thing was starting to fade away maybe? I don't know.

AK: Yeah, right.

RP: I mean my perspective is not right.

AK: I actually talk about the sort of evolution of the labels, and as a musician, how do you climb that ladder, you know, and in the '60s, Impulse Records, which was part of ABC, you know, the family labels, Ray Charles, that was the sort of mark of success, mark of arrival for Coltrane.

RP: That's where he went after he left Atlantic?

AK: Exactly, exactly.

RP: Well in England we all went "oh no" because we were getting [Ray Charles] mixed up a little bit with Gene Pitney and Kenny Dino. Going, "Oh wait a minute, what's he doing?" And then to do that *Modern Sounds in Country and Western* was . . . I mean now I think, wow that was—that's such a thing to do back then, it was so . . . well, proud and astute and daring and risqué and fantastic.

AK: And you did feel that way when the Ray Charles thing hit?

RP: I felt that the Atlantic years . . . I mean I was a bit young to really, really get it but I got it enough in the latter part of the Atlantic catalog to know that that was really cooking. And the studio sound was great, you know? The actual sound in the room.

AK: Tom Dowd?

RP: Yeah and the room. A big hand for the room and the mic placement and stuff like that . . . I worked with an engineer about four years ago when I made *Dreamland* and this guy is very slow and very irritable, this engineer. Very funny. And he worked on *Zeppelin III* or something like that, he's older than God's dog. But he knew exactly where to put the mics, you know, the mike placement was great. Didn't say much, just kept rolling hand-rolled cigarettes and looking pensively into the near distance.

AK: [*To the producer.*] Yeah. I think we're all set, Anya, thumbs up? Okay.

RP: Oh what's the score, USA? Can she talk to us on the screen? USA 2?*

AK: No, Ghana is 2, USA 1.

RP: Oh no. Oh sugar. Wow.

AK: We'll keep you up-to-date. Why don't we just launch in and talk about the solo legacy? Seeing it all in one box, I mean, when I got it, the advance, this nine-disc thing and then the bonus tracks and of course the booklet, etcetera, what emotion for you is in the lead when you look back on this stack of, this body of work?

---

*Here Robert is inquiring about the World Cup game.

RP: Wow, you know, I come from a very strong and demonstrative lineage and as well as coming from the land of ice and snow. And I guess that I was looking at the stuff and thinking from the inception, from the beginning of a solo career in 1966, pre–Led Zeppelin, all I wanted to do was to try and emulate a black sound. My very first single on CBS was a [Young] Rascals track called "You Better Run" and I really wanted to get that black sound.

And all the way through Led Zeppelin I was trying to develop a style which was part black, influenced by record collection and stuff. And also looking at the Americana, the music of the American youth. And when Led Zeppelin was no more I was very powered and determined that I must make a new stand and continue this sort of process, which I think was very evident in Led Zeppelin, of constantly changing, of enjoying my whim and letting fate and whatever it might be and chance a little bit of creativity lead me for whatever I'm going to go for the rest of my career, if it is a career.

So I look at the collection and I say yeah, I had romances with different technologies, with different sonic nuance and the whole idea of sound being courted by contemporary sounds in each era and I can hear that on this collection. I can hear the different sounds and the different ways that we were looking at the studio and the tools that we had to make sounds. Some of it has, it definitely has a time about it. You see in the notes that I say that every piece, every collection of songs should be looked at for what they were at that time in amongst everything else that was going on.

So I look at it amazed 'cause, I mean, it's like it's nine different moments of great power and thrust—sometimes understated, sometimes blasé, sometimes coquettish. And later and later on as the time has gone on much more focused and rounded and stated and opinionated. My lyrical capacity improved, my opinions became more focused. I began to leave Dion and the Belmont's behind and the whole "baby baby" a bit. Doesn't mean after a couple of gin and tonics it doesn't come back.

So I look at it with amazement really because I was left entirely to my own devices bringing in friends and new musicians and engineers and new environments like some kind of panacea or tonic. So everything was new every time. And now, looking back at it, I sort of go wow, I remember the energy in this stuff. It was great. Very good. I'm quite amazed at it really.

AK: So amazement is really the emotion that kind of leads you when you think back over the past?

RP: Yeah, because it's all so varied. I didn't ever want to get one sort of signature tune, signature mark sonically or vocally and just hang onto it. I wanted to keep moving around. And I mean from where it began recording in 1981 to where it is in 2006, where I've just come from working on the side of a mountain Wales to come here, and the music that we're making now sounds as if it's just crawled out of the Sahara and crashed through into a kind of a grunge, hip-hop dance floor. The journeys are quite spectacular.

AK: You mentioned that the amazement really comes from that sort of varied aspect and yet with all these incredible musical destinations that you're drawing from, whether it's delta blues, '50s R&B, Indian music, North African, etcetera: what is the common denominator for you between all this music?

RP: I have to surprise myself, I have to try and push myself into an area where I'm a little unsure. I mean the pastiche, the '50s stuff is maybe what I should have heard on the radio if I was a little bit older. But I could always go back to it and my relationship with Atlantic Records and my record collection and the whole CBS-FM on a Friday night, *The Doo Wop Shop*, all that stuff that I know about everything from the Jive Five to the Phantom on Dot [Records] in 1958. I know all about that and that is going into character.

But the great big thing is to take myself out of character and surprise myself. You know, just try and make it really, really like it's a proper adventure for me.

AK: You mentioned that there was a point when you sort of left Dion and the Belmonts and the "baby baby" stuff behind. When you look over these nine albums and this 25-year spread, is there a moment when you feel like, and what song would it be if you had to pick a moment where you feel like there is a maturity and you had really arrived as your own musical personality apart from Led Zeppelin and you still look back and you say "I'm really satisfied with where I was on that album or that tune"?

RP: Well, I have to say that I'm really satisfied with it all but by the same token there was always a sort of reflective contribution within all of the records. But I think probably by the time I got to *Fate of Nations* and I was writing stuff like "Network News" and "The Greatest Gift," and "Great Spirit," I thought that then I was able to . . . I wasn't missing any beats at all at what was going on around me. But, I mean there are other adventures back down the line that were not just evocative about personal discovery. But I think *Fate of Nations* was a major turning point.

And also one thing that it did, I've always felt a loyalty and an obligation to the people that I work with as if it must always be like that. I think coming from Led Zeppelin there were only four of us and that sort of, despite the comings and goings and the adventures of Led Zeppelin, there were only ever going to be four of us. So every time I have a band I keep thinking it's forever, you know?

But I think when I got to *Fate of Nations* I was suddenly encouraged by the producer and the record company to bring in people for particular roles within the record and I'd never done that before. So Richard Thompson arrived, who is . . . His guitar playing I always really respected but I could never see it fitting in with the way I project. But it worked, amazingly. And then I had a hurdy gurdy player, Nigel [Eaton], and the girl from Clannad [Máire Brennan] arrived.

People were coming in to color various elements of the record and it was a . . . And Nigel Kennedy, who is sort of a crème de la crème solo violinist worldwide comes in and creates violin parts and harmonies . . . He came in about two or three hours after a group of Indian classical violinists were in who couldn't get it right, who were sitting cross-legged on the floor looking very serene and otherworldly but they couldn't do it.

So Kennedy arrives, who really should have fell out of the Sex Pistols with his violin under his arm and a car painted multicolored supporting his local soccer club parked outside, and just kills it. And then joins me on one of the most fascinating videos called "Calling to You."

And I think really that record [*Fate of Nations*], I didn't feel any longer that I had to feel responsible for the emotions of the musicians around me, I became more capable of explaining that I needed this color or that color. Other people do it from day one. But I think because of my legacy and my sort of camaraderie that I was involved in for such a long time I didn't really want to ever change it. I always thought that the guys who were there in the beginning could do the lot.

AK: That's very interesting. That sort of goes very counter to the idea of a general sound that's the band's signature sound and more like a Steely Dan experience of picking this color and adding that element.

RP: Yeah, but *Fate of Nations* is quite emotive and rather like my vocals on something like the "Rain Song" with Zeppelin or "All My Love" or even "Babe I'm Gonna Leave You." The actual emotive, the vocal deliveries were nevertheless and always were charged. I mean on *Mighty Rearranger*, the most recent record, "All the King's Horses" and "The Enchanter" are singing about love, not quite in the street-corner, Brooklyn style but that's . . .

I mean I wrote these lyrics for those two songs in character imagining a very simplistic, absolutely beautiful time, which comes at an earlier age than I'm at now and I never really realized that I could ever go back there but I did. I suddenly started living out those two songs in real life but I had only written them in character thinking, "Oh man." They have very strong emotive lyrics about relationships—ambiguous, abstract but needing and very needy. And no sooner had I written them and recorded them and was almost embarrassed by them, then the whole property of the songs became real to me.

AK: Can you tell specifically what couplet or what lines come to mind as having that quality for you?

RP: The whole thing about "The Enchanter," the whole idea of this enchantress who has an abstract and fantastic relationship with the elements and animals and the whole otherworldly thing that Tori Amos often talks so adeptly about, I put into the song. And then suddenly everything that was either present in the song, either evidently lyrically or in intention suddenly became real. I met somebody who . . . my songs actually came to life and I was blinking and running away from the light going . . . I'm just doing this as a pastiche but it's real. And that was quite something to find that I was actually tapped on the shoulder by my own songs.

AK: That's incredible.

RP: Yeah.

AK: Congratulations.

RP: That's okay, it's a very short moment but it actually . . . everything was fulfilled and I thought if I keep writing like this I can write about things and they're always going to come to me. How weird is that?

AK: World peace please?

RP: Yeah, oh yes please. Well that's quite a few songs.

AK: Yeah. And I do want to come back to *Mighty Rearranger* for sure. One thing I've got to ask you is—and I've sort of been following the various interviews along the way of the past twenty to thirty years with your former partner in crime, Jimmy—I never really got a feeling for how he looked upon what you were doing with your years since Led Zeppelin. I'm just curious, did you ever get comments from Jimmy on any specific tracks, specific albums?

RP: Not unless I went out and fished for them. I mean, he did play with me on *Now and Zen* on the "Tall Cool One" and "Heaven Knows." And that was in a particularly '80s techno period. So listening to it now, it's very brittle sounding. I'm very pleased to say that it's not me that's going "there's a gerbil!"

AK: Sorry about that.

RP: [*Laughing*] I think that's great.

AK: Yes. Usually I have that taken care of.

RP: Yeah. I guess. I mean his performance and presence on those two tracks in the midst of that kind of techno outrage was a long way from our sort of organic Led Zeppelin root. And I think he really enjoyed it. I know that he was very dubious when I started sampling Led Zeppelin on

"Tall Cool One," but I said, "Look, you know, if the Beastie Boys can do it, I guess everybody can do it, you know?" And then at the end they use that "Kashmir" riff for the P. Diddy thing which wasn't—it didn't have the same sense of humor, I don't think. And then he played with me on the Honeydrippers stuff, "I Get a Thrill," the Wynonie Harris thing, you know.

But I don't know, you know? I mean the thing is I wouldn't say that I'm precocious but I do forge ahead and I do move and I have two or three things that are moving at the same time. And then I suddenly throw my hands up in the air and scream "I can't do this!" I'm supposed to be working for Ahmet Ertegun next week in Switzerland at the Montreux Jazz Festival and then there's something else and something else. And my guys are on the side of a Welsh mountain, writing.

And I like this sort of idea of having a hot seat and rushing to things and keeping the plates up in the air by wiggling the sticks and keeping an energy level going so that if only 40 percent of it becomes tangible, that's OK.

So with Jimmy I guess he moves at a totally different speed and tempo. I mean we did spend quite a bit of time in between *In Through the Out Door* and *Fate of Nations* working together but it was quite evident that we definitely had gone into different areas. And I expect a totally different bunch of realities in a twenty-four-hour period. I like to do what I like to do at a certain tempo. I mean I don't have the musicality or the skill but I have a lot of energy.

AK: That multitasking rate that you're talking about, as far as your career, was that not much like the Led Zeppelin years too? Was there a lot of that or was it just Led Zeppelin?

RP: No, it was just Led Zeppelin, yeah. And sometimes not much of that. But then when it was hot, when it was on. I mean we were young men, barely anything more than boys really. I was 19 when I met Jimmy and 20 when I persuaded Bonzo to come with us from the Band of Joy. And so your overview of life and the experiences that you gain give you the capacity to make decisions about how much you want to be involved. I mean "needs must" is quite an interesting term because it's not just based on monetary gain, it's based on feeding the soul.

AK: Right. I'd like turn to a very specific moment and ask you first a general question. After Led Zeppelin, what was more difficult or more challenging for you to do: think about going back into the studio or on the road?

RP: Oh, the studio because that's where your whole justification for everything comes from, to be on the road, to actually have the audacity to get a monolithic record company, a great corporate surge, you can't promote rubbish, although maybe you can. I mean the whole deal would be to write with conviction, to perform with integrity and real power and zeal and then to put it in the hands of people who can do the job, which is becoming more and more difficult now. And then if you want to play, play.

I was talking to Dave Gilmour, we were playing in Europe six weeks ago. I got into Paris at about 3:00 in the morning into the hotel and there is David Gilmour at the reception trying to get a drink. I said, "Hey, how are you doing?" And he said, "Oh Percy, I knew you were on the road but I thought you were somewhere in China or something." I said don't be facetious. I said how long are you playing for? How long are you out for? He said, "Three weeks. And you?" I said, "Well it's 128 shows in and I can't see it ending."

So I mean it depends on what you want to do, whether you actually just do a few gigs to please the record company and go back to the fortress . . .

AK: To Wiltshire or wherever?

RP: Yeah. Or you find that your home is everything, everywhere, and everyone.

AK: That's a great way of putting it. I think Bob Dylan would agree, a never-ending tour.

RP: Yeah he had his own bus, yeah.

When I play tennis, people say, "Hey, I haven't seen you for three months. Where have you been?" And I scratch my head and I go "Um, you don't want to know where I've been. How about Tunisia playing or Carthage, the Roman ruins on the African coast?" And they look at me and blink. It's like showing somebody holiday photographs: they're not really impressed, they just want to go away.

AK: Especially when the quantity of destinations is just . . . it changes every day.

RP: That's right. Actually two came in in the last twenty-four hours, one in Corsica and one in Malta. You can't get more obscure than that really.

AK: That was the one within the last twenty-four hours?

RP: Yeah.

AK: Wow. Well thank you for resting for a little while for us. Can you recreate for us that first moment when you actually hit the road for the very first time, the very first concert you did as a solo artist? How did it feel, what emotions were going through you?

RP: Well in the afternoon of that day in Peoria, Illinois, one of my best friends . . . who was working for Ahmet, was with me and he knew that I was really emotional and I was hopping up and down and pacing around. So he took to one of the most dreary shopping malls I've ever been to in my life and we walked round and round it pretending to be interested in this sort of rubbish that was on sale just to try to keep me moving and keep my head off the . . .

Well, it was not even the enormity but I mean in those days Led Zeppelin was . . . It wasn't that it was legendary, though I guess it was, but it also was still alive, kind of thing and I knew that. It was part of me and it still is, but I knew that I had to go on, like I was saying earlier, I had to forge on. So there were mixed emotions.

In one way I thought maybe I shouldn't do this, I should just quit, 'cause nothing could be like that. But on the other hand the great challenge was it's never going to be like that, but what's it going to be like? You know? And that was Peoria, Illinois. And I walked onto the stage and I was absolutely drowned, my whole being was, I was reduced to the size of a mouse because the response from the audience was amazing.

And it was such an emotional thing to be there without those guys, without the whole security blanket of belonging to this back there in the womb with the boys. I was just standing there alone and it was a brave new world and it's ridiculous because I was thirty-two years old, I mean I wasn't a baby. But I guess by contemporary standards I'd had two careers by then, two whole . . . the pre-Zeppelin and the Zeppelin eras were really charged, both of them for different reasons and now I was embarking on a third one. And it was quite something, yeah.

AK: Do you remember what tune that was that you launched into?

RP: I think it was "Burning Down One Side," which is the opening track on *Pictures at Eleven* which was pretty good 'cause I guess it was quite '80s rock but very early '80s so there was a big guitar presence and Robbie Blunt was a . . . he's a fine guitar player. And his delivery and solo work was near enough to a blues base that it wasn't too foreign to anybody.

AK: That's great, thank you for sharing that. Journalists get to play the game of naming styles or putting artists into categories. If you had to choose a name for where your music is now or where it's been over the past 25 years, how would you categorize it, what sort of description would you give it?

RP: I suppose off road. Taking terrain. Yeah, music for all terrains I guess because it's always been . . . My music has always been in the shadow of the great music of Led Zeppelin but it's always kind of been apart from The Honeydrippers, which was a kind of a done deal stylistically, it does go off road. It's 4x4.

AK: Four wheel drive, that's great. There's definitely . . . Led Zeppelin, as you were saying, had their sound. And yet now later in your career you have much more of a transparency where you can really see what you're pulling from and drawing from and that seems to be the reverse of what many other musicians' careers are. Would you agree with that?

RP: Well, I don't know really, it's a matter of—for you, for everybody—it's personal opinion. I mean I think in a way the filigree and the detail . . . I mean even in an album like *Manic Nirvana,* which I think was, well I'd say incredibly brittle and precocious, and risqué with so much humor in that record, you know? But you could see through it, you could look into it, you could go past Wavy Gravy and into a kind of dreamscape of the post-Woodstock period. But at the same time you can look through it all. And you can see the different layers of music.

I think in a way, as far as going for the kind of commercial jugular of trying to write hits and get big radio that's a kind of . . . it's not a successful way of doing it. One should keep it very simple and make it very evident and obvious that this is what it is and you're not giving too much information. Otherwise it does get to be multidimensional and that's what that music has become, even more so now with *Mighty Rearranger*, where one part of the song is taking you, is beckoning you towards the Sahara, while another part is taking you into San Francisco in '67.

So it's almost like musical references and then the vocal and the melody and the lyrics. So it's quite detailed. And, yeah, everybody says to me, "Hey man, next album you've got to keep it really simple."

AK: That's great. I have two or three quick questions about Led Zeppelin and then I'd like to wrap it up with *Mighty Rearranger*. Is there a Zeppelin signature tune for you? I mean if you met someone who you had five minutes with them, they had no idea what the whole rock 'n' roll tradition was about and you wanted to, you had the chance to play one Zeppelin track for them, what would it be?

RP: Wow. Well I think "The Ocean" would be a great track because it has the kind of uniqueness of the rhythm section, Bonzo and Jonesy, it has a hugely powerful riff and it has a kind of a bleak, willing vocal that talks about bringing people together. It's not quite Jesse Colin Young but it's cool.

But on the other hand, I guess you could say that if you wanted to know about the full sort of sovereignty of Led Zeppelin, you'd have to use "Kashmir" for obvious reasons because it's just so big and proud. And it doesn't care about whatever terms may be used later on to describe it. Because when you write and you record and you do it in the present tense, you do it for now.

So if ever people complained about the bombast of Led Zeppelin or whatever it might be in particular periods, who cares? I mean nobody could write a song like that, you know? With the kind of background that Jimmy and I had had through our travels and through Morocco and the Atlas Mountains. I mean it was so much of the feeling of actually being exposed to those cultures in that music and yet it was rock.

AK: That's great. I love the unapologetic aspect.

RP: Well, it only became unapologetic later on when we could dissect it. But at the time it was just what it was. It was part of *Physical Graffiti*, which was a bunch of songs which we came upon with enthusiasm and zest and great power and we didn't think about whether it was going to be considered six months later. The most important thing was what happened that day, yeah.

And that's what my whole deal is about for me continuing. I mean I may be a shadow, really, of what that great thing was, but I'm very confident and focused on the way I go about it and thank God for that, otherwise I would be wasting my time.

AK: I can't help but . . . I loved that album from the day I heard it and I still walk down East 8th street right here in New York and there is that building, you know?*

RP: Oh yeah.

AK: That is on the cover and in fact a historical and physical graffiti on the street level.

RP: Yeah. Well you know the guy [Peter Corriston] who did that album cover and so many of the other ones, you know, *Presence, In Through the Out Door, Zeppelin IV*. I mean he helped me put together this whole project, the *Nine Lives* project, he did all DVD stuff and interviewed people.

He's very funny because we've kind of rattled down through time and through history together and he's a very refined and genteel guy but he's also a sort of part-time crook. He's always hanging out with Floyd, he works with Gilmore and myself. He's doing this current Who thing at the moment and we have so many recollections of the absurdity of this game, of us. I mean, the sense of humor is fantastic. I guess he and I are the only two people left from that whole regime who meet regularly and continue to laugh about it.

AK: I remember hearing tales of *Houses of the Holy* and how they couldn't get the orange correct, how the covers kept getting sent back.

RP: Oh we spent . . .

---

*The buildings from the *Physical Graffiti* album cover are located at 96 and 98 St. Mark's Place.

AK: Hipgnosis, right?

RP: Yeah, yeah, that's right. Storm [Thorgerson], Aubrey Powell, and Hipgnosis. In fact, the credit on this box, it's the first time that Hipgnosis has appeared as a credit anywhere for years. So the old bastard is back. But yeah, quirky stuff but good.

AK: Knowing what you know today would you have done anything differently?

RP: Absolutely not. Because it's all, it's not even existentialism, it's just what it is, when it is and my limitations and so obvious and vast. I couldn't hope to put anything right that's already gone.

AK: That's great. The last Zeppelin question is: was there a sense of competition while you guys were growing form '69 into '70 and then through the early '70s with—

RP: No, no.

AK: With other bands at the time?

RP: Oh. The Stones, yeah.

AK: With like where Deep Purple was at the . . .

RP: Oh no, they didn't count. I mean there were so many bands that just didn't, just were nowhere near . . . it was about energy, really. Energy and creativity and I guess it wasn't even about material success, it was about divergence, about the whole thing that we've been discussing about creative rebirth and not hanging onto one or two plots and sticking with it. So there was nobody . . . There was nobody around.

The Stones used to get a lot of publicity but we . . . And there was a bit of sort of, to say the least, rivalry I guess . Yeah, there was. But we all knew where we fit in the game and it was a game and it is a game.

AK: And you left it to Peter anyway, right?

RP: No, no, no. No we didn't leave it to anybody really. I mean we just kept moving in the grooves that we were in and watched everybody discussing it all.

AK: Interesting, that's great. Let's leave that behind. *Mighty Rearranger.* It's the last album in the box; it's sort of like the bookend.

RP: Yeah.

AK: And in a way sonically, the size of the sound and feel of it, it has a feel, at least to me, that it's got . . . things are coming full circle for you.

RP: Maybe. I mean it's very stated and . . . but it's come about in a totally different way because the process of creativity in this contemporary world means that we can do things on the fly, on the run. We can bounce, we don't need a studio. We have a laptop and two mikes and that's how we got the drum sound on three of the tracks on that album. Just in somebody's garage. It's back to Gary US Bonds again, you know.

It's really like a thousand ideas can be turned over and mulled over really quickly, very quickly, and eliminated as we would wish. I mean the remixes that we've got from this stuff you can give it to DJs, to Uncle, James Lavelle, all these various people, DJ Shadow, whoever it is, and you can actually create, you can have other personalities make it into another part of the tapestry.

So although it sounds . . . it's big and strong and powerful, that's its relationship with Led Zeppelin, you know, and there's a lot of stuff that's African based which is Mississippi based. But where this is going is a different place and the method and the means are quite different.

AK: Perhaps this should've been close to my first question. Why now? Why do a box set now? Because there's a certain sense of finality to it where that a period of time is now closing when you do a box set like this.

RP: No, not really. I mean yeah, I know, I take your point. But I was encouraged because the metamorphosis, the kind of creative surge of my music has been what it's been up to this point and the record companies and everybody said, "Hey look, this is great." And they know that I'm spending more and more time working with [non-western] musicians and leaving kind of mainstream—well, not even mainstream, but almost dissolving into another world if you like musically.

So I guess their encouragement was, you know, you want to get these things into some kind of perspective now and then I think they quite expect me to disappear into the desert for years on end and come out with a beard down to the floor going, "Hey you'll never guess, I found a new scale."

AK: How jazzlike.

RP: Yeah, yeah. Oh, don't say that.

AK: Well, I mean that's the same thing, you know . . .

RP: Yeah, yeah.

AK: They're always looking for different sounds, different approaches.

RP: That's right, yeah.

AK: The last couple of questions are just like, what's a typical day for you like in Wiltshire? You might have answered this already . . .

RP: Well, I haven't been to Wiltshire very often because it's Saxon country and I get quite twitchy when I'm . . . But a typical day is to assail the night before, to try and figure out where it ended and where this day begins. And to visit all those plates that I have in the air that I told you about, you know, the guy that you see on the TV desperately running around the line making sure that all the plates are spinning so that none of them fall on the floor.

So I'm quite proactive, which means that I would travel probably. My band operates out of Bristol and Bath, which is in the southwest of England. A very prolific area there with Massive Attack on a . . . guys down there. So I go, I travel a lot to there and I go, believe it or not, where my guys are today, they're in the Misty Mountains. Believe it or not, it's still true. Creating. So there's a lot of that going on and that's basically about it really. I play quite a bit of tennis if I can.

AK: Which your son does, too?

RP: Yeah, yeah.

AK: And is the family man, the nonmusical side of you, the nonprofessional side of you, is there much time that you have, too?

RP: Oh sure. Yeah. I mean my two older kids have got kids of their own now but they're all musical. Two of my grandchildren are musical. Yeah, in the family we have people teaching Arabic, North African dance at WOMAD festivals and stuff like that. The family is really quite . . . I think they have heard so much Egyptian music in their childhood and so it's really had a great effect on them. Subliminally I've saved them from the land of the discotheque.

AK: Congratulations on that, too. Last question, Arthur Lee, who is he and why is he important? And why is he important to you?

RP: Well, Arthur Lee is an American heirloom. He was one of the sort of main movers in around the Summer of Love, after the Summer of Love, living on the West Coast. His group, Love, had a huge following in L.A., swamping the progress of the Byrds, Buffalo Springfield, and the L.A. bands of the time. Everybody wanted to be as big as Love.

They cut four very, very progressive albums for Elektra and their third album, *Forever Changes*, became in Europe one of the most I think in a poll that was run by *Q* magazine or whatever it is with *MOJO*, a big, big music magazine, I think it was in the top ten most important albums out of one hundred albums of all time. It's ironic really.

I mean I'm playing in New York tomorrow night. People's awareness of what he's done is negligible; nobody really knows here. I think it's because once artists have either peaked or have reached a certain age, their very well-known songs become the diet of a particular radio. So if Love made five or six albums, you're only ever going to hear three tracks. So people never actually . . . they may listen to these tracks and go "oh." But the whole intention of going out and finding out what else there is not the way it works here.

AK: And what was your discovery of Arthur Lee's music that was important to you?

RP: Oh yeah, sure, before . . . pre–Led Zeppelin, when I was in the Band of Joy with John Bonham, we based a lot of our music around Buffalo Springfield, Jefferson Airplane, and Love and . . . We were drinking from the same chalice as Led Zeppelin, it's just that we didn't have the power and the amazing skill of Jimmy and John Paul. So it was the same sort of thing but it was more . . . less stated.

So Arthur Lee was there. You know, when I was seventeen, eighteen, I was listening to Love and it's ironic really, all the people that I know listen to it all the time. It's like, it's there alongside Pearl Jam or Staind or whatever it might be, there's a whole lot of room for Love where I come from.

AK: That's great. Mr. Plant, thank you for making the time and coming out. It's a real honor.

RP: It's a pleasure. Thank you very much for having me and thank you for giving me that great book that you put together on John Coltrane [*A Love Supreme: The Story of John Coltrane's Signature Album*].

GETTING THE LED OUT: JIMMY PAGE AND JOHN PAUL JONES ON LED ZEPPELIN'S HISTORIC REUNION

Alan Light | November 13, 2007, MSN Music

The former members of Led Zeppelin had a lot on their plates in 2007: They wanted to remaster *The Song Remains the Same* into the latest audio format, 5.1 Surround Sound. They also were compiling a new "best of" collection to replace the two that Atlantic had put out—one that they had control over. So the business meetings happened fairly frequently. With the passing of their mentor, Ahmet Ertegun, the previous year, they wanted to do something in his name, especially Plant, who was very close to the Atlantic Records founder. They set up an educational foundation as a tribute to him, and to finance the fund, they decided to do a one-off concert at London's O2 Arena. —Ed.

It is a rock 'n' roll fantasy that most people had abandoned. On Dec. 10 at London's O2 Arena, the three surviving members of Led Zeppelin—Robert Plant, Jimmy Page, and John Paul Jones—will take the stage accompanied by Jason Bonham, the son of their late drummer, John Bonham. The concert marks the first time Led Zeppelin has performed together in almost 20 years, and only the third time the lineup has appeared since Bonham's death in 1980.

Anticipation for the event has spurred an avalanche of ticket requests, followed by fresh suspense when the group was forced to reschedule from the original concert date of Nov. 26. Guitarist Page reportedly fractured his finger, prompting the delay. The concert is a benefit supporting a scholarship fund created by Atlantic Records co-founder Ahmet Ertegun, who passed away last year [2006].

When the show was announced, the website on which tickets were being sold was so overloaded that it crashed. In the end, 20 million people around the world entered the lottery for the arena's 18,000 tickets. The response was incredible, but not shocking: Led Zeppelin is one of only two bands to sell more than 100 million records in the United States (the Beatles, of course, are the other, while Elvis Presley and Garth Brooks are the only solo artists to hit that number). The aura surrounding their majestic recordings—eight studio albums released between 1969 and 1979—seems only to have grown over the years.

Speaking on the phone from London's Landmark Hotel a few days before beginning rehearsals for the reunion show, guitarist Page and bass/mandolin/keyboard player Jones made it clear that they're not taking this event lightly. "This is a really serious commitment," says Jones. "We need to get so familiar with this material again [so] that we're not just re-creating a show, but doing something that's genuinely good."

The O2 performance will follow directly on the heels of several new Zeppelin projects. In October, the band announced that its music finally would be available for digital download, ending one of music's highest-profile holdouts. A new two-CD "best-of" compilation titled *Mothership* is being released Nov. 13, followed the next week by a remixed and remastered version of their 1976 concert film and soundtrack *The Song Remains the Same* with six previously unreleased tracks (including such skull-crushers as "Black Dog," "Misty Mountain Hop" and "Heartbreaker").

Song, which was recorded over three nights at New York's Madison Square Garden in 1973, isn't generally considered a first-rate document of live Zeppelin; *The Rolling Stone Album Guide* dismisses it as "desultory." But the remastering is a revelation, the DVD includes such extras as news coverage of the famous robbery that took place at the band's Manhattan hotel during one of the shows, and the sheer scarcity of material from these towering rock superheroes makes any new recordings significant.

The future of the 21st century Led Zeppelin seems very much up in the air: Plant has said that he considers the O2 show a one-time thing, while Page has left the door open for more work going forward. For now, though, Page and Jones sound genuinely excited about the band's return to the stage, raving about a secret rehearsal they did in late spring to test the waters.

"We're right on the brink," says Page. "Next week we start, and I'm really looking forward to it. If it's anything like the little things that we've done, then this is going to be a terrific journey."

Alan Light: How does it feel to be playing together again?

Jimmy Page: Well, earlier this year we had this clandestine get-together. There had been a bit of a rift between us, so we had to find out if it could work, or was there too much water under the bridge? And that session felt absolutely fantastic—it was urgent, vibrant, everything you might have hoped for and then even a bit extra, a bit more than that.

When the Ahmet thing came up, it was a call to arms. It gave us the opportunity to come together.

AL: John Paul, I saw you this past June at the Bonnaroo festival, and you were having a blast sitting in and jamming with everyone. Have you been able to bring that spirit and enthusiasm into these rehearsals?

John Paul Jones: To be honest, though, it went the other way as well. We had done this few days' rehearsal with Jason Bonham just before then, to see how it went. It felt really, really great playing with Jason, and with the others, really satisfying. It clicked immediately, it sounded tight—I was surprised how many of the keys we remembered! So I was there at Bonnaroo fresh from the excitement of that.

AL: How did the timing come together? Was it planned that *The Song Remains the Same* reissue, the *Mothership* collection, and the digital catalog announcement would all happen leading up to the show?

JPJ: The timing just kind of fell into place. We'd been working on *The Song Remains the Same* 5.1 mix for quite a long time, and we'd gotten lots of requests from the record company for a good compilation. We were never really happy with (the 1999–2000 collections) *Early Days* and *Latter Days*, and this will replace those. It's really kind of a chronological sampler—there are songs from every one of the studio albums, so that's kind of cool.

The online stuff we started talking about not so long ago, and the O2 show was just decided on, quite late—and that's part of it, we were having so many meetings about everything else, this just got on the agenda and then started to receive more serious talk. The time seemed right to do it.

AL: But why was this the right time?

JPJ: I don't know why! It seemed sort of organic. These things appear at the right time. The last time it came up was quite some time ago, and then it didn't seem right. This time it came up and everyone said, "Well, why not?" That's kind of how it's always been with Led Zeppelin. There never has been any great strategy or great planning.

AL: How is it being under so much media scrutiny for this show? When Led Zeppelin was actually making records, you never really received that much attention or mainstream exposure.

JP: I don't really want to give the media the benefit of the doubt, but each of our albums is so radically different, I just think that the reviewers didn't have a clue as to what we were doing. They were totally perplexed and bewildered. The passage of time, though, has shown what it was that the fans could connect and relate to.

In the late '60s and early '70s, there were other bands that had virtuoso players within them, but to have four virtuosos who could truly play as a band—that was the important thing. So we had four guys on top of their game, straightaway, and then those four combined to make a fifth element, which took them even further.

The level of playing is so fine, it travels across so many musical landscapes. Anyone who wants to play an instrument inevitably comes to Led Zeppelin because it is such a remarkable textbook, it's a diamond with so many facets. And the spirit and the honesty of the playing translates across generations.

JPJ: It's very nice that everybody is so interested. It's astonishing, overwhelming, to get 125 million hits or whatever for the tickets. But the music is what it's all about, and we have to just get to that.

AL: Do you think that the media's lack of interest worked to the band's advantage in the end? Certainly no one could ever say that Led Zeppelin was overexposed.

JP: We were always underplayed in press, to the point of annihilation, really negative press. But each tour, we couldn't meet the demand for people in each city. If we sold as many tickets as we could, we could have kept touring forever. So because of being so underplayed, it really relied on people's spirit coming to it, to access Led Zeppelin through the records. And like anything that's any good, it spread by word of mouth.

AL: Is that why there's still such reverence for the music? Why do you think the allure is still so strong for younger listeners?

JPJ: I'm not entirely sure. We made the records in the '70s, but they're not really of the '70s. It was a pretty unique band; it didn't really fit into any categories. Which is part of why the press didn't really get what we were doing, which was really their problem—it certainly wasn't a problem for the fans who were buying the records or coming to the shows. So I think the records aren't dated because they weren't of their time in the first place.

Young kids, especially young musicians, really recognize the truth and the integrity of the music. So many people tell me, "My son or daughter has taken up an instrument and they want to play like you." It's nice to be an inspiration. I was certainly inspired by my heroes, and it's nice to pass that along.

AL: *The Song Remains the Same* isn't generally considered to be an example of Zeppelin at its live peak. What do you think of that reputation—do you think it gets a bad rap?

JP: Listen to [the 2003 live album] *How the West Was Won*—that was done a year earlier and we were really firing on all cylinders, but, you know, I could be critical of those performances, too. [*Song*] is taken from across a couple of nights, at the end of a long tour. It was pretty happening, really happening. It wasn't [sic] the best shows we did on that tour, but I don't know which ones were.

JPJ: I never thought it had a bad reputation. I always thought it was a good gig, but now it sounds bloody good as well. I think the record companies, as they will do, when they put the film on VHS and on DVD, they just did the transfer directly, straight to video, with no consultation with us.

Everything we've ever done was a statement of where the band was at the time. It was the end of a tour, the New York crowds were always very responsive. I'm sure I saw the same faces in the first rows from night to night. I think we played well—I don't know how it came across, but I have no hesitation saying that.

AL: Was there anything that surprised you in the performances while you were doing the remixing and remastering?

JP: The remix was related to having up-to-the-minute 5.1 surround mix on the film. But we couldn't change a frame on the film once it was copyrighted. So unlike the [2003 live retrospective] DVD, where we could overlay visuals to the sound, the exercise was that the film was out of sync and we had to actually adjust the music. We couldn't just go slow motion on the film. With the aid of Pro Tools, [engineer] Kevin Shirley did a fantastic job with that. And everything just sounds so much better. You have techniques today that weren't dreamt of back then.

Also, the whole of the set is included now. It goes in the way we envisioned it, how we would really pace a show. The only addition was "The Ocean"—that was the encore, but we put it into the set.

AL: John Paul, what stands out to you when you go back and listen?

JPJ: How good it all was. I hadn't played the records much since those days—or even in those days. As soon as one was finished, we would start work on the next record or the next tour or whatever. Now I hear them and think, "Oh, I forgot—that was really good!"

AL: What is it like to watch the movie's famous "fantasy sequences" now?

JPJ: Well, we did look young! It was supposed to be a concert film, but when we went through it, there were these holes in the film, when they were changing reels or something. So then there was a bit of panic. I don't know whose idea it was to do the fantasy sequences—but Jimmy and I were just talking about it, and we realized that Bonzo's wasn't actually a fantasy sequence, it was a reality sequence!

It was all fun, but in the end, not to sound like a broken record, it still comes down to the music. There were some embarrassing moments, but some good fun, too.

JP: We all went off our own merry ways, but Bonham just carried on in his usual way while we did these weird depictions of whatever. It was very much for the time and of the time. It was courageous, on one hand—on the other hand, we managed to be Spinal Tap [*laughs*]. But we did it first!

AL: What is the biggest misconception about Led Zeppelin?

JPJ: A lot is made of the salacious reputation of the band, which always detracted from the music. That was always disappointing—especially newspapers, they would always start talking about sharks or whatever, and I would always think, "Oh, God, why does nobody mention how good the band was?"

JP: The biggest misunderstanding [*long pause*] . . . I could be trite and say that people think the robbery in the movie was a fake, that we did that to add drama to the film. But now, by including the local coverage from the New York news [in the *Song* DVD's bonus footage], you can see that it was very real.

I don't know—I don't care what they think about the band, or about me, or whatever. That will all be eradicated by listening to the music. If you really listen closely and hear what it was that we were doing, all the rest goes away.

COMMUNICATION BREAKDOWN

"We did about four days' rehearsal in total secret—just to see whether we could play together—and it was fantastic. We played through a couple of well-known numbers, and it was amazingly tight. So we decided to go full swing with rehearsals right through until the show . . . To me, Led Zeppelin was a live performance band. We would make a record and that would be the blueprint. Then we'd go off and play the record live, and it would move on from there. I'm pretty used to recording studios, so it was no big thing to be in the studio. Playing live was the most fun for me; I think that was the best of Zeppelin."

–John Paul Jones to Brian Fox, *Bass Player*, February 2008

COMMUNICATION BREAKDOWN

"Just before we were going to go on [at the O2 show], I looked out across that corporately sponsored VIP enclosure, watching everyone with their shimmering camera phones held aloft . . . I thought to myself, "Blimey, we've come a long way since me and Jimmy rented a cottage up in Snowdonia and took just a guitar and a little Philips cassette recorder.'"

– Robert Plant to Simon Mills, *GQ*, September 3, 2008

COUNTRY ROCKS; ROBERT PLANT AND ALISON KRAUSS TEAM UP

Charles Osgood and Katie Couric | October 12, 2008, *CBS Sunday Morning*

Very soon after the O2 gig, the musically peripatetic Plant was on to his next adventure, working with American bluegrass icon Alison Krauss. On paper, an odder couple would be hard to think of, but when they started to harmonize . . . –Ed.

[*Audioclip of "Whole Lotta Love" plays.*]

Announcer: It's Sunday morning on CBS, and here again is Charles Osgood.

Charles Osgood: Concert halls rocked for years to the music of Robert Plant of Led Zeppelin. Today country rocks as Robert Plant, still going strong at age 60, joins forces with country singer Alison Krauss, who's 37. Between them, they have won 22 Grammys and sold 30 million records, and they're only getting warmed up. With *CBS Evening News* anchor Katie Couric, we take note.

[*Concert footage of Led Zeppelin performing "Black Dog" in 1973 plays.*]

[*Concert footage of Led Zeppelin performing "Black Dog" in 2007 reunion concert plays.*]

[**Katie Couric, voiceover**] When Robert Plant reunited with Jimmy Page and John Paul Jones for this one-night-only concert last December, Led

Zeppelin fans hoped it would spawn the reunion tour they've waited nearly three decades for.

[*Concert footage of Robert Plant and Alison Krauss performing "Black Dog" plays.*]

[**KC, voiceover**] Instead, the golden god of rock 'n' roll has teamed up with the string band belle of bluegrass, Alison Krauss.

[*Footage of interview with Alison Krauss and Robert Plant plays.*]

Robert Plant: [*Affecting an American accent.*] Look at these boots, them's real good boots. I know how to wear boots, just got to learn the harmonies.

Alison Krauss: [*Bemused.*] Huh.

[*Footage of Plant; excerpt from Plant and Krauss music video for "Gone, Gone, Gone"; footage of audience; photo montage of Plant and Krauss.*]

[**KC, voiceover**] Along with those boots, Robert Plant can hang his ten-gallon hat on a critically celebrated CD that's gone platinum, a string of sellout shows, and this year's Grammy Award for Best Pop Vocal Collaboration.

[*Interview footage with Katie Couric, Robert Plant, and Alison Krauss plays.*]

KC: You do come from two very different worlds. Obviously, you two attract very different audiences. So who's buying this CD? Who's coming to see you perform?

RP: Well, we're sponsored by Geritol, so I mean, we get—we're getting [*laughing*] a lot of people stopping by for a minute, but they have to go to the toilet.

[*Footage of Plant and Krauss walking across stage together and chatting plays.*]

[**KC, voiceover**] A twenty-three-year age difference notwithstanding, theirs is a partnership that seemed improbable to everyone.

[*Concert footage of Plant and Krauss performing "Rich Woman" plays.*]

[**KC, voiceover**] Everyone but them.

AK: When I did finally meet Robert, our first conversation was about Ralph Stanley, and Robert talking about experiencing the Appalachian mountains and listening to Ralph at the same time. I thought, "Ah. I know a little about you now."

[*B-roll of mountains, and buildings in England rolls while "Little Maggie" (performed by Ralph Stanley) plays.*]

[**KC, voiceover**] In fact, Plant's eclectic influences date back to the early '60s, where a gloomy post-war England was lit up by the music of the Mississippi Delta.

[*Photograph montage b-roll of Robert Plant as a young man plays.*]

[**RP, voiceover**] As an English kid growing up in '61, there was no radio. There was just the American Forces Network and Voice of America.

[*Interview footage of Robert Plant and Alison Krauss plays.*]

RP: *Every* English group was playing Bo Diddley songs. We *all* wanted to be black Americans.

[*Photograph montage b-roll of Bo Diddley, Little Richard, and Sleepy John Estes plays.*]

[**KC, voiceover**] And, Plant says, the likes of Little Richard and Sleepy John Estes were welcome distractions from British blue-collar blues.

RP: The breaking from the monotony in whatever it is, from, you know, from the steel mills or from, you know, sharecropping or wherever it was.

KC: And you worked for a British construction company for a time, right?

RP: [*Jokingly incredulous.*] I never saw you there.

[*Couric laughs.*]

RP: Yeah, I was—I asphalted the roads while my contemporaries, other musicians, used to stand on the sidewalk and go, "Oh, you're going to be famous, aren't you?" as I was raking out the macadam. And I said, "Yeah, it's just a matter of time."

[B-roll footage of Led Zeppelin performing in concert plays.]

[KC, voiceover] That prediction came true in spades. As Led Zeppelin's lead singer, Plant became the poster boy for the rock 'n' roll excess of the '70s.

[B-roll plays of photograph of young Alison Krauss with her older brother.]

[KC, voiceover] But in Champaign, Illinois, a Led Zeppelin poster wasn't hanging on Alison Krauss's wall . . . it was on her older brother's.

AK: He would be in the other room, "Ah, ah, I can't deal with this. This is so great, I just can't believe it." Yeah, so.

RP: He was meditating.

[B-roll plays of old photographs of Krauss playing the fiddle.]

[KC, voiceover] Instead, Alison was taking violin lessons at five and winning fiddle contests by the time she was eight. She joined her first band when she was just ten. And while Robert was selling out stadiums, Alison was packing them in at the VFW.

AK: I'd come play fiddle tunes and I'd sing "Paper Roses" [Loretta Lynn] and some Hank Williams songs.

[B-roll plays of old photographs of Krauss.]

[KC, voiceover] And like Robert, Alison was a superstar at 21.

[B-roll footage of Krauss being welcomed by Garth Brooks as an official member of the Grand Ole Opry plays.]

Garth Brooks: The newest member of the Grand Ole Opry is Miss Alison Krauss.

[B-roll footage of Krauss performing "Forget About It" plays.]

[KC, voiceover] As she and her band, Union Station, helped bluegrass expand beyond its cult following . . .

[B-roll footage of Plant's musical video for "In the Mood" plays.]

[KC, voiceover]Robert Plant was enjoying a prolific post-Zeppelin solo career.

[*B-roll footage of Plant performing "Burning Down One Side" plays, followed by performance footage of Krauss and Plant singing "Gone Gone Gone" live.*]

[KC, voiceover] Pairing up was an opportunity for Plant to stretch his legs—and his voice.

RP: What greater test could there be than to actually sing with somebody who can really, *really* hold a note? I've never held a note in my life!

[*B-roll footage of Plant and Krauss practicing onstage plays.*]

[KC, voiceover] But mixing her mountain soprano with his Mississippi soul would require a maestro.

[*B-roll footage of T Bone Burnett playing guitar in concert plays.*]

[*Interview footage of Robert Plant and Alison Krauss plays.*]

[*Interview footage of T Bone Burnett plays.*]

T Bone Burnett: They say "angelic" for Alison, and they say, you know, "demonic" or something for Led Zeppelin or for Robert. You know, it's like the marriage of heaven and hell, right?

[*B-roll footage of Burnett, Plant, and Krauss discussing musical arrangements plays.*]

KC: Legendary producer T Bone Burnett was called upon to officiate that marriage.

[*Interview footage of Robert Plant and Alison Krauss plays.*]

AK: Robert and I sent things back and forth. He was not so thrilled with what I sent, and then he'd [*laughing*] send me something and I'd go, "Huh." And then T Bone sent a big bunch of tunes and both of us went, "Ah, this sounds like a record already."

[*"Stick With Me Baby" plays over b-roll montage of Krauss, Plant, and Burnett recording and arranging* Raising Sand *album.*]

[**KC, voiceover**] Raising Sand consists of 13 obscure covers, from the Everly Brothers to Tom Waits to Mel Tillis in between. Recorded in Nashville, this collection of half-remembered hits was T Bone's way of taking two icons out of their comfort zone.

KC: What were you afraid of? [*Gestures to Krauss.*]

AK: Well, he'd picked some songs, I thought, you know, "I'm so white. You know, this is really not such a good idea."

KC: What were you afraid of? [*Gestures to Plant.*]

RP: Not being good enough.

[*"Please Read the Letter" plays over b-roll montage of Krauss and Plant's concert at Madison Square Garden.*]

[**KC, voiceover**] They drew mostly rave reviews this past summer as they played to more than a quarter of a million people.

[*Interview footage with Madison Square Garden concertgoers.*]

Concertgoer One: I want a Zeppelin tour.

Concertgoer Two: I want a Zeppelin tour, but it's good to see this. This is very good quality music. This is really great.

KC: After this experience, can you ever see yourself singing with Led Zeppelin again?

RP: You got lovely eyes. I don't know who that guy was, honestly, because it all changes. That's what I live for, musical stimulation and change.

KC: So going back to singing with Led Zeppelin doesn't feel organic or forward enough for you, or . . . ?

RP: I can't even think about it. It's just not on my radar right now.

[*B-roll footage of Plant and Krauss performing with Burnett plays.*]

[KC, voiceover] Instead, Robert and Alison have hinted another album could be on the horizon.

AK: Seeing what T Bone would come up with this time and what we might find could be very interesting. I'd love to see what would happen.

[*B-roll footage of Krauss and Plant performing in concert.*]

[KC, voiceover] Whatever happens, this partnership is proof the song doesn't have to remain the same.

RP: I mean, because it doesn't matter about getting old. What it matters about is getting new.

[*B-roll footage of Plant and Krauss performing in concert.*]

[RP, voiceover] I'm glad you brought me here. I think it was one of the major moves of my late middle age.

[*B-roll of Plant and Krauss walking away.*]

COMMUNICATION BREAKDOWN

"Dave [Grohl]'s a bit funkier now. We listen to each other. There are a lot of parallels [in Them Crooked Vultures] of how Bonzo and I worked. It's invigorating."
—John Paul Jones to Austin Scaggs, *Rolling Stone*, April 20, 2010

COMMUNICATION BREAKDOWN

"A lot of this album is acoustic-based stuff along with adventurous rhythm. . . . It creates excitement with restraint, which pleases me no end, like we did back on *Led Zeppelin III*. A song like "Gallows Pole" was all about the dynamism, the way it unfolds and opens up and becomes more interesting rhythmically. When we made that record, we knew that we had to change the way people viewed that band or we would start becoming a bit of a parody."
—Robert Plant to Alan Light, *New York Times*, September 5, 2010

COMMUNICATION BREAKDOWN

"The entire complexion of this adventure, really, it's definitely made in America. Because as a kid and all the way through my time—and most of us British musicians, in all of our times—we felt the resonance of American music, and the influences within that. Whether they be from the Mississippi Delta and all the journeys I've made down there where, you know, I'm looking for ghosts, really. 'Cause I can hear all that stuff that affected me and made me quite emotional when I was a kid—the great voices down—you know, all that great stuff. Mix it and twirl it around, if you like, with the—kind of more glossy, American doo-wop pop, which you can hear on *Band of Joy*. If you listen to the Kelly Brothers song "[I'm] Falling in Love Again," you hear that kind of side of—the sweet side of the sound."

— Robert Plant to Melissa Block, NPR *All Things Considered*, September 20, 2010

COMMUNICATION BREAKDOWN

"I don't know that [Robert] doesn't want to [play together again]. We were aware that he was going to do the Alison Krauss project. So, I suppose one might have thought, "Well, let's see what he's going to do after that." And then he did another project and another project after that. There always seems to be another project coming out, and here we're talking five years later, well we haven't done another concert, have we?"

— Jimmy Page to Kirsty Lang, BBC TV4's *Front Row*, November 16, 2012

LED ZEPPELIN SUNDAY MORNING

Anthony Mason and Charles Osgood | December 16, 2012, *CBS Sunday Morning*

Things seemed to come in bunches for Led Zeppelin, even more than three decades after the group had officially broken up. The O2 concert had excited both fans and at least two-thirds of the remaining members. They had no plans to do anything beyond fund the foundation they had started, but they kept the digital video shot for the onstage video screens. Page started to review these images and discovered that they were of very high quality and could be spliced together to make the O2 experience available to all the fans who had tried to get tickets to the show and couldn't. The release of the video and music from the show coincided with the band joining Buddy Guy, David Letterman, Dustin Hoffman, and others among the 2012 recipients of the Kennedy Center Honors. –Ed.

[*"Kashmir" plays while a montage of Led Zeppelin performance photos rolls.*]

Narrator: When they were devouring the world in the 1970s [*concert footage of Led Zeppelin performing "The Ocean" plays.*] with their thunderous sound, and their wicked ways, the members of Led Zeppelin seemed the *least* likely musicians to expect an invitation to the White House.

[*Footage plays of President Barack Obama's introductory remarks at the presentation of the 2012 Kennedy Center Honors.*]

President Barack Obama: It's been said that a generation of young people survived teenage angst with a pair of headphones and a Zeppelin album.

N: But there they were this month, the band's three surviving members: John Paul Jones, Jimmy Page, and Robert Plant celebrated recipients of the Kennedy Center Honors.

[*Group interview with Anthony Mason, Robert Plant, Jimmy Page, and John Paul Jones.*]

Anthony Mason: Have you ever been there before?

Robert Plant: No, you're joking!

Jimmy Page: No, no.

[*Mason laughs.*]

RP: We were hardly the toast of American political—

AM: Establishment?

RP: Yeah.

AM: You weren't getting any White House invitations then.

RP: No. We were being questioned quite often.

[*Concert footage of Led Zeppelin performing "What Is and What Should Never Be" plays, followed by a montage of vintage behind-the-scenes footage of the band.*]

N: Led Zeppelin notoriously took sex, drugs, and rock 'n' roll to epic extremes.

AM: It was Joe Perry of Aerosmith who said that you were like Lord Byron: mad, bad, and dangerous to know. [*Laughs.*]

[*Plant raises an eyebrow; both Plant and Jones look closely at Page, seated between them.*]

JP: That must've been you, John.

John Paul Jones: [*Snorts.*] Yeah, it must've been me.

[*Montage of vintage Led Zeppelin photographs plays.*]

N: It's been more than three decades since the group disbanded after the death of drummer John Bonham in 1980.

[*Interview footage of Plant and Mason walking down the street plays.*]

RP: I think we all agreed unanimously that that was that.

N: But take a stroll with lead singer Robert Plant, now sixty-four.

[*B-roll footage rolls of Plant walking down the street.*]

Fan 1: [*Hurrying after Plant.*] Can I shake your hand? You're a god. You're a god!

N: And you'll get the picture quickly.

RP: [*Joking with a fan who has asked for a photo*] Come along into my office.

N: That Led Zeppelin's allure endures.

Fan Two: I think you're so hot still, and my sister's gonna be so jealous!

[*B-roll plays of Led Zeppelin performing "Good Times Bad Times" in 2007.*]

[**Narrator, voiceover**] The band sold more than 300 million records and when Led Zeppelin reunited in London for one night only in 2007, more than 20 million people applied for the 18,000 passes.

[*Footage plays of interview with Jimmy Page.*]

JP: What we achieved was to change the, the blueprint of a lot of things. We changed the, the sort of where the horizon was; we moved it on.

N: The band's founder was guitarist Jimmy Page.

[*Vintage photograph of Page appears onscreen.*]

N: At age fourteen he was already appearing on British TV shows.

[*B-roll footage plays of Page's 1957 appearance on the BBC's* Huw Wheldon Show, *performing "Mama Don't Want to Skiffle Anymore."*]

Huw Wheldon: What are your two names? Yours is?

JP: James Page.

[**Narrator, voiceover**] Soon, he was the most sought after session guitarist in Britain. In the early '60s he played for the Who, the Kinks, even on the theme song to the James Bond film *Goldfinger*.

[*Footage plays of interview with Jimmy Page.*]

JP: Well, it was exciting because it was right on the crest of the cutting edge of everything that was going on.

[**Narrator, voiceover**] He joined the Yardbirds, until the band fell apart in 1968.

AM: You knew you wanted to form another band.

JP: Yeah and I knew what sort of band to make, too.

AM: You did?

JP: Yeah, absolutely!

AM: You knew exactly what you wanted?

JP: Absolutely!

[**Narrator, voiceover**] His first recruit was bass player John Paul Jones.

AM: You knew Jimmy through session work.

JPJ: [*Nodding.*] We were the young guns, yes.

[**Narrator, voiceover**] Jones had written the string arrangements for Herman's Hermits and Rolling Stones records. When he heard Page was forming a band, he wanted in.

JPJ: He said "I'm going up to the Midlands to see a singer and we think he knows a drummer. I'll tell you what they're like when I get back."

[**Narrator, voiceover**] The singer was nineteen-year-old Robert Plant and his friend, drummer John Bonham. Within weeks the four got together.

AM: What do you remember about those first rehearsals?

JPJ: Just instant "this is fantastic!" [*Laughs.*] They just counted it "three, four!" bam! [*opening chords to "Good Times Bad Times" plays*] and just like "whoah!" The room just exploded.

[*"Good Times Bad Times" continues to play.*]

JP: And it was just so powerful. It just [*interlocks hands*] locked together like some—like something that was pretty scary, but had to be.

[**Narrator, voiceover**] Led Zeppelin was born.

[*B-roll concert footage plays of Led Zeppelin performing "Misty Mountain Hop."*]

[**Narrator, voiceover**] The band's debut album would spend seventy-three straight weeks on the chart, but the rock press was unimpressed. *Rolling Stone* magazine called it "self-indulgent" and Page a "writer of weak, unimaginative songs".

[*Group interview with Mason, Plant, Page, and Jones.*]

AM: Did that bother you in the beginning?

JP: No.

RP: No.

JPJ: It mystified me. I read that first *Rolling Stone* review, I thought "Did they mean us?"

RP: Oh, they were on Geritol, though . . . mainlining Geritol. I mean . . . they were some old farts.

JP: No, I think it just went down to their heads.

AM: Went over their heads.

JP: Absolutely, sir. Absolutely. It went way beyond them.

[*B-roll footage plays of Led Zeppelin in concert.*]

[**Narrator, voiceover**] But by the mid-'70s, Led Zeppelin was the most popular rock band in the world. In 1973, in Tampa, Florida, they played to more than 56,000 fans, breaking the Beatles' Shea Stadium record.

[*Vintage footage of a WTVT-CBS news report plays.*]

WTVT Reporter: Good evening! It really was the biggest crowd ever assembled for a single performance in one place in the entire history of the world.

[*B-roll concert footage plays of Led Zeppelin performing "Black Dog."*]

[*Footage plays of interview with Jimmy Page.*]

JP: I guess we would be on a roll. [*Both laugh.*]

AM: And you, by all accounts lived a pretty wild life while you were doing it as well.

JP: I don't know.

[**Narrator, voiceover**] Which brings us back to that quote from Joe Perry, the guitarist with Aerosmith.

[*Group interview with Mason, Plant, Page, and Jones.*]

JP: What, what, what did he say again, I'm—I'm, uh—

[*All laugh.*]

AM: He said that you were like Lord Byron; that you were mad, bad, and dangerous to know.

JP: And also to hear.

[*Montage of vintage Led Zeppelin photographs rolls while "Whole Lotta Love" plays.*]

[**Narrator, voiceover**] For more than a decade, Led Zep were the dark gods of rock. But in 1980, when drummer John Bonham died after consuming forty shots of vodka in twenty-four hours, it all ended unexpectedly.

AM: That must've been an incredibly difficult decision.

JPJ: No, it was an easy decision; it was an incredibly difficult time.

AM: Yeah.

JPJ: But . . . I couldn't imagine it without him.

[**Narrator, voiceover**] The band members went their separate ways.

[*Interview footage of Plant and Mason walking down the street plays.*]

RP: I've never felt so out of place and vulnerable and out of time and all that stuff. It was . . . nerve-racking, but that's what nerves are for.

[**Narrator, voiceover**] Led Zeppelin would reunite publicly only twice before 2007, and with disappointing results.

[*B-roll concert footage plays.*]

[**Narrator, voiceover**] So when the concert to honor Ahmet Ertegun, the late head of Atlantic Records was planned, Plant worried about recapturing Led Zeppelin's old magic.

AM: Did you have to work pretty hard to put yourself back there?

[*Footage plays of interview with Plant.*]

RP: I knew I couldn't go back there but I had to be comfortable with where I met it.

AM: And where was that?

RP: Ahh . . . it was just left of extreme fear [*both laugh*] and trepidation.

AM: What fear? Why?

RP: Well, because it's a big—it's a tall order, you know?

AM: Uh-huh.

RP: The thing is that everything that's . . . that's magnificent whatever it might be—

AM: Uh-huh.

RP:—a great moment in sport, a great moment in literature, um . . . can people actually ever go back and touch that again? You just know that once upon a time you could kick ass together and that's about it.

[*Concert footage plays of Led Zeppelin performing "Stairway to Heaven" at London's O2 Arena in 2007.*]

[**Narrator, voiceover**] But as *Celebration Day*, the new film of the concert shows, for that one night with Jason Bonham taking his father's place on drums, Led Zeppelin would soar again.

The band's performance raised hopes of a reunion tour, but at the premier of *Celebration Day* and the DVD release press conference last month, the question—

[*Footage of Q&A session at* Celebration Day *DVD release in 2012.*]

Audience Member: Why is it so hard to come together again?

[**Narrator, voiceover**]—was met with silence. They didn't like it when *we* brought it up either.

AM: I'm sure you've been offered a great deal of money to get back together.

RP: Are you still on about it?

AM: Yeah!

RP: Oh what a shame, he was doing so well.

JPJ: Yeah, yeah.

[**Narrator, voiceover**] Away from the band, Jimmy Page was more receptive.

[*Footage plays of solo interview with Page.*]

AM: My sense is that you're saying that you're open to the idea, but you think it's unlikely?

JP: I've *been* open to it and . . . I'm just looking at the past history of it.

[*Footage plays of solo interview with Jones.*]

AM: Do you think that's likely your last show?

JPJ: Likely, yeah, I think so. But I've said it before. [*Laughs.*]

[Narrator, voiceover] But if this was Led Zeppelin's last set, they went out with thunder and all.

[*Concert footage plays of Led Zeppelin performing at London's 02 Arena in 2007.*]

COMMUNICATION BREAKDOWN

"I mean, the great thing about what happened in 2007 when we played together again was that we were back, even though we were in a reasonable size venue, we were close together, really listening intensely. And intently to the interplay between the four of us with John playing. And that was exactly kind of how we started off, you know?"

– Robert Plant to Charlie Rose, *Charlie Rose Show*, January 5, 2013

COMMUNICATION BREAKDOWN

David Letterman: To hear your music coming at you from other musicians in the same building . . . is it exhilarating, does it make you nervous, is it . . . what is the reaction there?

Jimmy Page: Well we didn't know what was going—it was quite a surprise, what was gonna happen. So it was quite exhilarating to hear the different approaches people had to the songs. It was . . . yeah, Kid Rock was fantastic. He did a version of "Stairway [to Heaven]" that had a choir and an orchestra and then after the guitar—well, it was with Ann and Nancy Wilson. They did a superb job to start it off, and it started building and building, and then after the guitar solo, there's a screen that goes up and you see these. . . . They'd already had a small choir on the stage already, but a *huge* one at the back. And they started *really* rockin'! It was great!

DL: It was lovely. And then there were *more* people onstage doing your music than actually in the audience. [*Audience laughs.*] It was a huge, huge production. And then, the Lenny Kravitz also was tremendous.

Robert Plant: And what about the Vikings? Did you see them?

–David Letterman interview with Led Zeppelin,
Late Show with David Letterman, January 7, 2013

CODA: IN WHICH A GUITAR HERO PAYS TRIBUTE TO HIS YOUTH PLAYING SKIFFLE, AND ONE OF HIS INSPIRATIONS

Jimmy Page: When did I first discover [Hank Marvin]? That's a good question, isn't it? [*Laughs.*] When I was about fourteen, because in those days it was really skiffle for young kids who wanted to learn three chords and have a good time. But going past that, more into the world of the American rockabilly 'n' rock and roll was starting to seduce us all as kids. Then you had Cliff Richard and the Drifters at that time, putting forward a really, really damned good rendition of it, but it still had that sort of grit identity to it.

So, really it was a question of seeing Hank playing with Cliff as a kid, looking at Hank on the television. He was good, but he came alive with the Shadows. I mean it was such a . . . a really, really good band and Hank was such a stylist. He had such a—I mean, he was so cool. He was and still is. He had this image. He just looked as though . . . he was such a fluent player.

John Sugar: You said that you thought Hank was very cool in those early days, and yet he was wearing the geeky Buddy Holly glasses. For you, that obviously worked, Jimmy.

JP: Well they're not so much geeky glasses, they're the *Buddy Holly* glasses. I'm not having "geeky" said about Buddy Holly. For all of us sort of rock fanatics, Buddy Holly was a serious god to all of us, living up there on the rock 'n' roll Mount Olympus. And you could see, certainly obviously was for Hank, so that was a cool passport to have. And Hank was a very fluent player and of course he had a *marvelous* sound.

In those early days, teenage years, all of us—Jeff Beck, myself, Eric Clapton—we all played things like "Apache," "Man of Mystery," "FBI," those sort of hits.

JS: Are they easy to do?

JP: No, not if you're going to play it properly.

JS: Like Hank.

JP: Like Hank. There's a serious technique going on there with Hank. You can get through, but you won't sound like Hank. It all came into the same compartment of learning music from a record. And so it's all a matter of being able to sort of *play* something and show off a bit.

They did it well, what they did. The Shadows, and in particular Hank, they were in a class of their own. When you start to look more in the area of all the instrumentals that they did, from "Apache" onwards, you know all the way through, a marvelous catalogue of songs, really positive stuff. It *really* puts a smile on your face, and it's a positive guitar style that he has.

Hank managed to come up with this unique sound, and that sound is just *so* recognizable. He inspired so many guitarists in those days as kids, kids who had no idea they may even be rock stars themselves one day. [*Laughs.*]

They had more than one walk, actually. They had these routine moves that were employed in a really cool way. I mean, certainly in its day, it was quite something to see all these guitarists going into synchronicity. And on most television appearances, the Shadows, they were a cool band. I don't know how much we want to be owning up to whether we had to do it as a teenager [*laughs*], in early groups or something similar.

JS: So has our other guitar superstar, Jimmy Page, found himself in a huddle with Hank Marvin?

JP: I'm not trying to blow my own trumpet here, but I actually did a session in the days when I was a studio musician. And that was during the time that you didn't know who you were going to be with when you walked through the door. It just happened to be Cliff [Richard] and Hank was there. I got a chance to meet him. It was a real thrill to meet him. That's the first time I got to meet . . . all of them, really. They called me in to play harmonica. I wasn't on guitar, obviously, but I played harmonica on "Time Drags By." It was cool!

The Shadows, and in particular Hank's guitar sound that you could recognize it straight away, and I think that says a lot. The thing about Hank, you know, in those very early days of learning the guitar from records and by word of mouth and that, he didn't let anybody down. He always did some wonderful work. And still does.

—John Sugar interview with Jimmy Page,
BBC Radio 4, October 11, 2011

CONTRIBUTORS

Author, broadcaster, and *NME* features editor **Keith Altham** interviewed the likes of the Beatles, the Rolling Stones, Jimi Hendrix, Ray Davies, Jim Morrison, and the Beach Boys on innumerable occasions. In the early '60s, he wrote for the legendary fan magazine *Fabulous* from its inception. Subsequently he became England's most successful independent rock press agent for three decades beginning in the early '70s, representing most of those artists he had previously interviewed. He appeared frequently on BBC 2's *Scene and Heard* and contributed to BBC Radio 2's program *The Changing Styles of Music Journalism, Music Hype,* and Virgin FM's *Tribute to Jimi Hendrix.* Altham is also accountable for giving Hendrix the idea of setting fire to his guitar. In addition to radio, he has worked as a contributor on film and TV. Altham is the author of *The PR Strikes Back* (John Blake, 2001) and is currently working on a book about his life in the '60s as well as a biography of a well-known superstar.

Widely recognized as one of the most culturally influential, politically trenchant, and innovative artists of the twentieth century, **William S. Burroughs** became a key figure in the generation of writers that emerged in the early 1950s. He is the author of *Queer* and *Naked Lunch,* among other works, and collaborated throughout his life with many artists in various media, including Brion Gysin, Allen Ginsberg, Jack Kerouac, Ian Sommerville, Throbbing Gristle, Nick Cave, Tom Waits, and Sonic Youth.

Lon Cabot spent twenty-one years as a senior chief photojournalist for the US Navy. He worked at *All Hands* magazine, the Pacific and European editions of *Stars and Stripes*, and served as print media and broadcast journalist aboard ships and at shore bases in the US and overseas. He currently works for FEMA.

Chris Charlesworth was a staff writer on *Melody Maker* magazine between 1970 and 1977. He has been editor-in-chief at Omnibus Press, the world's biggest book publisher specializing exclusively in rock and pop titles, since 1983. Much of his work can be found on the website www.rocksbackpages.com.

Thor Christensen is an award-winning writer, journalist, music critic, and editor whose work has appeared in dozens of newspapers and magazines worldwide. He is a former staff writer at the *Dallas Morning News* and the *Milwaukee Journal Sentinel*, and his stories included one-on-one interviews with Paul McCartney, Aretha Franklin, Mick Jagger, Ray Charles, and Bono. He was a contributing author for the book series *Musichound Rock: The Essential Album Guide*. Christensen won a Katie Award for Arts Feature Writing, a Milwaukee Press Club Award for Arts Criticism, and was nominated for a Pulitzer Prize by the *Milwaukee Journal Sentinel*.

Katie Couric is an award-winning journalist and TV personality, well-known cancer advocate, and the *New York Times* best-selling author of *The Best Advice I Ever Got: Lessons From Extraordinary Lives* (Random House, 2011). Couric joined the Disney/ABC Television Group in Summer 2011, contributing to *ABC World News, Nightline, 20/20, Good Morning America, This Week*, and primetime news specials. She hosted the syndicated daytime talk show, *Katie*, from 2012 to 2014. Couric was the first female solo anchor of an evening news broadcast, the *CBS Evening News with Katie Couric*, and she also contributed to *60 Minutes, CBS Sunday Morning*, and CBS News primetime specials. Previously she served as coanchor of NBC News' *TODAY* show. Currently Couric is a "global anchor" for *Yahoo! News*. She lives in New York with her two daughters.

Dave DiMartino is the executive editor of *Yahoo! Music* in Santa Monica. He is a former editor of *CREEM*, West Coast bureau chief of *Billboard* magazine, and senior writer at *Entertainment Weekly*. He is the author of *Singer Songwriters: Pop Music's Performer-Composers, from A* to *Zevon* (Billboard Books, 1994), consultant editor of *Moonlight Drive: The Stories Behind Every Doors Song* (Edition Olms, 1995), and US editor of *Music in the 20th Century* (M.E. Sharpe, 1998). His writing has appeared in *The MOJO Collection: The Ultimate Music Companion* (Canongate, 2003) and *The Pop, Rock, and Soul Reader: Histories and Debates* (Oxford University Press, 2004), and in numerous publications including *Rolling Stone, MOJO, Musician, Spin*, and the *Village Voice*.

Geffen Records Publicity department serves in creating press releases, press kits, and electronic press kits to get media coverage for their artists. Geffen is now part of Interscope Records.

Danny Goldberg began his career in 1969 as a music journalist for *Rolling Stone, Circus, Crawdaddy, Record World, Billboard*, and the *Village Voice*. Later he wrote about culture for the *Los Angeles Times, The Nation*, and *Tikkun*. From 1974 to 1976, Goldberg was vice-president of Led Zeppelin's Swan Song Records, and in the early 1980s he co-owned Modern Records, which released Stevie Nicks' solo albums. From 1983 to 1992, Goldberg was the founder and president of Gold Mountain Entertainment, a personal management firm whose clients included Nirvana, Hole, Sonic Youth, Bonnie Raitt, and the Allman Brothers Band. Subsequently, Goldberg became chairman and CEO of the Mercury Records Group, chairman and CEO of Warner Bros. Records, and President of Atlantic Records. He formed the indie label Artemis Records in 1999, which ran until 2005. Artemis releases included Warren Zevon's Grammy-winning album *The Wind*, Steve Earle's Grammy winner *The Revolution Starts Now*, and the Baha Men's *Who Let the Dogs Out*. Goldberg is currently president of Gold Village Entertainment, managing the careers of The Hives, Steve Earle, Martha Wainwright, and many others. He is author of *Bumping Into Geniuses: My Life Inside the Rock and Roll Business* (Gotham, 2008) and *How the Left Lost Teen Spirit* (Akashic Books, 2005), and he coedited the anthology *It's a Free Country: Personal Freedom in America After September 11* (RDV Books, 2002).

Tom Hibbert was a brilliantly funny contributor to *Q* magazine, *Smash Hits, MOJO*, and other publications. He was also the irreverent brain behind Q magazine's "Who the Hell . . ." series. He died after a long illness in September 2011.

Adam Howorth's work has appeared in *Billboard*, the *Times (of London)*, the *Guardian*, *Independent*, and many other publications. He is currently the director of publicity, EMEIA for Apple (Computers) in London.

Ashley Kahn is an author, educator, music journalist, and concert producer. A professor of music history and criticism at New York University who lectures at other institutions as well, his books include *A Love Supreme: The Story of John Coltrane's Signature Album* (Viking, 2002) and *Kind of Blue: The Making of the Miles Davis Masterpiece* (Da Capo Press, 2000). Kahn's writing has generated two Grammy nominations, three ASCAP/Deems Taylor Awards, and two Book of the Year distinctions from the Jazz Journalists Association.

Nick Kent was one of the most important and influential music journalists of the 1970s, and remains a hugely respected commentator to this day. He wrote for number publications, including *NME*, and he is the author of *The Dark Stuff: Selected Writings on Rock Music* (Da Capo Press, 1994), which boasts a foreword by Iggy Pop. Kent's autobiography, *Apathy for the Devil: A 70s Memoir* (Faber, 2010) was published to great acclaim. Kent lives in Paris with his partner, Laurence Romance, and their son.

Liam Lacey served as the rock critic at the *Globe and Mail* in the 1980s; currently he serves as the newspaper's film critic. He lives in Toronto.

Matt Lauer is the coanchor of NBC News' *TODAY*. Since joining NBC News, Lauer has conducted a number of remarkable and newsworthy interviews. Lauer lives with his wife in New York City.

A reporter since he was fifteen years old, **Robin Leach** launched his first monthly magazine at seventeen years old, and a year later he joined the prestigious *Daily Mail* as Britain's youngest page-one reporter. After immigrating to the United States, he wrote for the *New York Daily News*, *People*, and other publications before launching his own *GO Magazine*, *R 'n' B World*, and *Stereo Review*. He also acted as the show business editor of *The Star* and Rupert Murdoch's worldwide publications for ten years. Leach's television career began simultaneously on KABC-TV in Los Angeles and WABC-TV in New York. In 1980, he joined CNN's *People Tonight* and helped launch CBS's *Entertainment Tonight*. Then in 1983, Leach created *Lifestyles of the Rich & Famous*, which ran for an unprecedented fourteen years. Leach has subsequently produced and hosted over three hundred hours of TV series and specials. His newest series is VH1's *Fame Games*. He is a lifetime board member of the New York based Citymeals-on-Wheels charitable home food delivery organization; among his numerous charitable activities, he works for Alzheimer's charity Keep Memory Alive and Opportunity Village.

Arthur Levy, a twenty-year veteran of Atlantic and Columbia Records, is a Grammy-nominated independent music press writer, publicity and public relations consultant, record collector, historian, educator, archivist, and founding member of the Traveling Jewburys rock band. His music career began in college, and he was later an editor of *Zoo World* (whence comes his Led Zeppelin interview of 1973), in the first golden age of tabloid rock papers. He served on the select Curatorial Committee that helped design and build the Rock and Roll Hall of Fame in the early 1980s, and has been a member of the Hall's prestigious Nominating Committee since its conception.

Alan Light is a former editor-in-chief of *Vibe* and *Spin* magazines, and is a frequent contributor to *Rolling Stone* and the *New York Times*. He is the author of *The Holy or the Broken: Leonard Cohen, Jeff Buckley and the Unlikely Ascent of "Hallelujah"* (Simon and Schuster, 2012).

Anthony Mason is the cohost of *CBS This Morning: Saturday* and he also acts as *CBS News'* senior business correspondent. Additionally, he is a frequent contributor of cultural stories to *CBS News Sunday Morning with Charles Osgood*. Mason has spent more than thirty years as a television journalist and has won seven Emmy Awards. He has profiled politicians (Bill Clinton), business leaders (Henry Paulson), and musicians (Bruce Springsteen, Paul McCartney, and Keith Richards.) He and his wife, Christina, have three children and live in New York.

Patrick McDonald is the chief arts writer for the *Adelaide Advertiser*.

For more than fifteen years **Mark McEwen** has served in a variety of high-profile positions at CBS, including anchor of *CBS This Morning* for three years. But he is perhaps best known as the weatherman and entertainment reporter for *The Early Show*. Named one of the country's "Ten Most Trusted TV News Personalities" in a *TV Guide* survey, Mark also served as a correspondent on the CBS News show *48 Hours*. During his extensive career, Mark has traveled the world as a prominent newsman. McEwen lives in central Florida with his wife Denise and his children.

Rick McGrath was rock critic of the Vancouver underground newspaper the *Georgia Straight* from 1969 to 1971. He also wrote for *CREEM*, the *Terminal City Express*, and *The Grape* before moving on to become an advertising agency creative director. Now retired, McGrath continues to add to his own website and contributes features, as well as music, book and movie reviews for the media analysis website http://culturecourt.com.

Melinda Newman worked at *Billboard* magazine for eighteen years, starting as associate editor in New York and rising to West Coast bureau chief in Los Angeles. She currently writes for the *Washington Post, Los Angeles Times*, Associated Press, *Variety*, MSN, AOL, Hitfix.com, *M-Life*, *M*, and many other periodicals. Her work for Associated Press, Hitfix.com, AOL, and MSN has also taken her into the realm of video journalism.

HP Newquist is the author of more than two dozen books, hundreds of magazine articles, and several music documentaries. He was the editor-in-chief of *GUITAR* magazine, and has written extensively about guitars and guitarists for the last three decades. Newquist is also the founder and executive director of the National GUITAR Museum, the first museum dedicated to the world's most popular instrument.

Broadcasting Hall of Famer and four-time Emmy Award winner **Charles Osgood**, often referred to as CBS News' poet-in-residence, has been anchor of *CBS News Sunday Morning* since 1994. He also anchors and writes *The Osgood File*, his daily news commentary broadcast on the CBS Radio Network. He has been an anchor and reporter for many CBS News broadcasts, including the *CBS Morning News*, the *CBS Evening News with*

Dan Rather, and the *CBS Sunday Night News*. Osgood recently made his big-screen debut as the narrator of Dr. Seuss' *Horton Hears a Who!*, the animated feature film adaptation of the beloved children's book, voiced by Carol Burnett, Steve Carell, and Jim Carrey. He also wrote *A Funny Thing Happened on the Way to the White House: Humor, Blunders, and Other Oddities From the Presidential Campaign Trail* (Hyperion, 2008), a compendium of anecdotes from the last seventy years of presidential campaigns, in addition to six other books. Osgood was born in New York, where he currently lives with his wife, Jean. They have five children and three grandchildren.

Chris Salewicz, who lives in London, has documented world popular music and culture for over three decades, both on television and in print in *Time Out*, the *Sunday Times Magazine*, *Q* magazine, *The Independent*, *The Face*, and many other publications. As a senior features writer for *NME*, he saw service at the frontlines of glam rock, punk rock, reggae music, and the Los Angeles and New York music scenes and their subcultures. He also wrote for and syndicated to countless publications worldwide. He worked on *DOA*, the definitive US film about punk rock. He has written many books, including biographies of Jimi Hendrix, George Lucas, and Paul McCartney. Other books include *Rude Boy: Once Upon a Time in Jamaica* (Orion, 2000), *Reggae Explosion: The Story of Jamaican Music* (Virgin Books, 2001), *Mick and Keith: Parallel Lines* (Orion, 2002), the best-selling *Redemption Song: The Definitive Biography of Joe Strummer* (HarperCollins, 2006), and *Bob Marley: The Untold Story* (HarperCollins, 2009). Salewicz also edited *Keep On Running: The Story of Island Records* (Universe Publishing, 2010).

Mat Snow was a regular contributor to *NME* in the '80s as well as a feature writer for *Sounds*, *Q* magazine, and many other publications. He served as the editor of *MOJO* from 1995 to 1999. He is also the former editor of soccer monthly *Four Four Two*. Snow currently serves as editorial consultant to *Rock's Backpages*.

Denny Somach is a Grammy Award recipient, author, producer, and owner of Denny Somach Productions (DSP), a major producer of syndicated radio programming. DSP's shows include *Legends of Rock*; *Live* *from the Hard Rock Café; The Classics*, a weekly show on over 130 rock radio stations; and *Get the Led Out*, which currently airs on more than 100 classic rock radio stations. Somach helped create the TV shows *Solid Gold*, the concert series *Hot Spots*, and NBC's *Friday Night Videos*, conducting interviews including the Robert Plant piece in this book. He was an original consultant to MTV, director of Turner's Cable Music Channel (which became VH1), and a consultant for XM Radio's debut. Somach produced recordings and/or videos with Johnny Winter, Yes, Todd Rundgren, and others. He also produced guitarist Eric Johnson's *Ah Via Musicom*, which went platinum, and he won a Grammy for the song "Cliffs of Dover." Somach has appeared on numerous television shows, including: *TODAY, Larry King Live, The Early Show on CBS, Showbiz Today*, and *The Big Breakfast Show* (UK). He is also the author of *Ticket to Ride* (Time Warner Paperbacks, 1990), *Meet the Beatles . . . Again!* (Musicom International, 1996), and *Get the Led Out: How Led Zeppelin Became the Biggest Band in the World* (Sterling, 2012). Somach is the founder of the Classic Rock Society of America.

Neil Spencer wrote for *NME* in the 1970s and '80s, and acted as the magazine's editor from 1978 to 1985. His writing has appeared in publications including *The Independent, MOJO*, and *Elle* magazine. Currently Spencer is a writer and an astrologer for *The Observer* and lives in London.

John Sugar has been in broadcasting for thirty years and has worked in various capacities within the radio industry, launching the UK radio station BBC Radio 6 Music. He currently runs his own production company providing programs for BBC Radio and has, in his time, interviewed many leading music figures, including James Brown, John Lydon, and Paul Simon. Sugar has produced programs on Radiohead, the Beatles, and Bob Dylan. For more information, visit www.sugarproductions.co.uk.

John Swenson has been writing about popular music since 1967. His account of musicians returning to New Orleans after Katrina, "The Bands Played On," appeared in *Da Capo's Best Music Writing 2007* (Da Capo Press, 2007); his "Every Accordionist a King" won the 2008 Best Entertainment Feature award from the Press Club of New Orleans. Swenson has been an editor for *Crawdaddy, Rolling Stone, Circus, Rock World, Offbeat*, and other publications. He is the author of *The Rolling Stone Jazz and Blues Album Guide* (Random House, 1999), *Stevie Wonder* (HarperCollins, 1986); and *Bill Haley: The Daddy of Rock and Roll* (Stein and Day, 1983). His most recent book is *New Atlantis: Musicians Battle for the Survival of New Orleans (Oxford University Press, 2001)*.

Chris Welch joined *Melody Maker* as a reporter and features writer, and soon became the features editor. During the '60s and '70s he interviewed and wrote about major artists and bands including Jimi Hendrix, Marc Bolan, David Bowie, Paul McCartney, the Rolling Stones, the Who, Cream, and Led Zeppelin. Later he became assistant editor of *Musicians Only*, then a reviews editor and feature writer for *Kerrang!*, editor of *Metal Hammer* and *Rock World* magazines, and a contributor to *The Independent, Daily Mail, MOJO*, and *Record Collector*. He worked at Repertoire Records as a researcher and editorial consultant. Welch has written more than thirty books including *Hendrix: A Biography* (Quick Fox, 1978) and *Ginger Geezer: The Life of Vivian Stanshall* (Fourth Estate, 2001) as well as books on Led Zeppelin, Black Sabbath, John Bonham, David Bowie, Marc Bolan, Steve Winwood, Tina Turner, Cream, and the Who. In the 2000s he wrote scripts and conducted interviews for filmed documentaries on Yes, the Moody Blues, and Cream in the *Classic Artists* series and has frequently contributed to radio and TV programs. His latest book is *Eric Clapton: Treasures* (Carlton Books, 2014).

Steven P. Wheeler is an award-winning journalist who wrote about the music industry for a variety of publications—both offline and online. He rose to senior editor of *Music Connection* magazine and started his own political/entertainment magazine, *L.A. Vision*. Expanding into video and the web, he became vice president of content programming and marketing for Tonos Entertainment, heading the video production, content programming, artist development, and marketing departments. He was also the producer of the American Rock Connection concert showcase, a monthly, live event held at the legendary Palomino Club in Hollywood, which resulted in publishing deals and recording contracts for some of the handpicked talent that performed at his shows. He joined the online division of Warner Brothers in 2004, and is now the senior content producer responsible for creating and programming all content for Warner-Bros.com, and an endless stream of other related WB sites, applications, and initiatives. Wheeler maintains his residence in Southern California, where he lives with his wife, Maggie, and a seemingly endless series of feline adoptees.

David White worked in Australian radio and television for more than thirty years. He held a range of positions including deejay, news director, program director, music director, news anchor, TV reporter, documentary writer, and producer. A multiple award-winning journalist, he earned a Walkley (radio's version of the Pulitzer), a dual UN Media Peace Prize, gold medals at the New York International Radio Festival, and the Australian National Science Week $10,000 Eureka Prize for Environmental Journalism. He has interviewed political leaders, scientists, movie stars, and rock stars including John Lennon, Led Zeppelin, the Rolling Stones, Fleetwood Mac, David Bowie, Steely Dan, Jack Nicholson, and George Harrison, to name a few.

Mark Williams has spent his entire career in publishing. He is a respected, if sometimes controversial, journalist and columnist in the disparate fields of rock music, film, and automotive media. Williams also conceived of, launched, and/or edited several periodicals, including *Strange Days, Bike* (still the UK's best-selling motorcycle title), *New Music News,* and *Jalopy.* A successful publishing consultant, Williams has continued to write for *Rolling Stone, Melody Maker, Top Gear, Motorcycle Rider, Time Out, Condé Nast Traveller,* the *Guardian, London Evening Standard, Daily Telegraph,* and *Used Car Buyer.* He has also produced books on film, music, and motorcycling topics, plus two anthologies of material from *The Week.* He has been involved in running several musical events, most notably Sheep Music, the annual world music festival in Wales.

Sue Williams works for the *Derby Telegraph* in Derby, England.

World renowned British writer and photographer **Val Wilmer** has been following and documenting blues, jazz, African, and Caribbean music for more than fifty years. Wilmer's work has run in *Melody Maker, Down*

Beat (as UK correspondent), and *The Wire*. She is the author of several books including *Jazz People* (Bobbs-Merrill Co., 1970), *The Face of Black Music* (Da Capo Press, 1977), *As Serious As Your Life* (Allison and Busby, 1977), and her memoir *Mama Said There'd Be Days Like This: My Life in the Jazz World* (Women's Press Ltd., 1992), that contain her iconic black and white photographs. These images have been exhibited extensively and are held in photographic collections including the Arts Council of Great Britain (Victoria and Albert Museum); Musée d'Art Moderne (Paris); Smithsonian Museum (Washington, DC); Schomburg Center for Research in Black Culture (New York Public Library), and the National Portrait Gallery. Wilmer regularly contributes informative obituaries of musicians to *The Guardian*, and is working on five more books. She lives in London.

Gail Worley is a veteran rock journalist. She contributed to *Modern Drummer Magazine* for thirteen years and penned monthly columns in *Request* and *Metal Edge* magazines, among many other print and online outlets. Worley is also the proud author of the pop culture blog http://worleygig.com, which covers classic rock, the contemporary art scene in NYC, food, design, and lifestyle topics. Her favorite bands are still Led Zeppelin and the Beatles. She lives in New York City.

Music commentator **Ritchie Yorke** has been described by Led Zeppelin member John Paul Jones as "the band's champion." Singer Robert Plant has noted: "Ritchie was one of us from the very beginning." When Zep's first album was released, many critics panned it. Yorke was a dedicated supporter, right from the start. Writing in the Toronto *Globe and Mail* and the UK's *NME*, Yorke predicted the supergroup success of Zeppelin. Yorke often traveled with the band as their guest and was located side of stage during the filming of *The Song Remains the Same* at New York's Madison Square Garden in 1973. Yorke authored the first book biography of the band, *The Led Zeppelin Biography* (Methuen, 1976). Since its initial publication, it has been updated in several editions and is published in English, Japanese, Swedish, and Hebrew. More information can be found on www.ritchieyorke.com.

CREDITS

I appreciatively acknowledge the assistance of everybody who gave permission for their material to appear in this book. Great lengths have been taken to find the copyright holders. If an error or omission has been made, please notify the publisher.

"Jimmy Page Is Just Wild About Led Zeppelin." Originally printed in *Go!* magazine, December 27, 1968. Copyright ©1968. Reprinted by permission of Robin Leach.

"Led Zeppelin Climbs Before Its First LP," by Ritchie Yorke. Originally printed in the *Globe and Mail*, January 11, 1969. Copyright ©1969 Reprinted by permission of Ritchie Yorke.

"Led Zeppelin: Plant," by Mark Williams. Originally published in *International Times*, April 11, 1969. Copyright ©1969. Reprinted by permission of Rock's Backpages.

"Forget Blind Faith, Led Zeppelin's the Biggest," by Ritchie Yorke. Originally published in the *Globe and Mail*, August 14, 1969. Copyright ©1969. Reprinted by permission of Ritchie Yorke.

"Jimmy Page Talks About Led Zeppelin," by Valerie Wilmer. Originally published in *Hit Parader*, 1970. Copyright ©1970. Reprinted by permission of ©Val Wilmer/CTSIMAGES.

"Ask-In with a Led Zeppelin: Bassist John Paul Jones—'Motown Bass Deserves a Lot of Credit,'" Ritchie Yorke. Originally published in *NME*, April 4, 1970. Copyright ©1970. Reprinted by permission of Ritchie Yorke.

"Ask-In with a Led Zeppelin: Thinking As A Sex Symbol Can Turn You Into a Bad Person—Robert Plant," by Ritchie Yorke. Originally published in *NME*, April 11, 1970. Copyright ©1970. Reprinted by permission of Ritchie Yorke.

"Ask-In with a Led Zeppelin, Part Three: John Bonham, Drummer Extraordinary Known as Bonzo," by Ritchie Yorke. Originally published in *NME*, April 18, 1970. Copyright ©1970. Reprinted by permission of Ritchie Yorke.

"Jimmy Page Answers the Questions in the Final Led Zeppelin Ask-In," by Ritchie Yorke. Originally published in *NME*, April 25, 1970. Copyright ©1970. Reprinted by permission of Ritchie Yorke.

"Jimmy Page: Zep Come to the People," by Keith Altham. Originally published in *Record Mirror*, February 27, 1971. Copyright ©1971. Reprinted by permission of Rock's Backpages.

"Robert Plant." Originally published in *Rock Magazine*, August 14, 1971. Copyright © 1971. Reprinted by permission of Larry Marshak.

"Led Zeppelin: Vancouver 1971," by Rick McGrath. Originally published in the *Georgia Straight*, 1971. Copyright ©1971. Reprinted by permission of Rock's Backpages.

"Led Zeppelin Radio Interview, Sydney Australia," by David White. Originally broadcast on Radio Station 2SM, on February 27, 1972. Copyright ©1972. Published by permission of David White and the National Film & Sound Archive, Australia.

"'Don't Label Us': 'Zeppelin' on Japan Tour," by Lon Cabot. Originally published in *Stars and Stripes*, September 30, 1972. Used with permission. Copyright ©1972, 2014 *Stars and Stripes*.

"Plant Back on Track," by Liam Lacey. Originally published in the *Globe and Mail*, June 26, 1982. Copyright ©1982. Reprinted by permission of the *Globe and Mail*.

"Robert Plant with Denny Somach, First US Solo Tour," by Denny Somach. Originally broadcast on NBC *Friday Night Videos*, August 1983. Copyright ©1983. Published by permission of Denny Somach.

"From Hot Dog to Big Log: Robert Plant Hits the Road," by Dave DiMartino. Originally published in *CREEM*, October 1983. Copyright ©1983. Reprinted by permission of Dave DiMartino.

"Jimmy Page On Stage '85," by Chris Welch. Originally published in *CREEM*, April 1985. Copyright ©1985. Reprinted by permission of Rock's Backpages.

"Rockin' Robert likes 'A Bit of Grit Below the Waist,'" by Liam Lacey. Originally published in the *Globe and Mail*, June 8, 1985. Copyright ©1985. Reprinted by permission of the *Globe and Mail*.

"Robert Plant: Guilty!," by Tom Hibbert. Originally published in Q magazine, March 1988. Copyright ©1988. Reprinted by permission of Rock's Backpages.

"Emerging from the Shadows: Jimmy Page" by Patrick McDonald. Originally published in the Advertiser, July 7, 1988. Copyright ©1988. Reprinted by permission of Copyright.com.au.

"Robert Plant Keeps the Faith," by John Swenson. Originally published by UPI, October 14, 1988. Copyright ©1988. Reprinted by permission of UPI.

"A Decade Later, Plant Refuses to Live His Past," by Thor Christensen. Originally published in the *Milwaukee Journal Sentinel*, July 22, 1990. Copyright ©1990. Reprinted by permission of the *Milwaukee Journal Sentinel* via RightsLink.

Coverdale/Page Electronic Press Kit Video, by Geffen Records Public Relations. Originally published March 1993. Public domain.

"Robert Plant, Jimmy Page, and John Paul Jones Discuss Their Led Zeppelin Careers and Their New Tour Footage DVD," by Matt Lauer. Originally broadcast on the NBC *Today Show*, May 29, 2003. Copyright ©2003. Published by permission of the NBC News–NBCUniversal Archives.

"Atlantic Captures Plant's Solo Side on Compilation," by Melinda Newman. Originally published in *Billboard*, October 11, 2003. Copyright ©2003, 2014. Reprinted by permission of Prometheus Global Media.

"Robert Plant: Starting Over After Led Zeppelin," by Ashley Kahn. Originally broadcast (in excerpt) by NPR *Morning Edition*, June 22, 2006. Copyright ©2006. Published in full by permission of Ashley Kahn.

"Getting the Led Out: Jimmy Page and John Paul Jones on Led Zeppelin's Historic Reunion," by Alan Light. Originally published by *MSN Music*, November 13, 2007. Copyright ©2007. Reprinted by permission of Alan Light.

"Country Rocks; Robert Plant and Alison Krauss Team Up," by Charles Osgood and Katie Couric. Originally broadcast on *CBS Sunday Morning*, October 12, 2008. Copyright ©2008. Published by permission of CBS News Archives.

"Led Zeppelin Sunday Morning," by Anthony Mason and Charles Osgood. Originally broadcast on *CBS Sunday Morning*, December 16, 2012. Copyright ©2012. Published by permission of CBS News Archives.

"The Thing About Hank," by John Sugar. Originally broadcast on BBC-Radio 4, October 11, 2011. Copyright ©2011. Published by permission of Sugar Productions.

INDEX